Screening
Difference

D0943355

Screening Difference

How Hollywood's Blockbuster Films Imagine Race, Ethnicity, and Culture

JAAP VAN GINNEKEN

ROWMAN & LITTLEFIELD PUBLISHERS, INC.
Lanham • Boulder • New York • Toronto • Plymouth, UK

ROWMAN & LITTLEFIELD PUBLISHERS, INC.

Published in the United States of America
by Rowman & Littlefield Publishers, Inc.
A wholly owned subsidiary of The Rowman & Littlefield Publishing Group, Inc.
4501 Forbes Boulevard, Suite 200, Lanham, Maryland 20706
www.rowmanlittlefield.com

Estover Road, Plymouth PL6 7PY, United Kingdom

British Library Cataloguing in Publication Information Available

Library of Congress Cataloging-in-Publication Data

Ginneken, Jaap van, 1943–
   [Exotisch Hollywood. English]
   Screening difference : how Hollywood's blockbuster films imagine race, ethnicity, and
culture / Jaap van Ginneken.
      p. cm.
   Includes bibliographical references and index.
   ISBN-13: 978-0-7425-5583-9 (cloth : alk. paper)
   ISBN-10: 0-7425-5583-6 (cloth : alk. paper)
   ISBN-13: 978-0-7425-5584-6 (pbk. : alk. paper)
   ISBN-10: 0-7425-5584-4 (pbk. : alk. paper)
   1. Exoticism in motion pictures. 2. Race in motion pictures. 3. Motion pictures—
United States. I. Title.
PN1995.9.E95G56 2006
791.43'6552—dc   222007011064

Printed in the United States of America

⊗™ The paper used in this publication meets the minimum requirements of American
National Standard for Information Sciences—Permanence of Paper for Printed Library
Materials, ANSI/NISO Z39.48-1992.

For Antjenidevi and Anand

Contents

Preface   ix

1   The Loud and the Silent: Global Film in the
Twenty-First Century   1

2   Children and Adults: Animated Cartoons   19

3   Civilized and Savage: Antiquity Movies   43

4   The Tamers and the Wild: Wilderness Adventure   63

5   The Prolific and the Idle: Westerns and Southerns   83

6   The Prude and the Lewd: Romantic and Erotic Encounters   107

7   Helpers and Helpless: Colonial Adventure   127

8   Friends and Foes: Spy, Action, and War Movies   151

9   Believers and Heathens: Religious Films   177

10   The Advanced and the Backward: Science Fiction and
Space Adventure   201

11   Other People's Dreams   223

Glossary   235

Notes   243

References   257

Index   269

About the Author   281

Preface

The top two hundred best-selling movies (earning between $250 million and $2 billion at the box office) come mostly from the Anglophone world—with only very few exceptions. Many of these films deal with encounters or confrontations between Westerners and non-Westerners. But in many such cases, the story has somehow been slightly twisted, designed to please the primary audience groups in North America and western Europe. For example, did you know:

- That the "Indian princess" Pocahontas did not at all fall in love with John Smith, as the Disney movie and many others pretend? At their supposed first encounter, she was only ten or twelve years old, and he twenty-seven. She was made a prisoner by the British at seventeen, may have been abused, and was subsequently married off to an almost-thirty-year-old burly widower.
- That the persistent myth about the mummy and "the curse of the pharaoh" in books and films derived from a simple mosquito bite? This bite contributed to the death of Lord Carnarvon, the British Egyptologist who financed the excavation of royal tombs, after he and Howard Carter opened Tutankhamen's grave, with its hundreds of pounds of pure gold.
- That *Godzilla* was originally an antinuclear and anti-American movie from Japan? Bought by an American company, the film was censored for American audiences, with many scenes suppressed and many others added. Even the latest major new version of 1998 had a subtly changed political orientation (see chapter 4).

- That the Californian hero Zorro was not invented by a twentieth-century American author? He was outlined earlier in nineteenth-century Mexico, and his roots go back to the earliest stirrings of Mexican independence movements centuries earlier.
- That the myth of the eager half-naked hula girls on South Sea Islands, as depicted in all versions of *The Mutiny on the Bounty*, goes back to the accounts of earlier European explorers who probably misunderstood the meaning of the encounters to the locals?
- That the supposedly autobiographical story *Anna and the King* was largely invented—first by Anna Leonowens herself and then by others—and further embellished by theatrical and musical producers? She was only briefly a schoolmistress at the Thai court and never the forbidden love interest or diplomatic adviser of the king.
- That *Black Hawk Down* and many other American war movies were subject to censorship and propaganda by the Pentagon? In exchange for low-cost provision of materials, personnel, and advice, the Pentagon imposes changes on many such scripts.
- That the Bible never claims that Moses was the prince of Egypt or supervising architect of the realm, as he is portrayed in the films *The Prince of Egypt* and *The Ten Commandments*? It turns out a minister's wife changed the Bible story to make it more attractive.
- That the first and second *Star Wars* trilogies, with their "missile shields" and "evil empires" became closely intertwined with the public perception of the foreign and defense policies of the Reagan and both Bush administrations, even after the turn of the twenty-first century?

ABOUT THIS BOOK

Much of the initial material and ideas for this book[1] were accumulated during the dozen years or so that I lectured a video-illustrated academic course titled "Eurocentrism in the Media." The other part of the course was based on my earlier book *Understanding Global News*. It was a very stimulating experience: Students for these courses in English came from the United States, the U.K., and continental Europe, but also from dozens of countries in Africa and the Middle East, Asia and the Pacific, the Caribbean, and Latin America. The course was taught within the framework of the International School for the Humanities and Social Sciences at the University of Amsterdam, but I received further input during occasional guest lectures on similar subjects elsewhere.

Over the years, I have taken great inspiration from some earlier authors: my friends and colleagues Cees Hamelink, who authored *The Politics of World Communication* and a range of other texts on international communication, and Jan Nederveen Pieterse, whose book *White on Black* set a standard; and Ella Shohat and Robert Stam, whose earlier book *Understanding Eurocentrism in the movies* I used in my class for many years.

This book is about the residue of ethnocentrism in recent blockbuster movies circulating in movie theatres and on television screens around the world. Not surprisingly, the vast majority of these global successes are American, but some are coproductions with major European countries such as Great Britain, Germany, and France and occasionally other countries as well. It turns out that many such movies about the encounters between Western heroes and strangers derive from a limited number of "classical" characters, situations, and themes. Many of these are a hundred or more years old, going back to colonial or segregationist days and often still bearing their invisible traces.

The book was written with a relatively broad and twofold audience in mind. On the one hand it is aimed at students of communication and culture, in the humanities and social sciences, and also at teachers and trainers in related fields. It is academically sound, refers back to sources and literature, and explains analytical notions. On the other hand, it is also aimed at a somewhat larger educated general audience. I have tried to make it easily readable, understandable, and vivid and to build on the everyday media experience of a young audience in the age of globalization. I have also provided ample leads for further individual projects and group discussions.

The book focuses on recent blockbuster movies familiar to everyone, rather than on older art house or "alternative" films familiar only to academic scholars, professional reviewers, and amateur cinephiles. I have tried to use plain everyday language as much as possible, steering clear of film-studies jargon most of the time, while still discussing some of its key notions. This text privileges concrete and easy-to-recognize examples over abstract and hard-to-follow interpretations.

In view of the topicality of the subject, I have deliberately included information from reviews, news items, and background stories in newspapers of record, primarily the American general quality newspaper most widely available overseas, the *International Herald Tribune*, abbreviated as *IHT*. *IHT* is now owned and published by the *New York Times*, until recently together with the *Washington Post*. Whenever an item was attributed to either one of those two I have indicated so, but the date always refers to the *IHT* version. Other general quality newspapers of record that I have frequently used as trustworthy sources are the French *Le Monde* and the Dutch *NRC Handelsblad*. Numbers and listings for budgets and box office revenues usually come from reliable movie data websites such as www.the-numbers.com and www.imdb .com and were last updated when this manuscript was completed.

The period of research and writing on this book was facilitated by a small grant from the Netherlands National Commission on Sustainable Development (NCDO), in addition to some of my Amsterdam university research time. I was encouraged by Betteke van Ruler, then head of the Department of Communication Science, Liesbeth van Zoonen of the Centre for Popular Culture, and Jeroen Jansz and Ed Tan, who led the Entertainment Section. A number of academic colleagues took time to provide me with useful criticism and feedback on the manuscript: David Barnouw, Enrique Gomezllata, Cees Hamelink, Jeroen Jansz, Jona Lendering, Irene Meijer, Jan Nederveen Pieterse, Joost Smiers, Lidewij van Gils, and Jan Wieten. Needless to say, they cannot in any way be held accountable for the final decisions I made on the material and its presentation.

Over all these years, many students have provided me with useful input by challenging my assertions and by providing me with new leads, both during class discussions and in written form. A few even wrote their master's theses on these or adjacent subjects under my supervision. All students submitted papers at the end of the trimester term. Whenever some of the material or ideas contained in them proved helpful, I have included their names in the text and references. Wherever I could, however, I have checked their use of sources against the originals.

Special thanks go to intern Elske Oranje and documentation assistant Kyra Storm van Leeuwen, who helped track down material.

Most of all, I wish you as much fun and surprise in reading this book about the overly familiar characters of our popular culture as I had in writing it.

Jaap van Ginneken
early 2007

The Loud and the Silent: Global Film in the Twenty-First Century

What are the movies shown all around the world today? Do they come from all continents, or just from the developed world, and, more particularly, from North America? Why is Hollywood so effective, how is it organized, and what are its key recipes for blockbuster successes? Why do its movies cross cultural borders so well, both within the United States and abroad? To what extent can various genres be distinguished? Do these very diverse movies still share some common cultural point of view? What are the many different ways in which ethnocentrism can creep into a movie?

This is a book about very popular movies, commonly called "blockbusters." I am a great admirer of blockbuster directors such as Steven Spielberg—who is said to have "invented" the new Hollywood blockbuster with his movie *Jaws.* I greatly admire his cinematic craftsmanship as an effective storyteller in early optimistic sci-fi movies such as *Close Encounters of the Third Kind* and *E.T.* and in later social dramas such as *Schindler's List* and the less successful *Amistad,* even if adventure films such as the *Indiana Jones* series are full of stereotypes and shockers such as *Jurassic Park* seem overly exploitative. In his eagerness to remake some of the great interwar genre movies, he was apparently insufficiently aware that the Indiana Jones character and archnarratives were closely intertwined with the Western ethnocentrism of the colonial era.

The same thing has happened to many other blockbuster directors, who simply meant to recycle, renew, and revive some of the great megamyths of the cinema, comics, and literature: about Aladdin, James Bond, the mutiny on the

Bounty, the geisha, the mummy, Tarzan, Zorro, and many others. Most of the time neither they nor their viewers were immediately aware of the many different ways in which these themes are traditionally interrelated with the white superiority complex. Often, the hidden dimensions of these megamyths become apparent only after one takes time to track down the history of these stories, going back to their roots and successive transformations.

This is also a book, then, about how prejudice survives in such adaptations. It is a book about the representation of "other" ethnicities and cultures in present-day blockbuster movies, which are widely shown in theaters, on television channels, and in home video around the world, with a few excursions into the adjacent realms of television reality shows and stage musicals. This first chapter seeks to clarify what is specific about "representation" of "ethnicity and culture" and also about blockbuster movies. Thereafter we will look in some detail at successive genres.

WORDS AND IMAGES

One evening, after putting the final touches on this book, I sat in front of the television set and watched a trailer for the miniseries *Into the West*, produced by Steven Spielberg. It did indeed look like a giant leap forward from the traditional Western, even though some of the scenes and themes still remained mired in the old mythology. My nine-year-old niece Tara was sitting next to me with her back turned, occupied with a computer game. Suddenly she turned around, flabbergasted, having caught some of the commentary: "What? Do they mean to say that Indians actually existed? I always thought they were super-phony!" She apparently believed they were just invented aliens, like E.T. or Darth Vader. I was dumbfounded.

The next day, I asked my nine-year-old son, Anand. "Do you think Indians actually exist?" He did not hesitate for a moment. "Of course they do," he said, in a triumphant tone, "in India!" The two of them surprised me. I had silently taken for granted that they would have learned this, halfway through primary school, but apparently the subject had not yet come up and has also largely disappeared from popular youth culture. We supposedly live in a multimedia and in an information society, but how well-informed are we really, even as adults? How balanced is the information we get—what makes a big impact and what does not?

Until fairly recently, the written word prevailed. Books, newspapers, and magazines provide strings of words or concepts, organized in linear order, with a certain detachment. Gradually, they have been superseded by sounds and images. Records and radio, film and television, present a much more forceful substitute reality. They seem to provide us with much more direct windows into "real life," while mediation and conceptualization fade into the background. Sounds and images about other times and places convince us much more easily that this is how it probably is or was, and it is hard to extricate oneself from their suggestive power. Even the Bible itself has long been superseded by Bible films, as we will see, and their scenes simply have more salience and impact in our minds.

Even within the audiovisual media, there are huge contrasts in style and impact among different categories of film and television: fact and fiction, documentary and drama, dramatized documentary and documentary drama. A plain documentary rarely has the same impact as a dramatized documentary, as in the former the rational logic of the presentation of the facts and of the available material usually prevails, while in the latter the emotional logic of the distribution of roles, stirring our sympathies and antipathies, is artfully heightened. In spite of all claims to "thorough research" and "expert consultants," the contested facts are usually arranged in such a way that one "preferred reading" gains disproportionate force. This is what filmmaking is all about.

The living room was traditionally a "socially controlled" environment, with the eldest male present monopolizing the remote control during the prime-time evening hours. This is one reason why women's programs prevailed during the day, and why children wanted televisions in their own rooms and later turned to viewing, chatting, and gaming over the Internet. The movie theater, by contrast, has traditionally been designed to allow for maximum emotional involvement and release. Projection and sound have been optimized to trigger immediate responses. The large group present and its compact seating facilitates intense experience and reaction. One sits in the dark with total strangers (or alongside intimate peers), so that thresholds are lowered. Cinema is a highly emotional experience.

Just like an amusement park, Russian film pioneer Sergei Eisenstein said, the cinema should be considered a "montage of attractions," an assembly of "strong moments," leading to "the molding of the audience in a desired direction" (Maltby 2003, p. 13). One American screenwriter added that the audience "wants something that will pleasantly excite it, amuse it, wring it with suspense, fill it with self-approval, or even arouse its indignation. . . . It looks to the photoplay to provide it with a substitute for actual life experience" (p. 10). Richard Maltby concludes with director James Cameron (of *Titanic* fame) that paradoxically, "audiences go to the movies to consume their *own* emotions" (p. 14). This is a very important point.

Media formats must by their very nature be extremely condensed and thus stereotypical, as director Martin Scorsese recently admitted, since they range from the ninety-minute feature movie to the thirty-second television commercial. Maltby also agrees with media critic Richard Dyer that escapist entertainment has "more energy and more abundance than the 'real' world . . . its issues, problems, and conflicts are clearer and more intense than those we experience in our day-to-day reality" (Maltby 2003, p. 37). And one anthropologist wrote, "Man, according to Hollywood, is either completely good, or bad. His personality is static, rarely showing any development." This holds in particular for movies aimed at the largest possible audience, but the question is, of course, how realistic or truthful this is (Maltby 2003, p. 39), because in real life all people are complex and contradictory.

This has always been a characteristic of very popular culture: It is usually a kind of puppet theatre of just good and bad, white and black. But in the age of globalization, blockbuster movies require astronomic budgets, and only a handful of corporations have the means to put such productions together. Their prime target audiences are those with the largest purchasing and decision-making power, in the richest, largest countries of the world. Douglas Kellner sums up: "In order to resonate to audience fears, fantasies, and experiences, the Hollywood genres had to deal with the central conflicts and problems in U.S. society and offer soothing resolutions" (Miller & Stam 2004, p. 211)

THE GLOBAL FILM INDUSTRY

In a wider sense, the term "global film industry" means the fully professional production, distribution, and exhibition of films around the world. In a narrower sense, it limits itself to those of its constituent parts that really carry global weight. But how is this decided, and on the basis of what criteria? One approach is to focus on those national film industries that turn out the largest number of feature films per year and reach the most populous countries or language areas.

India (with Bombay/Bollywood) and China (including Hong Kong) would be good candidates. But much of their exports are limited to those countries' emigrant populations abroad. Only very few of their productions actually reach other audiences every year, and fewer have a major impact on them. Likewise, Egyptian films hardly travel beyond the Arab world and Mexican films—even the famed *telenovelas*—hardly beyond the Latino world. So far, only Western films are exported significantly across national, linguistic, and cultural borders to consistently reach global audiences. They are the only ones to really have a transcontinental impact on images of "us" and "them."

The major European nations have a respectable moviemaking tradition. Great Britain, Germany, France, and Italy were early producers and exporters of noteworthy features. They boast an impressive film history, with many big names among directors and actors. In spite of half a billion Euros in European Union (EU) subsidies per year, however, no European country is today a major exporter of feature films in its own right. (At the time of the completion of this manuscript, 1 Euro corresponded to approximately 1.30 American dollars and 0.66 British pounds).[1] Only a few productions get some exposure in neighboring countries every year, but hardly any of them has a real global impact—unless they are coproduced by Hollywood. In these countries, filmmaking is often primarily considered a (partly subsidized) national art form; many films are rather highbrow and/or mean to insert themselves into the national cultural tradition. There is nothing wrong with that; it just does not favor a major impact abroad. In European movies, directors have considerable artistic autonomy; in American ones, producers do often intervene openly to safeguard commercial viability. An interesting example is the recent European movie *Perfume* (2006), based on the best-selling novel by Patrick Süskind. It had some crucial shortcomings in the way the story was told by the director, but most could easily have been corrected even after the film had been completed. The producer should obviously have intervened.

The situation in America is quite different. In the United States, filmmaking is primarily considered a form of commercial popular entertainment, aimed at everybody—even if the prime target group is much more limited. It is a business that has learned how to use considerable investments to turn a hefty profit by taking calculated risks. It has learned how to maximize audience "uses and gratifications" of a film in many different ways. Since the United States is an immigrant society, where many newcomers long remained only semiliterate in English, it has always tried to do this in an all-inclusive way. That is to say, it built in strong appeals and special effects that easily crossed cultural borders. Once it had thus succeeded at home, it often succeeded abroad as well.

But there are other reasons for the global appeal of American films. The United States may not be the most populous nation on Earth, but it is the richest big nation on Earth and therefore has the largest national market. Furthermore, American films do not need any translation to export to some other key rich nations, where many people are native speakers of English—that is to say, in other settler states left over from the British Empire such as Canada, Australia, and New Zealand, as well as Great Britain itself, with Ireland as a special case.

English does not have the largest number of primary (native) speakers; Indian Hindi and Chinese Mandarin have more. But these primary (native) speakers of English are richer, and therefore they form a larger market together.

If one adds secondary (non-native) speakers, the English-language market is even bigger (by far). Furthermore, the area with primary (native) speakers of English shares more than just a language, a literature, a culture, and a history. It shares a present and past of economic, political, and military hegemony, bringing material benefits as well as a pragmatic mentality and social stability at home. Because of this potential reach, U.S. companies can make much bigger investments in the development of the "first copy" of an information, media, or cultural product. Finally, it is in the nature of these products that after the first copy, an unlimited number can be produced at virtually no cost. This is one set of reasons why the United States has a further decisive competitive advantage in these markets worldwide.

Today, copyrighted material and entertainment thus have become the country's largest export category—right after military hardware. Hollywood already gets half of its income and most of its profits from foreign markets. One rule of thumb is that if the original production costs can be earned back in the home market, then further exports to foreign markets amount to almost pure gain. No less than 71 percent of all movies tickets sold within the EU in 2002 were for American films (with 8 percent for films from other European countries, a dismal 1.3 percent from the rest of the world, and only 19.5 percent on average for national productions).[2]

A large proportion of the movies shown on television in many European and Asian countries, particularly in prime time and on prime dates, are also American. Although there is a definite preference for local programs, they cannot easily deliver the same production value for the same price. A significant number of the extra thematic channels with animated cartoons for children, music for adolescents, and news, history, and geography for adults—available to cable and satellite viewers elsewhere in the world—are also of American origin, as are most licensed magazines, books, comic strips, CDs, games, toys, computer programs, Internet providers, websites, and so on.

It should be added, however, that Hollywood and the U.S. culture industry have always attracted ample foreign input, thrived on it, and rewarded it as well. They have always welcomed talented writers, directors, actors, and performers and given them largely equal opportunities: whether refugees, migrants, or people with temporary work permits. In recent years, some studios have been bought by foreign (e.g., Japanese) companies, and many projects have been financed by foreign (e.g., German) investors. Much of the actual filming is also increasingly done abroad, often in less-developed nations of eastern Europe or North Africa, which may provide great historical or natural settings, willing crews, and cheap extras. As is increasingly the case in other advanced industries, California is sometimes a mere "design and management center" where projects are put together, while much of the actual work is out-sourced abroad.

To what extent does it make sense, then, to continue to consider these products primarily American or Hollywood movies? It makes sense because their production mostly follows the American and Hollywood mold outlined below. Key elements in this whole process continue to give them a primarily American and Hollywood flavor, even if the scope has somewhat broadened in recent years, with an eye on rising sales overseas. Coproductions with Great Britain (for instance, in the James Bond franchise) or with Germany (in some recent antiquity blockbuster movies) also carry this same stamp. So what is specific about "the new Hollywood"?

THE NEW HOLLYWOOD

At first, the U.S. film business was mostly concentrated on the East Coast, in New York, which was also where most of the new immigrants from Europe ar-rived. Jewish entrepreneurs and talents were particularly prominent in cul-ture, media, and show business, for reasons related to the previous impact of anti-Semitism on the sociology of that group in Europe.[3] Filmmaking, how-ever, needed good and constant lighting conditions, a varied landscape, spa-cious lots, and cheap labor, none of which were available in the bustling metropolis of New York. So the center of the emerging film industry soon moved to Los Angeles on the West Coast, and particularly to its suburb, Hol-lywood. The "dream factories" built there soon turned it into the worldwide capital of make-believe.

But today's Hollywood is not the same as the earlier Hollywood of the 1950s or even the 1930s. After its first golden age between the two world wars, the postwar movie industry was hit by a succession of two crises. The first cri-sis was related to form: As the rise of television from the late 1940s on tended to make people stay at home to watch movies on the small screen, Hollywood came up with wide-screen spectaculars to continue to draw them to the the-atres. But as costs rose, audiences still became somewhat wary of these for-mulas: with their monumental historical settings and large number of grimed extras. (This will be discussed in greater detail in chapter 3.)

The second crisis was related to content. As Hollywood continued to use the same old recipes, it initially missed out on the cultural revolution among the baby boomers of the 1960s. *Easy Rider* was an early example of an inde-pendent counterculture success, but meanwhile the studios accumulated duds and their profits fell. But a new generation of "movie brats" came up with a series of highly personal hits: Francis Ford Coppola with *The Godfather*, William Friedkin with *The Exorcist*, Martin Scorsese with *Taxi Driver*, and many others. This led to a certain popularity of the French auteur theory of filmmaking, according to which the director is considered the primary creative force in making a movie.

But two directors did more than just make a few hits: They revived the entire system and ultimately also gave the studios a completely new lease on life. Steven Spielberg with *Jaws*, George Lucas with *Star Wars*, and their collaboration in *Indiana Jones* fundamentally changed the rules of the game and placed the dream factory business on an entirely different footing. Although it took decades for the entire pattern of new exploitation strategies and tactics to unfold, the revolution did indeed take hold—and it changed the industry forever. This new blockbuster approach focused on the "shock and awe" introduction of a new pop-cult phenomenon, its exploitation by multiple means, and an endless recycling of the same themes. But in order to be able to exploit this phenomenon, one needed more than a good movie; one needed both vertical and horizontal integration with a wide range of other activities, largely within the broader framework of a major corporation.

We have already mentioned that—for a variety of reasons—Jewish immigrant entrepreneurs happened to become particularly prominent in early show biz. Five out of the big major studios or film production companies were founded (or cofounded) by Jewish pioneers: Carl Laemmle with Universal, Adolph Zukor with Paramount, William Fox with Fox, Louis B. Mayer with MGM, and Benjamin Warner with Warner Bros. (Gabler 1988, p. 3). Latecomer Walt Disney resented their preeminence and was said to have occasionally made anti-Semitic remarks about them. Only later did the group of owners and directors become broader in composition.

The original studios continually split and merged, but most survive to this day in one form or another. Today, the major studios control almost 80 percent of the movie business in the United States, and 50 percent in many European and Asian countries (Stringer 2003, p. 77). One of their roles is the milking of their great heritage of films—but also of stories and characters, some newly adapted to the television and video age. With the explosion of television channels that needed to be filled, the value of film libraries has risen twenty-fold in only twenty years, to an estimated $8 billion around the turn of the twenty-first century.

But the independence of the studios has gone, and they have become embedded within much broader corporate frameworks. The movie studios are now linked in one way or another to the major U.S. television and cable networks—as well as to theme parks, Internet providers, record companies, video game producers, and book and newspaper publishers—all within the framework of enormous media empires such as News Corp, Viacom, or AOL Time Warner.

Some of these media empires, in turn, belong—partly or wholly—to *Fortune* 500 companies with considerable nonmedia interests, such as General Electric. Sony and Matsushita, Japanese producers of consumer electronics, have entered the fray to have more clout in the battle over standards such as HDTV. The German publisher Bertelsmann has moved into the audiovisual field. But there is constant change, buying and selling of assets, in search of optimal synergy.

Since the movie studios are now part of much larger media empires, they can mobilize much larger budgets to try to create a successful film. The average cost of production and marketing for major studio pictures had shot up to well over $80 million by the beginning of the twenty-first century, and some films command double that sum or more. In his 2006 book *Bambi vs. Godzilla*, David Mamet, movie critic for the British daily *The Guardian*, complained that Hollywood was making films of increasing expense and diminishing worth. Six out of ten fail to return their costs, while another one or two break even. So the remaining two or three relative hits are the "tent poles" supporting the rest. It is clear that only huge corporations can support such risks.

But the investment may also bring a hefty profit. Top earner *Titanic* has brought in almost $2 billion—so far. The top ten earners all brought in close to a billion dollars. This covers only the total box office. The top ten sellers on the all-time hit list all date from the last decade. The top two hundred sellers all date from the last three decades, with only two exceptions. These top two hundred all earned $250 million or more at the box office alone; in comparison, the highest-grossing real foreign-language film, *Crouching Tiger, Hidden Dragon*, earned only half that sum in the United States. The most successful French films of recent years made only between $30 and $60 million in the United States.

Although fewer Americans go to the cinema than they did decades ago—and those who do go less often—the theatrical release of blockbuster movies is still decisive for the whole pattern of exploitation that follows. Around the last turn of the century, less than a third of the U.S. population over age twelve went to the movies once a month, whereas more than a quarter never went at all. Children, adolescents, and young adults prevail. Blockbusters are mostly seen by the less educated; college students often favor art house films. (But hardly anyone in my ten-year class, with students from all over the world, remembered having seen a film from a fundamentally different continent).

Paradoxically—in view of some of what follows—minorities are avid movie-goers. But what formats are used to reach these groups?

THE BLOCKBUSTER ECONOMY

Today the vast majority of the movie industry is geared to churning out so-called blockbusters. In the past, if a movie was a hit, it was called a "bombshell." Today, a movie that is a super hit is called a "blockbuster," after the extra-heavy bombs that are used against enemy bunkers of reinforced concrete. Other types of smaller-scale, special-interest movies have become increasingly marginalized. So some movie voices are overly loud, in the theaters around the world, whereas others are almost silent. This is because, although the studios ultimately aim at producing lasting and worldwide successes, their original focus in developing a new project is much narrower, as they must first conquer a very well-defined U.S. target group during a very short period of time.

The most coveted release dates in the United States are in December for the Christmas/winter season and near Independence Day for the summer holiday season, with Memorial Day and Thanksgiving as alternatives in spring and autumn. These release dates also favor American family and patriotic themes in blockbusters. Traditionally, the U.S. opening weekend "take" is widely considered the best predictor for further success. In order to capitalize on their own marketing efforts, and to dodge possible negative reviews and/or negative word-of-mouth, the studios have increasingly moved from a "road show" or gradual release pattern to saturation of one, two, or even three thousand theatres at the same time.

The economic and media deregulation of the Reagan-Bush era has facilitated this, as it allowed chains to concentrate on the one-third of screens that cover 80 percent of the box office. Today these are usually multiplex theatres at key locations, exploiting a number of screens with a limited staff. Since they are usually located in the most strategic and fashionable regions, they also influence what people in other regions will want to see. Even as early as the mid-1990s, the 150 major movies per year that followed a wide-release pattern garnered a whopping 95 percent of all theatrical revenues.

By 2005, total U.S. box office revenue was almost $9 billion—almost 40 percent of the worldwide total of slightly more than $23 billion. Ten years earlier, the cinema share of the home box office take in the total revenues from a film had already fallen to as little as one-sixth (Stringer 2003, p. 70). Traditionally, release in domestic theatres was followed by release in foreign theatres, first in the more important and then in the less important markets overseas, but there is now a tendency toward near-simultaneous release of mega-blockbusters worldwide, accompanied by a global publicity tidal wave.

This used to be followed by release on VHS (now on DVD), but also digitally and on pay-per-view channels. At the height of their popularity, DVDs earned half a movie's revenue for the studios. This was followed by release on pay television, cable and satellite, and ordinary broadcast and network television, first at home and then abroad, with biannual repeats for most major movies. But theater owners are feeling the pinch. They are complaining that the time window between theatrical and DVD releases is continually shrinking. Even online video distribution is taking off rapidly and is expected to be an $11 billion business by 2011. In the end, viewers who are even remotely interested cannot escape seeing the movie sooner or later. This is another reason why American blockbusters increasingly belong to the "cultural baggage" of most citizens of the developed world, and much of the semideveloped world as well. Their reach and impact cannot be overestimated.

But concurrent with a movie's release, a wide range of ancillary products is released as well, from the promotional "making of" documentary for television to textbooks and picture books, comics and theme park rides, music records and video games, clothes and gadgets, premiums and toys. As a matter of fact, this is today part of the financial and marketing plan from the very beginning. It adds up to a worldwide promotional tsunami that quickly affects hundreds of millions—or even billions—of people worldwide. In 1999, the total retail value of the licensed product market was already estimated at $70 billion per year. A year later, the *Jurassic Park* franchise alone had already generated $5 billion (Maltby 2003, pp. 190, 208).

Today, children's channels often get their broadcasting material relatively cheaply, since most television series and movies for kids also serve as promotion for licensed toys. Classic story characters are updated to make them easier to produce and more inviting to play with. Disney, for instance, had a ten-year licensing contract with McDonald's—to their mutual benefit. The deal brought Disney a huge fee of $100 million, with considerable free marketing and advertising exposure, but it also helped McDonald's sell Happy Meals to children—and made the fast-food chain nominally the largest toy outlet in the world.

THE BLOCKBUSTER FORMAT

The key problem of movie exploitation is balancing complexity and simplicity and determining how to effectively communicate the latter to the diverse groups involved. The blockbuster solution to this problem is called "high concept": a straightforward idea. This basically means that it must be possible to "pitch" the (appeal of the) movie in only one unique image and only one alluring sentence to everyone involved, taking no more than the equivalent of thirty seconds, the length of a television spot. The pitch should be able to trigger attention, interest, desire, and action—to use the terms of the classical AIDA marketing model—get people to buy a ticket and go see the film. Whether they will actually like it is quite another matter.

Another aspect is the involvement of "big names" in the project. Viacom president Sumner Redstone fired actor Tom Cruise in 2006, after bad publicity related to his involvement with Scientology damaged the gross of the third installment of *Mission: Impossible.* There is no value to a studio to retain an actor demanding high fees who no longer has a positive impact at the box office. This may be partly true in the United States, but it is not always true for the overseas markets, where big names and familiar faces make it easier to sell a film, particularly in an unfamiliar environment.

The notoriety of star actors and actresses is maintained and enlarged by popular magazines, paparazzi pictures, and gossip columns. Industry publications continually rate their A-status and earning power not only on the basis of past successes, but also on the basis of current visibility. Premiere and gala nights, award ceremonies, and festivals attract further media attention to these stars and "their" films. They may even emphatically court controversy and tweak social mores to get free publicity: for instance, by doing films dealing with relationship and sexual themes in ways that are sure to stir the outrage of conventional citizens, as in the succession of mid-1990s movies *Basic Instinct, Indecent Proposal, Disclosure,* and *Striptease.*

More recently, Hollywood has discovered that there is something even better than stars: disguises. Disney had already found that animated cartoon characters do not run the risk of spurring controversy, particularly if the copyrights of the original creators and their descendants have run out. Others have chosen to recycle a whole range of classic American superheroes and supervillains: Batman, Spider-Man, Superman, and company. Star actors are hired to provide voices in animated films or act in the moves, but they command much lower fees and are easily replaceable. This also allows producers to make endless sequels, designing and redesigning the characters, costumes, and props in such a way that generates maximum spin-off opportunities. New developments in computer-generated synthetic images also make it ever easier to merge real actors with virtual characters.

Another way to milk a franchise is to release sequels, one after another. By 2007, the three *Lord of the Rings* movies had brought in $2.9 billion, the first three *Harry Potter* movies $2.6 billion, and the three *Matrix* movies, the first two *Spider-Man* movies, and the first two *Pirates of the Caribbean* films $1.6 billion each. The advantage of this is that some costs can be written off on several installments, whereas the marketing hype benefits all of them. These super-blockbusters have only limited resonance with the ethnicity and culture divide as such, so they will not be discussed elaborately in this book. By contrast, we will return to the *Jurassic Park* and *Star Wars* cycles, even if their reflection on ethnicity is also only implicit.

A final and key ingredient in blockbuster movies is the spectacular. In the old days, this derived primarily from large numbers of extras moving in great and expensive sets against wide and impressive backgrounds. Today, however, these can also be generated by computer and can be endlessly enhanced by special effects—as, for example, in the *Matrix* movies. Only Hollywood studios are able to invest in the costly equipment needed to outrace the competition and come up with new and mind-boggling spectaculars that "blow the audience out of its seat," time and again. Director James Cameron is planning to make full use of new synthetic techniques for the supermovie *Avatar*, to be released in the summer of 2009. These are also elements that travel extremely well across cultural borders, both within the United States and outside it.

The rise of broadband connection to the Internet is now giving impetus to the further transformation of the film industry—now, movie material can be delivered instantaneously, anywhere in the world, for high-quality viewing at home, in the theatre, or anything in between. Douglas Gomery concludes that "nothing looms on the horizon to alter this business," since "A handful of companies . . . still have hegemony over the creation of the movie blockbusters and their distribution in all technologies around the world. . . . These companies may have new owners, but they show no sign of weakening. Indeed, if anything, they are getting stronger. . . . The Hollywood oligopoly has learned to thrive in an age of advanced technologies, based on skilled use of media economics" (Stringer 2003, p. 82). In Hollywood, it is clear: bigger is better.

GENRES

The rest of this book is devoted to a discussion of ethnocentric elements in blockbuster movies. In order to discuss such a large body of past, present, and future films in an orderly manner, they are here divided into different sorts and categories, which cultural observers traditionally call genres (Browne 1998; Creeber 2001). The term "genre" was long used by film reviewers and scholars as if it were completely self-evident and nonproblematic. Everybody seemed to agree on the existence of a limited number of film genres and subgenres, but in recent years has this use been questioned (Altman 1999; Neale 2002).

Once we recognize that genres simply provide a convenient way of sorting films into some kind of order, it becomes immediately apparent that there are many different ways of categorizing films, books, or "texts" in such a way. We can sort films according to the technique used (for instance, "animation"), the costumes and setting (for instance, "peplum" for antiquity movies), the approach and style (for instance, "film noir" for certain hard-boiled crime movies), the intended target audience (for instance, children's or women's movies), or the intended emotional effect (for instance, thrillers or horror or comedies). Since all these aspects overlap, the traditional grid turns out to be contradictory and shifting.

From a social-scientific perspective, therefore, a better question may be, What are these labels meant to achieve? Upon closer inspection, they are meant to facilitate communication about a type of media product or project. This is related to the ever-growing complexity of the business.

With books, it is still relatively simple at the outset. A writer develops a book on his or her own, a unique, individual product. The complications arise when he or she contacts a publishing house. The publisher must determine whether it belongs in a series, what cover and design and "appearance" to give it, what reviewers and booksellers to approach, and so forth. This is all communication within strict limits; therefore, it needs to be straightforward and effective. With movie production, this becomes much more complex as it may start with just producers and investors but ultimately involves crews of hundreds of people from many different fields. With television programming for commercial channels, the specific appeals to a target demographic group need to be outlined, as this is the only basis on which advertising space can be presold.

So genres are a convenient kind of label, giving hints about what to expect from a media product. In filmmaking and television, they are needed to help connect three worlds: those of producers, consumers, and the intermediaries between them such as distributors and broadcasters, press and reviewers. This is done with the help of a very limited set of words and images that stir expectations about the entire movie itself by relating it to a set of similar previous movies in the very small space allowed for blurbs, ads, programming schedules, and television guides. Of course, sellers may try to hype their product and deceive the buyers, but they do so at their own expense.

Since genre labels are only a pragmatic communication device, the understanding the public has of them may shift over time. So genres are not a fixed category but whatever the relevant groups take them to be. Old genres may almost fade away, such as the Western, and new genres, such as the space adventure, may supersede them. In today's hectic media world, there is a continuous quest for new successful formats—including many second-rate imitations and predictable recombinations.

Whereas yesterday's audiences were still primarily oriented toward text and book genres, today's audiences are oriented toward image and movie genres.

One of the pleasures of being familiar with a genre is that one can recognize even minor similarities and differences with previous productions relating to a similar character or situation. Many productions are full of such subtle hints to the initiated, warranting even a second or further viewing. Since movies are called media "texts," this phenomenon is called intertextuality. All texts of a culture in some way or another implicitly refer to (or merely resonate with) many other texts, so attributed meaning may also differ, depending on the context in which the viewer places a text. This produces endless possibilities for both conventional and critical interpretation of such texts.

CULTURAL STRUGGLE

This book is about a twofold question. On the one hand, we have seen that the vast majority of the movies with the biggest impact are made by a relatively small group of people, namely, those at the top of the economic, social, and cultural pyramid in a globalizing world. Our lore masters and major producers of popular culture are people in and around Hollywood and New York, with some further input from other major Anglo-Saxon countries and other major continental European countries. They are mostly men, mostly white, and mostly multimillionaires—although most also consider themselves somehow "enlightened." On the other hand, they also form a kind of prism, a system of cultural lenses that distorts the historical and global reality in a very specific way, because the blockbuster makers largely belong to the same cultures and subcultures.

Culture is a set of *hidden* assumptions a group uses about what is taken for granted: what is considered natural, logical, and self-evident in everyday life and work, in conversations and the media. Most of the time, we do not consciously realize that we belong to a culture, but we may experience a vague unease whenever these hidden assumptions are challenged. Ethnicity refers to the external traits certain categories of people share. According to the American sociologist William Graham Sumner, ethnocentrism is the phenomenon by which everyone takes his or her own ethnic group and culture as a yardstick against which other ethnic groups and cultures are measured. In most cases, this results in us seeing our own values and norms, our own customs and habits, as somehow better than those of others; though sometimes, it should be added, the reverse occurs.

According to a famous study by the Palestinian-American intellectual Edward Said, this phenomenon applies to the views that successive Western travelers, writers, and artists—but also scholars and experts—developed about the Arab world, the Middle East, and the Orient beyond it. According to a 2004 essay written by Israeli philosopher Avishai Margalit and Dutch author

Ian Buruma, in turn, anti-Western agitators and propagandists (such as Osama bin Laden and al-Qaeda) cultivate an even more stereotypical and prejudiced view of the West. Both Orientalism and Occidentalism make an overly simplistic distinction between the East and the West, then enlarge and generalize it in a way that severely distorts a multifaceted reality.

During the modern age—since the Enlightenment—elites and masses within the Western world increasingly adhered to one all-embracing grid of interpretation and valuation that could easily classify any human phenomenon as either high or low, left or right, advanced or backward. It was the epoch of the all-embracing "big stories." From the postwar period on, however, and during the 1960s and 1970s, women and workers, ethnic minorities, and overseas peoples increasingly challenged this hegemonic view for the premature value judgments contained therein, which further contributed to the perpetuation of their underprivileged position. Since then, postmodernism and relativism support the view that the same reality may legitimately be seen in different ways by different people.

This resulted in a critique of the overemphasis on the sole achievements of a male, white upper class. At times, however, this critique became overly shrill and one-sided, and beginning in the 1980s and 1990s, a reaction set in against those who were derogatively labeled the "multicultis" and the "politically correct." After the turn of the twenty-first century and the terrorist attacks by fundamentalist Muslims, this countermovement reached its apparent apex. In 2006 the Jewish-British comedian Sacha Baron Cohen did a hilarious spoof of a "Kazak" television reporter, Borat, in what was probably the most un-PC movie ever made. *Borat* illustrates that the general and abstract notions about political correctness are too facile because images may be layered and contradictory. In this book, I want to investigate a broad range of concrete cases and precise details with regard to feature films.

The multimedia industry is extremely complex, just like processes of intercultural communication in which one culture forms an image of the next. In a previous book, *Understanding Global News* (1998), I tried to dissect this for everyday news: about whom and what, where and when—and, most of all, why—successively looking at the philosophy, economics, sociology, politics, historiography, linguistics, semiotics, and psychology of international newsgathering. It turned out that there are at least ten different mechanisms at work in ten different fields. Together they result in a "selective articulation" of certain facts and relationships in the everyday "naturalization" of the Western ethnocentric view. A hundred and one tiny little forms of bias of 1 percent each thus result in a gross distortion of sometimes even 100 percent.

This book, about the exotic megamyths of Hollywood, has a somewhat different approach. The chapters focus on respective genres in which the encounter between Westerners and "strangers" somehow plays a central role. On some occasions the movies claim historical veracity, on others they are admitted fiction, but they are usually an ill-defined mixture of the two. Within this framework, we are going to put "cases" of subgenres, series, or individual movies under the microscope. These are not primarily old, small, or arty films known only to a small group of initiates, but rather recent, big, and very commercial ones familiar to most: blockbusters from the top two hundred best-earning features of all time.

The making of such huge movies demands the input of tens if not hundreds or even thousands of people: producers and investors, scriptwriters and directors, set makers and prop designers, costume makers and hair dressers, actors and extras, stunt doubles and experts, camera crews and lighters. For days, weeks, and months, they have to make decisions, often in a split second—based on intuition, expertise, and experience—about plausible characters and situations, dialogue and text, accents and intonations, looks and make-up, frames and sequences, sounds and music. At the end of the line is a final series of decisions about presentation, distribution, and promotion of the film.

Since all this is also related to our own and other cultures, it is almost inevitable that a certain degree of ethnocentrism does somehow silently creep into the final product. It is no use to be overly judgmental about that. The point of the exercise is to study the myriad ways in which this happens—most of the time completely inadvertently—in order to learn from it and to heighten our sensitivity on this score, even if it is true that many such details remain polysemic. That is to say, they can always be interpreted in different ways: One may adhere to the dominant view, to an opposing one, or even try to "negotiate" the meaning one wants to assign to any such detail.

The final chapter will bring some of these lines of observation together again, to make an inventory of the many ways in which such a blockbuster can become colored or rather "whitened"—often against the express intention of the makers. Readers may then try to apply this same grid on their own to new releases.

But let us first take a closer look at one of the most endearing and "innocent" genres, also one of the most widely spread and influential: the full-length animated cartoons of the Disney Studios.

Children and Adults: Animated Cartoons

What are the first words we get to hear, the first images we get to see, about other ethnic groups and cultures? To what extent do the terminology and iconography of a different day and age survive in present-day versions of children's "classics"? Do American, British, and some continental European creations take up a disproportional share of this supposedly "universal" heritage? How does this translate into the current body of cinematic and blockbuster productions? What about the key role of Walt Disney, his studio, and its continuous output of new animated cartoons? What about its efforts to "go global" during the last decade preceding the turn of the century, with films about Aladdin, Simba the Lion King, Pocahontas, and Mulan?

Socialization is "growing into" one's own culture and learning to use its hidden codes. This also entails getting to know key words and images, anecdotes, and stories about other cultures. So try to bring to your mind the earliest words and images you heard and saw associated with other ethnical groups or cultures: about blacks and Africa; about Arabs and the Middle East; about great civilizations of South, Southeast, and East Asia such as India, China, and Japan; about the tropical islands of the Pacific Ocean and the Caribbean Sea; about Latinos and the native population of the Americas; and about Inuit peoples in the far north.

At home, fairy tales and classic children's stories have been read to us—a large part of which stemmed from the era of the so-called voyages of discovery and the subsequent eras of colonialism and segregation, a time when Europeans dominated other continents and peoples, enjoying many more rights than those they dominated, right up to the anachronism of South African apartheid. The same holds for many classic comic strips.[1] Even at school, we learned geography on the basis of ethnocentric maps and ethnocentric names for regions and places, for majorities and minorities, and history on the basis of an ethnocentric choice and framing of noteworthy people and events.[2] It is true that since the 1960s these versions have evolved, but they are often still far from ideal.

ANIMATED CARTOONS

Whereas early children's literature simply described other lands and peoples in words, illustrations showed them in pictures—that is to say, in emphatic shades of white and black, of brown, red, and yellow—and even more so in early comic strips and animated cartoons. As opposition against ethnic stereotyping rose in North America and in western Europe, however, there was a silent shift to animal characters depicting interaction and confrontation between species, rather than people. They were made to seem "natural" even though the storylines often resonated obviously with real-world conflicts between races or classes (another taboo in commercial popular culture).

A pioneer in animated film, Walt Disney was not so much a genius as a storyteller or as an artist, but rather as the inventor and supervisor of the large-scale industrial production and reproduction of children's lore, from the systematic collection of individual texts and illustrations abroad, to the optimization and recombination of usable elements therein, to the creation and protection of new copyrights and their additional exploitation through merchandising and theme parks. This process of course also entailed "recycling" preexisting ethnic stereotypes, for instance, in early animated cartoons such as *Peter Pan* and *The Jungle Book*, based on the British colonial-era books of James Barrie and Rudyard Kipling.

One of my students noted about *Peter Pan* that "Neverland is portrayed as a classic tropical paradise with blue water, palm trees, mountains, waterfalls, forests and lagoons. It promises all the right adventures for the children: pirates, Indians, mermaids, and a 'cannibal cove.' Like Barrie's work, the Disney version treats Tiger Lily differently than the other 'redskins.' She is very attractive, a nice shade of light brown, innocent, proud, and stoic [compare Pocahontas, discussed later], whereas the other Indians are introduced as sneaky, hidden, threatening, and ultimately all look the same with some variation of body type. They have exaggerated features, big noses, wagging tongues, funny bodies, and appear very red. They speak 'stupid' broken English and words like 'ugh' and 'how.' The usual symbols are here: tee-pees, tomahawks, buckskin outfits, arrows, drums, bare feet, war cries, hand signals, a peace pipe, and allusions to impending human sacrifice—if Peter does not save the day" (Maas-Despain 2003).

During the 1990s, Disney Studios charted a new course: The largest producer of children's movies in the world released a rapid succession of four animated cartoons featuring exotic characters: *Aladdin*, *The Lion King*, *Pocahontas*, and *Mulan*. All four films were listed among the top hundred highest-grossing films, and made between $300 and $800 million each at the box office. There can be no doubt that they were not only commercial but also artistic successes. Their visual representation of exotic natural and cultural environments was very impressive and poetic.

Three out of the four films received Academy Awards for musical score and/or original song. Yet their greatest achievement is no doubt the direction and orchestration of so many separate teams for major characters and storylines, of the hundreds of people involved in such productions over a number of years. But what motivated this "exotic offensive," and how did it fit into the strategy of Disney?

After Walt's death, his son-in-law Ron Miller and his brother's son Roy Disney initially took over the reins. But in spite of continuing expansion during the 1970s, the empire's profitability fell, and corporate raiders began to prey on its stock. During the early 1980s it became increasingly clear that younger, more professional, and more aggressive management from outside was desperately needed. After the Gulf & Western conglomerate bought Paramount Studios, Paramount CEO Michael Eisner and production president Jeffrey Katzenberg were lured to Disney.

Eisner and Katzenberg soon realized that the recent home video revolution provided an excellent new opportunity to exploit Disney's vast film library of 250 features and 450 shorts. But they also realized they had to get back on mainstream television, both to get regular exposure for their characters to new generations and to garner free publicity for the Disney theme parks—the most profitable branch of the business. During the second half of the 1980s, these new policies boosted the company's gross from $1.7 to $5.8 billion, and personnel increased from 30,000 to 52,000 (van Willigen 1995, p. 167).

At the same time, however, new feature-length animated cartoons were needed, to expand and update the catalog with new "classics" and characters. As Disney seemed to be rapidly nearing its limits of growth in North America and western Europe, a major effort had to be made to break into the emerging markets of Africa, Arabia, Asia, and the rest of the Americas. Of course, exotic characters were not entirely new to the Disney universe. But there was a need for different material on (and for) non-European peoples and continents. That is where *Aladdin, The Lion King, Pocahontas,* and *Mulan* came in—and they became huge successes.

Yet there is also a downside to this industrial approach to storytelling for children. It always begins with extensive research, making a complete inventory of all the anecdotes and stories, stills and sequences ever produced on such characters and settings. The most impressive of these ideas often creep back into their final product: knowingly or unknowingly, lawfully or less so. This is doubly ironic because the Disney Corporation itself is eager to mobilize huge teams of well-paid lawyers to sue anyone thought to infringe on their copyright. Another problem is that the vast majority of this material usually emerges from the distant past of Europe and America, even if it deals with other continents. It inevitably includes a heavy dose of ethnocentric thinking, even if this goes against the conscious and expressed desire of the makers.

Janet Wasko summarized: "In certain cases, representatives of the Disney company have responded to criticism by explaining that they did not intend to misrepresent minorities. The problem is that even though creators of popular cultural products may have admirable nonracist goals, nevertheless we are left with their creations, not their intentions" (2001, p. 139). As the leading creators of such fantasies, as well as their prime targets, are primarily white Americans and Europeans, there will always be a tendency to adopt a Western perspective, with the concerns of others of only marginal concern.

Let us take a closer look at how this worked out in the case of each of these four productions. How did ethnocentrism seep and creep into them: in the most familiar versions of the original stories, in the embellishment or belittling of certain literary or historic characters, or even in arbitrary changes further making caricatures out of them?

DISNEY AND EXOTIC BOYS

Interestingly, the four films can be assigned to two different categories. During the first half of the 1990s, two animated cartoons constructed around exotic boys were released: *Aladdin* and *The Lion King.* These were followed in the second half of the decade by two animated cartoons constructed around exotic girls: *Pocahontas* and *Mulan.* In spite of the seeming diversity of the subjects, they have certain ideological subtexts in common: all four of them, and then two by two as well. We will delve somewhat into the original historical circumstances, the original stories, and the original fantasies related to each story, and we will find that in each one of these cases, the characters have been flagrantly altered to suit white pride and prejudice.

Case Study: Aladdin and the Middle East

Throughout the 1960s the Israeli-Arab conflict persisted stubbornly, the 1970s had brought two major oil price hikes, and the 1980s had revealed a sudden wealth in some Gulf states. There was a rise of interest in the region and its emerging middle classes, both in North America and in western Europe. So it seemed perfectly natural that when the popular-culture industry and Hollywood started looking for exotic material, they would turn to the Middle East. Disney Studios undertook its first major project ever based on an exotic source, with the first major leading role for a nonwhite character since Mowgli in *The Jungle Book*. Studio chief Jeffrey Katzenberg said that he had been fascinated by the *Aladdin* story since his childhood and had always wanted to make a film about it.

"Aladdin" was one of the stories of *The Book of One Thousand and One Nights*, supposedly told by the beautiful young woman Scheherazade to keep a tyrannical sovereign spellbound. Another famous one, repeatedly and stereotypically filmed, was "The Thief of Baghdad." *The Arabian Nights* derived from a huge and ever-changing collection of anonymous folk tales In spoken language, passed on through the ages by storytellers in marketplaces (similar to the famous one in present-day Marrakech). Some stories came from as far away as India, the collection was originally Persian, was translated into Arab at the end of the eighth or beginning of the ninth century CE, and only took its Arab title, *Alf laila wa laila*, during the tenth century. According to Rana Kabbani's *Europe's Myths of the Orient* (1986), Christian Crusaders then brought some stories back home, where they influenced medieval European works such as the famous *Orlando Furioso*.

Antoine Galland, a diplomat at the French embassy to the Turkish court at Constantinople, first translated large parts of the collection in 1704, along with other classical texts. However, he changed and embellished them at will, for instance by expanding the famous Ali Baba story from a mere six to thirty-six pages. (Much of this inserted European material later turned up in Hollywood movies, as well as in Disney's *Aladdin* and its sequels). Galland later regretted that these fanciful *turqueries* became more successful than his more serious translations. In this form, the stories also influenced the ideas of eighteenth-century Enlightenment philosophers such as Montesquieu, Rousseau, and Voltaire. Henry Torrens later made a first English translation of *The Arabian Nights*, but such early translators were criticized by later ones for their further arbitrary injection of funny styles and accents (Arberry 1953).

This is how the imagined universe of sensuous women enclosed in the steamy harems of vengeful rulers residing in opulent palaces took further form. According to Edward Said's famous study *Orientalism*: "The Orient was almost a European invention . . . a place of romance, exotic beings, haunting memories and landscapes, remarkable experiences" (1978, p. 1). In this form, it had always provided attractive material for popular movies and animated cartoons. The Aladdin theme had earlier surfaced in the Donald Duck stories and was then elaborated in *Ducktales, the Movie: Treasure of the Lost Lamp* (1990). The development, production, and release of the feature-length animated cartoon *Aladdin* (1992), though, took place in a highly charged atmosphere of ideological confrontation, which left blatant traces in the film.

The United States had long supported the monarchical regime of the shah in Iran, but this had been overthrown by a popular revolt under the fundamentalist Islamic cleric Ayatollah Khomeini, followed by a decades-long confrontation between the new regime and the United States. The relative international isolation of the new regime was then exploited by Saddam Hussein, president of the adjacent secular republic of Iraq, who tried to settle old disputes by launching an all-out war, which ultimately victimized more than a million people. When it turned out he had miscalculated and was on the verge of losing, both the United States and major EU countries began in the greatest secrecy to help him with intelligence and the means to deploy weapons of mass destruction such as poison gas, delivery vehicles, and the like. But when he subsequently tried to use this newly acquired military arsenal against Kurdish separatists and to annex the "lost province" of Kuwait in 1991, the West turned against him and suddenly "discovered" his crimes.

This immediate context is made apparent in the Disney film in many different ways. The major "bad guy" in *Aladdin*, Grand Vizier Jafar, looked almost exactly like the hated Ayatollah Khomeini. And his stooge, perhaps added to the opening scene as an afterthought, looked very much like Saddam Hussein. The sympathetic king, by contrast, was emphatically de-Middle-Easternized into an Indian maharaja (with a tiger as pet). The unlimited treasure they were fighting over— in the cave of wonders deep under the desert—was an obvious metaphor for petroleum, and the villains were apparently also seeking absolute power through weapons of mass destruction as the final scenes show poison gas, nuclear energy, and bombs. The genie was once again let out of the bottle/lamp there and literally said, "I work for Señor Psychopath now" (Bernstein & Studlar 1997, pp. 193–94). These subliminal political messages were masked by the hysterically funny genie jokes and brilliantly executed scenes.

The subtext of such Hollywood movies is always that young people in exotic lands are innocent and open minded until they are corrupted by traditional and obscurantist elders. In this case, Aladdin followed the mold of the ideal suburban son-in-law, with the face of Tom Cruise or Michael J. Fox. In the character development department, a lot of thought had obviously been given to the exact shape of Semitic noses; the more important or sympathetic a character was to be to the American or European audience, the less "characteristic" the nose would be. Aladdin was given an almost perfectly straight nose; Jasmine's was only slightly bent. Ordinary people were given more "typical" Arab noses; brutes even more so; and Jafar's was completely crooked. But most people in the audience do not notice such subtle ethnic "signifiers" on a conscious level. Feminists pointed out that Jasmine sought her freedom by giving it up in typically romantic fashion—as the beautiful princess emancipated herself from the court by throwing herself in his arms of (literally) the very first common man to come along outside the palace walls.

The film is also packed with Orientalist bric-a-brac. I often play a little game with my students: They freely associate with the word "Arab," and I note down the list on the blackboard. They say: desert, sandstorm, earthquake; market, junk, haggling; poverty, starvation, opulence; gems, copper work, flying carpets; and so on and so forth. I then show them the first ten minutes of the film, where all these elements are already put in place, along with Indian fakirs alternately spewing fire, lying on a nail bed, or walking on hot coals, and other Orientalist clichés. And the Agrabah palace turns out to be an Orientalized version of the Disney logo itself.

Disney claimed it had consulted "a range of experts," but these had obviously not been very "culturally aware." Even the engaging musical score was blatantly stereotypical. The opening song, "Arabian Nights," contained a stanza about a faraway place with camel caravans "where they cut off your ear if they don"t like your face. It's barbaric, but hey, it's home." After protests from the American-Arab Anti-Discrimination Committee, Disney announced that the line would be replaced by something about immense heat and an intense sun, and that "barbaric" would become "exotic," or something of that nature. But the characters themselves and the storylines were, of course, going to be left untouched.[3] The main song, in turn, had as its engaging refrain a call for "a whole new world." America is widely known as "the new world,"

and President George H. W. Bush had just called for the establishment
of a "new world order"—meaning a Pax Americana.

In spite—or maybe because—of all of this, *Aladdin* was a huge success, not only at home but also abroad. It became the highest-grossing
film of the year, and Disney reported record earnings that year. It soon
produced a spin-off television series and two video sequels, *The Return
of Jafar* (1994) and *The King of Thieves* (1995)—the latter loosely based
on Ali Baba and inspired by *The Arabian Nights.* There also was a 2001
stage adaptation, a new parade and new attractions in the various Disney theme parks, and so on. So, taken together, this first stab at overseas exoticism had been well worth the effort—an enormous success.

Case Study: Simba the Lion King and Africa

The next major project for a feature-length animated cartoon was at
the same time more simple and more complex than *Aladdin*, as it was
not to focus on a human, but on an animal figure: the lion. Since time
immemorial, the lion had been a symbol of sovereignty, of the power,
justice, and wisdom of gods, prophets, and rulers in the religious cultures of Asia, Europe, and Africa ranging from Hinduism and Bud-
dhism to Judaism, Christianity, and Islam (Chevalier & Gheerbrandt
1969, pp. 575–77). But can there be ethnocentric aspects to the presentation of an animal—any animal? Maybe the answer should be yes.

The lion has always been thought to be the most awe-inspiring of all
land animals and mammals, particularly in Africa. It was therefore labeled "king of the Jungle." But as Paul Bohannan's book *Africa and
Africans* (quoted in Maynard 1974, p. 3) notes: "Lions do not live in jungles. In the first place, only about 5 percent of the African continent can
be called jungle in any case. What few lions there are live in the grass-
lands. But darkness goes with jungle and wild beasts, and the lions in
the jungles persist as a symbol for the unrecognized fear that Americans have for Africa" (and Europeans as well). On ancient maps, the
unexplored interior of the entire continent is marked: "This is where
the lions are," as the ultimate warning of a dark threat.

In the Western imagination, sub-Saharan Africa has always been
closely identified with splendid but "wild" nature. There has always
been a focus on virgin landscapes and unruly vegetation, as well as on
the presence of a wide variety of wonderful but also dangerous animals. Until fairly recently, European and American fiction and nonfiction, for both adults and children, treated the black natives as savages,
supposedly living in a "natural" state, without either a culture or a his-

tory to speak of. Over the last few decades, however, this whole approach had come under closer scrutiny. Thus, the emphasis on wild nature and wonderful animals remained, but people gradually became a possible source of embarrassment and were progressively evicted from popular texts and images (e.g., in Disney's later movie *Tarzan*, to which we will return in chapter 4), as there seemed to be no way to include them in a book or movie without being accused of condescension or prejudice.

This was particularly true in the United States, where the civil rights and black pride movements had given rise to significant lobby groups such as the NAACP, which also criticized the mainstream media for their portrayal of blacks, both at home and abroad. Disney, for one, increasingly tried to steer clear of this particularly sensitive subject, although commentators had already observed that the wide variety of animal species in the animated cartoons of Disney and its competitors often stood for different human races, as was obvious from their appearance, language, and other peculiarities. So Africans were written out of *The Lion King* (whereas they were still present in an earlier model, as discussed below). Even such ex-nominations or absences from a story may be revealing of underlying orientations, but there is more to the subject than this alone.

Whereas Western tourism elsewhere (for instance, in the Middle and Far East) also focused on local culture, the subject seemed to be largely absent from African tours—apart from a few fully contrived folkloric "song-and-dance" shows. This is, in part, because many sub-Saharan civilizations had built largely wooden cities, palaces, and monuments that had disappeared without leaving much of a trace. It is also true that the wealth gap between present-day Western visitors and local populations was appallingly large, so that exchanges and interactions were often even more problematic than elsewhere.

Yet the recent redefinition of sub-Saharan Africa as a giant "safari park" for game hunters and photo shooters, with many wonderful animals but no humans to take note of, is curious (see Nederveen Pieterse 1992, chap. 7). This was exactly the focus of Disney's *The Lion King*: the splendid nature and wonderful animals of Africa, particularly in Western-friendly and reputable "safari park" countries such as Kenya and South Africa (recognizable in the movie from their landscapes and species, and in the soundtrack from Swahili and Zulu expressions).

According to an authoritative film guide, the original "story for *Lion King* had reportedly been devised by Jeffrey Katzenberg," then head of the studio. Screenwriter Linda Woolverton was aware of her responsibilities: "When you take on a Disney animated feature, you know you are going to be affecting entire generations of human minds" (Kilpatrick 1999, p. 154), so the story might as well be original and correct. But one of those present at the June 1994 premiere was Fred Ladd, who had long been involved in adaptations of Japanese animated cartoons. To his great surprise, the "original" Disney film about Simba the lion borrowed very heavily from an earlier model, nowadays called *Kimba the Lion,* partly broadcast by NBC. It had been based on a comic strip about King Leo, a white lion, and was made by Osamu Tezuka, nicknamed "the Japanese Walt Disney," who had died five years earlier. His family and company did not sue,[4] but Ladd summed up a great number of close similarities between the two.[5]

I decided to take a closer look for myself and was able to get hold of a video with the first two installments of the Japanese television series. There can be no doubt that the Disney production was much better made than the smaller-budget Japanese one, both professionally and artistically, but there are indeed eerily close resemblances. The first installment of the Japanese television series was partly built around the different theme of white hunters and black helpers, but its generic opening scenes had many of the exact same visuals as the American movie: from the snowy top of Mount Kilimanjaro to the meandering form of the valley river and the impressive tumult of Victoria Falls further to the south—but most of all, the precise high and pronounced cliff that formed a kind of balcony and throne from which the king repeatedly contemplates his land, his subjects, and their tribute. (Disney even retained this for the later *Pocahontas,* to which we will return later). Other particular details also bear striking similarities, from the appearance of the bird and the baboon counselor to that of the wildebeest stampede.

The second installment of the Japanese *Kimba* series, furthermore, prefigures many of the key elements of the Disney storyline on Simba: two neighboring animal countries, the troubled succession of a lion king, the good lion in lighter colors and the bad one with black mane, the attempted murder of the former by the latter, and even some of the precise rendering of their fight—as well as the nail scratches, the fall from a cliff, the apparition of the deceased in a cloud, the young lioness in love, the treacherous role of the hyenas, the mass of threatening light eyes in the dark night, the thorny bushes, and so forth. Of course the archetypical royal succession struggle is quite familiar (see, for example, William Shakespeare's dramas, particularly *Henry IV, Henry V,* and *Hamlet*): A jealous and evil family member plots against the legitimate heir, stirring civil strife and outside intervention. The same theme runs through many medieval books and Bible stories, but in the Disney movie it is given an African and animal twist.

One of my students, born and raised in Kenya, did some further research on the subject. She told us that the elder king's name, Mufasa, was borrowed from that of the last king of the Bagada people, since dispersed, that the younger king's name simply means "lion" in the East African Swahili language, and that the monkey counselor's name, Rafiki, means "friend." She was surprised, at the same time, by the fact that the "making of" documentary on TV showed only white American experts, no black African ones (Schulpen 1998). The student also noted that, although there was bloodletting in the film, the story was carefully arranged in such a way that it was not Simba who killed his rival, Scar, but Scar's own stooges, the hyenas.

Ideological critique of the film by others focused mostly on the portrayal of this hyena rabble. Some pointed out that Scar himself was given a British accent, but others pointed out that there were resonances with the anti-British independence movement of Mau Mau guerrillas and traditional Kikuyu warriors of earlier days. At one point, the hyenas were even given all the paraphernalia and characteristics of Nazi thugs, always the most convenient bad guys—even if completely unrelated. But American blacks noted that these hooligans were placed in the jungle equivalent of an urban ghetto and given recognizable black and Hispanic accents (Wasko 2001, p. 141). Others noted that it was no mere coincidence that the songwriters had used the engaging "don't worry, be happy" theme of Hakuna Matata in an African context. Whatever the case, it illustrates that there is not—nor can there be— such a thing as "free fantasy" by a free-floating and socially unattached group of "creative people" in California, particularly on contested subjects, because there is always resonance with the real or imagined world within a dominant culture. No product stands completely isolated and alone.

There is a final detail that is ironic. Disney was not able to resist incorporating a few lines from the best-known song about an African lion into the film: the early 1960s hit "Wimoweh," featuring the famous line "In the village, the quiet village, the lion sleeps tonight" and a very characteristic yell. It was recorded by the folk singer Pete Seeger and his group the Weavers; Seeger had "found" the song on an old South African record and had transcribed its refrain into the famous "O Wimoweh" by ear. In fact, the earlier song was "Uyim Mbube," a Zulu

song recorded by the Manhattan Boys for the Gallo label in Johannes-
burg, just before World War II. Thus it became the first "African" top hit
in pop history.

The song was written by Solomon Linda, who died penniless shortly
after the song jumped to the top of the charts around the world. What
about his royalties, then? He had been told at the time that under the
South African regime blacks could not claim copyright to anything, period. He was later made to formally sign his rights over for less than
one dollar, and his illiterate wife and daughters were still later made to
reconfirm it. That is how the copyright was ultimately "consolidated"
in American hands. After the release of *The Lion King*, it took sympa-
thizers a campaign of a full dozen years and multiple lawsuits to finally
have the rights of the Linda family recognized.[6]

Meanwhile, the movie had become Disney's greatest success ever,
fourth on the all-time blockbuster list, with a gross global intake of
close to $800 million. Two video sequels were subsequently released,
as well as a wildly successful Broadway musical. In the eyes and minds
of many viewers, *The Lion King* was the most magnificent evocation
ever of the "real" Africa.

DISNEY AND EXOTIC GIRLS

The demographics of film and television audiences had begun to change. Until recently, most families had only one television set in their homes. It stood in
the living room, and the man of the house monopolized the remote control, at
least during prime time. Younger males had more leeway to go to the movies
with their male friends, and if they asked girls out they usually made the choice
for them as well (often with a hidden agenda about taking a macho pose and/or
scaring their date out of her wits). But over time, both adult women and girls
became more emancipated. The birth control pill and other devices had finally
given them some control over procreation and sex. They often had their own
money to spend, made their own choices with their female friends. Some romantic television series, soaps, and sitcoms—traditionally aired in the daytime
and targeted at a female audience—moved to prime-time evening hours.
"Chick flicks" came to occupy a prominent place in movie theatres.

All this had major strategic implications for Disney, and even for its animated cartoon franchise. As discussed earlier, old classics could be recycled for
every generation, but "new classics" also had to be made, and major theatrical
blockbusters were further exploited by bringing out a series of video sequels
for broadcasting or for the home market. They also generated a steady stream

of income through a range of toys, spin-off products, premiums, and theme park attractions. However, their target groups needed to be redefined. Not only did movies need to be made more appealing directly to children rather than to their parents, but they also had to be made more appealing to girls rather than just boys. This was also attractive for commercial allies and sponsors, advertisers, and marketers—as youngsters tended to elude them.

Another factor, already mentioned, is that the main body of white European and American children's literature had been more or less exhausted, leaving exotic lore to provide a fresh range of themes, characters, and stories. These would also help Disney break out of the rather saturated and overdeveloped markets of the North Atlantic and into the emergent and developing markets of the rest of the world. The changing world situation also played a role here: the end of the Cold War, new opportunities for overseas expansion and globalization, the emergence of China as future superpower, and so forth.

It is interesting to note, meanwhile, that Disney's earlier "exotic boy" and later "exotic girl" blockbusters were framed rather differently. The exotic boys Aladdin and Simba, the Lion King, were depicted as little macho men. The exotic girls Pocahontas and Mulan, in contrast, were portrayed as beauty queens. Even though both were also made "machas" or "powerrr girrrls," in line with the changing spirit of the times, strength and wits were mostly shown to be the ideal traits bringing social promotion to exotic boys, while beauty and character were the ideal traits bringing social promotion to girls.

Interestingly enough, the four movies also reproduced the classic fairy tale obsession with monarchies—with dynastic intrigue and court advisers, and with marriage as the ideal route to social promotion and riches for the ordinary poor boy as well as the ordinary poor girl. All the stories reverently embrace the original monarch as a wise and noble figure. Aladdin is a poor boy who comes to marry the princess, in spite of Jafar's court intrigue. Simba the Lion is a crown prince who goes through a period of poverty and destitution because of the intrigues of his uncle Scar. Pocahontas, by contrast, is said to be a Native American princess, but realizes social promotion by agreeing to marry a much older British elite colonist (under circumstances to which we will return). Finally, Mulan earns the recognition of the emperor and marries one of his top officers.

It is interesting that Disney should steer clear of the modern world and revert to such archaic themes in these four blockbuster projects of the globalizing 1990s, although it is in line with the overall ideology of its stories and of commercial popular and media culture in general, particularly in the United States: Riches are usually acquired in one lucky stroke (marriage, an invention, the lottery, a treasure found), and not through consistent hard work.

The sphere of modern production (the mine, the factory, the office) almost disappears from view, while the sphere of modern consumption (nice houses, cars, shopping, leisure, travel) is ubiquitous. Inequalities are a natural and eternal given, challenged only by criminals and revolutionaries. It is a world from which most hints of critical social reflection have disappeared.

Case Study: Pocahontas and Native America

Between the feature-length animated cartoons devoted to Africa, Arabia, and Asia, Disney also revisited the early encounters between Native Americans and the first British immigrants in North America. *Pocahontas* (1995) was released with great fanfare, including a premiere in New York's Central Park, with a two-and-a-half-hour "making of" documentary on television. It was promoted by the claim that it was "based on a true story" (of course, all fictional accounts are, to some extent), and this claim was at first accepted uncritically all around the world—even by quality dailies and weeklies around Europe.

American critics even claimed that the makers had been overly "politically correct," in view of the earlier controversies over *Aladdin* and *The Lion King*. Upon closer inspection, however, this was far from the truth, as the known facts of the Pocahontas story had been willingly muddled and twisted in the Disney version. Producer James Pentacost retorted: "Nobody should go to an animated film hoping to get an accurate picture of history" (Kilpatrick 1999, p. 154)—which is perfectly true. But Disney's "true story" is largely wishful thinking, as is evident from a wide range of both print publications and websites (see Zabus in Lie & D'Haen 2002; McIntyre 2003).[7]

Pocahontas was indeed a historical figure. She was born around 1595 as Matoaka, or "precious little white feather," the daughter of Powhatan, chief of eight Algonquin tribes in Virginia. It was he who gave her the affectionate nickname Pocahontas, or "the naughty one." When she was fifteen, she was promised to (or actually betrothed to) a fellow tribe member named Kocoum. But soon thereafter, she was coaxed onto an English ship. The British had just set foot on Virginia soil and founded their first permanent settlement Jamestown there but got into repeated skirmishes with the natives. Pocahontas had a habit of visiting them, but the captain now held her hostage for a year, demanding the return of prisoners and a ransom of food.

Some sources say she was probably abused or even raped during her captivity.[8] According to others, a burly widower and tobacco planter of almost thirty years old named John Rolfe negotiated her release in exchange for marrying him. (Note that the sequence of a kidnapping followed by a marriage was not unusual in those days, particularly in lawless regions throughout the world, as the girl in question would have "lost her honor" and thus be considered unacceptable to any other man). Pocahontas learned English, was baptized, adopted the Christian name Rebecca, gave birth to a son, and was later used as a translator and intermediary in negotiations.

Two years later, the family traveled to London to promote the Virginia Company, where she was presented to the king and queen as an "Indian princess." She was said to be homesick, but by the time they were to return she had caught some common European infection to which she had no immunity, died, and was buried in Gravesend. (Note that ninety-five thousand Indians had died from such an epidemic a few years before the Pilgrim Fathers set up a permanent settlement, leaving only five thousand Indians along the coast—thereby making room for the colonizers.[9] Millions of Native Americans died from European-induced illnesses before and after that).

One of the pioneers of the Virginia Company's Jamestown colony had been one John Smith, who also produced maps and histories of the region. He later published several books about his own heroic adventures, although much of it was later found to be embellishment or invention. One recurring theme was that he had almost been killed but had ultimately been saved by a beautiful girl—as they all fancied him. Since Pocahontas had remained a modest celebrity, even after her death, he also came up with a story involving her person. According to his belated account, he had been captured by the natives during the early days of the settlement and was almost put to death. But the "princess"—then at most twelve years old, whereas he was at least twenty-seven—had supposedly rescued him by covering his head and body with hers.

In settler lore, the stories of John Rolfe and John Smith then became further embellished and fused in the simplified claim that Pocahontas had obviously fallen in love with the first Brit she ever saw and that they lived happily ever after—just like the two communities, which she welded together in peace and harmony. Note that this archetypical theme of the native woman falling in love with an intruder, becoming a translator and intermediary, had run through such stories for several centuries. John Smith and others may already have been aware of those. A contemporary version was that of the Utica woman who had saved Juan Ortiz in Florida eighty years before; the earliest version related to La Malinche, the indigenous mistress of Hernán Cortés, the conqueror of Mexico, who reportedly helped him communicate with Aztec ruler Montezuma (Lie & D'Haen 2002, pp. 37 ff.).

The Pocahontas myth also resonated with, and became a complement to, the similarly ideological Samoset myth, which is even more at the heart of U.S. historiography. Only a few years after Pocahontas's death, around Christmas 1620, the Mayflower and other ships of the Pilgrim Fathers had landed in Massachusetts. They struggled through the harsh winter, and many died. According to the official version quoted in the *Encyclopaedia Britannica,* in spring "a tall, nearly naked Indian named Samoset confronted the haggard settlers with the peace cry in English, 'Much welcome, Englishmen! Much welcome, Englishmen!'"[10]

He and his friends also became translators and intermediaries with the native population: "Their common efforts at survival gave rise after the autumn harvests to the feast of Thanksgiving."[11] Note that the harvest festival based on an Indian tradition was thus ironically turned into the major settler holiday,[12] in which they thanked the Christian God for handing this wonderful continent to them, with its rich natural resources and its friendly natives. This idyllic story also had a dark and hidden counterpoint, however: As a first reaction against persistent British encroachment, there was a major Indian uprising near Jamestown the very next year. No fewer than 347 settlers—a third of the white population there—were killed.

This was of course ignored in the Pocahontas idyll, which subsequently became very popular in Anglo-American literature. Ben Jonson met her and wrote her into his comedy *The Staple of News.* Many subsequent authors also wrote about her, and John Davis even did a further eroticized account with a half-naked Pocahontas. In the end, she also turned up in the official art of the new republic. Among the eight hundred works of art displayed in the Capitol Building in Washington, DC, for instance, only twenty-eight show women (and only twenty-one African Americans), but no less than three show the mythical Pocahontas, "transformed, whitened, Europeanized"—according to Vivien Green Fryd, professor of art at Vanderbilt university. Another painting, by contrast, shows an apparently nontransformed "true" Indian holding a bloody knife, with a scalped white man at his feet.[13]

Over the years, then, *Pocahontas* came to occupy an ever more prominent place in U.S. lore: with hit songs (including Peggy Lee's famous "Fever"), musicals, plays, books, poems, and films. Strong writes, "The pre-Disney *Pocahontas* was already a highly mythologized heroine known only through colonial and nationalist representations—

from the beginning a product of Anglo-American desire" (in Walker 2001, p. 194). After long shunning every drop of nonwhite "Indian" blood, dozens of U.K. and U.S. citizens now proudly rediscovered they descended from the native "Princess." They were even interviewed as a kind of eyewitnesses and experts for a 1995 four-hundredth anniversary BBC documentary *Pocahontas: Her True Story.* But it recycled many of the same old fairy tales and ignored most of the critical historical information that was now available—because it would kill a favorite daydream.

As usual, the Disney team had surveyed the entire tradition of hundreds of books and illustrations for its feature, carefully selected what suited its purpose, and left out all the available facts that contradicted the preferred version. The twelve-year-old Pocahontas was of course made considerably older: She was turned into a sexy adolescent with a waspish waist and protruding breasts. She was redrawn in the mold of the stereotypical exotic (rather Asian) beauty, with long hair and incredibly long legs. The actor doing the voice of her counterpart conceded: "She's a babe." Others said Pocahontas had been turned into a Lolita, a Barbie doll, or a seventeenth-century "valley girl" with a deep tan in an off-the-shoulder (and suggestively short) leather dress.

The fused John Smith/John Rolfe character had by contrast been made much younger—light, blond Nordic demigod—to make their liaison seem more natural and more acceptable to present-day Western audiences. His voice was provided by Mel Gibson: probably the first Brit in history portrayed with an American accent. The interaction between the two was further mythologized: Pocahontas is shown having a utopian foreboding, a dream, that "something is coming," which turns out to be the British ship and the settlers. She then rejects her Indian lover, Kocoum, and literally falls in love with the very first settler she sees. Later in that very same first encounter scene they are shown kissing and fondling each other, probably a world record in the history of interethnic relations, indicative of the eagerness with which the harsh reality had to be painted over. But Jacquelyn Kilpatrick comments, "This film's pseudo-history will exist as 'fact' in the minds of generations of American children. They will believe in the Romeo and Juliet story" (1999 p. 151).

It must be acknowledged, though, that some room in the film is given to a slightly more critical view. The colonizers are sometimes painted as greedy, although a subtle distinction is made. The really bad white guy is the British governor and his immediate helpers flaunting the Union Jack: that is to say, the people the "real Americans" were soon to fall out with. They are just interested in gold digging and making an easy buck. The much better white guys, by contrast, are their younger and lower-placed companions such as John Smith, who are pursuing the American Dream. They are looking for "freedom," are willing to work hard for a better life and to teach the natives how to make better use of their rich resources. The natives, too, are split between cruel/vengeful and noble/forgiving people. There is even some attention given to the mirror-like nature of enemy images as the settlers and natives join each other in a final chorus line about each other: "They're savages, savages, barely even human." At the same time, the invaders and invaded are placed on the same level.

The immense tragedy of the encounter, followed by genocide and expropriation on an unprecedented scale, is of course passed over in complete silence, even though Disney had succeeded in recruiting a former leader of the American Indian Movement (AIM) as an actor, providing a moral guarantee. Russell Means provided both the voice and the toy model for chief Powhatan and declared the movie "the single finest work ever done on American Indians by Hollywood" (Rollins & O'Connor 1998, p. 197). Disney claimed that it had also involved a number of other native consultants, but some later said their advice had been completely ignored. Instead, Disney had drawn heavily on Gauguin-like renditions of native beauty in an idyllic environment. The narrative and visuals even hooked up with conservationist and New Age philosophies, which recent authors had come to ascribe to premodern peoples. The final scene ignores Pocahontas's tragic death, as she sees her lover off to England—temporarily.

In this fashionable form, *Pocahontas* proved a major success in the United States and abroad. There was a first video sequel called *Journey to a New World* (1998), an $8-million traveling ice-skating show, and so on. But in *Understanding Disney: The Manufacture of Fantasy*, Janet Wasko sums up: "The Disneyfied story excludes Pocahontas's kidnapping by the English, her conversion to Christianity, her marriage to an English aristocrat, and her death" (p. 142). Ella Shohat and Robert Stam had already concluded that the preferred U.S. reading of the Pocahontas story "excludes the narrative of rape, cultural destruction, and genocide" (1994, p. 44). And Robert Eaglestaff, the principal of the Indian Heritage School in Seattle, even went so far as to compare the Disney movie to "trying to teach about the Holocaust and putting in a nice story about Anne Frank falling in love with a German officer" (Kilpatrick 1999, p. 151).

Case Study: Mulan and East Asia

Meanwhile, Disney's focus had shifted back to overseas territories. The major area of rapid economic growth in the near future seemed to be East Asia. During the early 1980s, the company had already opened a Disney theme park near the Japanese capital, Tokyo, but during the early 1990s plans were made to also pursue one near the British "crown colony," Hong Kong, soon to be reunited with the vast Chinese mainland. The People's Republic was rapidly reverting to free markets and capitalist development, integration into the world economy and recognition of foreign copyrights. So Disney set up a *Mickey Mouse* magazine, offered its Donald Duck and other animated cartoons to China television at virtually no cost, just to prepare the ground, even though a spat over Touchstone's *Kundun* (Martin Scorsese's biopic of Tibet's Dalai Lama), followed by the Asian financial crisis, proved major obstacles.

In this entire context, it seemed a good idea to produce a major new feature-length animated cartoon based on some kind of ancient Chinese legend or fairy tale, although Disney would have to bend over backward this time to avoid even the slightest possible offense to an increasingly powerful and demanding partner. The story of the Mulan ("Lily Magnolia"), a kind of Chinese Joan of Arc, seemed the perfect candidate. It was first included in a collection of poems fifteen hundred years ago, had been translated into English by Han Frankel, had inspired a character in a book by Maxine Hong Kingston, which had also been turned into a play, and there already was a Chinese movie about Mulan. According to some sources she had belonged to a nomad minority; according to others she belonged to the ethnic Han majority, with the very common family name of Hua, still honored by monuments in a village near the seat of Yucheng county in the eastern Henan province, in the central plains.

Upon another outside invasion, the emperor had drafted one able-bodied man from every family. As her father was too old and her brother too young, Mulan reportedly dressed as a boy, reported for duty, and embarked on a twelve-year career as a brave soldier. In the end she was found out and reported to the emperor. One version has a sad ending: She is imprisoned and hangs herself. Another version has a happy ending: She marries her general.

Curiously, the movie was not produced in California (with its Asian orientation) but in Florida. Disney invested no less than $100 million in it: a measure of the importance attached to the project. Producer Pam Coats even led ten artistic supervisors on a three-week tour of China, "a country I knew nothing about before the beginning of this movie. . . . [But] it was fun to see, to try the food, just completely immersing ourselves in a culture" (Liu 2004, p. 1).

As always, the movie included as many "typical" elements as possible, deriving from restaurant, bazaar, and tourist familiarity with the culture: chopsticks and rice bowls, jade and laquerwork, calligraphy and watercolors, abacus and incense, rice fields and cherry blossoms, goldfish and cranes, bamboo bushes and misty mountains, red lanterns and butterfly kites, meditation postures and martial arts, circus acts and lion statues—and even the Forbidden City and the Great Wall (both built long after Mulan's time). Landscapes were rendered in signature Chinese style. An early plan to have a trademark Panda bear as comic relief was shelved, although he did have a minor role, and an early plan to include the dragon twins Yin and Yang was superseded by one that merged them into a single dragon, Mushu (named after a familiar Westernized Chinese dish), comparable to *Aladdin*'s genie, *The Lion King*'s monkey, and other similar Disney-formula sidekicks.

Yet a large number of elements and arbitrary changes to the original story were pointed out, particularly by younger female Sino-American media scholars, and, for instance, by Metzger (in Lie & D'Haen 2002, pp. 117–26). Some said the original theme of filial piety had been turned into one of "macha" rebellion and cross-dressing. In the Disney version, Mulan's elders wanted her to become an acupuncturist, just as many American parents want their children to be doctors or lawyers. Mulan's face was also adapted to Western beauty ideals by making her eyes larger and rounder. In the matchmaker scene (and the bride scene at the end), the applied white makeup was rather that of a Chinese opera singer or even of a Japanese geisha than that of an ordinary girl. In contrast to Pocahontas, however, Mulan's forms were flattened and desexualized (probably in view of Chinese Communist sensitivities). Yet in the end she happily marries, not an older general, but a younger captain.

Disney boasted that Sino-Americans did most of the voices, but in fact they filled only half of the dozen major speaking and singing roles, with a Filipino singing the main role (the same actress cast in Broadway's *Miss Saigon*) and a number of well-known Japanese American and Korean American actors. It is doubtful that such ethnic substitutions would have passed as easily with regard to major American or European roles. At one point, there even seems to be a typically Japanese sumo wrestler in sight. According to some critics, the musical score also contained a number of Oriental-sounding themes and instruments—but no otherwise identifiable Chinese songs. McDonald's served a Mulan

McNuggets with a (not so hot) "Szechuan" sauce for the occasion, whereas Disneyland introduced a Chinese dragon parade.

Chinese and other Asian students in my seminar wrote papers on this mishmash. They noted that ancient Chinese did indeed keep lucky crickets, but that the pet dog was a quite strange and typically Western addition. Mulan's contradicting the emperor, his bowing to her, and their finally hugging each other would have been completely unthinkable, of course. They also noted that the new technique for computer-generated images may have helped create impressive battle scenes in the snowy mountains and crowd scenes in the Forbidden City and Imperial Palace, but that its primitive use also helped reproduce the ancient Western stereotype that people of other races—Asians and especially Mongols and Chinese—"look completely alike," since apart from Mulan's very closest companions, they were drawn in near identical fashion. The ancestor party at the end, where they play volleyball with one of the heads, would futhermore be considered rather disrespectful (Liu 2004, Tanzil 2003).

Because of a temporary ban resulting from the spat over the Dalai Lama film *Kundun*, *Mulan* was not immediately released in China. But progress was made after a presidential visit by Bill Clinton, and a deal was brokered by Jack Valenti of the powerful Motion Picture Association, whereby the MPA would help China Film distribute some of its movies in the United States, such as *A Time to Remember*, a love story set during the Communist Revolution. Although the lucrative Chinese New Year holiday (preceding the fiftieth anniversary of the regime) remained reserved for local products, *Mulan* was finally released soon thereafter.[14] But reception of the movie was tepid. People recognized little of the original story, and one deputy to the National People's Congress referred to a "cultural invasion," claiming that Disney had violated and "raped" *Mulan* by using a Western approach, catering to Western tastes.[15] The movie did not do as well as other American blockbusters such as *Titanic*, therefore, but did better than Chinese animated cartoons such as *Monkey King*.

Mulan also broke the impasse over a Chinese Disneyland. After the Asian financial crisis and rising unemployment, Hong Kong authorities finally decided to sink $3.5 billion into a major foreign theme park that might restore and boost tourism. As usual, Disney invested only some 10 percent of that sum, but looked forward to a steady stream of revenue and promotion. Building on reclaimed land next to Lantau Island began in 2003, and the opening took place in September 2005. Both the layout and the dates were reportedly corrected in accordance with feng shui masters, but "shark fin" soup was taken off the menu due to Western pressure. Disney is discussing another theme park near Shanghai to be opened in 2010 or beyond. At the same time, its competitor Universal Studios has signed for a theme park near Shanghai and is considering another one near the capital, Beijing.

CHANGE

Over the next few years, Disney continued with blockbuster projects for animated cartoons with exotic content, some again harkening back to colonial days. A retouched *Tarzan* (1999), deriving from Edgar Rice Burroughs's famous book, was another great success. The space-age *Treasure Planet* (2002), based on Robert Louis Stevenson's classic *Treasure Island,* however, proved a major dud. These will both be discussed in more depth in chapter 4. But "handmade" films were increasingly enhanced in part, or replaced entirely, by computer-imaging techniques. The staff of the relevant department was ill equipped to make the change, however, and therefore many were laid off.

Disney had been forced to seek alliances with other companies that were better equipped for the innovation "arms race" of computer animation. As authors' descendants and copyright holders of classics had meanwhile proven to be demanding partners (on respecting original forms and atmospheres), it also proved easier and more lucrative to develop supposedly "new" stories around entirely new dolls and toys that could be marketed, merchandised and licensed at will. So Pixar (in which Apple founder Steve Jobs is a major shareholder) produced some new three-dimensional blockbusters for Disney, ranging from both *Toy Story* movies (released in 1995 and 1999) to *The Incredibles* (2004). Ultimately, Disney became so dependent on Pixar that it was forced to take the company over—and keep Jobs in a key role.

DreamWorks, meanwhile, had become a major competitor. Disney's successful studio chief Jeffrey Katzenberg had demanded a better deal after some time. When he did not get it, he left to found DreamWorks SKG with Steven Spielberg and David Geffen. It also launched into animated cartoons, some with exotic content. *The Prince of Egypt* (1998; a kind of remake of Cecil B. DeMille's classic *The Ten Commandments,* both discussed in chapter 9) was a major success. *Sindbad: Legend of the Seven Seas* (2003), however, was a major dud. From then on, Disney/Pixar and DreamWorks did successive competing projects: anti–fairy tales (*Monsters* versus *Shrek*), about insects (*A Bug's Life* versus *Antz*), about the underwater world (*Finding Nemo* versus *Shark Tale*). After a takeover battle with GE's Universal and NBC, DreamWorks was finally taken over by Paramount.

Yet the Disney Corporation still seems to hold a major trump card in its control of some key outlets for popular culture and family entertainment: that is to say, the very profitable Disney Stores and Disney theme parks in California and Florida, in Paris and Tokyo, in Hong Kong and maybe soon Shanghai. They also export a naive vision of the world abroad, for instance, in the *Pirates of the Caribbean* ride (further promoted by the 2003 movie), as the theme parks are implicitly organized around the development stages of humanity as Uncle Walt saw them, with the science-fiction world of Tomorrowland, the Wild West of Frontierland, the virgin forest of Adventureland, the traditional "Mainstreet USA" of Walt's youth at its very heart, and some knights' castles and princess' palaces as a token reference to previous European history.

Representations of Aladdin and Simba the Lion King, Pocahontas and Mulan, thus act to integrate Arabia and Africa, native America and Asia, into this infantile universe of the "Magic Kingdom." Alain Nadel concludes on the new world order put on display there: "The foreign locale merely flavors a set of familiar, safe, and ultimately predictable narratives to make them diverting, tasty, and consumable. . . . The foreign place itself becomes the medium that allows American cultural narratives—projected out onto the world as foreign policy, clothing styles, and social codes—to return, blessed by the imaginary Other, as a form of narcissistic confirmation" (in Bernstein & Studlar 1997, pp. 199–200).

3

Civilized and Savage: Antiquity Movies

Where do we come from? What are the roots of Euro-American civilization? Where and when did it first flourish? Were there antecedents? What about historiography and epic literature? Who were the major heroes, and what were their exploits? How did they confront the barbarians on the other side? To what extent are those stories still being told in the same old way by Hollywood today? What sentiments do we derive from them?

Let us first take a closer look at the geography and history of Western civilization as it was presented to us in school. It focused on Europe, but look at its map. Then focus on the areas where the first major growth spurts are supposed to have taken place, leading to golden ages in the successive major centers.

They are three: first, ancient Greece; second, ancient Rome, with a resurgence, long after its collapse, in the Italian Renaissance; third: medieval Iberia, with Spain and Portugal, where explorers took off to "discover" and exploit the "New World." It was only from 1492 onward that Europe decisively overtook civilizations on other continents in wealth and productivity, technology and science, and came to occupy a lastingly privileged place within the emerging world system. It was only thereafter that development shifted decisively to the Atlantic coast and the north—to the world powers that still dominate today.

Now what do Greece, Italy, and Spain have in common? What was the hidden secret of their early success? Take another close look at the same map. They are located on the southeastern, southern and southwestern shores of Europe, respectively. Moreover, they are all more or less peninsulas, sticking out into the Mediterranean, reaching out to the shores on the other side, literally forming bridges to the contemporaneous civilizations of West Asia and North Africa of those days, that is to say, to present-day Turkey, Tunisia, and Morocco, which are in turn "sticking out" from the other side. It was over these bridges that art and knowledge from equally developed "Oriental" countries flowed: from Persia and Mesopotamia, Egypt, and the great Arab and Islamic empires.

The peaceful exchange with that other side—of philosophy, science, and technology—is often largely left out from history lessons; where it is included, it is severely distorted. The focus is almost exclusively on the intermittent armed confrontations, on an endless succession of relatively short wars, battles, and commanders, with their eternal conflict between the civilized "good guys" and the barbarian "bad guys." Now think about popular films, old and new. Are they not mostly focused on these very same themes? "Our" stars, in the role of "our" icons, battle "illegitimate" incursions of the barbarians into the Balkans and even Austria, into Italy, into Spain and even France, alternated with "legitimate" European excursions to spread civilization into Turkey and Persia, into Palestine and Egypt, into Tunisia and Morocco. That is the hidden metanarrative.

In the revised 2001 edition of his overview *The Ancient World in the Cinema*, Jon Solomon noted that there had been already been some four hundred films about the subject: "An alluring, historical world well-marbled with graceful columns, gently folded togas, wine-filled goblets, racing chariots, divinely inspired prophets, golden idols of pagan gods, Christian-devouring lions, scantily clad slave girls, and brawny heroes" (p. 1). In this chapter, we will look more closely at two subgenres: those dealing with ancient Egypt and those dealing with Greco-Roman antiquity, emphasizing discontinuities and continuities with European developments.

We have already noted that from the very start cinema embraced its superiority over theatre, exhibitions, and literature in focusing on the exotic, the strange, and the spectacular. It had a predilection for things that were far away in time and space, things that were "hard to imagine"—not only to make them "easy to imagine," but to represent them in such an impressive way that these versions then became fully self-evident. Although filmmakers had to take extreme liberties in connecting the dots about the unknown, then, their versions were so overwhelming that they became "more real than the real." Audiences soon forgot their dull schoolbooks about geography and history and eagerly adhered to this Hollywood version of the world—filled in with believable characters and recognizable emotions.

Ancient history, and the encounter with strange cultures, provided an ideal canvas for painting the human condition in broad strokes. Lavish and spectacular productions about real or imagined antiquity had risen to prominence during the silent era, but they received a further boost after the spread of sound and color. During the 1950s the competition of the television "small screen" further drove filmmakers to bet on the cinematic "wide screen," on the panoramic and the monumental. In the arms race between studios, super-productions were followed by mega-productions, which were followed by giga-productions.

"Peplum" is the slightly derogatory label for the entire movie genre built around the literature and history of European antiquity. The word "peplum" derives "from the Latinized version of the Greek word *peplos*, meaning a woman's shawl or long hanging dress" (Elley 1984, p. 21). The films of course include ancient men dressed in tunics or a togas as well. The genre is some-times also labeled "swords-and-sandals." Derek Elley treats it as a subgenre of the epic, aptly defined in one dictionary as "a narrative of heroic actions, of-ten with a principal hero, usually mythical in its content, offering inspiration and ennoblement within a particular cultural or national tradition" (p. 9). Since most Westerners have been familiar with these stories and themes since their school days, it is an attractive subject to present, although American ac-tor Charlton Heston, who often played the principal hero, once observed that it is also "the easiest kind of picture to make badly," as undue attention to sets and costumes may distract from the characters and their psychological mo-tives.

Present-day Greece has only a very modest film industry, but present-day Italy has long had a major one. So it is not surprising that the antiquity genre flourished there. Cinema emerged only a few decades after the country was re-united and became obsessed with modern technology—but also with its glo-rious past. Ironically, the genre subsided somewhat under fascism, when strongman Benito Mussolini attempted to create a new Roman Empire.

But there was another golden age for Hercules, Maciste, and Ulysses and company between the mid-1950s and the mid-1960s. Over the latter five years, no fewer than 130 peplums were produced in Italy, one-seventh of total film production there (Pinel 2000, p. 168), including three on Julius Caesar, five on gladiators, and so forth (Elley 1984, p. 180). It has been said that the genre may have been particularly appealing in a country that had not only lost World War II but was also going through a severe sociocultural crisis that put the traditional cult of male strength under pressure and promoted fantasies about Italian superiority in distant times and lands.

An article in the French daily *Le Monde* on the subject was therefore aptly titled "The Psychoanalysis of the Poor Man."[1] Richard Dyer's study *White* noted in turn that "ethnically different people in pepla are generally played by white actors, but the differences signaled by mise-en-scène are those of racial difference in Eurocentric discourse. . . . There is a use of architecture, clothing, hairstyle, music, and dance gestures to create a broadly Oriental world, with luxurious court life and devilishly clever modes of torture. . . . In contrast there are the primitives. . . . The hero, who comes from without, comes to the aid of the good or rightful elements" (1997, pp. 177–78). American body builders were often imported to play the main roles, and these Italian films were exported abroad with some modest success, before the so-called spaghetti Western genre took over.

Meanwhile, Americans had shown that they could easily outdo Europeans on these scores. David W. Griffith, Cecil B. DeMille, William Wyler, and Joseph Mankiewicz had demonstrated superior skill in creating and re-creating blockbusters out of classical stories on the rise and fall of the Roman Empire such as *Ben-Hur, Quo Vadis,* and *Spartacus:* first silent and in black and white, then with sound and in Technicolor.

No antique ruler has ever fascinated popular audiences as much as Cleopatra, who stood at a unique historical intersection between the great Egyptian, Greek, and Roman empires. She became the last pharaoh of an independent Egypt, of the Ptolemaic dynasty that had been founded several hundred years before by a Macedonian general of Alexander. She first began a relationship with Caesar, the Roman statesman, and after his death with Mark Antony, one of the generals fighting over his heritage. The first relationship is often thought to have been motivated merely by power and the second more by love, but both were probably a mixture of the two. Cleopatra and Mark Antony committed suicide after their military defeat.

In these stories, too, it is emphasized that Cleopatra was sly and cunning, as she was portrayed by the propaganda of Octavian/Augustus (the rival of Mark Antony and ultimately the successor to Caesar), or that she was very sensuous and sexual (in line with the stereotype of surplus libido of tropical people, discussed in chapter 6). In Western popular culture her exotic appearance and presentation are always heavily emphasized, although her skin is often made whiter, her eyes lighter blue, and the hair of her son with Caesar lighter blond, than they probably were.[2]

But this emphasis on Cleopatra as a mere seductress is very stereotypical, somewhat sexist and racist, and overlooks that she was also a stateswoman and an intellectual. She was a fashion leader, all right, but also an author of books on hairdressing and cosmetics, as well as a scholar, author of books on gynecology and on measures and weights. Plutarch's *Life of Antony,* written well over a century later, said that she was not a striking or incomparable beauty, but possessed an irresistible charm—and also that she was a polyglot, very persuasive and stimulating in conversation.

In view of the appeal and potential of the subject, then, Cleopatra quickly became the most popular historical figure in early cinema. The first portrayal was that by French pioneer Georges Méliès in 1899; five more versions of her story were produced between 1908 and 1918 alone, and at least five more thereafter (Bernstein & Studlar 1997, p. 82; Solomon 2001, p. 62 ff.). She was played by female superstars ranging from Theda Bara (an acronym for "Arab death") to Elizabeth Taylor. The latter got involved in a stormy on-again-off-again romance with her counterpart, Richard Burton (who played Mark Antony), on the set, which further complicated the already catastrophic shooting of the 120 miles of film for Joseph Mankiewicz's 1963 version—but generated welcome additional publicity.

The production, which was said to have been originally budgeted at just a few million dollars, ultimately came to cost $35 million. It was also said to have almost bankrupted Fox, which it did not as it became the highest-grossing movie of the year. The entry of Cleopatra and her retinue in Rome in it remains one of the most lavish displays of exotic pomp and circumstance in movie history. But few dared to touch the subject again. Solomon notes, therefore, that "the financial scare . . . almost single-handedly killed a genre of film" (2001, p. 75).

EGYPTO-MANIA

The story of ancient Egypt has a strong trademark conveyed by unique logos: the sphinx and the pyramids, the temples and the tombs, the Nile and its various iconic Nile boats. It also has some potent arch-characters such as Cleopatra, and arch-stories such as those built around the myths of the pharaoh and the mummy, and their horrible revenge upon being disturbed by local gravediggers or foreign archaeologists. It is interesting that with regard to this archetypical "other" culture there should be so much consistent emphasis on darker sides such as mystery and horror, whereas with regard to our own chosen predecessor culture, Greece, there is greater emphasis on lighter sides such as achievement and heroism.

Egypto-mania made another major splash around the turn of the new millennium with *The Mummy* (1999) and *The Mummy Returns* (2001), both directed by Stephen Sommers, with Brendan Fraser and Rachel Weisz as costars. The films immediately shot into the top fifty films and together sold close to $1 billion in tickets for Universal. The theme was immediately recognizable for Western audiences, and the first story was loosely based on a cinematic classic from the early 1930s, with Boris Karloff as the the mummy in bandages.

In 2002 Egypto-mania really took off, with at least two major new English-language television documentaries about "the curse of the pharaoh." The

Discovery Channel broadcast a full "Egypt week," whereas the National Geographic Channel and the Fox network reported "live" on the much-hyped probe of a tiny robot into a narrow shaft leading to the interior of the Great Pyramid in Giza—which proved a nonevent, as the robot was blocked just a bit further down. Yet the obsession remains with these strange and colossal monuments, even though we should be aware that their survival is partly due to a mere coincidence—namely, that they were built in natural stone and not in brick (as many monuments, palaces, and temples in Mesopotamia were) or in wood (as many in sub-Saharan Africa were), of which little survives today.

Where should we "place" Egypt in the historical geography of the ancient world? Is it just the Nile Delta, a kind of extension of the Middle East, and thus a mere prelude to the emergence of Judeo-Christian civilization? Or did its supply routes go up the whole length of the Nile, far into Nubia and the Sudan, and on occasion probably beyond, as well as along the coast of the Red Sea up to Ethiopia, the Straits, and perhaps beyond—somehow making connections with trade routes into the black sub-Saharan interior? Were the ancient Egyptians all light-skinned, or were several major figures beige or brown—particularly during the century the Nubians and Sudanese reversed the roles and took over Egypt?[3] What about their religion and philosophy, science and technology? Critics have claimed that Egyptian (as well as Mesopotamian) influences on Greece and Rome have been unduly toned down in the past.[4]

Some of this is visible in the politics of casting, makeup, and dress in Hollywood. Despicable leaders and tyrants of ancient Egypt are actively "alienated": They are played by actors with nonwhite physical traits, which are further emphasized through hairstyles, makeup, and costumes. Admirable leaders and visionaries are actively "appropriated" instead: They are played by actors with Anglo-Saxon, northwest European, or generally "white" traits, which are also further emphasized through hairstyles, makeup, and costumes. The best and most recognizable example is the contrast between Yul Brynner as Ramses and Charlton Heston as Moses in Cecil B. DeMille's *The Ten Commandments*, to which we will return.

DeMille's blockbuster—and its contemporary remake *The Prince of Egypt*—also tend to take credit away from the impressive accomplishments of pharaoh culture by reassigning them to an entirely different lineage (this will be discussed further in chapter 9). Both blockbusters, as well as many other Egypt films, tend to stress the perpetual and massive cruelty of the builders of these impressive monuments: Their most dramatic and emotional images are those of fanatical overseers continually whipping thousands upon thousands of slaves on to a greater effort. This image is widely taken for granted in Europe and America, but it is somewhat improbable upon further consideration. Zahi Hawass, the Egyptian chief of antiquities, even claimed that farmers built the pyramids in parttime and alternating shifts, with good alimentary and health care.[5] This view may also betray a hidden agenda, but it must be considered seriously.

There is an interesting and recurring variation to this whole theme of an Egyptian supercivilization as a geographic anomaly. The Swiss author Erich von Däniken once wrote a worldwide bestseller titled *The Chariots of the Gods*. He dwelled on the unsolved mysteries of Egypt and similarly sophisticated early civilizations in order to suggest that they must have been planted there from outer space. This later led to the highly successful 1994 movie *Stargate* (where mostly white present-day Americans rescue poor dark ancient Egyptians from abject slavery) and to a subsequent successful television series.

This theme also recurred in other productions and was further stimulated by the findings of archaeologist Robert Bauval, who reported that the angle of some of the shafts of the pyramids at Giza pointed to the exact spot in the sky where the appearance of the constellation Orion would every year have announced the upcoming flooding of the Nile and the return of plant life.

Case Study: The Mummy and the Curse of the Pharaoh

To Europeans, an African or Arab country like Egypt was not only considered incapable of spawning such a superior ancient civilization, it was also deemed incapable of guarding its vestiges—so the European powers took over. France, with Napoleon and, in his wake, Champollion, who first deciphered the hieroglyphs. The Suez Canal, opened in 1869, was then largely taken over by Great Britain, as was Egypt itself. Europeans carried off many major artifacts, had much earlier begun to erect obelisks on the squares of their capitals, and now set up well-stocked departments in their national museums. All this was "naturalized" within their vision of history. Egypto-mania also seeped through into nineteenth-century popular culture: into traveling exhibitions, early light shows, fairground attractions, and other "protocinematic" experiences (Bernstein & Studlar 1997, p. 73).

A dispute over the strategic canal then became the pretext for the 1882 full occupation of Egypt and a first unsuccessful attempt to extend it into Sudan and the Upper Nile region. When the troops of Lord Kitchener finally retook Khartoum, they violated the tomb of their old adversary, the Muslim religious leader known as the Mahdi. "The body was seized and mutilated, the trunk cast into the Nile, and the head was sent to Cairo" to be further forwarded to London (Bernstein & Studlar

1997, p. 273). Such sacrileges provoked the wrath of some anticolonial avenger sects and further stimulated fantasies about a curse.

It was also during the early 1880s that the Valley of the Kings had been discovered, opposite the former capital of Luxor. It was estimated that at least ten thousand bodies were buried there, many of them pharaohs, high priests, and their families. Such bodies would normally have dried out in the desert, but embalming, as well as airtight sarcophagi and underground chambers, had improved preservation. The idea behind such preservation efforts was that the soul would be able to come and reinhabit the body, but the deceased would become "undead" or a zombie if the corpse was ill preserved or heavily mutilated (as in the case of murder). Some graves thus carried death threats and ingenious traps against grave robbers—yet when the tombs were explored, most had already been emptied. After one mummy was sent to the British Museum in 1889, there were already stories of a curse on the excavators. During the early 1890s, gothic novelist Bram Stoker was writing horror stories in a house and room in northern England that contained a sarcophagus, which may have inspired his later story about a curse by a pharaoh. Such stories were also stimulated by the popularity of Spiritism in Europe at the time.

One of the major British Egyptologists working in the field was Howard Carter. About the original discovery of the Valley of the Kings by Egyptians, he wrote: "Incredible as it may seem, the secret was kept for six years, and the family, with a banking account of forty or more dead pharaohs to draw upon, grew rich" (Bernstein & Studlar 1997, pp. 38, 63). Soon after the turn of the century, he found hints that there might be a grave of the young pharaoh Tutankhamen, that it might still be intact, and he convinced Lord Carnarvon to sponsor his search. After almost giving up the search, he finally found it in November 1922. He made a hole and inserted a candle: "At first I could see nothing. But as my eyes grew accustomed to the light, details of the room emerged slowly. Strange animals, statues and gold. Everywhere the glint of gold. I was struck dumb with excitement."[6] After the hole was enlarged, Carnarvon was the first to go in: "All that one could see was what appeared to be gold bars" (James 2001, p. 478).

But after returning to his hotel, Carnarvon fell ill, and he later passed away. The press immediately hyped the myth of the curse of the pharaoh and willfully ignored all other rational explanations, such as unusual microtoxins that might have been released upon the opening of the tomb. They may have caused blood poisoning through a mosquito bite he reported or may have aggravated pneumonia in someone already old and ill. But the story grew as later deaths were then brought under the same umbrella: those of a brother, a nurse, a secretary, the dog, a canary, and then an endless list of others, even those surrounding later travel around the world of Tut's mask and sarcophagus—more than a hundred kilos of pure gold.[7]

Even more than newspaper accounts and popular novels, photo reports and feature films provided the ideal platform for bringing such exotic fantasies to life. *The Haunted Curiosity Shop* (1901) had already brought to cinema audiences the image of a mummy emerging from a sarcophagus, and a dozen mummy films were produced before Karl Freund's 1932 classic *The Mummy*, featuring Karloff as the zombie of high priest Imhotep and his Arab incarnation Ardith Bey, created a sensation. It was followed by a seemingly endless series of sequels: *The Mummy's Hand, The Mummy's Tomb, The Mummy's Ghost, The Mummy's Curse,* and was revived again in 1959 with Christopher Lee. Meanwhile, legion other films using the mummy theme were released as well.

So the idea to revive the classic again in 1999, with a sequel in 2001, was not entirely original. The archaeologist character was rewritten to become a kind of Indiana Jones, and the story was rewritten to resemble his adventure in *The Lost Ark* (this film, and Lara Croft's similar *Tomb Raider,* will be discussed further in chapter 7). Adopting an ironic and slightly campy style also enabled the writers to maintain all the stereotypes by taking their edge off. The producers chose not to have big stars but employed mind-blowing special effects instead, with heaps of flesh-eating scarabs, and a gory corpse gradually restoring itself by feeding on its victims like a vampire, reincarnating itself in threatening mists, floods, and sandstorms.

There is also an interesting scene in which the mummy seems to hypnotize an insurgent crowd, in the same vein as Arab nationalist leaders seemed to do against the British colonial occupation (compare van Ginneken 1992). The 2001 Virgin *Film Guide* concluded: "The razzle-dazzle factor is high, and many viewers won't mind that it's all rather hollow, formulaic stuff any more than they'll be troubled by the offhanded treatment of Arabs as buffoons, exotics, and verminous riffraff. (It's one thing to set the movie in 1926 and another to appropriate the era's insidious racism). In all, it's the quintessential summer movie: noisy, spectacular, and disposable" (p. 541).

THE GRECO-ROMAN SUPER-PEPLUM

After Cleopatra, few other major projects about ancient Greece and Rome were set in motion by Hollywood for a very long time. It took two generations before Steven Spielberg accepted a pitch on the subject. His reaction, according to the screenwriter was to ask, was it "about ancient Roman gladiators? Yes, I said. Taking place in the ancient Coliseum? Yes. Fighting with swords and animals to the death and such? Yes. Great, let's make the movie" (Winkler 2004, p. 2). Spielberg was very much aware of the attraction of such older popular formats but also of the fact that new movie techniques, such as CGI (computer-generated images), now made it possible to further trump the wide-screen spectacles of the 1950s and 1960s.

So DreamWorks (and Universal) commissioned blockbuster director Ridley Scott to make *Gladiator*, with Russell Crowe in the main role. It had a budget of more than $100 million and was shot in four different countries—but not in Rome itself. In the spring of the 2000, it was released simultaneously in no fewer than three thousand theatres in North America and four hundred in Great Britain. It immediately shot up the charts, making almost $500 million worldwide during its first box office run, followed by the bestselling DVD and even a video game. It also received relatively sympathetic reviews and was nominated for a dozen Oscars, winning five: best film, actor in a leading role, visual effects, sound, and costumes (Kochberg 2003, pp. 26–28). It was also followed by a number of television features and documentaries on the subject in Europe.[8]

This success apparently broke the evil spell on the genre and triggered the go-ahead for a whole series of other similar projects in Hollywood. Whereas the United States identified more closely with ancient Rome, some Europeans—and particularly Germany—identified more closely with ancient Greece. Two new Hollywood super-peplums on Hellenic civilization thus depended heavily on German input. (A new tax law enabled Germans to invest $10 billion in risky Hollywood projects over six years).[9]

The 2004 movie *Troy*, on Achilles, had a $175-million budget and was shot by German director Wolfgang Pedersen, while *Alexander*, also released in 2004, had a $150-million budget and was produced by German Thomas Schuely (although Schuely reportedly had difficulty restraining and disciplining American director Oliver Stone, as both critics and audiences saw the latter movie as somewhat incoherent).

All three new blockbusters about Greco-Roman antiquity were double-length features, built around "lone white male heroes" venturing into the "wild southeast" of the day and deriving much of their appeal from a rapid succession of fighting scenes. The number of people involved in these scenes was impressively multiplied through new computer-imaging techniques.

There is something curious about the genre of Greek and Roman antiquity narratives. During some eras in some countries, these themes became more or less prominent—often as part of a reflection on past and future, of current empires and regimes. Eighteenth- and nineteenth-century British literature was preoccupied with the rise and fall of the Roman Empire, as was twentieth-century American cinema. The emergent and virtuous empire was implicitly depicted as a forerunner of Anglo-Saxon democracy (with august speeches about "individual freedom"), the vicious and decadent empire instead as a forerunner of fascism and communism (with despicable scenes of tyrant demagogues and domesticated masses).

At the same time, movies about ancient Rome tend to focus on a very limited set of themes. More than a dozen feature films have been made about Julius Caesar alone, indicating a tendency to focus on the political rulers, the emperors and the senate, dynastic intrigue and palace life, its duplicity and hypocrisy, and its luxury and decadence, with the occasional orgy thrown in for good measure. At the same time, there is comparatively little about the fascinating lives of the middle classes and ordinary citizens, in the capital or outside it—little on traders, craftsmen, farmers, and their like. (The successful early twenty-first-century big-budget television series *Rome* is an interesting deviation).

On the other hand, there is often a focus on "the people" and the lower classes, but these are mostly presented as rabble, mobs, and crowds—as a potential threat to be contained by the rulers. There is relatively little on the daily life in the outlying provinces and colonies, except in the context of war and rebellion. The only exception is Palestine at the time of Christ (which will be discussed further in chapter 9).

If ancient Rome has always been the subject of European literature and art, plays, and operas, the specific possibilities of blockbuster cinema have always tended to shift the focus to occasions where the emperors and "the people" met face to face, as in large-scale public ceremonies and parades (think of Cleopatra's triumphant entry into to the city), and most of all to the huge stadiums of the day, where the rulers distracted the masses with popular games. The Circus Maximus was a racetrack with room for 150,000 spectators; the Coliseum in turn was an arena with stands for fifty thousand, where full-day programs with wild animlas, comics, executions, and gladiators were regularly featured. On special occasions, the latter fought to the death over prizes equaling the annual salary of a common soldier; they could thus become superstars, cheered on by admiring fans. This was show biz in the year zero. Several classical scholars have written monographs about Hollywood's depiction of these subjects.[10]

The scriptwriters for *Gladiator* took inspiration from historical characters and events but changed them at will to fit the Hollywood mold. The supreme bad guy is Commodus, the son of a just emperor who kills his father to usurp the throne (a complete invention, according to Meijer 2003, p. 217). The supreme good guy is Maximus, a brave general who is sold into slavery but makes a glorious comeback as a prizefighter and "restores democracy." ("Much of the world is brutal and cruel and dark; Rome is the light," he says at the very beginning of the film). Yet his revolt is not driven by a struggle for social justice (as in Stanley Kubrick's earlier *Spartacus*), but by mere "family values" and a desire to be reunited with his wife and son. His friendship with a black comrade is likewise "privatized."

Implicitly, the cruelty of the fights is associated closely with exotic lands and peoples. Maximus "the Spaniard" is trained among Arabs in the film, in the North African province of Zucchabar. The first of three fights in the Roman Coliseum is announced as a re-creation of a war against Carthage (in modern-day Tunisia), where the Roman general Scipio Africanus confronted "the barbarian hordes" of Hannibal, according to the announcement, with his "ferocious mercenaries and warriors from all brute nations, bent on merciless destruction." The battle scenes also emphasize the superiority of the arms and tactics of the Romans over those of their primitive enemies. Unnoticeably, then, some observers noted, the Pax Romana of those years already came to resonate with the Pax Americana of the year 2000 (Winkler 2004). But this tendency only grew further thereafter.

Case Study: The Supermen of Ancient Greece

Many of the "classical tales" about European antiquity are seen and treated as if they were "recorded history," but they were not, or they were only partly so. This is particularly true for the myths and legends emerging from the mists of time, such as those about the earliest conflicts of Europe with the outside world: in Greece, in present-day Turkey and with Persia, or during the Roman Empire in West Asia and North Africa. Very often, we only have one side of these stories, unconfirmed by neutral—let alone by hostile—sources. One interesting recent example was the Iranian protests over Zack Snyder's ultraviolent 2007 movie *300*, based on an earlier comic strip about the famous 480 BCE battle of Thermopylae with the Spartans and full of stereotypes.

These "classical tales" are often incomplete or contradictory but tend to embellish the European role and downgrade the Asian or African roles in the events of those days. Two thousand years of Western historiography, literature, art, and their "cult of the ancients" have further "connected the dots" and "filled in the gaps" along these very same ethnocentric lines. Who invaded and who was invaded? Who were the heroes and who were the villains? Who proved noble and who proved cruel? Books and plays, operas and paintings, tended to bolster an "us versus them" picture of antiquity—well before popular filmmaking came along.

Older and newer European and American films—but most of all recent Hollywood blockbusters—also share a "perspectivistic slant" in other respects. That is to say that they often tend to project typically contemporary Western (and particularly American) views, feelings, and behavior back upon these supposed historic events. Sometimes this is an explicit and conscious decision, but often it is not. The scriptwriters, designers, producers, directors, and actors use their own grids to "make sense" of the scattered bits and pieces about original events.

The ancient Greeks and Romans are often made to look like northwestern Europeans in these movies, sometimes more like Celts or Vikings. The main protagonists are selected and grimed to look whiter than they probably were, with blond (often light blond) hair and blue (often light blue) eyes. Noteworthy recent examples are Brad Pitt as Achilles and Diane Kruger as Helen in *Troy*, and Colin Farrell as Alexander. It is true that descriptions of the former have long been taken to mean that Achilles and Helen had somewhat yellowish and somewhat reddish hair, respectively, and somewhat bluish eyes, but considerable doubt has been cast upon the connotations of these translations elsewhere. It is now understood that only between 2 and 7 percent of the Greek people then (as now) were of a somewhat lighter type and that the colors should rather be understood as nuances within a light to dark brown spectrum.[11] By contrast, the Greeks' "exotic" partners or enemies have often been made much darker in these films, both physically and psychologically—for instance, Alexander's Persian love interest Roxane (played by a black actress) or his enemy Darius (who is further Osama-ized).

On the one hand, the creators (for instance, in *Alexander*) go out of their way to make certain characters mutilated, ugly, or coarse—even on the "civilized" side of the distribution. On the other hand, they cannot keep themselves from selecting actors with "magazine model" looks and grooming: shampooed hair (particularly for distinguished gray elderly gentlemen), lotioned skin (without any rashes or pimples), shining white teeth (perfectly complete), and even surgically improved faces (such as female stars' collagen-enhanced lips). It may seem nitpicking to point this out, but it is not: It is just a more visible example of the tendency to bring historical "reality" in line with modern tastes, produced within a media landscape dominated by a star system and a consumer culture sponsored by commercial advertising—largely for fashion and fads, cosmetics, and hygienic products.

It is interesting that within this genre, the young male body has always been presented in a highly sexualized way, both in partial nudity (the body-builder shoulders, arms, and chest; the six-pack abdomen) and in skimpy clothing (the short leather skirts). Homosexual and bisexual practices were widespread in ancient Greece, but of course this does not go down well in present-day Middle America. So Wolfgang Pedersen wisely chose to present Achilles' intimate friend Patrocles merely as his "nephew"; but Oliver Stone stubbornly decided to have Alexander caress, embrace, and kiss his lover Hephaistion in full view. In fact, one of the main reasons his movie was not very successful in the United States, Stone claimed with some exaggeration, was the "raging fundamentalism in morality" at the time.[12]

It is also interesting that the young female body, by contrast, is not always presented in a sexualized way here. Of course she is often made to be a slim weight watcher rather than a plumper figure. The worthy "white" woman is often shown in a long, flowing robe, in an attractive but rather dignified pose. The man and the woman are shown as romantically in love, and once they are united they also display a tender parental love for their offspring in ways that are more twenty-first century CE than thirteenth century BCE. By contrast, it is often the "nonwhite" woman who is the bearer of rampant sexuality, waiting to be released, and who is shown fully nude in scenes of violent passion—for instance, the Persian Roxane, played by the "ethnic" actress Rosario Dawson, in *Alexander.*

The ancient legends are already full of boasts about small armies under heroic leaders crushing armies ten times larger under cowardly leaders, through mere courage and wit. Technological and technical breakthroughs on the European side may have played a role, but such extreme numerical contrasts have not always been confirmed. Yet huge armies do, of course, make for great production value, particularly when equipped with strange-looking gear. Hollywood has always tried to impress cinema audiences with vast numbers of extras (often hired at minimal expense on exotic shooting locations), but in recent years computer-generated images have made it possible to further multiply these numbers electronically—so that the Greek landing near Troy comes to resemble the familiar images of the D-day landing in Normandy at the end of World War II; and Alexander's battle of Gaugamela comes to resemble the massive onslaughts at the height of

World War I, whereas they must in reality have been much more modest affairs.

The morality or immorality of the leadership is often intertwined with the safeguarding or loss of empire. This was the case in Victorian-era British literature on antiquity and in modern American movies; there is a tendency in them to equate white imperial power with superior civilization and thus morality. Before the Great Battle in the Middle East, director Oliver Stone has his Alexander make a bombastic speech about "freeing" the region's peoples from slavery. (Note that the Greek Athenians were and remained slave keepers when they supposedly "invented" democracy and human rights—as did the Americans, the British, and the French millennia later). Earlier movies implicitly equated decadent or hostile empires with fascist or Communist totalitarianism (for instance, in the on-screen "preface" to Cecil B. DeMille's *The Ten Commandments*, to which we will return later).

The Greek and Roman societies are implicitly secularized in many of these movies. Their religion is toned down and becomes a relatively private rather than a very public matter. Certain ceremonies and rituals are shown, but they are somehow Christianized or even made humanist. By contrast, the religion of their enemies in West Asia and North Africa is made to look more superstitious and cruel (such depictions of Babylonia and Egypt will be discussed further in chapter 9). Ancient notions of chance and fate, honor and revenge, are also silently replaced by a more familiar quest for wealth, power, and fame as the major psychological and social driving forces (for instance in *Troy*'s Achilles and in *Alexander*).

PRESENT-DAY AUDIENCES

It is noteworthy that the "Greek antiquity" movies *Troy* and *Alexander* did better in western Europe, particularly Germany, but that they were made possible by the previous success of the "Roman antiquity" movie *Gladiator* in North America. The "ancient Greece" craze in Germany went back to the eighteenth-century work of Johann Joachim Winckelmann. The nineteenth-century amateur archaeologist Heinrich Schliemann excavated layers of the fortified town of Troy, on the extreme northwestern tip of Anatolia, in present-day Turkey, where trade routes to the Orient originated in ancient times (before Constantinople/Byzantium/Istanbul at the other extreme of the Sea of Marmora took over that role).

If indeed there ever was such a prolonged siege of Troy (later called Ilion) in those days, it was rather an episode in the "tribal warfare" between

competing villages, small towns, and surrounding areas on either side of the
Aegean Sea between Europe and Asia with some support of fishing fleets—not
a world war. (In these super-peplums, Greek buildings and cities are also consistently made more grandiose than they probably were at the time). The siege
reportedly lasted ten years and supposedly took place during the thirteenth
century BC, but the heroic exploits were transmitted orally over many generations and were probably aggrandized and embellished. The epic *Iliad*, supposedly written with the *Odyssey* by the Greek poet Homer many centuries
later, covered only two months of the battle. The twin texts became a key reference and are said to have founded Greek, antique, and European literature
and culture. Millennia later, Hollywood further condensed the entire siege of
Troy into a battle of just a few weeks.

The movie *Troy* also transformed a dark and complex tragedy into a simple action movie *cum* love story. In the original story the beautiful Helen
was married to the brother of King Agamemnon when the son of the king
of the competing realm of Troy then kidnapped her. The original story did
not say in so many words she had an unhappy marriage and eloped—although she ultimately is supposed to have fallen in love with her abductor
(there are various more or less original versions). She was carried off,
forced to leave her child behind, and was later said to have longed to return
to her original husband, her family, and her home. Confused and torn between contradictory feelings, Helen was the first femme fatale in European
popular culture. Agamemnon reportedly used her abduction as a pretext
for a naval expedition and siege. He also enlisted the "blond" superman and
demigod Achilles for this purpose but later took his prize—another captive
female beauty—from him. The recurring theme of the capture and rape of
such female prizes by the heroes is of course mostly avoided in Hollywood
movies.

The movie *Alexander* is an even more interesting case than *Troy*. It was not
the first movie on the subject, emerged from a series of many contemporaneous projects on the subject, and it may soon be followed by another major
movie on the same subject. It is characterized by an oversized ambition and
huge budget, by the hubris of both the producer and the director, as both had
a boyish fascination, since grammar school, with the hubris of Macedonian
emperor Alexander. According the movie's main historical adviser, he was
"encouraging the idea that he was the begotten son of Zeus," although one
Macedonian general wryly observed that his family were rather "the grand-
sons of goat-herds."

Stone had previously proven to be a worthwhile filmmaker, but he may
have been done in here by some tendencies that have marked his life and

work: the combination of hero worship and enemy images (already notable in his visions of Kennedy, Nixon, and Vietnam). Apparently he could not keep himself from attempting to tell Alexander's entire life, furthermore, which makes the film of ten thousand seconds last twice too long. He then tried to add more psychological drive by inserting a Freudian-type arch-conflict, with a brutal father and a domineering mother (probably based on Fox 1973, pp. 18–21). But the big question remained why, between twenty-five and thirty-three years of age, Alexander succeeded in conquering "most of the known world" (known by a few in ancient Europe that is) and prefiguring much of the later Roman Empire. The answer is that we do not really know; the original sources are too few and limited, and other unknown factors may simultaneously have weakened rivals.

According to the film's main historical consultant, Alexander scholar and Oxford professor Robin Lane Fox, his "horse bound charges" were essential, providing the "shock and awe" tactics of the day.[13] According to others his phalanx-type defenses against lances and arrows played a key role: the "missile shield" of the day. That is to say, his success depended on factors of intellect and courage. Although still others maintain that not military but economic (or even climate) factors were decisive in the end. The problem is that there is little we know with complete certainty. None of the twenty accounts of Alexander's life believed to have been written by his contemporaries have survived. The closest extant accounts were written four centuries or more after his death, even though Fox's study mentioned no fewer than 1,472 books and articles on him published over the preceding century and a half alone.[14]

The problem is that this paucity of original sources leaves ample room for both Fox and Stone to prolong the hero-worshiping tendency of previous Western historiographers. The Greeks' superiority over the Persians and other Oriental enemies may have been exaggerated by them, from the very first major battle at Gaugamela, where forty thousand soldiers reportedly beat an army of 250,000. In the film, Darius flees first as a stereotypical exotic coward, although the record says that it was his troops that deserted when they began losing. Babylon, and Alexander's entry and welcome there, are an earlier Hollywood invention, copied straight out of D. W. Griffith's 1916 film *Intolerance*. The belly dancers, and Darius's harem with 365 girls (one for every day of the year) are unsupported by the evidence. The account downplays the fact that Alexander also gambled (and lost) many of his Eastern conquests by stubbornly pushing forward in pursuit of a reported "Eastern edge of the world," which he always thought to be near.

A Dutch Alexander scholar, Jona Lendering, who also spent years researching and retracing Alexander's campaign, noted that Alexander was far from the imagined and depicted "noble" hero fighting for "freedom." He refused his opponents' peace proposals because a war would bring better spoils; he spied on his own generals and men and had them killed at the slightest expression of doubt; he did not always leave conquered armies intact, as the film claims, but sometimes massively killed his prisoners of war even after they had rendered themselves. He had civilians murdered by the thousands and reveled in torture.[15] He was exceptionally cruel—even for that time and place—but little of that is actually shown in the film. We choose to project those kind of things upon ethnic "others."

But Alexander is obviously one of those historical figures whose role can easily be adapted to fit the epoch and concerns of his historiographers. (The same can be said about Caesar, and also about Napoleon, for instance). So in this case, too, there is a strange resonance with current events. "He's a dashing warrior-king who had a vision of compassion, generosity of spirit, and peace," the unfazed Stone thus told the Associated Press upon the release of the movie. "He was not a needless killer, he was not a butcher. At times, he did massacre, but these were hard times. He did so with a purpose, with a reason. He did not have the Genghis Khan or Attila the Hun mentality."[16] Of course his Asian enemies of the day may well have felt that the exact opposite was true.

The film also falsely claims that Alexander treated Persian and other cultures with great respect. The largest Dutch daily newspaper, *De Telegraaf*, was taken in to such an extent by Stone's noble flight of fancy that it wrote: "For Alexander Muslims belonged to a much older and more developed culture than his own compatriots"—not accounting for the fact that that Muhammad and Islam were not born until a full thousand years later.[17] A review in the *Washington Post* commented on Stone's "notion that Alexander was a mere multiculturalist, who wanted to 'unify' the globe." It said, "He seems not to recognize this as a standard agitprop of the totalitarian mind-set, always repulsive, but more so here in a movie that glosses over the boy-king's frequent massacres." The *New Yorker* magazine noted the interesting coincidence that at the elite university of Yale, the now somewhat liberal filmmaker Stone had been in the same class as the conservative president George W. Bush and added that Stone uses Alexander "to offer a strident argument in favor of unilateral aggression against foreign powers, on the ground that—guess what— it's good for 'em."

Surprisingly, the AP dispatch quoted Stone as commenting on the reelection of Bush the younger: "Often second-term presidents do become better presidents. . . . If Bush manages to transform Iraq and Afghanistan into secure, democratic states, if he can negotiate with Iran to disband its nuclear weapons program and calm Islamic radicalism," he may earn the legacy of the ancient hero of Alexander. "It's a grand scheme," Stone acknowledged. But "if he pulled it off . . . in twenty years maybe he would be considered Bush the Great."[18] Other media had meanwhile noticed that same hidden subtext in *Alexander*, that of the most powerful leader of the most powerful country in the world claiming to bring freedom and civilization to the Middle Eastern heartland of Iraq, Iran, and Afghanistan—and thus change the course of history.

We could continue this reflection by scrutinizing the Hollywood depiction of successive historical epochs, its continuities and discontinuities, as some film scholars have done (see, for example, Bourget 1992, Searles 1990). But this book rather focuses on genres, their hidden focus and ethnocentric subtexts, so we will not continue with the Middle Ages, the Crusades, the explorers, the pirates, and so on, although such themes do indeed occasionally return within the framework of the successive chapters.

4

The Tamers and the Wild: Wilderness Adventure

What are our prime fantasies in relation to wild and distant lands? Would we be able to confront the terrible and outsized monsters that are no doubt lurking somewhere deep in the interior? Could we master the world of strange plants, animals, and savages in the jungle? Could we even survive on our very own, on the deserted shores of an uninhabited island, without the help of natives? How does ancient seafarer lore translate into present-day Hollywood blockbusters? What about the themes of ethnicity and culture: Have they simply disappeared?

We often wonder who we really are, deep down, stripped of all the make-believe—what we are really capable of, left to ourselves, without fancy devices or outside help, after shedding our culture, confronting nature in the raw. That kind of wilderness is hardly there anymore, within the framework of the developed world. Of course there are the interior valleys of the Rocky Mountains in North America or of the Alps in western Europe, but in those places, we would have a vague idea of what plants to eat or to keep away from. There are few dangerous animals, as even the few remaining wolves or bears are mostly afraid of humans. There are no threatening tribes. Yet the fascination remains.

Millions of children are enrolled in the international scouting movement, with its emphasis on "wilderness survival skills," or in one of its many imitations and variations. They usually know that it was founded in Great Britain by R. S. Smyth Baden-Powell, but not his precise backgrounds and intentions. (This will be discussed further in chapter 7). Germany and other countries built similar youth movements at the time based on fitness and a natural lifestyle.

Today, even adults do all kinds of sports, individually or in teams. Often we devote entire holidays to exercising ourselves deep inside some forest or far outside some shore. Commercial companies and civil services have learned to occasionally tap into our physical fitness and group sentiment, staging out-door "survival games" or "treasure hunts" in a natural environment, in order to build department morale and cohesion. We test our endurance and skills together, and we are supposed to carry some of our newly acquired feelings of competence and common ambition back with us to the office. This kind of ac-tivity is very familiar to everyone.

It also taps into an old fount of myths, legends, folklore, archaic stories, and classic tales—about monsters, as in *King Kong, Godzilla,* and *Jurassic Park*; about children lost or abandoned in the wild, suckled by wolves or apes, as in *The Jungle Book,* or *Tarzan*; about castaways surviving on deserted shores or uninhabited islands, as in *Robinson Crusoe.* These themes stir some of our deepest fears or proudest hopes, so it is no wonder that new movies about them often have blockbuster ambitions, and television formats derived from them become ratings hits. Let us take a closer look at the popular culture tra-dition of the wilderness genre, its various subgenres, and their hidden ideo-logical subtexts.

MONSTER MOVIES

Humans are not alone as major protagonists in movies; on occasion animals are as well. Yet they are often "humanized" in both appearance and behavior and given a specific personality. Like humans in popular movies, they are of-ten portrayed as either all good or all bad, with nothing in between—that is to say, neither psychologically complex nor realistic. It is either *Flipper* or *Jaws*, either *Free Willy* or *Moby Dick.* The most unusual monsters live in hiding, somewhere deep under the sea or far into the interior of an island or conti-nent, until unconscionable people come to disturb and release them. The most famous such movie monster, and a classic pop icon, is *King Kong.*

The latest version of 2005 cost more than $200 million and brought in $550 million. It had spectacular special effects and was made by New Zealand director Peter Jackson, whose 2002–2003 *Lord of the Rings* series had received many Oscars and became the best-selling trilogy of all time, earning $2.9 bil-lion at the box office. He said that he wanted the new *King Kong* film to be faithful to the 1930s original, "the last period when one could still believe in mysterious islands and unexplored regions"—even though he acknowledged that "the story lends itself to multiple interpretations: sexual, racial, etc."[1]

Case Study: King Kong the Dark Brute

The 2001 Virgin *Film Guide* characterized the original 1933 version of *King Kong*, by directors Merian C. Cooper and Ernest B. Schoedsack, as "the ultimate monster movie and one of the grandest and most beloved adventure films ever made." The film reportedly grossed almost $2 million, at the time considered a colossal amount, which "by itself saved the studio that produced it from bankruptcy" (p. 409). The movie was released in 1933, at the height (or depth) of the Depression in the United States. That very same year the Nazis came to power in Germany, and there was a substantial subliminal link between German brutes and a giant gorilla in the minds of both the directors and the audience.[2]

Directors Cooper and Schoedsack had for many years been traveling around the world to film exotic environments, for instance, in the Middle East and South East Asia, which could then be enriched with storylines and characters to produce features. They had seen material about an island with large reptiles in Indonesia, and they had seen a huge gorilla in the Barnum & Bailey Circus. In the mid-1920s, there had been media hype over the notorious "missing link" between ape and man, and an American court actually condemned a man for teaching evolution theory in school. Meanwhile, a Russian scientist tried to inseminate apes in Africa with sperm from local blacks and then to inseminate a woman with monkey sperm from Cuba until an outcry in the United States stopped the experiments.[3]

Together with British writer Edgar Wallace, Cooper and Schoedsack came up with the idea of an encounter with apes and other gigantic prehistoric animals that had somehow survived on an isolated island. Advances in building miniature models, slow motion, and background projection made filming the story a feasible option. The intrigue was about a filmmaker, just like themselves, bringing a starlet to meet such a monster, namely, a giant ape on "Skull Island" that demanded regular human sacrifices from the native tribe living on the island. This King Kong is thus a kind of outsized "missing link" or supercannibal (even though most such apes prefer fruit under normal circumstances).

As always, the myth derives its strength from opposite extremes. On the one hand is the setting of a primitive "heart of darkness" in some unexplored interior: the natural habitat of the archaic animal. On the other hand is the setting of the (literal) peaks of civilization—the highest skyscraper at the time in Manhattan, where Kong is ultimately brought as the "eighth wonder of the world." The city is the natural habitat of his opposite numbers, the most advanced humans. After rampaging through New York, King Kong climbs the Empire State Building, is attacked by fighter planes with machine guns, and ultimately plunges to his death on the sidewalk below. The showman protagonist concludes, however: "It wasn't the airplanes. It was Beauty killed the Beast."

Other opposite extremes play an even more important role. On one side is an overpowering figure, considerably larger and stronger than average: a dark brute, albeit with occasionally touching human sentiments for the girl. The ape was made very realistic by the patient alternation of shots of dwarfish puppets and of giant hydraulic hands holding the girl. On the other side there is her ethereal figure, considerably smaller and weaker than average: a very white young woman, drawn between utmost horror and pity. The actress was even made to wear a light wig for contrast, because "gentlemen prefer blondes." Both the black tribe and the black monster were ready to trade one such white woman against six black "brides," it was said. She was also shown with provocatively naked shoulders, in wet clothing, and in suggestive poses.

Note that this was in the midst of a racist and segregationist era when blacks were still widely compared with apes, blacks were considered extra-big and supersexual in the minds of many white men and women, and romantic or erotic encounters between black men and white women were the ultimate taboo, automatically defined as involuntary, therefore as rape and meriting lynching on the spot.[4] So both audiences and critics experienced weird associations during the provocative scenes in which the anthropomorphic King Kong fancies the heroine, unpeels her white virgin clothing, while she screams hysterically and almost orgastically. (One thing is emphatically missing in all these movies, I realized after seeing all these versions: his genitals. But they would indeed have posed a big problem, particularly once he got aroused.)

The Virgin *Film Guide* (2001) sees "the re-emergence of suppressed desire" at least "on a psychological level," and counsels "don't think too hard about the racist subtext." Allan Hunter's *Film and TV Handbook* (1991) mentions "the outpouring of all our socially repressed sexual and violent urges" in the film. The year after its release, the enforcement of the new Hollywood Production Code against race mixing, sex, and excessive violence led to a suppression of some of King Kong's "clothes-peeling" and "man-eating" sequences, whereas other scenes were darkened so that offending details became lost to the viewers. Meanwhile, the director had already made an unsuccessful sequel, *Son of Kong* (1933).

A more recent big-budget remake was *King Kong* (1976), with John Guillermin as director and Jessica Lange as the dark beast's ethereal love interest. It gave the story the slightly different pretext of oil exploration and ultimately petrol ads (like Exxon/Chevron's "put a tiger in your tank"), but it also made the erotic dimension even more explicit: the monster actually bares her breasts (a scene censored in many early versions), and she is shown naked. But the dialogue seems to suggest that she not only sweet-talks to calm him, but really fancies him and enjoys his outsized attentions—like blowing her dry after a bath. Note that it is only the cartoonlike difference in size that makes it possible to play with this theme at all. Had they been even remotely similar, it would have been unthinkable to tolerate such suggestive sexual scenes in a mainstream movie. The movie was moderately successful and is still regularly repeated on television, but its sequel *King Kong Lives* (1986) was a dud.

Peter Jackson's 2005 version meant to top them all, although its persistent AD/HD would cause a slight headache in the viewer.[5] It is a perfect example of the synthetic mix of real and animated images of people and animals, virtual monsters, and horrible insects. Opposite the ape, it placed an intellectual who had to compete with him for the love of the girl. The movie had a number of brilliant twists and daring scenes, with many winks to the viewer: references to earlier super-blockbusters (such as *Jurassic Park* and *Titanic*), earlier celebrities (a director resembling Orson Welles, a writer resembling Arthur Miller, a starlet resembling Marilyn Monroe, etc.), and many jokes about the opportunism and cynicism of show business. But the archetypical nineteenth-century storylines about cruel tribes (think of *Heart of Darkness* and *Apocalypse Now*) and about the remains of an extinct civilization (think of Allan Quatermain and Indiana Jones) were still there. We will return to these themes in chapter 7.

Meanwhile, others had joined the fray, with movies on other outsized monsters. The original *King Kong* script had contained elaborate scenes of King Kong fighting with a dinosaur and other archaic monsters, but they were mostly omitted from the final version. The Japanese filmmaker Inoshiro Honda, a protégé of the better-known Akira Kurosawa, had visited Hiroshima and had wanted to make a film about the horrific devastation caused there by the atomic bomb. Somewhat later, the United States tested an even more powerful hydrogen bomb on the Bikini Atoll in the Pacific, contaminating Japanese fishermen and fish and stirring a new surge in anti-American sentiments. It was these precise circumstances that made the filmmaker and the Toho studio go ahead with a related monster film.

The original 1954 Japanese film was called *Gojira,* after a mythical sea dragon in mariners' songs. A U.S. company bought the rights and garbled the name to *Godzilla.* It inserted scenes with its own actors and expressly censored both the anti-American and antinuclear message of the film, since these were the McCarthy years, with their witch hunts against "unpatriotic" people—most of all in Hollywood. It was in this amputated version that the movie became known and circulated around the world. Only a half century later was the uncut version made available to the rest of the world on home video.[6] Meanwhile, there have been twenty-five Japanese sequels and variations; one was even called *King Kong vs. Godzilla* (1962).

The most recent version was made in Hollywood by director Roland Emmerich (of *Independence Day*). His 1998 *Godzilla* immediately shot into the top fifty of the charts and made $380 million at the box office. The film was critical of American institutions and authorities, but the original story was once again grossly altered and changed to spare American sensitivities. The nuclear explosions triggering the mutation were not American, but French, and nuclear contamination itself was also associated with the Soviet Union (via a detour to the aftermath of the Chernobyl disaster). The victims of the monster, by contrast, were no longer Japanese, but American. So the original message was put on its head. Later critics even saw an entirely different theme—related to terrorism.[7]

Renewed American interest in the theme had of course been stirred by Steven Spielberg, who had said he had been inspired by the American *King Kong,* but of course meant he (and best-selling author Michael Crichton) had been inspired by the Japanese *Godzilla,* to come up with the 1993 blockbuster *Jurassic Park. Jurassic Park* cost close to $200 million to make but immediately shot to the very number-one spot on the charts, made close to $1 billion, and was followed by two sequels that together made almost another billion dollars. It was simultaneously made as and for a Disney theme park ride and a Nintendo video game and made further billions of dollars on derived products: The usual plastic figurines in Happy Meal boxes at McDonald's outlets; food products for children; T-shirts, boxer shorts, and sneakers; calendars and school supplies; hygienic and cosmetic products—an avalanche of products, at 10 percent royalties apiece. European countries were completely surprised and overwhelmed by the dino tsunami. The film had 6.5 million viewers in

France, some seventy licensing contracts, even with some very French brands such as La vache qui rit and La pie qui chante.[8]

It proved very difficult to claim every dino icon as "copyrighted," and Asian knock-off products soon flooded the markets as well. Disney also made an animated cartoon *Dinosaur* in the year 2000, which brought in $360 million at the box office, in spite of its tepid, predictable, and formulaic characters. In view of the persistent bombardment with miniature models, many confused toddlers asked their parents for a Tyrannosaurus Rex as a live pet. Ultimately, the dinosaur replaced furry animals as the most popular creature for kids.

Children, too, are easily fascinated by exotic supermonsters, suddenly springing forward from the darkest of times in prehistory and the darkest of places on Earth, to stir fears that were quietly hiding in the darkest corner of our own souls. Strange is scary. Or, as some Asian maps used to note: "This is where the dragons are."

JUNGLE MAN MOVIES

Another recurring theme in ancient heroic myths of all cultures is that of the baby abandoned or lost in the wild (see Rank 1964); the child either survives on its own or is suckled by wild animals. One early example is the Roman story of Romulus and Remus, supposedly adopted and raised by a wolverine. Later examples of famous wild children were the French Victor "de l'Aveyron" (who inspired François Truffaut's arty movie *L'enfant sauvage*) and the German Gaspar "von Nürnburg" (who inspired Werner Herzog's *Gaspar Hauser*). Very often, extraordinary origins and/or extraordinary destinies were ascribed to such infants—usually men.

The underlying philosophical theme is, of course, that of nature versus nurture. Two of the most famous stories of this kind with an ethnic angle are *The Jungle Book* and *Tarzan*. The former story, by British writer Rudyard Kipling, had the ordinary Indian child Mowgli as its major protagonist; the latter, American writer Edgar Rice Burroughs, by contrast, featured a very aristocratic white child left to his own devices in the black environment of Africa. So race—as well as class and gender—inevitably play a major role in such tales, even if this is toned down or carefully hidden in recent versions.

Disney had already done well with its 1967 version of *The Jungle Book*, the last animated cartoon personally supervised by Walt himself before his death. Disney did even better with the 1994 version, conceived to inspire further theme park rides and merchandising spin-offs. Both portrayed the jungle as a somewhat unruly garden and the animals as mostly sweet. The 1999 version of *Tarzan* had a much more tragic and violent opening, but it immediately became one of the best-selling Disney animated cartoons ever, with total box office revenues of some $450 million. Only *The Lion King*, released five years earlier, fared better. But whatever happened to the race factor, which had been so prominent in the Tarzan tradition from the very start?

The original author, Edgar Rice Burroughs, was the son of a car manufacturer, ill at ease with his father's unheroic ambitions for him as some kind of future office supervisor. He tried a military career and even sought an overseas command, but failed. He then moved into popular writing and fantasy adventure, where he found success. The first installment of the Tarzan of the Apes/Lord of the Jungle series appeared in the *All Story* pulp magazine and was soon followed by the first book, on the eve of World War I.

The stories were immediate hits, and the publishers asked for more. Burroughs was happy to oblige. But he was also one of the very first authors to register his character as a trademark and to rent it out to advertisers. In his later years, he merely supervised his own work and hired ghostwriters to fill in the story outlines. There would be twenty-six Tarzan novels in all, translated into fifty-eight languages, which sold well over fifty million copies (Seesslen 1996, p. 207). They were soon followed by Tarzan comic strips, Tarzan radio series, and Tarzan movies.

The Tarzan stories were to become the best-known white fantasies about the "black" continent. Author Kenneth Cameron observed: "Both Americans and Europeans carried a set of pictures in their minds right into films, done by people who had never been in Africa. You get an emphasis on thrills and so on. Filmmakers are kind of left with that as baggage, especially if you're doing commercial film. Where you're supposed to please an audience—that thinks it already knows what Africa is—danger, disease, snakes, insects and so. That's what you give them."[9]

Case Study: Tarzan the Superior Native

The background of the Tarzan character is often misrepresented and misunderstood today. Burroughs tried to emulate the contemporary imperial adventures published by British writer Rudyard Kipling and his compatriot H. Rider Haggard. Around the turn of the century, Burroughs had also read Darwin, and he was an adherent to social Darwinism, an ideological creed emphasizing the "struggle for life" and "survival of the fittest," not only among human individuals and classes, but also between nations and races. In particular, he adhered to the American version of social Darwinism, pleading for a combination of selective immigration restrictions and international power politics, in reaction to dire warnings in Madison Grant's 1916 book *The Passing of the Great Race* and Theodore Lothrop Stoddard's 1920 book *The Rising Tide of Color against White World Supremacy* (Slotkin 1998, pp. 195–202). In this specific context, there also was a call for ruthless new "white barbarians," because only they would be able to resist the threatening rise of colored barbarians: a call for white supermen to hold back the colored undermen.

The first Tarzan film, released during the last year of World War I, was an immediate success and was one of the few silent movies at the time to bring in more than $1 million. It was immediately followed by sequels, often more than one per year. Altogether, there would be at least forty-eight Tarzan films and at least two television series, but there were hundreds if one includes the imitations made worldwide under other names: about kings of the jungle, swinging around between lianas, and queens of the jungle, scantily clad in the skins of wild animals. This became a genre in itself, with seminudity as a major appeal (think of the role of the blonde sex symbol Bo Derek in the 1981 version of *Tarzan*).

The golden age of the Tarzan movie arrived in 1932, when the first sound version introduced the character's trademark yell. He was one of the first major body builder heroes (Dyer 1997, chap. 4), hailed as an "American Adonis": hairless, clean, aseptic, a kind of running ad for early male body-care products, the office worker's fantasy answer to the challenges laid down by the flappers of the interwar years and by feminism.

The actor who became the quintessential Tarzan was Johnny Weissmuller, born in Timisoara, Romania (near Hungary), but claiming to have been born in Pennsylvania in order to be able to represent the United States in the 1924 Olympics. While working at a gym, Weissmuller had become very good at swimming. He won almost all freestyle competitions in which he participated during the 1920s before catching the eye of an MGM representative, among 150 other possible candidates. They were looking for someone with a perfect body, not necessarily with any acting skills, as most Tarzan movies had only around a hundred short lines of spoken text, composed from a vocabulary of only a few hundred words. Weissmuller made a dozen Tarzan films in sixteen years, half of them opposite Maureen O'Sullivan as Jane. But as he became older and more burly, he was dumped by the studio. He then made another sixteen films in seven years as Jungle Jim, posed in ads for GM's rather unsexy German Opel Kadett car, and tried a "Jungle Hut" fast-food franchise, but accumulated debts and quickly went downhill.[10]

What about the hidden ideology of the Tarzan stories, comics, and films? Their original setting was supposedly sub-Saharan Africa, but it was mostly the contrived cardboard Africa of studio sets, as not a single Tarzan film was shot in Africa over the first half of the twentieth century. Burroughs himself had never been to Africa, nor did he ever travel there. One of his main sources was the explorer H. M. Stanley's 1890 report *In Darkest Africa*. Much of his other background material referred to the British colonial empire in South, Southeast, and East Africa. But Tarzan's jungle cannot be pinpointed on any one map, as it is a fantasy mix, stretching to cover entirely different regions, and on occasion even entirely different continents. Once again, Africa is presented as a mere safari park or even a giant zoo. And once again, Hollywood portrayed lions living in the jungle rather than in the savannah. For good measure, it sometimes even included tigers and Asian rather than African elephants (Melis 1998).

White explorers are usually portrayed as smarter than either animals or natives—and of course also better armed—but some may turn greedy and cruel, spellbound by possible treasures of ivory and gold. In the first Weissmuller movie, Jane carries six trunks of fashionable clothes into the interior, but it is the porters who are repeatedly flogged as lazy and recalcitrant—and this is made to seem perfectly justified. The natives are a composite of the dark, primitive, and superstitious tribes that supposedly live deep in the interior of such continents: almost nude, rigged out with the usual paint, feathers, and bones. There are occasional hints they may be cannibals. Their drums and chants always denote danger. They carry funny fantasy names, have only a very limited vocabulary, and speak primitive and incomprehensible languages. If their ways need to be explained to the cinema viewer, this is not done by the natives themselves but by the white explorers or experts in the scene. But there is something else: The blacks in Tarzan films seem to carry some kind of mysterious hereditary disease, as they seem scarcer with every new version.

The name Tarzan, we hear somewhere, means "white skin" in the local black and/or ape tribe language. He did not have a real tan at first, even after years under the burning tropical sun—but that must have been due to the dense trees providing an eternal shade. He is, of course, a completely unskilled immigrant but apparently adapts rather easily to the jungle thanks to his superior body and mind, to the extent that he soon becomes a much better native than the natives themselves in a wide variety of indigenous skills ranging from the building of a tree hut to fighting of any kind of exotic animal. At the same time, however, he proves to be a "natural" leader. The vast majority soon recognizes him as such, so that he is accepted as "lord" or "king" of the jungle—almost as if he were elected.

But he cannot possibly fall in love with, or even feel sexually attracted to, a black girl—however scantily clad she might be. Nor can he adopt a black orphan. He has to wait until a white expedition ventures into the forest to supply him with a partner and a child. The minute he sees a white girl, he snatches her away; he immediately falls in love with her, and she with him. But he behaves like a born gentleman— which he is, as we will see. They become a new Adam and Eve, perhaps populating Africa with a different breed—as in apartheid fantasies—although the blacks do occasionally threaten her, and he acts out the classical white rape-and-rescue fantasy. In some stories and films they have a child—naturally, a boy—together; in others they adopt one. But in the end they become a fully functional family in the treetops, a kind of Flintstones of the forest.

After so many decades of "anything goes," the 1984 movie *Greystoke: The Legend of Tarzan, Lord of the Apes* (with Christopher Lambert in the title role) did a believable job in returning to the original stories and to the story origins of the hero. It had long been forgotten that he actually was not merely a white newborn who had survived a shipwreck and the death of his parents on the coast of Africa, who had been adopted by apes and had gone on to become the ultimate self-made man. He had all along remained the heir to the aristocratic title of Lord of Greystoke Manor, a vast country estate in Scotland, to which he returned in this film, but where he could not feel at home. So it was his superior stock, after all, that predestined him to rule over inferior beings.

The 1999 Disney film *Tarzan* retained some of this class contrast in its opening scenes but had civilization erased in a violent early fight. Tarzan was given archetypical aristocratic traits—a long, pinched face; a long, straight nose—with only his unruly long hair reminding viewers he is in the jungle, later turning into Afro locks (not so much an African as rather an American fashion). Jane becomes a kind of Diane Fossey/Jane Goodall character, a WWF animal protection saint.

Burroughs's black tribes are reduced to a minor role in the soundtrack and are replaced on the screen by apes and monkeys—both good and bad. But whereas the blacks used to speak incomprehensible local gibberish, the monkeys suddenly speak English. So where the color lines seem to have been displaced and almost made invisible, they continue to shine through. The Virgin *Film Guide* concludes: "Disney is faced with retrofitting a reactionary and essentially racist source material to suit its far more liberal agenda . . . [but] it's hard *not* to read the film in racial terms" (2001, p. 811).

The rest of the whole animal world familiar from Disney movies ranging from *The Jungle Book* to *The Lion King* is inserted into the original story: mostly cuddly and made for merchandising, with just the occasional bloodthirsty monster for dramatic contrast. The 1900 imperial jungle story has further been adapted to the 2000 urban youth culture; for instance, Tarzan swings his exotic lianas as if he were riding the more familiar skateboard (Lie & D'Haen 2002, p. 99). There is also an emphatic attempt to make Tarzan more or less "politically correct" by transforming him from a Victorian disciplinarian into a kind of softie forest ranger and game warden, secretly carrying a Greenpeace membership card somewhere inside his tiny loincloth.

A year earlier, another international feature by Carl Schenkel for Alta Vista tried to revive *Tarzan and the Lost City* by inserting a sprinkle of Stargate and Lara Croft into the formula. But Casper Van Dien and Jane March looked unconvincing: worn heroes of another age.

THE CASTAWAY, ROBINSON, AND SURVIVOR THEMES

Let us now look at blockbuster television formats. The turn of the twenty-first century was characterized by scares and hypes, both related to new communication technologies. There was a scare around the supposed Y2K bug, which, it was feared, might make computers mistake the year 2000 for the year 1900, and thereby cause a chain reaction of malfunctions in automated systems.

There also was hype about "reality TV," a new genre focused on following the everyday interactions of small groups of (mostly young) ordinary people in (almost) real time, through multimedia ranging from webcams and the Internet to hidden cameras and television. This undermined traditional and taken-for-granted distinctions between private and public, fiction and nonfiction, and even between consumers and producers (Hermes & Reesink 2003, p. 229). They triggered an intense wave of controversy and interest, particularly among adolescents, a group that both the networks and the sponsors had appeared to be on the verge of losing forever and were therefore eagerly trying to win back.

Whereas the *Big Brother* format, originating in the Netherlands (and most popular in western Europe), focused on a suburban home, the *Castaway* format, originating in Great Britain (and most popular in North America), focused on an uninhabited island instead. On the European continent the latter format was mostly called *Expedition Robinson*; in the United States it was called *Survivor*.

The last episode of the first *Survivor* series in the United States reached an unprecedented 51 million viewers, almost as much as the annual peak event of the Super Bowl. CBS demanded no less than $600,000 to broadcast the briefest thirty-second commercial during such events. The *Castaway/Robinson/ Survivor* theme was one of the oldest and most forceful stories in the world. But where did it come from, how had it become so popular, and what were its hidden ethnocentric subtexts?

The folklore and literature of seafaring cultures has always abounded with stories of shipwrecks, of sailors put overboard by pirates or after a conflict with their own captains, and washing up on deserted shores. The most archetypical case (and the subject of endless jokes) is that of the "uninhabited" island, far from trade routes, which one cannot leave unless one succeeds in attracting the attention of the crew of a stray ship. Some early examples come from ancient Egyptian, Greek, and Arab literature.

The theme turned up in northwestern Europe after these nations took to the high seas during the sixteenth century. William Shakespeare's *The Tempest* had the dark and primitive castaway Caliban (an anagram for "cannibal") subdued by the white and noble Prospero. The late-seventeenth-century Glorious Revolution saw Protestantism, meritocracy, and individualism triumph in Great Britain, preparing the ground for further overseas expansion. Of course, the possession of guns played a key role but was minimized in heroic survival stories such as Daniel Defoe's famous *Robinson Crusoe*.

Detailed stories about shipwrecks and marooning had already played a major role in the early written reports of the Dutch East India Company, particularly those about the discovery and exploration of "New Holland" or "Southland" (Australia) during the early to mid-seventeenth century, although many details were omitted or distorted for reasons of colonial rivalry. They inspired the 1708 novel *Krinke Kesmes* by Hendrik Smeeks from the small port of Zwolle, who may have been a ship's doctor.

A very detailed study by David Fausset claims that it was in reality this unknown book that inspired Defoe's 1719 *Robinson Crusoe*. Defoe was of Flemish origin, his library had Dutch titles, and he may have understood some of the language. In view of William of Orange's claim to the throne, he briefly worked as a spy in Holland for Robert Harley, who had himself ordered a copy of Smeeks's book. The link had been pointed out earlier but was dismissed on the false ground that Smeeks's *Der holländische Robinson* had only appeared in 1721; but this was in fact a later German translation. Similar

French travel reports and a book reprinted in 1723 as *Le Robinson français* may also have inspired Defoe, according to Fausset.

The most widely accepted theory, however, is that Defoe was inspired by a later, similar British event. After run-ins with the law, the Scotsman Alexander Selkirk had enlisted for a privately financed expedition to prey on Spanish ships, and particularly on the great trading galleon that plied from the Philippines to Mexico each year in the early summer. But after criticizing the captain, he was put overboard and left on the uninhabited island of Juan Fernandez, off Chile, where he spent the next four years and four months. His later rescuers described him as "a man clothed in goat skins, who looked wilder than the first owners of them." After his return, the story was written down by Richard Steele and published as *The Englishman* in 1711. The title and text tended to link his survival to qualities claimed to be "typically British," such as ingenuity and endurance (Porybná 2003).

There can be little doubt that Defoe had heard about this story. He had been unsuccessful in manufacturing and trading, but his 1697 *Essay upon Projects* is sometimes portrayed as one of the earliest management books. After dabbling in politics and religion, he tried to eliminate his debts by turning to popular writing. His 1719 book *The Strange and Surprizing Adventures of Robinson Crusoe of York, Mariner* was entirely fictional but was presented as factual—namely as an autobiography, based on the diary of a castaway who had supposedly survived twenty-eight years on an abandoned "Island of Despair" somewhere near the mouth of the Orinoco River, near present-day Trinidad and Tobago, off the northern coast of South America.

Robinson Crusoe was one of the first real novels in the English language, catering to the new reading public that has arisen after the initial spread of printing and education. It went beyond previous literature of the supposedly factual travelers' tales or the fantasized philosophers utopias, yet its description of physical objects and events lacked in sensual quality. It hardly had any characterization or dialogue and was largely an interior monologue without much form or rhythm, let alone a plot. It largely centered on a stream of moral and religious reflections, with older Christian themes such as that of the Prodigal Son and newer ones of the Puritan variety (Crowley in Defoe 1972). It also "exemplified a type of practical, self-reliant Briton who would go to the New World, make a fortune, and . . . help to found a global empire" (Fausset 1994, p. 137).

Robinson Crusoe became an immediate bestseller, with seven official editions during the rest of Defoe's lifetime, several pirated ones, and a noteworthy serialization in the *London Post*. There have been more than seven hundred editions since, and one reviewer claimed it was reissued more often than any other book except the Bible. Its success was not limited to colonial and settler countries, either; it was translated into virtually every written language, paraphrased in children's books, and represented in works of art, including an opera by Jacques Offenbach. One scholar catalogued no fewer than fifteen hundred later stories on a similar theme, now labeled "Robinsonades."

Robinson Crusoe thus became one of the major myths of British, Western, and universal civilization. The story is charmingly naive, yet of course it conveys a very specific view of the faraway world. Let us look at some elements: the introduction of nature, of animals, of natives. Although the island is apparently rich in nature, Robinson immediately defines it as a "wilderness" to be cultivated. Although the animals may well be nonthreatening, furthermore, he is ready to kill them at first sight. And when he first sees a footstep in the sand of the uninhabited island, he immediately assumes that the visitors must be cannibals. Of course, he later confirms this and helps one of their victims escape.

Defoe/Robinson's account of their encounter is as follows: "I smil'd at him, and look'd pleasantly, and beckon'd to him to come still nearer; . . . [he] laid his Head upon the Ground, and taking me by the Foot, set my Foot upon his Head; this it seems was in token of swearing to be my Slave for ever." The same scene is emphatically repeated a few pages further down, and Defoe/Robinson concludes that he had "made all the Signs to me of Subjection, Servitude and Submission imaginable." But he adds, sentimentally, "never Man had a more faithful, loving, sincere Servant . . . his very affections were ty'd to me, like those of a Child to a Father" (Defoe 1972, pp. 203–209).

Rather than presenting himself to the newcomer and somehow asking for the other's indigenous name and identity through gestures, Robinson tells him to call him "Master" and gives him an arbitrary English name—after the day of the week. "Friday" thus became one of the first of many ethnic sidekicks to white adventurer heroes in Western explorer literature. Robinson also converts Friday to Christianity and thus makes it easier to control his behavior. It is the history of the colonialism the next few centuries in a nutshell, built on the supposition of a "natural inequality" of the races. This is, of course, polished away in all recent versions, including a 1997 film with Pierce Brosnan as Robinson, who suddenly considers Friday just "a very close friend."

Slavery is indeed one of the themes recurring throughout the original book. Robinson had originally gone on a trip to buy slaves in Africa but was in turn enslaved by a pirate. He escaped together with a Moorish slave, but rather than becoming his friend, he first made him his servant and then sold him back into slavery. He later regretted this when he needed cheap labor for his Brazilian plantation. Therefore: "The first thing I did, I bought me a Negro slave." Of course this was the mentality of that age, but this whole subtext of the book is entirely glossed over in present-day versions, which means that the theme remains inscribed into the structure of the story but has been made subliminal, almost invisible, in recent versions.

The book ends with the observation that he later revisited the island he now considered his property to install settlers there. He says, "Besides other Supplies, I sent seven Women." But there is a fear of miscegenation, and he hastens to reassure his readers: "As to the *English* Men, I promis'd to send them some Women from *England*" (p. 306). He also wrote a first sequel, *The Farther Adventures of Robinson Crusoe*, and then a second sequel, *Serious Reflections of Robinson Crusoe*, which were far less successful than the original.

Other, similar books were often even more extreme in caricaturing overseas realities, either to stir readers' curiosity or to criticize home realities. In 1726 Jonathan Swift published *Gulliver's Travels*, with seafarers alternately visiting the dwarfs on the island of Liliput and the giants on the island of Brobding-nag. A much later example was Robert Louis Stevenson's 1883 *Treasure Island*, about the hidden riches waiting to be unearthed and appropriated overseas. Although they sometimes dealt with adult themes, such stories were increasingly framed as "mere" children's books, which was also a way to maintain them as innocent fantasies, with few links to the real world of overseas exploration. *Robinson Crusoe* shared the same fate.

At the same time, the simplified (because decontextualized) situation of mere survival on a deserted island became the key setting for Western reflections on the relations between nature and culture and what pioneers and settlers could do to change them. Johann David Wyss's 1812–1813 novel *The Swiss Family Robinson* had a pious preacher family overcome a similar ordeal; William Golding's 1954 *Lord of the Flies* (another name for the devil) by contrast had a group of schoolboys descend into hell. More recently, Michel Tournier's 1967 novel *Friday* reversed the roles of the slave and the master, whereas John Coetzee's 1986 novel *Foe* introduced a woman into the equation. Over the years, the Robinsonade developed into a very popular genre, alternately reaffirming or challenging established views of "the white man's burden" overseas.

It also inspired many films, from a 1916 silent version to Luis Buñuel's 1952 surrealist version and the 1977–1979 trilogy *Mountain Family Robinson*. Latter-day Robinsons crashed on the island with an aircraft and did not keep dark slaves, from the 1960 Byron Paul version for Walt Disney with the popular Dick van Dyke as Lieutenant Robin Crusoe (meeting the beautiful Nancy Kwan as "Wednesday") to the Robert Zemeckis's 2000 blockbuster movie *Castaway*, starring Tom Hanks. Still other Robinsons landed with a space ship on the planet Mars. There were also television series: *Robinson Crusoe* in France and *The Swiss Family Robinson* in the United States, Canada, and Great Britain (also incorporated into the various Disney theme parks). It is not entirely surprising, then, that the archetypical theme turned up again in the late-1990s rush to find new settings for reality television.

The trend to "reality" had been noticeable for some time. One early forerunner was the fascinating BBC television series *7-Up*. Filmmaker Michael Apted made extensive interviews with and reports about a varied group of British children from 1964 on, returning to them at seven-year intervals. At the time of writing, the sixth sequel, *49-Up*, is being broadcast. A more recent forerunner was the MTV series *The Real World*, which began in 1992, in which a group of young adults sharing a house was followed for an entire season.

A new threshold was crossed in 1999, when Dutch television producer John de Mol conceived *Big Brother*, a show that would follow a group "everywhere, always" and almost live, around a specially built port-a-cabin house. This program stirred a huge controversy and moral panic in both the media and public opinion—which was most welcome, as it helped to draw further attention and sell the format worldwide. I covered these developments as a psychologist for a major daily in the Netherlands and subsequently contributed a chapter to the first academic book about the entire new phenomenon (Meijer & Reesink 2000).

Case Study: The Invisible Fridays

A slightly older format began to attract even more attention. The British production company of Bob Geldof, known for his role in the Boomtown Rats pop group and the Live Aid concerts for Africa, had developed the *Castaway* format, wherein a group of people with only primitive supplies was placed on a desolate island off Scotland. Their survival skills, their loves and hates, were filmed the whole time by camera crews. Even before the first broadcast, rights were sold to a Scandinavian production company that began to produce it for Sweden (where the first contestant voted off the island by the other contestants later committed suicide). Over the next few years, Denmark and Norway also adopted the format.

The later productions made a key decision in changing the venue, however, from the cold north to the warm south and naming it *Expedition Robinson*. In this way, the format linked up with the older popular myth about civilized Western settlers domesticating a wild tropical environment through sheer drive and skill. This caught on immediately, and over subsequent years a range of other European nations bought the format as well. Of course, the original narrative was censored to make it more "politically correct." Most participants were white, but occasionally a few minority representatives were included as well. And there was no dark servant in sight, let alone a personal slave.

The Swedish production company Strix rented a dozen tiny islands between Sumatra and Borneo in the South China Sea, some of which had earlier harbored large numbers of Vietnamese boat refugees. The company learned how to stage a South Sea paradise and hell on them, with the right props and camera angles. The filming of an average episode for a small language market would cost several hundred thousand Euros, an entire series several million Euros, and an entire season for a range of countries tens of millions of Euros. The annual turnover of the production company thus shot up from almost 9 million to nearly 40 million Euros in only five years' time, with an estimated 3 million flowing back into the local economies. The islands were in fact transformed into one big open-air studio lot, as it were. But this, of course, was kept out of sight, as it spoiled the entire "lonely castaway" illusion.

Some European newspapers, however, published reports on the secrets of the production after some time. Throughout each summer season, the majority of the islands were occupied by groups from several different countries simultaneously, as teams competed and participants were voted off, until only one winner was left. But neither the teams nor the "survivor" were even remotely alone: There were camera and production crews during the day, and a local babysitter/troubleshooter during the night. So much of their extraordinary "courage and ingenuity" was carefully staged every single day. Sixteen boats and a helicopter shuttled people and equipment around from dawn to sunset. A television and production team of two hundred stayed in a resort on one of the islands, and a thousand or more locals were involved in servicing and supplying the entire European invasion. And this present-day version of Robinson consumed not only a hundred thousand liters of fresh water every season, but also half a million liters of fuel.[11] Of course only the heroic Western participants were highlighted in the show's coverage—not the scores of "Fridays" behind the scenes.

Things got into an even higher gear when the United States joined in and CBS adopted the format for its program *Survivor* in the year 2000. Again, a moral panic fed the media hype, and backstabbing escalated as the million-dollar prize came nearer: "In her final statements to the entire group—and to much of the nation—Sue labeled Rich a 'snake' and Kelly a 'rat.' She called Rich 'a very openly arrogant, pompous human being' and Kelly 'very two-faced and manipulative,'" the *Washington Post* reported. "Sean, a doctor voted off earlier, said the final choice was not for a winner but for which of the final two survivors proved 'least objectionable.'"[12] The winner turned out to be Richard: a gay father, formerly a cadet at West Point, and now a suave company mediator.

The second series was filmed on a private bush terrain in Australia, the third in a savannah nature reserve in northern Kenya, as producer Mark Burnett wryly observed that "surviving in Africa always has an extra dimension." Indeed it has. People of the local Samburu tribe (cousins of the Masai) wondered how the Americans could possibly survive on the semiarid land without their own cattle, or without occasionally drinking goat's blood—as they themselves used to do. But they did not realize that a huge infrastructure was being built, with an elaborate camp of comfortable tents for a crew of three hundred, including air conditioning and a swimming pool.[13] Meanwhile, major projects for development aid to the area got by with considerably more modest budgets.

In each and every case, then, the *Castaway/Robinson/Survivor* experience was carefully stage-managed for the home front to project an image of European and American daring overseas, so dear to Western television audiences, while at the same time completely overlooking the real achievement of local people, who were *actually* surviving, year in and year out, with much more limited means—often less than a euro or a dollar per day—with no major improvement in sight, for the next few decades.

In the wake of the success of these programs, there was a boom in new reality formats, not only of the "stay at home" type, but also of the "daring travel abroad" type. Even in a relatively small market like the Netherlands, where *Robinson* was broadcast by Net 5, almost all other major channels followed with similar "heroic discoverer" formats. In one, *Mount Kilimanjaro*, participants had to climb the legendary African mountain—of course accompanied by a long row of black porters with all their amenities, just as in the old days.

Another variation to the theme was *Temptation Island*, introduced in 2001 on the Fox network owned by Rupert Murdoch, whose worldwide group had mostly thrived on a peculiar cocktail of high-minded patriotism and low-minded trash. A *New York Times* editorial comment noted that it was obviously not the pretended effort "to explore the dynamics of people in serious relationships," but rather one in which they "find their commitment tested on a tropical island by a harem of well-built, scantily clad members of the opposite sex, all certified by Fox to be free of sexually transmitted diseases."[14] The series catered to the exhibitionism of the participants and the voyeurism of the audience. The first three American seasons were filmed on the coast of Central America (in Belize, Costa Rica, and Honduras, respectively); later European producers vacillated between the Caribbean and Southeast Asia.

In the framework of this book, the question is, of course, why it necessarily had to be a "tropical" island. The answer is that in the mind of northerners, travel to the south is associated with libidinous release, not only because holidays in general are often taken there, but also because warmth seems to imply skimpy clothing, sunbathing, and swimming, alternated with exotic food and heavy drinking, in a general atmosphere of sensuousness. It also implies low wages and therefore great service by local personnel in luxurious hotels. It is closely associated with casual sex as well, both between tourists themselves and with "willing" locals to whom "surplus libido" is ascribed. We will return to this last theme in the chapter on romantic and erotic movies.

5

The Prolific and the Idle: Westerns and Southerns

What is the next step in the confrontation between Western heroes and the great non-Western unknown? How does our popular culture depict the adventures of the pioneers and settlers in their takeover of new continents? How is the reaction of the natives to the loss of their lands and resources portrayed? By what devices did Hollywood put things on their heads, turning the invaders into the invaded, and the other way around? How are we made to identify and sympathize more with the former rather than the latter, even if both attract and fascinate us? Have the arch-characters become part of our worldview, and, if so, in what way?

Tomorrow's children and young adults will be mostly socialized through computer and video games designed to stir emotion and close identification—but also hostility. "Shooter" games demand split-second reactions; the need for immediate action overwhelms reflection. Most are built around an "us" versus "them" theme in which "we" are legitimate and mandated to use overwhelming force and violence, whereas "they" are illegitimate and must be eliminated at all cost. "We" may not always be white anymore, but "we" are lighter and brighter than the others. "They" range from unscrupulous drugs dealers with vaguely Latino or Asian traits to dangerous terrorists with vaguely Arab traits. Fortunately, they usually lose out in the end. We will discuss this theme further in chapter 8.

Yesterday's children and young adults, by contrast, were still mostly socialized through films and "stand-alone" toys. When I was a kid, these were mostly explorer and Western films and their paraphernalia. This was the immediate postwar period, when the European colonial empires began to crumble and

American pop culture was eagerly adopted on the old continent. I remember playing "explorer" with a plastic white adventurer doll leading an expedition of plastic brownish porter dolls into the dark forest under the couch in the living room, or joining other boys outside to play "cowboys and Indians."

In "cowboys and Indians," the former had hats and guns, while the latter had feathers and paint. Cowboys and Indians were icons in a literal sense: the headgear produced an easily recognizable profile against any background, making it extremely easy to separate friend from foe during the fight. This was one of my earliest experiences of being enlisted to take part in ethnic confrontation. Of course, it seemed completely natural and logical, and we thought nothing of it.

The most famous analyst of hidden consumer motives at the time, Ernst Dichter, was asked to study the appeal of the Western. In his 1969 book *The Strategy of Desire*, he explained that they represented "an interesting aspect of ritualization of one phase of American life and history. They are basically morality plays, where everything is clearly structured into good and bad people." But he was still surprised to see that his French nephew, who hardly spoke any English, was glued to the television set and spent a large part of his two-month holiday watching Westerns on the small screen. He concluded that they had a universal aspect as well: "In the morality play, pure virtue is extolled and some of this virtue rubs off on an audience waiting to be reminded that these are the only worthwhile and eternal moral values. The response to a morality play is something close to a religious experience" (pp. 200–203).

French critic Bernard Fort noted, in turn, that "the Western is a modern version of the chivalric epic. Its hero, the dashing cowboy of the twentieth century, is the exact copy of the brave wandering knight of the thirteenth century. In this way, the presence of the sacred is what would explain the pleasure it gives us and the fascination it exerts on us" *(Encyclopédie Alpha du Cinéma, vol. 6, p. 35)*. The pleasure derives from feelings of moral and cultural superiority over others, in reality. The chivalric epic with its horses and swords flourished in the wake of the Christian Crusades against the Islamic infidels (and European travelers in fact imported the literary genre from Arab lands). Watching or playing cowboys and Indians, too, stirs such feelings, even if both children and adults have of course tried to twist or change this message numerous times.

Both genres are profoundly Manichaean, as was originally underlined by having the good guys wear white outfits and ride white horses, and the bad guys black ones. Richard Slotkin explains: "The premise of 'savage war' is that ineluctable political and social differences—rooted in some combination of 'blood' and culture—make coexistence between primitive natives and civilized Europeans impossible on any basis other than subjugation. Native resistance to European settlement therefore takes the form of a fight for survival; and because of the 'savage' and bloodthirsty propensity of the natives, such struggles inevitably become 'wars of extermination' in which one side or the other attempts to destroy its enemy root and branch" (1998, p. 13).

The key ideological operation of these stories is a travesty and projection, ultimately resulting in role reversal. The original inhabitants of the country or region in question are transformed into aggressive intruders, whereas the real intruders are transformed into peaceful inhabitants. Every characteristic detail of the genre derives from this twisted premise. In the Western such details are the visual emphasis on impressive nature and its virginity, the lack of scenes in which preexisting domestic life of the Indians is shown, and their replacement with scenes in which peaceful families of the women and children of the encroaching settlers are emphatically shown—followed by the focus on the sneaky and cruel attacks of the Indians and on the ultimate rescue by the white cavalry—depicted as the only "legitimate" force.

A number of other obvious travesties derive from this, although they too have become so ingrained that we fail to recognize them. The word "Indians" actively makes them exotic and originally defined them as strange Asians. The word "Americans," by contrast, has primarily come to denote the immigrants, not the natives. It has also come to denote the citizens of only one nation, on a double continent of that name with dozens upon dozens of other nations. The United States was founded and dominated by settlers or colonists, who replaced most of the original inhabitants, but because the settlers later declared independence, they also saw and presented themselves as "anticolonial." As one commentator put it: "In essence, the viewer is forced behind the barrel of a repeating rifle, and it is from that position that he receives a picture history" (Shohat & Stam 1994, p. 120 n53).

At the same time the true sources of the nation's wealth and power are systematically obscured in such accounts. The "American Dream" and the "manifest destiny" of European settlers was originally also driven by the quest for an El Dorado or a Bonanza, from gold mines to oil wells and other mineral resources. As the Indians could not show written land titles, these resources were considered up for grabs. The same held for forests and wildlife, and for the agricultural land in the Great Plains of the Midwest, once it was cleared of buffalo herds and native hunters. Of course that resulted in a very quick accumulation of wealth and an accelerated rise of investments and productivity throughout the nineteenth century, catapulting the United States into the position of prime industrial and world power.

But in the Western this is completely painted over, emphasizing only one aspect of the whole exercise in a mythical tale of daring and enterprise, of hard work and great inventiveness of the settlers themselves. The Hollywood version of history is so effective that generations overseas were easily seduced into embracing it as well. Anticolonial writers reported their astonishment when they realized that colonial subjects of the mid-twentieth century mostly identified intuitively with the cowboys rather than the Indians. As Daniel Boorstin noted in his influential study *The Image*, "The making of illusions which flood our experience has become the business of America" (1980, p. 5). It has also become its major export product.

The Western was one of the earliest of such commodities. It reproduced the myth that the Anglo-Saxon colonists and settlers made America prolific, whereas the Indians and Hispanics had left it mostly idle.

THE WESTERN GENRE

Since the Western used to be so much at the heart of Hollywood adventure movies, let us delve further into its exact prehistory and history.

It has been said that when it declared its independence, the United States turned its back on the Old World in the east and turned its face to the New World in the West. After Great Britain had already given up much of its hold on the Americas, the French Revolution and the Napoleonic Wars forced France and Spain to follow suit, enabling weaker independent nations to spring up in Latin America. But the Monroe Doctrine quickly claimed primacy for the Anglo-Saxon north, and a long succession of territorial wars ensued: the Mexican Wars, the Civil War, the Indian Wars, the Spanish-American War, and the annexation of other overseas territories such as Hawaii. Sometimes they resulted in unequal "treaties" and in the nominal "buying" of new land, often followed by the withering away of the former inhabitants' rights or even their "legal" expulsion.[1] This continuing expansion further propelled the United States to a position as a prime world power in its own right.

In 1892, on the occasion of the four-hundredth anniversary of Columbus's landing in America, the United States celebrated its achievements with a World's Fair held in Chicago, the industrial boomtown of the Midwest. An "ethnic pavilion" displayed live Indians and other exotic species. Among the many conferences the city hosted (the very next year) was a meeting of the American Historical Association, where Frederick Jackson Turner pronounced an extremely influential speech, *The Significance of Frontier in American History*. The speech entailed a forceful reinterpretation of U.S. history as a linear trajectory by linking its geographic expansion with social progress and a pioneer mentality, a movement that had gradually opened up the Great Plains, penetrated the Rocky Mountains, and finally attained the West Coast—with just parts of the Pacific to be conquered and Asia on the other side. Over many millennia, some said, civilization had thus come full circle around the globe.

In an article devoted to Turner's speech, Vernon Mattson noted that subsequently "Turner became the high priest of American nationalism because of his talent for investing the West with a soaring idealism that gave the American Dream its vision, dynamism, and mission." His colleague Ronald Carpenter had already noted that Turner became the nation's most famous historian because his eloquent mastery of a rhetorical style empowered him to make a "profound . . . impact upon our national psychology" and also because of his use of the frontiersman as the "cornerstone of mass persuasion" about American greatness. Mattson added that "interest in the West as myth intensified after Turner announced that the frontier was closed" (Mattson 1988).

Turner's thesis gave a wholly new dimension to American popular culture about the frontier and the West, both in literature and in the visual arts, as it linked the scattered anecdotes and characters from its emerging folklore with a unifying ethos, a claimed set of moral values. One early literary example is provided by the work of James Fenimore Cooper, the first major novelist of the American nation, also considered the inventor of the frontier and "pre-Western" genre. He wrote the famous series *The Leatherstocking Tales*; the most famous of the five books is *The Last of the Mohicans*.

But it was only toward the end of the nineteenth century that a really popular mass literature emerged. The year after Turner's speech was the first during which more American than foreign novels were published (Leutrat 1987, p. 8). Pocket books of a dime apiece were aimed at wider audiences, but were also more simplistic and stereotypical. One of the early pulp fiction writers was Zane Grey, whose turn-of-the-century *The Spirit of the Border* was followed by no fewer than 53 other popular novels, selling a total of 15 million copies. Such books were to inspire most of the early movie Westerns soon thereafter.

Meanwhile, painters had already begun to develop the stylized iconography of the Western genre, whereas photographers continued to capture documentary images. Managing large stocks of cattle in wide-open spaces demanded a range of special skills from "cowboys": taming wild horses, throwing a lasso, riding bulls, wrestling them to the ground. Demonstrations and competitions were set up on holidays and at fairs. Gradually, they developed into a Western corrida-like rodeo ritual of masculinity and virility, attracting large crowds. They were further embellished by the display of wild animals and sharpshooting. Ultimately, they developed into major fairground and circus acts and were "exported" back to the urban areas of the Midwest and the East Coast.

The inventor or major propagandist of this "Wild West" genre was William Frederick Cody. He had begun his career as a messenger and later become an accomplished horseman and hunter. He said, "I stood between savagery and civilization most all my early days" (Saunders 2001, p. 7). On one occasion he won an eight-hour shooting match of buffalo; on another occasion he claimed to have shot a record 4,280 buffalo in 240 days, which he sold to the railroads to feed their construction crews, hence his proud nickname, Buffalo Bill. (Altogether, an estimated 25 million buffalo were killed in just a few decades, without replacement). Cody also worked as a scout for the U.S. Army, participated in sixteen Indian fights, shot the Cheyenne warrior Yellow Hair, and proudly dispatched the scalp in an envelope to his own sister. These widely publicized exploits transformed him into a true popular folk hero.

Cody became an actor, engaged other well-known Wild West characters, staged familiar scenes with them, and finally organized a permanent show with cowboys and Indians and the whole repertory of a Pony Express ride, a buffalo hunt, fancy shooting, and so on. It came to camp in Chicago, in the vicinity of the aforementioned World Fair, where Turner held his famous frontier speech. Janet Walker noted: "With its 600 men, 500 horses, 11-acre mobile showground, and 25,000 yards of tent canvas, Buffalo Bill's Wild West company needed 52 train cars to travel. And travel they did, on the European tour of 1895, for example, to 131 sites in 190 days, covering 9,000 miles. The German Army was ordered to study the operation 'as a logistical feat'" (2001, p. 17).

Buffalo Bill even enlisted Indian leaders like the famous Sioux chief Sitting Bull, who had defeated General Custer but had later been defeated by his successors. Buffalo Bill later spoiled an assignment to mediate with Sitting Bull when U.S. troops were dispatched to put an end to a Sioux revival of the "ghost dance" on their reservation, as it was associated with mobilization for war. Sitting Bull was subsequently killed during the police arrest, which further worsened the situation. A few days after Christmas, the Seventh Cavalry fired on a crowd at Wounded Knee, killing several hundred mostly unarmed men, women, and children. Buffalo Bill then offered to take some of the prisoners, and the reenactment of the "battle" subsequently became part of his show (Kilpatrick 1999, pp. 12–15, 120; Simmon 2003, pp. xi–xii; Walker 2001, pp. 11ff.). Commemorations of the event led to renewed outbreaks of violence, as long as eighty-three years later (Biagi & Kern-Foxworth 1997).

A number of years earlier, Buffalo Bill engaged stage director Steele Mac-Kaye to help develop *The Drama of Civilization*, consisting of a series of consecutive live tableaux: first the primitive forest with Indians fighting, then the migrant caravan with a prairie fire, a cowboy ranch attacked by Indians, a miners' camp with a stagecoach holdup, and so forth. (The tableaux format may well have helped inspire the later "worlds" format in the Disney theme parks.) During the World's Fair, MacKaye proposed that the Chamber of Commerce build a special "Spectatorium" for such shows, in a step toward the modern movie theatre.

The cinema was about to be born. The Chicago World Exposition itself had displayed a tachyscope, a zoopraxiscope (with the famous pictures of movement by Edward Muybridge), and a single Kinetoscope on the second floor of the Electricity Building (Leutrat 1987, pp. 9–10). The latter was rather a simple viewer for a one-person audience, with film loops only a few seconds long. The very first items produced for the Edison Company included several frontier subjects, including *The Hopi Snake Dance* (1893) and *The Sioux Ghost Dance* (1894). Another one was *The Life of Buffalo Bill* (1898). Whereas European cinema was from its very beginning "naturally" drawn to colonial adventure, American cinema was from its very beginning drawn to colonists' adventures. From the very start, imagining the unknown—the exotic—was the major attraction of the movies.

The first projected and edited silent ten-minute film shorts by Edwin Porter also favored Wild West subjects, such as *The Great Train Robbery* (based on a real holdup committed by Butch Cassidy and his bunch years before) and *The Life of an American Cowboy*, both released in 1903. One hundred years later, the centenary was commemorated with a host of special editions, film festivals, conferences, and exhibitions around the world. In subsequent years, Siegmund Lubin had made *The Great Bank Robbery* (1904), David Wark Griffith made *The Redman and the Child* (1908), *Crossing the American Prairies*, and *In Old California* (both 1911), and Cecil B. DeMille made *The Squaw Man* (1913). Scott Simmon reports that by the beginning of that decade, the Western had come to account for at least one-fifth of all U.S. releases (2003, p. 3); Ella Shohat and Robert Stam report that between 1926 and 1967, the Western accounted for one-quarter of Hollywood's costume film output (1994, p. 114).

Famous cowboy actors were Tom Mix, Roy Rogers, Gary Cooper, Jimmy Stewart, Henry Fonda, and John Wayne; famous Western directors were John Ford, Howard Hawks, Anthony Mann, and Sam Peckinpah. Paul Newman, Clint Eastwood, and others doubled as both. One of the most memorable Westerns of the interwar period was *Stagecoach*, directed by John Ford and derived from the earlier story *Boule de suif* by French novelist Guy de Maupassant. John Saunders quotes various specialized scholars saying that just before World War II the low-budget Western B-film industry turned out eight films a year and kept thirty stars in regular employment, that even as late as 1958 some fifty-four new feature-length Westerns were released, and that a full study of the genre required viewing some eight thousand films (2001, pp. 3–4).

In her book *Westerns*, Janet Walker notes that these Westerns can be taken as an object of historical study on various different levels: from interpretations blatantly linked to the preoccupations of the creators, to attempts at a faithful rendering of an earlier age. "Westerns incorporate, elide, embellish, mythologize, allegorize, erase, duplicate, and rethink past events that are themselves— as history—fragmented, fuzzy, and striated with fantasy constructions" (2001, p. 13). In *The Western Genre*, Saunders in turn quotes scholars who claimed that there are only seven basic Western plots: "The Cavalry and Indians story, the Union Pacific or Pony Express story, the Homesteaders or Squatters theme, the Cattle empire story, the Lawman story, the Revenge story, and the Outlaw story" (2001, pp. 5–6). "Genre memory" and "intertextuality" play a big role, as one of the main pleasures of such familiar genres resides in the viewer recognizing and anticipating particular characters and plot lines and savoring minor allusions or variations.

At the heart of the storyline, there is always an interaction between the same four or five protagonists. On the surface, there is the confrontation between the outlaw (Jesse James, Billy the Kid, Butch Cassidy, the Daltons) and the law, as represented by the sheriff and his posse. Yet Philippe Jacquin and Daniel Royot report that during the second half of the nineteenth century, there were only 219 vigilante movements in the West, killing only 527 suspected criminals (1993, p. 53).

In the space between law and outlaw operate two archetypical categories of Western heroes. On the one hand are the wildlife trappers, belonging to the earliest stages and farthest regions of the Wild West, often identified by a fur hat. And on the other hand are the cowboys, belonging to the later stages and closer regions of the Wild West, identified by the trademark wide-rimmed hat. Richard Slotkin notes that these latter two categories are the mediators between wilderness and civilization, who sometimes find themselves on one side of the fence, sometimes on the other (1998, p. 14). John Saunders adds that they are paradoxical in the sense that they are often "caught up in the defense of the community while sharing some of the characteristics that threaten it" (2001, p. 10). Minor additional roles are those of the gold digger, the gambler, and so on. The most ambiguous character is the cynical gun-for-hire, who believes in (almost) nothing and became increasingly prominent during the latter decades of the genre.

The story always alternates between male bonding and conflict. The heroes are tough, courageous, and adventurous, but fate forces a close togetherness.

In the absence of women, their male solidarity often carries somewhat homo-erotic undertones, but the emphasis is on machismo. The confrontation with other males is violent, and this violence is aestheticized in both the staging and the filming. Westerns seem like a protracted commercial for the Colt revolver and the Winchester rifle: a spot lasting not thirty seconds but a full one-hundred years or more. Slotkin has written a brilliant trilogy on these themes resulting in a cultural history of the gunfighter nation, showing in great detail how the myth of the frontier affected political rhetoric throughout twentieth-century America: from Franklin Roosevelt and Kennedy to Reagan and the Bushes. Within this universe, women are usually just a distraction, as either sa-loon whores or housewives.

On a different level, the Western genre is on the one hand about wide-open and empty spaces with just the occasional ambush, and on the other hand about how the settler society slowly emerged. The circling of the wagons is just the first representation of embryonic communal life involving innocent women, children, and elders assaulted by the savages for no reason at all. The next phase is the idyllic homestead or ranch, threatened by the approach of strangers. Then there is the village or small town, at first with one main street, a saloon, and a bank, but later also with a telegraph office and a station along the railroad. Incoming visitors and valuables trigger new storylines. Cowboys and Indians on horseback chase the speeding trains.

Jacques Mauduy and Gérard Henriet's *Géographies du western* (1989) is a fascinating study on recurring patterns in the archetypical organization of ge-ographic space in Western movies. One overwhelming theme is the visual rhetoric of breathtaking images of unspoiled nature: from mountains and forests to valleys and prairies. These landscapes always seem to offer them-selves for exploration and cultivation, as there is hardly any possible owner in sight. The landscape theme gradually became more prominent as the film crews left the studio to film outdoors in the open air. A large part of John Ford's many Westerns was even filmed in the same dramatic landscape: Mon-ument Valley.

In the accounts of the settlers, their trek was often presented in religious terms as that of God's own chosen people through the biblical desert to the "promised land" of milk and honey, where they were to found a new nation in His name. (This will be discussed in more depth in chapter 9.) They chose to forget that surveyors and geometers immediately followed in their footsteps, to name and measure this "no man's land" and gradually take control and pos-session of it. Then followed the real estate agents, who further divided up the lots. If individual Indians could not show a preexisting land title on legal writ-ten paper, they could claim no rights to it and were effectively expropriated.

From the mid-1950s onward, simple Westerns tended to be overshadowed by wide-screen spectaculars in the movie theatres, but the formula still proved ideally suited for daily or weekly serials on early television: first in black and white, then in color. The genre was hardly controversial, stirring consensual and patriotic feelings, and was thus ideally suited for commercial sponsoring. One subgenre was that of children's Westerns—for example Disney's series around the fur trapper Davy Crockett, which caused a worldwide hat craze, and another around the cavalry dog Rin Tin Tin. Still another subgenre became that of "adult" Westerns—for example, *Cheyenne* and *Gunsmoke*, the latter with no fewer than 633 installments.

William Boddy reports that in the 1957–1958 season there were fifteen new television Western series, in the next season there were twenty-four, and the next season twenty-eight (in Creeber 2001, pp. 14–17). During that last season, eight of the ten top-rated shows were Westerns, and no fewer than thirty Westerns were broadcast in prime time; over these three consecutive seasons nearly one-third of network prime time consisted of Westerns alone (Goldstein 1991, p. 160; Saunders 2001, p. 4). The boom did not stop there: *Bonanza* became a popular "family" Western, with 430 installments of fifty minutes each, followed by *Rawhide* with 217 and *The High Chaparral* with 98. Note that many of these series reached Europe and other continents only many years later and that Westerns dominated the early age of television there as well.

But from the 1960s on, with the original countryside withdrawing and suburbia advancing in the United States, the popularity of the genre began to wane, even though the emergence of the comic strip–like Italian spaghetti Western (Frayling 1998) gave it a temporary new impulse. The rising controversy over excessive violence in the media and the war in Southeast Asia gave the "shoot 'em ups" a bad name. Slotkin notes that in the meantime, Western-speak had become increasingly popular in military circles and that at first American troops described Vietnam as "Indian country" and search-and-destroy missions as a game of "cowboys and Indians" (1998, pp. 3, 627).

But that then seemed to backfire as the United States began to lose the war: Slotkin also reports that from 1969 to 1972, American producers released an average of twenty-four feature Westerns per year, but that in 1973 only thirteen were released and in 1974 only seven. Saigon fell in 1975. After a brief resurgence, the number further dropped to an average of four per year from 1977 to 1982, and two years later, market share of the Western had fallen to zero (Neale 2002, p. 29). Later there was a brief revival, but no Western became a real blockbuster any more. Saunders called Clint Eastwood's *Unforgiven*, released in 1992 and the recipient of four Oscars, "the last truly memorable Western" (2001, p. 124).

The archetypical characters, themes, and storylines of the Western had meanwhile deserted to other genres: Rambo was basically a white Indian, and Indiana Jones an American cowboy who got lost in a European-style colonial adventure. *Star Trek* always called space "the final frontier," and *Star Wars* was clearly made as a galactic Western. Yet the Western genre proper had always proved extraordinarily resilient and had often risen out of its ashes again like a Hollywood phoenix. Simmon notes that its first "premature obituaries" had been published as early as seventy years before (p. xv), but Saunders notes some of its "continuing appeal" today (p. 3).

Western Indians and the Revisionist Wave

During the 1980s there were few or no Western blockbusters; the genre seemed extinct as a major box office draw. But during the first half of the 1990s there was the surprising success of *Dances with Wolves*, immediately followed by other so-called revisionist pro-Indian (or even pro-black) Westerns. They tried to overcome—or even reverse—the stereotypes that seemed built into the genre. But this was easier said than done, and in many different ways they remained mired in some of the same old mythical themes.

Dances with Wolves (1990) seemed "the kind of reckless gamble that Hollywood is no longer supposed to make" (Hunter 1991, p. 77). Although actor Kevin Costner was quite bankable in the main role, the film was also his debut as a director. The original novel was by Michael Blake, who also wrote the script. The movie was more than three hours long, and the subsequent extended television version even slightly under four. It cost "only" $18 million to make, but soon shot into the top ten of the all-time charts and ultimately brought in well over $425 million. It had been almost a quarter century since a film had received more Oscar nominations; it received seven. It was a true triumph.

Although Indians had been major characters in about one-fifth of Westerns and minor characters in many more (Walker 2001, p. 9), it was exceptional that more than one would be shown as an individual, with proper character and motivation. In many dime-novel B-film and television series, Indians were simply the sidekicks of white trappers or cowboys. Few Indian roles were played by Indian actors, and few actors playing Indian roles made a name for themselves, as actors playing cowboy roles did. One of the earliest noteworthy non-Indians in "redface" was Anthony Quinn. Of Mexican lineage, he became one of those all-around actors for "ethnic" roles. He seemed the perfect choice for an Indian in *The Plainsman*, and also later became Cecil B. DeMille's son-in-law. Raquel Welch (also of Mexican heritage) on occasion played squaws and other ethnic roles.

Indians could hardly convey any articulate motives, as they were mostly limited to pidgin speech or Tonto-talk at first, if not to a mere oft-repeated "Ugh!" Relatively little was shown of their domestic life or tribal culture in peacetime, even though Ella Shohat and Robert Stam quote various scholarly sources saying they invented some of the democratic ways subsequently borrowed by the United States (1994, pp. 86–87). Nor is there any hint in the movies that American Indians had a history of thousands of years (without either horses or guns) or that there were some two thousand different Indian cultures. Those of the fifty years of "the frontier" in the United States belonged to at least seven very different groups with radically different lifestyles (Kilpatrick 1999, p. 1; Mauduy & Henriet 1989, p. 209). All this teeming diversity was imploded into one muddled image of the mere "other," often stuck with arbitrarily invented appearances and mores.

Native Americans had also been depicted as a uniform threat, since whites had consistently projected their own encroachment and aggression upon them—particularly in popular culture. More than 250,000 migrants trekked over the Oregon and California trails of the far West during the early days of pioneer expansion between 1840 and 1860, yet only four hundred were killed in skirmishes with (not necessarily by) Indians (Maxwell 1995). An official 1869 report by the Board of Indian Commissioners appointed by the president observed, by contrast: "There is a large class of professedly reputable men who use every means in their power to bring on Indian wars, for the sake of profit to be realized. . . . The testimony of some of the highest military officers of the United States is on record to the effect that, in our Indian wars, almost without exception, the first aggressions have been made by the white man" (Kilpatrick 1999, p. 10).

Apart from Tecumseh's abortive attempt, Slotkin notes that from the eighteenth century onward "no tribe or group of tribes pursued (or was capable of pursuing) a general 'policy' of exterminating or removing white settlements on a large-scale basis" (p. 12). Yet this is the image provided by the overwhelming majority of "cowboy and Indian" movies until well after World War II.

How did this state of affairs come about? John O'Connor notes: "In spite of a more or less subtle racial bias, Hollywood is presumably not filled with Indian-haters intent on using their power to put down the natives. . . . significant elements of the Indian image can be explained best through analyzing various technical and business-related production decisions that may never have been considered. . . . Film is a collaborative art; it requires the creative contributions of dozens of people" to coordinate "camera angles, composition, lighting, editing and a host of other factors. . . . For a mass audience, for example, the dramatic situation should be straightforward and unconfused. . . . In the studio tradition, 'moral ambiguities' were kept to a minimum" (Rollins & O'Connor 1998, pp. 30–33). But as the "real" Wild West faded and the Indians just withered away in their reservations, there was room for change.

Some of the very earliest shorts and silent films had been somewhat pro-Indian, in one way or another. But from the late 1940s on, both the anticolonial and the civil rights movements began gathering steam. An early trio of films somewhat sympathetic to the Indian cause were *Fort Apache* (1948) by John Ford, *Broken Arrow* (1949) by Delmer Daves, and *Bronco Apache* (1954) by Robert Aldrich.

From the mid-1960s on, the Vietnam War and the black civil rights and the Indian movements led to a further radicalization and to a renewed scrutiny of the settlers' literary and historical canons. A further trio of films sympathetic to the Indian cause were *Tell Them Willy Boy Is Here* (1968) by Abraham Polonsky, *A Man Called Horse* (1970) by Elliot Silverstein, and *Buffalo Bill and the Indians, or Sitting Bull's History Lesson* (1976) by Robert Altman. The latter was an enlightening reconstruction of what the relations between those two archetypical figures might have been (see its detailed analysis in part 2 of Janet Walker's overview). But Kevin Costner's *Dances with Wolves* went much further.

Case Study: The White Guy Dances with Wolves

Dances with Wolves is a sympathetic feel-good movie, although it is not particularly riveting. It received widely varying reviews from film and cultural studies scholars and American and Indian studies scholars. Allan Hunter's *Film and TV Handbook* (1991) calls it "an astonishingly accomplished début"; the Virgin *Guide*, by contrast, calls it a "plodding vanity project" and "not a great film by any standard." It was "hailed as a landmark" by some reviewers (Kilpatrick 1999) but put down as a kind of "Lawrence of South Dakota" by others. Ted Jojola said that "it was apolitical and subconsciously plied its appeal by professing a simple New Age homily about peace and Mother Earth" (Rollins & O'Connor 1998, p. 17).

Press releases proudly trumpeted the fact that the Sioux Lakota tribe had made Costner an honorary member because of the film but did not mention the reaction of the Pawnee tribe, which had been painted in a rather less sympathetic light by him. In her overview *Celluloid Indians*, Jacquelyn Kilpatrick pleads for some indulgence, however, "given that the film attempts to undo in a little over three hours stereotypes developed over hundreds of years." She says Costner made a serious attempt at getting things right: "Though not perfect, this film deserves a few points" (1999, pp. 127–29).

Interestingly enough, the film returned to some of the oldest and most central myths of the Wild West: that of the white man going pink or red and of the white girl abducted or adopted by the Indians after her entire white family had been slaughtered by them. These are myths not in the sense that none of this ever happened but in the sense that a few isolated incidents of this nature occupy a disproportionate space in Western literature and cinema, retaining the fascination and obsession of entire generations. Robert Baird published an interesting essay (1998) showing that the first theme was at the very heart of the American Dream: the utopian fantasy of the emergence of a "new man" and a "new world." Europeans left their troubled histories, their cultural identities, and often their original names behind when they migrated to America. They shed their skins, in the words of D. H. Lawrence, "to grow a new skin underneath" (Baird 1998, p. 154).

But Americans on the developed, urban, and industrializing East Coast in turn fantasized about the regenerating influence of a "return to nature" in the Wild West. Baird also notes (on pp. 156–57) that Thoreau's famous essay on utopian natural life in *Walden* "strikes me as a case study of the limits of how far a Harvard man can 'go Indian'" (and indeed that particular title ultimately refers to an old squaw). The whole literature on the frontier, from Fenimore Cooper's early nineteenth-century *Leatherstocking Tales* to the New Age *Dances with Wolves*, is shot through with the motive of the civilized white man "going native"—and becoming better at it than the natives themselves. Baird quotes studies saying that many contemporary Americans fantasize about a distant drop of Indian blood or native roots (Virginians in particular, after the release of Disney's *Pocahontas*), just as others fantasize about descending from noteworthy historical figures or victims as a way to "virtually" extract themselves from constraining social circumstances.

At the heart of Blake's novel and Costner's film is what we might call a "resplitting" operation. In the archetypical Western, the white cavalry are the good guys coming to the aid of the main character. An individual Indian may be a good guy when aspiring to become the white man's friend, but this necessarily involves betraying his tribe, since they are the bad guys. *Dances with Wolves* uses a similar cake but flips it over and cuts it differently. The cavalry are the bad guys, but one or two of its individual members are good guys as they aspire to become

Indian friends, even if this involves betraying their cavalry. But as a corrective, the Indians are also split this time: between the Lakota Sioux, who turn out to be noble and straightforward, and the Pawnees, who turn out to be cruel and sneaky. The Manichaeism—the polarization and extremes of black and white—remains; it has just been arranged somewhat differently.

The hero of the movie is Lieutenant John Dunbar of the Union army, played by Costner himself. During the Civil War, he is injured in the foot, and the surgeons decide to simply amputate it, as an operation would be too costly and time consuming. This makes him desperate, and when they retire for a coffee break, he escapes. He rides to the front, gallops toward the enemy with his arms spread wide like a true Christ-on-the-cross, determined to die—but he miraculously survives. Others take this as an act of bravery, feel encouraged, change the tide, and win the battle. He is then allowed to choose an assignment and says: "I've always wanted to see the frontier before it's gone" (a first example of anachronism—looking at the past through the eyes of the present—in the dialogue).

Dunbar is first sent to Fort Hayes, with a commander gone crazy (reminiscent of the one in Francis Ford Coppola's Vietnam film *Apocalypse Now* or Joseph Conrad's earlier Congo novel *Heart of Darkness*). He is then sent onward to Fort Sedgewick, a tiny outpost that has just been deserted. After cleaning out the mess, he bathes naked in a pond—and then sees a Lakota Sioux in full gear. The scene kind of re-baptizes him, as he will soon adopt the same gear and acquaint himself with the tribe. As they have seen him approach an animal, they call him "(He who) Dances with Wolves."

The Indians speak Sioux-Lakotan, with subtitles throughout the film. On the one hand this helps make them even more genuine, but on the other makes it harder to empathize with them. The film depicts relatively little on the daily life of the tribe from their own perspective but inserts a few recognizable details (e.g., child's play) to make it easier for present-day suburban viewers to identify with them. These details include the usual hilarious incidents with the surprising contraptions of civilization, such as a coffee grinder. Later, Dunbar even breaks the prime directive of the cavalry, by procuring them rifles and ammunition. This brings us closer to the eternal settler theme of the massacre.

Costner is more effective than his predecessors by insisting less on the gratuitous violence of the cavalry against Indians and more on that against furry animals. The cavalry are shown to arbitrarily kill his pet wolf, his dear horse, and entire herds of buffalo (just for their tongues and skins, not even for their meat). They also massacre Indians, and the bad Pawnees massacre them in turn. When Dunbar's love interest is shown, there is a flashback to the "original" massacre—when her family was eradicated by the Indians and only she survived. The good Lakotas, by contrast, kill only in a just bid to prevent Dunbar from being taken away as a deserter and a traitor. Robert Baird notes that this turns ninety years of Hollywood Westerns on its head, as "we have here the same cheer for the good guys, the skilful and precise application of violence to right the world, the promise of 'regeneration through violence,' which Richard Slotkin has so eloquently elaborated" (Baird 1998, p. 160).

It is true that the movie makes us sympathize with the Indians—at least with the long-haired Lakota Sioux, if not with the partly shaven and near-skinhead Pawnees. Yet the two main Indian protagonists are not "real" Indians, but whites dressed as Indians: Dunbar's love interest is the eternal white orphan, adopted when still a child. So an Indian in the film says about their relationship: "It makes sense. They are both white." One commentator observes: "This could be seen as a characteristic evasion of the racial issue" (Saunders 2001, p. 111). A second notes that it "accomplishes, I think for the first time in our American imagination, the transmigration of the white family unit [pair] into the mythical hunting ground of The Indian" (Baird 1998, p. 163). And another comments: "The difference is that she does not die at the film's end. Instead, they ride off together" (Kilpatrick 1999, p. 128). In spite of all its daring multicultural intentions, then, the story remains caught in some of the oldest stereotypical themes.

At the same time, the film contains several further examples of anachronism. Dunbar exclaims that he has become a "celebrity." He and his love kiss and hug in quite contemporary ways; they are formally married with a speech, a white dress, and a discussion over whether to have a child right away, and so forth. There is also an emphasis on waste, pollution, and the environment that seems rather modern. Meanwhile, the film makes no reference to the current condition of Native Americans, as the epilogue on the title scroll at the end on the ultimate subjugation of the Lakota Sioux safely contains the problem to the "comfort zone" of the nineteenth century.

The worthwhile 1992 thriller *Thunderheart*, by British director Michael Apted, did, however, address the current situation. It was situated on a 1970s North Dakota reservation, where an activist movement confronted illegal test drillings for possible uranium by outsiders, aided and abetted by some government agencies. Val Kilmer played a

highly believable role as a "Washington Redskin"—that is to say, a fed-
eral agent with some Indian blood, guided by visions of his forefathers.
Other movies, however, have also focused on rewriting the past.

The unexpected success of *Dances with Wolves* (paired with the
quincentennial of Columbus's landing) facilitated the realization and
completion of other films with more or less sympathetic Indians, like
the classic *The Last of the Mohicans*—although Walker and Kilpatrick
claim that the original plot was twisted to accommodate white viewers.
Another early 1990s Indian movie was Walter Hill's new version of
Geronimo: An American Legend (1994), which made him less of a cruel
savage and more of a noteworthy leader. The very next year, Disney
came out with the blockbuster *Pocahontas* (1995), discussed in chapter
2, which meant to be "Indian friendly" but twisted the historical facts,
as we have already seen. So in spite of all the good intentions, such revisionist pro-Indian movies remained caught in some of the same old
preferred Western myths, like an unsuspecting insect caught in a spi-
der's web.

THE SOUTHERN

There are other genres closely related to the Western—for instance, that of the
confrontation of the cowboys and the cavalry with the Spaniards and Mexicans
rather than with the Indians. Their underlying logic is partly the same, partly
different. Feelings of Anglo-American superiority remain, but the "other"
groups consist of southerners of European, or at least mixed, stock. These stories are less overtly racist and they have survived better in recent years.

The year 1998 even saw the revival of a major pop-cult icon with the release
of the midsummer blockbuster *The Mask of Zorro*, directed by Martin Campbell and produced by Steven Spielberg, which made almost $250 million.
Spanish actor Antonio Banderas played the young Alejandro, who wanted to
avenge his murdered brother, the Californian social bandit Joaquin Murieta.
Welsh actor Anthony Hopkins played the elderly Don Diego de la Vega, a.k.a.
Zorro, who prepares Alejandro to take over his mantle, and Welsh actress
Catherine Zeta-Jones played Zorro's murdered wife, Esperanza, as well as his
abducted daughter, Elena. A first sequel was *The Legend of Zorro*, released in
2005.

The project was preceded by the release of an animated television series
and followed by a whole new range of novels, comics, toys, gadgets, and other
merchandise, as copyright holder John Gertz had urgently "devoted his time
to building the worldwide Zorro licence," according to his wife, Sandra Curtis

(1998, p. 197). Curtis—herself author of seven new Zorro stories—published *Zorro Unmasked: The Official History*, which meant to provide a complete overview of the phenomenon. She also made much of the paradigmatic "dual identity" Zorro shared with the slightly older Scarlet Pimpernel (as well as the later Superman character, among many others).

Both the new film and the overview book, however, clung to two major misconceptions, which were once again widely and uncritically copied in press reviews around the world. One major misconception was that the Zorro character had been "invented" by American author Johnston McCulley, whereas it was in fact based on a much older Mexican legend involving such a double identity. The other major misconception was that it had been in-spired by the resistance of poor local peasants against the succession of Span-ish, Mexican, and Californian landowners' rule, implying that they were better off with the adhesion to the United States, whereas the original story had in-stead been inspired by the resistance of Mexicans against Spanish rule—and against all other kinds of foreign domination.

Not only did the gringos thus "steal" a major Mexican story and a major Mexican subject, but over almost a full century their Zorro industry also used it to recycle many Anglo-Saxon stereotypes of Hispanic people. Some of these were positive, it should be acknowledged: the chivalrous hidalgo, the roman-tic poet, the Latin lover. But many were negative: the corrupt public servants, the brute military, the stupid ordinary men. It is therefore important to rec-ognize that the Zorro character is not just another free fantasy, because just underneath the surface there are accumulated layers of a more ethnocentric nature. They basically show two major cultural fault lines.

The stories are built around the opposition between superstition and ra-tionality, between the Catholic and Protestant faiths, between feudal and cap-italist society, and between arbitrary absolutism and human rights. But by subtly changing the context, McCulley decisively shifted the ideological impli-cations of Zorro's quest, detaching him from the Mexican and tying him to the American Revolution. Of course this suited the American popular culture industry and Hollywood, as it primarily catered to white Anglo-Saxon Protes-tant tastes at the time, and not to those of the Hispanic minority, even if Lati-nos subsequently embraced the twisted Zorro story as their own.[2]

So let us go back to the first phase: that of the colonization of Mexico by Spain and its search for treasures and gold mines located in the mythical country of El Dorado more to the south. According to some studies, the in-digenous population dwindled from some 25 million to a mere 2 million in-habitants after the European conquest. By the mid-seventeenth century, this figure had returned to 3.5 million, along with two hundred thousand mestizos, or "half-bloods," and blacks, but they were exploited by only two hundred thousand people of Spanish stock (first considered *Peninsulares*, then Criollos). A rebellion began to brew, as only a few in the upper aristocracy and the higher clergy recognized the necessity of reform.

One relative insider was accused around the mid-seventeenth century of planning a palace revolution and the proclamation of a kind of bill of rights, in order to first have himself elected viceroy by the local population and then declare independence thereafter. His name was Guillèn Lombardo, but this was the Spanish translation of his Irish name, William Lamport. He came from the ranks of the lower aristocracy in Ireland, had a good education, and wrote and spoke several ancient and modern languages. But as he hated the English, he turned into a pirate and a mercenary. After some time he ended up in Spain, enlisted in its army, and fought in various battles against the Protestant countries of the north. He also fostered relations at the court before traveling onward to try his luck in "New Spain," or Mexico. But he soon began to lead a double life there: circulating in elite circles during the day, and getting together with radical schemers at night.

When he was about to strike, he was caught, but escaped again. He was then betrayed, incarcerated, and tried by the Inquisition. He was accused of heresy, sorcery, and astrology—as the judges tried to conceal the true grievances from their superiors. In the end, he was burned at the stake. Court documents regarding his trial survive in several archives and libraries in North America and western Europe; it turns out he was a real revolutionary, long before the American and French revolutions, even though he was long thought to only have been a dreamer. His story soon turned into an enduring popular Mexican legend—the legend of the refined aristocrat who came to the aid of the oppressed poor—that resurfaced in many subsequent popular rebellions.

In 1998, when both Spielberg's film and Curtis's book came out, the Italian scholar Fabio Troncarelli published the detailed study *La spada e la croce*, later translated into French and other languages. It proved beyond doubt that Guillèn Lombardo had indeed been the original model for Zorro and his alter ego Don Diego de la Vega, as the epilogue of the book listed no less than a dozen precise features the two characters shared: leading a double life, as a poet and a ladies man as well as good fighter and an escape artist; leading a plot of noble men abetted by Franciscan friars; posting manifestos taking the defense of the indigenous people against the local tyrants and corrupt judges; and so forth. We will later see there are further precise reasons to consider Don Guillèn the historic model for Zorro.

Over the next century, Spain further extended its control from Mexico City to the northern territories, and even to faraway California. Spain set up a string of settlements with familiar names like San Antonio, Santa Barbara, Santa Cruz, San Diego, San Francisco, San José, and (Reina de) Los Angeles, connected through El Camino Real, the royal "highway" (in reality more of a dusty track). These included four presidios, or fortified settlements; a string of pueblos, or civic communities; and twenty-one Franciscan missions employing a workforce of baptized Indians. Later land grants created large ranchos in private hands. Curtis quotes historical studies noting that "no white man had to concern himself greatly with work" and that "the Indians of California were hardly less enslaved than were the blacks of the South" (1998, pp. 63–65).

It was in this general context that McCulley later placed his stories: Zorro would confront the military, the governors, and the rich to help the friars, the natives, and the poor. Sometimes it was suggested that he confronted Spanish rule, sometimes that he confronted Mexican rule, and later versions suggested that he confronted the California landowners. Imperceptibly, this shifted the setting by almost half a century, completely changing the sociopolitical context and the regime he was fighting and therefore the implications of his actions.

All these regimes were made interchangeable, from the perspective of the local peasants, so that they would be better off seceding and adhering to the United States—as some finally did by the mid-nineteenth century when the sudden discovery of a real El Dorado and subsequent gold rush made the local white population in California swell from 15,000 to 250,000 and made the Hispanics further lose control to the Anglo-Saxons. Within ten years, the number of Indians also dwindled from an estimated 150,000 to 30,000 (Jacquin & Royot 1993, p. 50). The original population lost access to agricultural land, and Mexican mineworkers were evicted (and replaced by Asians), whereas bandidos such as Joaquin Murieta came to embody the peculiar type of social rebellion extensively analyzed by British historian Eric Hobsbawm (1959, 1969; see also Lie & D'Haen 2002).

Now let us look at the second stage in the prehistory of the Zorro legend. After the American and French revolutions, the Napoleonic invasion had made the Spanish regime collapse, leading to popular insurrections, to palace revolutions and military coups in the Latin American colonies, and to the declaration of Mexican independence in 1821. Over the next hundred years, the regime vacillated between conservative/clerical on the one hand and reformist/secular on the other. Peasant revolts were meanwhile led by such famous rebels as Emiliano Zapata and Pancho Villa.

European powers intervened to try and restore a monarchy, but the United States had declared the Monroe Doctrine immediately after Mexican independence, whereby it opposed the interference of all other than themselves. They first encouraged immigration into, and then secession of, the neglected

Mexican border states in the north (as well as in the south), and then the adhesion of the former to the United States, thereby effectively reducing its giant southern neighbor to half its size, further doubling its own size, and thus decisively changing the existing balance of power (for more details, see Jacquin & Royot 1993, pp. 30–69). Not only California, but also Arizona, Nevada, New Mexico, Texas, and Utah ultimately changed hands. This feat was lionized in American popular culture through the Alamo story.[3]

One of the Mexican fighters for social justice and against foreign interference was Vicente Riva Palacio, grandson of one of the founding fathers of the country and himself a famous general, governor, and ambassador.[4] He had been fascinated by the aforementioned story about the earliest stirrings of an independence movement since he was a boy and came across some of the relevant court papers in later life. In 1872 he published the historical novel *Memorias de un impostor* about *Don Guillèn de Lampart, Rey de Mexico* (I looked at the reedition of 1946), which closely followed the original accounts, but also noted a "Don Diego" as one of his closest friends. It further developed the Romanesque "double life" theme as well as the "secret society of noble plotters" theme. A central chapter of the first book had the title "Zorro y lobo" (The fox and the wolf). He had earlier written fictional adventures and greatly admired the French dime novelist Alexandre Dumas, père. One of those tales had a Martin Garatuza, "called El Zorro," as the main character, who happened to be a master at the sword, disguise, and farce.

In the former book, Don Guillén already plies himself into a Z when he escapes through a narrow window. Troncarelli points out that like so many other Mexican Republicans and reformers in catholic countries, Vicente Riva Palacio was a Freemason, was read by Freemasons abroad (also think of Rudyard Kipling and his Freemason story *The Man Who Would Be King*, discussed in chapter 7). Like so many Americans with an active interest in events further south, Johnston McCulley was a Freemason as well (Troncarelli 2001, pp. 300–302). Troncarelli concludes there can be little doubt that the American author McCulley must have been aware of the Mexican Zorro legend.

Case Study: The Masking of Zorro

This brings us to the third and final stage in the development of the Zorro story, which finally transposed it from Mexico to California, to Los Angeles, and close to Hollywood, where the American film and popular culture industries were going to arise.

Around the turn of the century, the United States further drove Spain out of Cuba, Puerto Rico, and the Philippines, carving out territories for the construction of major naval bases (such as Guantánamo and others) to further reinforce its military grip on the region. After the acquisition of the Panama Canal Company and zone, it also reinforced its presence in Central America. The Mexican Revolution stirred a considerable interest. World War I further entrenched the Monroe Doctrine of American hegemony throughout the Western hemisphere. During the conflict, the army employed many former journalists and reporters as information officers and PR men; one of them was Johnston McCulley.

Even before the war, McCulley had been a prolific writer of pulp fiction and had traveled abroad. According to Troncarelli, he "pirated without scruples" Vicente Riva Palacio's Mexican adventure novels (2001, p. 300). In 1919 *The Curse of Capistrano* transposed the original Zorro story to California at the time of the settler resistance against Latino rule, on the eve of its adherence to the United States. The five installments appeared in the *All Story* weekly of Frank Munsey, who also made Tarzan and other popular heroes a success (and may have been related to McCulley's wife).

The cinematic potential of the story was immediately recognized by Douglas Fairbanks, who had just founded United Artists (with his wife, Mary Pickford, and Charlie Chaplin, among others). He turned it into the silent film *The Mark of Zorro* the very next year and seemed to create a wholly new genre—although it actually derived in part from the preexisting popular French "cape-and-sword" genre (Pinel 2000; Seesslen 1996). Fairbanks and Pickford used some of the proceeds to try to revive an early Californian rancho for themselves.

McCulley then released a new edition with the new title, deriving from a famous line at the end of the story: "Like the tongue of a serpent, Señor Zorro's blade shot in. Thrice it darted forward, and upon the fair brow of Ramon, just between the eyes, there flamed a red, bloody, letter Z. 'The Mark of Zorro!' the highwayman cried. 'You wear it forever now, commandante,' the hero replied" (Curtis 1998, p. 16). The mark and the mask, the hat and the suit, the sword and the whip soon gave the character an iconic status, as did his character of rebel and provocateur, poet and lover, leading a double life. All these elements together stirred the rise of a true Zorro industry.

Over the years, McCulley published sixty-three more Zorro stories (apart from many others and film scripts). There were thirteen further Zorro films in the United States before the latest productions, and thirty-seven Zorro films were made abroad, mostly in Mexico, Spain, and Italy. There were six major television series, including two live action ones by Disney Studios, and hundreds of comics, from daily strips to albums.

There also was a never-ending range of Zorro toys, and even theatrical shows and museum exhibits, like the one in the Los Angeles Western Heritage Museum that reportedly also "examined the origins of negative Hispanic imagery from bandidos, cantina sluts, and lazy peons to heroic figures such as Zorro" (Curtis 1998, p. 245). Zorro was used in advertising for Citroën, Coca Cola, Duracell, Euro Disney, Ford, Fujitsu, Trivial Pursuit, and many other companies. One Heinz spot depicted Zorro tasting its salsa and slashing his famous *Z*, and then added the letters *H-E-I-N* in front of it (pp. 239–40).

Although Zorro had become the first Hispanic Hollywood hero in 1921, Antonio Banderas was the first Spanish actor to actually play him in the 1998 Hollywood production of *The Mask of Zorro*. The script and the film were indeed reasonably well done, although few viewers were aware that this was largely due to the lifting and insertion of complete storylines from a range of other novels and films, such as *The Count of Monte Cristo*, the popular French novel by Alexandre Dumas, père, and an entire scene from *The Temple of Doom*, with Indiana Jones rescuing poor little colored kids kept as slaves in a mine.

The Zorro industry thrived on eternal recombinations of eternal Hispanic images: duplicitous Old Continent aristocrats pursuing dark ladies with mantillas and fans in their elegant haciendas lined by monumental palm-trees; secret meetings in dark churches and confession boxes, the hero sometimes disguised in the simple habit of a friar; markets with poor ladies surrounded by their too many children busily selling tropical fruit, while their men dozed off under their large sombrero hats next to a cactus; stirring Latino party music, even ranging as far as flamenco tap-dancing and Argentinean tangos—the whole familiar universe.

6

The Prude and the Lewd: Romantic and Erotic Encounters

What about intercultural encounters between men and women? Is the attraction lessened or heightened by ethnic difference? In what sense, and under what circumstances? What are the situations with which Western popular culture and Hollywood movies seem to be fascinated or even obsessed? Does the white male gaze prevail? How is sexual eagerness projected upon the "other," the nonwhite female, in such cases? Can this be shown to dominate in certain kind of films—about certain regions and certain situations? Where does this entire theme come from? And does it extend to other forms—for instance, to classical opera and modern musicals?

It is (by definition) very hard to probe one's own unconscious and the oft-denied drives that make us tick. Drives such as hunger and thirst are relatively simple and straightforward: most of the time they are soon satisfied; appetite and longing are usually temporary and low-key. Drives such as sex, eroticism, and romance, however, can be much more pliable and pervasive. Even the slightest hint or distant fantasy of a possible flirtation with a desirable partner at some distant point in time may color our relationship in marginal but persisting ways. We may daydream about others without even being aware of it, sometimes becoming completely obsessed.

Sex, eroticism, and romance are par excellence about mysterious combinations of sameness and otherness. Some people are homosexual and primarily feel attracted to their own sex; most people are heterosexual and primarily feel attracted to the other sex—or rather, to their own or the other gender, that is to say, a role largely defined by culture and socialization. The contrast in

107

gender roles is larger in some societies and epochs, smaller in others. Most heterosexual men traditionally find women attractive for being slightly smaller and softer, caring, and nurturing, among other things. Most heterosexual women traditionally find men attractive for being slightly larger and stronger, secure, and protective, among other things. We are educated and learn how to meet these expectations, even though there are a dozen different ways of attaining this. These different ways may also "resonate" with other contrasting roles—for instance, those of parents and children, elder or younger, higher or lower in social hierarchies. ("Lower" is often associated with uncivilized or natural, animalistic or bestial, savage or primitive, infantile or immature in this context.)

But there is a lot of ambivalence and paradox here. The criteria for an official long-term stable relationship between people belonging to the same social category may not be the same as those for a clandestine short-term passionate fling transgressing conventional group boundaries of age, class, or ethnicity—of the "forbidden fruit" type. Ethnicity is associated with external markers of cultural belonging such as skin, hair and eye color, facial and body forms, and so on—differences that may in turn be highlighted or toned down by hairstyle, dress, and adornments. Importantly, much of it can and will be noted and categorized "at first sight"—that is to say, even before we engage in conversation and further meaningful interaction where language, dialect, and other elements may further modify such impressions.

It is not surprising then, that sexual, erotic, and romantic preferences are often intertwined with ethnic ones and that there is a whole fantasy world surrounding them. The first level is that of physical build. From the point of view of the average white person of European stock, most people of African stock are built somewhat larger and stronger on average, whereas most people of Asian stock are somewhat smaller and weaker. This simple observation has translated into the notion that black "studs" might on occasion be physically more attractive to white women but also physically overpowering in a confrontation with white men; or that petite Asian women might on occasion be physically more attractive to white men but also "cunning" in a confrontation with white women.

The second level is that of underdressing or overdressing. The dress codes of Europeans originating from moderate climates often became the implicit norm for judging others living in warmer tropical climates. If they lived primarily in dense and shadowy forests, they were often half naked or minimally dressed, which was taken as a sign of their shamelessness and therefore probable promiscuity. If they lived primarily in scorching wide-open deserts or fields, by contrast, they were often dressed from top to toe—which was then taken as a sign of their repressive mores, with passions smoldering just beneath the surface. Whites even felt these same forces tugging at themselves when they underdressed or overdressed to adapt to the climate. Other aspects of diet, housing, culture, and religion were similarly judged from a European perspective.

But the third and most important level is the history of power relations between ethnic groups. For several centuries, whites have ruled most of the world. They saw themselves as proper and monogamous, and others as debauched and polygamous. But that was theory, of course; practice was often just the opposite, as white men often used their power to abuse nonwhite women: as slaves, servants, or prostitutes. In the official discourse of individuals and institutions, however, this was consistently covered up. In their unofficial discourse and popular lore, furthermore, "surplus libido" was projected upon their victims: They could not always resist their temptation, they said, as it was forced upon them on an everyday basis.

Today there is a considerable literature, from anthropology to media studies, documenting both these long-hidden realities and the twisted imagery deriving from them, beginning with images of the Holy Virgin that are so central in the Christian faith, and images of overdressed Victorian middle-class women that long were the icons of respectable society. In his study *White*, Richard Dyer has further dissected both the recurring visual elements staging their etherealness and the suggestions contained therein (1997, pp. 28–30). Of course these arch-images were a double-edged sword, as this image of propriety and frigidity also drove their men to go look for transgression and passion elsewhere—that is to say, in other classes and ethnic groups.

In his study *White on Black*, Jan Nederveen Pieterse has spelled out how this worked out in the context of white planters holding black slaves in the Americas. They frequently abused their young female slaves and impregnated them, thereby expanding their "livestock" and creating an oft-denied category of "half-bloods" around the house. He also shows how this logic persists to this very day; pretty black women from Josephine Baker to Grace Jones in turn exploited the image of their supposed surplus libido (1992, chap. 12).

But pretty young women and men were also often kept away from the respectable house, because they posed a sexual threat. Desexualized elderly black servants like Uncle Ben and Aunt Jemima instead became icons for homely conviviality and good cooking (as well as famous brands for rice and pancakes). Also think of the related racist imagery in film classics such as *Birth of a Nation* (1915) and *Gone with the Wind* (1939), often included among the "best movies of all time." At the same time, young men were seen as a possible threat; only when constantly laughing and clowning, or when contained to the worlds of entertainment and sports, were they easily accepted. It is easy to still fit the vast majority of black media personalities today into these same old and well-defined categories.

In *Visions of the East*—in the introduction by Ella Shohat and various chapters by other authors—it is shown how colonialism did in its turn affect the gender images of Asia (see also Hagedorn in Biagi & Kern-Foxworth 1997). Think of the imagery of Arab sheikhs and harems and "a thousand and one nights," recycled to this very day, but also think of the steamy images of light-brown Pacific belles suddenly emerging half-naked from crystal-clear blue water or thick green undergrowth. Of course the first generations of sea-farers, traders, and settlers consisted primarily of men, who took the habit of contracting informal "temporary marriages" with locals, if not abusing them outright. Here again, the victims were blamed for the transgressions, and the same patterns persisted long after proper European wives were brought over to form proper European families with proper European children.

After colonial rule began to recede, successive "allied" wars brought waves of millions of Western soldiers to the Pacific Rim. Their hard currencies in turn lured millions of poor women into prostitution. But here again, the harsh realities of the sex industry were glossed over by images of local girls who were just "happy go lucky" and "eager to please." European popular novels from the nineteenth century on—and American movies from the twentieth century on—are shot through with marked versions of these same themes and characters to this very day, to such an extent that both directors and audiences have come to think of them as "real" and "natural," and are often unaware of where these fantasies come from.

Of course moralists did fight back. The Legion of Decency forced a production code on Hollywood during the 1930s that forbade adult nudity, suggestive dancing, and interracial sex but was later replaced by a mere rating system. Segregationist laws forbidding coeducation and interracial marriages persisted in many states well into the late 1950s and early 1960s. A 2002 article in the *New York Times* recalled that even as late as "1963, 59 percent of Americans believed that marriage between blacks and whites should be illegal. At one time or another, forty-two states banned intermarriage. The Supreme Court finally invalidated these laws in 1967."[1] And it was only in 1969 that nonwhites were admitted into some of the major American beauty contests.

This is where the "Suzie Wong syndrome" of those years fits in. In a discussion on "women of color" and "the Asian mystique," Lena Chao quotes San Francisco news anchor Wendy Tokuda about "the fascination that Americans have with the geisha girl—or Singapore girl—and [which] is rooted in the experiences U.S. servicemen had with Asian women while overseas in China,

Japan, Korea, the Philippines and Vietnam. Those experiences, however, were primarily with prostitutes, 'a very select strata of the society overseas, and they bring those images home'" (Wilson, Gutiérrez, & Chao 2003, p. 202; see also Negra 2001).

This heritage of double standards on interracial sex shines through in a wide range of popular movie themes, from *Mutiny on the Bounty* and the South Sea "hula girl" genre to the pleasure girl theme in the famous opera *Madame Butterfly* and the well-known musical *Miss Saigon.*

Case Study: The True Causes of the Mutiny on the *Bounty*

One of the most frequently filmed South Seas stories is that of the mutiny on the *Bounty*, about the 1789 revolt on board a British ship meant to bring a bounty of bread tree seedlings from Pacific Tahiti to the West Indies in order to feed the black slaves there. Its captain, William Bligh, was also its purser; that is to say, he sold food and drinks to the crew on board. But as he had to wait for the last supplies, their original departure was delayed by three weeks, meaning they arrived late and had to stay over an entire season of five months on the islands, waiting for proper winds to sail onward. This facilitated overly close ties between the crew and the local population, resulting in an unwillingness to continue the voyage.

They had heard about the alluring Tahiti women even before they left, and even before their arrival the stern captain had his men inspected for venereal disease by the ship's surgeon. Soon after he had ordered the ship to leave again, a mutiny broke out. He concluded: "The Circean blandishments of the Otaheitan [Tahiti] women had prevailed on them to return to scenes of *voluptuousness unknown to any European country*" (Bligh n.d., pp. 43 and x, my emphasis). Bligh and a few others were put overboard in a longboat but miraculously made it back to London for a trial. The mutiny leader, master mate Fletcher Christian, wanted to return to his local mistress; the rest of the crew ordered him "to get them each a woman to live with," and when he refused they proceeded without him at first.

The dramatic story later inspired a romantic poem by Lord Byron (1823) and a book by Sir John Barrow (1831) but was only reworked into a popular novel a full century later by Charles Nordhoff and James Norman Hall, two military officers who had retired to Tahiti. They began with contributions to the *Atlantic Monthly.* The book was published in 1932, had no fewer than eleven editions in two years, and was then reportedly read by no fewer than 25 million people. At least half a dozen films were made of it. The three major Hollywood productions were those of 1935 by Frank Lloyd (with Clark Gable opposite Charles Laughton), 1962 by Carol Reed and Lewis Milestone (with Marlon Brando opposite Trevor Howard), and 1983–1984 by Roger Donaldson (with Mel Gibson opposite Anthony Hopkins). The prime island belle was first played by the Mexican actress Movita Castaneda, then by local novices Tarita Tariipaia and Tevaite Vernette. Each film was shot against a background of azure seas, white beaches, and green palm trees—a paradise familiar from tourist brochures.

The films reinforced a fascination, if not obsession, with the carefree Pacific paradise, not only in the audience but also in the cast. Actor Marlon Brando, for one, was already married to an exotic beauty when he divorced her to remarry the somewhat elderly 1935 *Bounty* star Movita, and then divorced again to marry the much younger 1962 *Bounty* star Tarita (he was thirty-eight, she was half his age). He even acquired an island property to retire there with her. The relationship was turbulent and occasionally violent. Their children were equally handsome "half-bloods," but the son later murdered his sister's lover in a fit of rage, and she committed suicide: The Hollywood obsession with Polynesian beauty had turned into a Shakespearean drama. Recently, Marlon Brando's successor, Mel Gibson, also bought an island near Fiji, although the acquisition was challenged by a local landless tribe.[2]

The signature scene of the arrival of the male crew of the *Bounty* and the welcome by the female population shows progressing states of undress with each subsequent version. The 1962 version with Brando depicted huge crowds of half-naked girls but was still prudishly shot from the back. Whenever there were full-frontal shots, the girls were strategically covered by flower garlands. Only the outlines of the side and underside of the breasts was occasionally showing, which was, however, considered a major breach of propriety—and therefore also a major attraction, particularly as the commentary in the spirit of the captain's report intoned that the Tahitians considered "light skins a mark of beauty" and "love-making a gesture of good will." Wow! It fired up the daydreams of another generation of draft-age American military men on the very eve of a major new engagement in the Pacific.

The 1984 version with Gibson, by contrast, is noteworthy for its drawn-out display of female nudity, free love, and orgies with at least a hundred of the most beautiful girls in the galaxy. The hypocrisy lies in the fact that it would have been unthinkable to show so many naked white breasts in a major mainstream Hollywood film at the time, but light brown ones were thought to be acceptable. As in other similar cases, the local extras were of course selected for youth and vigor, whereas older, flabby women were weeded out.[3]

The story of Polynesian promiscuity went back to the first European explorers there. Polynesia is a huge triangle of island groups next to the 180-degree international date line, stretching from American-controlled Hawaii near the Tropic of Cancer in the north to Samoa near the Tropic of Capricorn in the south and from this archipelago in the west to the French-controlled Tahiti and British-controlled Pitcairn in the farthest east. Their original religion was governed by the concept of mana, or all-pervasive energy, which also manifested itself in sex. Sex also played a role in maintaining social harmony as well as resolving tribal confrontations; young women were sometimes offered to conquerors in order to avoid rape and plunder.

British explorer Samuel Wallis first "discovered" Tahiti and what were later called the Wallis Islands in 1767. As the mist lifted, he was struck by the stunning beauty of the sunny island and its lush vegetation. A large number of praus, or small local boats, approached his ship. His crew, after a long time at sea, was immediately mesmerized by the pretty, half-naked women. Because of their facial form, body shape, and skin color, they looked more attractive to them than others—for example, Melanesians—to such an extent that the crew was caught off-guard by some skirmishes, then overreacted by firing their muskets and cannon into the crowds, which left many dead and wounded. In order to reestablish the peace, the locals then reportedly offered their girls, and the Europeans eagerly had sex with them.

French explorer Louis-Antoine de Bougainville in turn discovered Tahiti the very next year (and also what was later called Bougainville Island and the Bougainville flower). This time the locals did not want to risk guns and sent their women right away to placate them—as he reported in his *Voyage autour du monde* (1771). This was translated the very next year into English as *A Voyage around the World,* albeit with a curiously chauvinist British preface. He reported: "The periaguas were full of females, who, for agreeable features, are not inferior to most European women. . . . Most of these fair females were naked, for the men and the old women that accompanied them, had stripped them" (1967, pp. 217–18).

He added that they "soon explained their meaning very clearly. They pressed us to choose a woman and to come on shore with her; and their gestures, which were nothing less than equivocal, denoted in what manner we should form an acquaintance with her. It was very difficult, amidst such a sight, to keep at their work four hundred young

French sailors, who had seen no women for six months. In spite of all our precautions, a young girl came on board . . . carelessly dropped a cloth . . . and appeared to the eyes of all beholders, such as Venus shewed herself. . . . At last our cares succeeded in keeping these fellows in order, though it was not less difficult to keep the command of ourselves" (1967, pp. 217–19).

Of course this scene in the book dumbfounded Paris and London, particularly as de Bougainville inferred a culture of free love. This was an Eden, he said, where the senses flourished rather than the intellect. He therefore called the island *La Nouvelle Cithère*, after the mythical love island in Minoan times, planted the flag, and immediately claimed paradise for France. His account played a major role in further accrediting the myth of the noble savage in the salons and among Enlightenment philosophers such as Rousseau. Immediately after the publication of the book, de Bougainville was promoted to adviser at the court, and he later commanded a navy squadron in support of the American Revolution. A few decades later the French established a naval base and a mission post on Tahiti, which, of course, had contradictory effects on Polynesian promiscuity, now notorious.

After the invention and development of photography during the nineteenth century, Tahiti also became a major source of the quasi-ethnographic pictures of nude colonial belles for the French market. This further stirred many artists and intellectuals to go there and see for themselves. One of them was the impressionist painter Paul Gauguin, who meant "to confront rotten civilization with something more natural."[4] After seeing the Colonial Exhibition of 1890 in Paris, he finally made up his mind: He left his Danish wife and five kids and sailed to Tahiti, where he successively "married" two fourteen-year-olds, hired a long string of other underage models and lovers, and carelessly spread his acute syphilis. Yet local writer Chantal Spitz caused quite a stir when she called him a "racist" and a "pedophile" at an international colloquium on the centenary of his death, celebrated by a major commemorative exhibition in the Paris Grand Palais.[5]

In 2004 the mutiny on the *Bounty* in turn had a sobering sequel. Fletcher Christian and some of his British men had originally returned to Tahiti immediately after the mutiny to pick up Polynesian women and also some men to work for them. They inspected thirty islands before settling on a 2.5-square-mile speck, the island of Pitcairn, as they found it was marked incorrectly on the maps of the admiralty and would therefore long remain untraceable. Pioneer John Adams promoted a religious revival there, but long after his death the appropriately named Adamstown saw a forceful return of the repressed. The men revived the notion that young Polynesian girls were extremely precocious and eager and created a culture of abuse that continued into the late twentieth century. It was only during the late 1990s that Britain began an investigation, assisted by New Zealand.

In 2004, legal proceedings were begun against fifty-three-year-old mayor Steve Christian and a network of half a dozen relatives known as "the boys" for crimes of rape, indecent assault, and gross indecency, consistently committed against girls between five and fifteen years of age. The prosecutor said, "This group of distant cousins has spent at least forty years using any woman they wanted for sex, at any time, at any age." Someone who had been raped at eleven said: "It just seemed to be the normal way of life on Pitcairn, how the girls are treated as though they are a sex thing. Men could do whatever they want with them."[6] But only those who had since emigrated abroad dared speak out, and local women retracted their testimony. Six of the seven men were convicted but remained free pending appeal. Otherwise, life would have come to a complete standstill—as they formed half of the adult male population and of the irreplaceable boat crews.

HULA HULA GIRLS

The idée fixe and idée-force of Polynesian promiscuity in a perfect paradise not only inspired the renewed popularity of the *Bounty* story from the 1930s on, but also inspired an entirely new Hollywood genre: the South Sea movie, of which new exemplars came out almost annually. These films are usually about a Western man (planter, artist, soldier) fleeing civilization and meeting a local girl (preferably a superior one, that is to say a chieftain's daughter or "princess"). They settle and live a moment of timeless bliss, after which she is left behind or dies conveniently, and he returns home.

A fascinating television documentary about this theme was made by Trevor Graham in 2004.[7] It includes fragments from a range of relevant Hollywood films released before, during, and after World War II, as well as commentary by experts from the region, like Los Angeles film historian Ed Rampell, who notes that "South Sea cinema without sex is like Aunt Jemima's [all-American] pancakes without the syrup. The films are suffused with sexuality and sensuality, with nubile naked nymphs inhabiting the natural nirvana. . . . It was just natural for Hollywood, that always peddled sex, [that it] would peddle paradise." Of course, these movies were mostly inspired by the American Pacific.

Eleven years after European explorers had first set foot on Tahiti, British explorer James Cook landed on Hawaii, during the local Makahiki festival. He, too, reported that he was greeted with excessive enthusiasm by the local natives—who had climbed aboard his ship in such numbers that it almost capsized. It was assumed that they saw him not merely as the captain of a foreign ship but as their own god, returning on a floating island during a holiday (although he was killed in a fight with natives a year later).[8] Cook and his men also said they were shocked when the Hawaiians performed a ritual hula dance, whereby they bared and shook "everything" in front of their eyes. He also noted seemingly permissive attitudes toward sex. But Anne Salmond, professor of history and anthropology, noted in the television documentary, "It was not the case that sexuality was totally free and available to everybody. It was seen as a power in the world that linked people to their ancestors and to their gods."

Yet the idea persisted, in the United States and elsewhere. Polynesian promiscuity was even enshrined in early social science by Margaret Mead. She was a student of the founding father of American anthropology, Franz Boas, who had sent her to Samoa to investigate these fascinating South Sea mores. This led to the famous 1928 book *Coming of Age in Samoa*, which claimed that adolescents there were relatively carefree in their peaceful exploration of sex— a true example to the uptight West. Australian Derek Freeman (1983), however, claimed after verification half a century later that she had paid only a very short visit there, had reported very selectively, and had relied on only two girls as her prime informers. He was later able to track one of them down, at ninety years of age. Giggling, she reportedly conceded that they had taken the young scholar for a ride at the time and had just told her what she obviously wanted to hear (see also Freeman 1999).

Meanwhile, the island of Hawaii had increasingly become a favorite hub for traders and fleets. In the late nineteenth century, the United States overthrew the king, annexed the islands, and made Pearl Harbor its largest navy base in the Pacific and in the outside world. Plantations attracted foreign workers, who soon outnumbered the original population. Prostitution, nightlife, and the hotel and tourist industry flourished (see the hula tourist ad in O'Barr 1994, p. 28). They were all attracted by the image of the familiar exotic paradise studded with palm trees, an eternally smiling population, and inviting beautiful ladies. The popular culture industry of films and television, music and dance further built on these same stereotypes to such an extent that the hula girl became a local icon comparable to the Paris Eiffel Tower or the London Tower Bridge.

One early film was the movie *Tabu* (1931), filmed on location on Bora Bora Island by the American documentary filmmaker Robert Flaherty and German feature director Friedrich Murnau, as a seemingly realistic but instead heavily romanticized story. A typical example of the entire genre was *Bird of Paradise* (1932) by King Vidor. Many such films had Latino protagonists; Caribbean island movies later copied some of the same formats. They all tried to circumvent censorship rules on nudity and interracial romance laid down in the Hollywood Production Code. During World War II, a million G.I.'s moved through Hawaii (a thousand times more men than women); thereafter the number of tourists quickly climbed to a million per year. The late 1950s even saw a worldwide hula craze, which reportedly sold 100 million Hula-Hoops at two dollars apiece (Panati 1991, pp. 264–65; see also Jansen van Galen, Schreurs, & Smink 1999, p. 58). It accompanied movies like the Rodgers and Hammerstein musical *South Pacific* (1958) and *Blue Hawaii* (1961), starring Elvis Presley.

Just as Hawaiian dance had come to mean any kind of hip wiggling in a flower garland and a grass skirt, Hawaiian music came to mean any kind of balmy song accompanied by ukelele, guitar, and other strings—even though these were recent imports to a largely percussionist Polynesia. According to Rampell, "What Hollywood did was it coopted indigenous dances and turned them into these huge production numbers, with a kind of orgiastic undertone."[9] Katerina Teaiwa, a lecturer of Oceanic studies in Honolulu, added ironically, in the same documentary: "It is funny that Europeans focused on the lower regions," even though a 1966 hula song counseled to "keep your eyes on her hands" as "she's telling a story." But males around the world could think of nothing else but "that," whenever the subject was Polynesia.

THE FASCINATION WITH GEISHAS

The year 2005 saw the release of the movie *Memoirs of a Geisha*, with great popular appeal. It told the story of a poor girl, born during the depression years in a Japanese fishing village, who was subsequently trained in the refined tradition of female entertainment and who ultimately became the mistress of some of the country's most powerful people.

The movie was based on a best-selling novel of the same title by Arthur Golden, which sold no fewer than 4 million copies worldwide over the first few years after its publication. It presented itself as the life story of a famous geisha as told to a professor of Japanese studies. The author's postscript said: "I am indebted to one individual above all others. Mineko Iwasaki, one of Gion Kobu's top geishas" (1998, p. 433). However, the retired lady soon filed a lawsuit in New York, claiming that her anonymity had been breached and that the book disparaged her by "repeatedly stating that she was sold into the geisha world by her parents and that her virginity was auctioned to the highest bidder" (BBC News, April 25, 2001). The author and publisher maintained, however, that the biographical portrait had been a composite story of the accounts of several people.

The movie was hailed in the United States for its visual beauty, but it was disparaged in Japan because the main actresses were foreigners who had received only a six-week training course in the subtleties of Japanese culture. It was also disparaged in China because all three main actresses were Chinese. The authorities in China even forbade the showing of the movie, as it risked opening an old wound—namely, the controversy over the thousands of Chinese "comfort women" who had been abused as sexual slaves by the Japanese imperial army during the war.

Memoirs of a Geisha was not the first Hollywood geisha film, nor will it probably be the last. One of the first was *The Barbarian and the Geisha* (1958), with macho John Wayne as an early American consul charmed off his feet by such a hostess. An Internet search produces several further titles, but if we extend our search to major geisha roles in popular movies, it turns out that similar characters turn up in many films or television series about other Western male heroes visiting Japan, either in ancient or in modern times. Some were inspired by the popular romantic and Orientalist adventure novels of bestselling writers such as James Michener (*Sayonara*, 1957) and James Clavell (*Shogun*, 1980). Still others recast the eternal geisha theme in a Chinese context (*The World of Suzie Wong*, 1960; *Taipan*, 1986). Note that American and European films had largely given up depicting white "pleasure girls" in this way, that is to say, as naive and eager to please rather than calculating, asocial, and opportunistic.[10]

But let us stick to Japan. Ever since Japan opened itself up to the outside world, Westerners have basically seen geishas as sophisticated whores, even though other books argued that the tradition was much more complex and subtle than that: that it was an art of personal female entertainment, helping men relax, feel at ease, and rebuild vigor. Sex was not always the first—or even the final—goal. For her study *Geisha* (1983, 1998), American anthropologist Liza Dalby even went so far as to train as a geisha, in order to be able to fathom this mysterious world. The figure of the geisha is most familiar to educated Westerners through the character of Madame Butterfly in the famous opera by Italian composer Giacomo Puccini. One very impressive minimalist staging was realized by Texan director Robert Wilson in 1993 and again represented in 2005 on the New Stage of the Bolshoi Theatre in Moscow. An elaborate Orientalist staging by British film director Anthony Minghella (of *The English Patient*) for the English National Opera in London received tepid reviews, by contrast, but was soon sold out as "the hottest ticket in town." When the New York Metropolitan Opera opened its season with a new gala production (for the first time in two decades) in 2006, it chose this same work. It was simultaneously shown on the giant Panasonic, NASDAQ, and Reuters screens in Times Square, as well as on Lincoln Center Plaza. John Galliano, the chief designer for the Paris haute couture house of Dior, even decided to make Madame Butterfly the fashion trend for the spring and summer seasons of 2007. So the classical opera remains very much alive and appealing.

Meanwhile, it had also inspired the blockbuster musical *Miss Saigon*, a major hit in North America and western Europe. The musical became the sixth-longest-running show on Broadway in New York and ran for more than ten years in London. Its websites reported that some twenty-one companies made eleven cast recordings and played it in nineteen countries and ten languages. They reached 31 million people (40 percent in the United States alone) during nineteen thousand performances in 138 cities. It even spawned a *Miss Saigon* study guide for educational purposes, addressing some of the intercultural aspects. The musical grossed $1.3 billion worldwide, more than most movies mentioned in this book. But where did this story come from?

Case Study: The True Story of Madame Butterfly

Madame Butterfly is a story about the archetypical and tragically unequal relationship between man and woman, white and nonwhite, rich and poor, powerful and not—conveniently situated in a faraway time and place. Its roots go back to the early days of the renewed encounter between Japan and the West. After the European powers imposed their "unequal treaties" upon China, gained concessions, and opened ports to their drugs and trade through the "Opium Wars," the United States wanted to claim its "equal share" of trade in the Asia-Pacific region. It twice sent threatening fleets to Japan under Commodore Matthew Perry to force it to give up its two centuries of isolation. The port of Nagasaki was then further opened to trade, and the island of Dejima hosted a growing expatriate community. Foreign sailors and merchants waiting for repairs or deliveries took up the habit of contracting so-called temporary marriages with poor local girls in exchange for money. The opening up of the country also led to a coup and the so-called Meiji Restoration, followed by the adoption of foreign science and technology, and rapid modernization.

The rapid growth of the exchanges with Japan stirred considerable interest in western Europe and North America and to a wave of Japanophilia. Artists such as Hokusai were discovered in the West, emulated by the French impressionists and the Dutch artist Vincent van Gogh. The French Goncourt brothers were fascinated; Judith, the daughter of Théophile Gautier (and supposed mistress of Richard Wagner) wrote novels about Japan. Librettists and composers such as Pietro Mascagni developed operas about Japan, and a host of lighter and more popular musical plays, with costumes and ballets, were performed in vaudeville theatres.

The most famous and influential of these operas would be the gripping and melodramatic *Madama Butterfly*, by the Italian Giacomo Puccini, widely performed throughout the world to this very day. After a "temporary marriage" to U.S. Navy lieutenant Pinkerton, Madame Butterfly is abandoned, but she hopes for his return—even more so, because she expects and then bears a son, named Trouble. But when Pinkerton returns, his new American wife proposes to adopt the child, and Butterfly commits suicide so as not to stand in their way. Many scholars have wondered whether the character Cho-Cho-san had been modeled after a real-life example. Their tracking down of possible candidates often reads like a detective story.

One of the oldest of such stories already dated from a previous period and centered on Philip Franz von Siebold. He was a German medical doctor, sent to Nagasaki/Dejima by the Dutch East Indies Company (the only traders allowed in Japan at the time), where he collected Japanese plants, objects, and knowledge. He became one of the forerunners of Western Japanology and was even read by Commodore Perry before his naval expedition. Siebold contracted a "temporary marriage" with a "pleasure girl" called O-Taki-san, who bore him a daughter. Back in Europe, he married a German woman who bore him another five children. He later returned to Nagasaki, where his Eurasian daughter had become a midwife, and helped further educate her to become the first female doctor in Japan. So the ending of this story is still a relatively happy one. Siebold was said to have inspired one of the main characters in a later opera by French composer Camille Saint-Saëns, *The Yellow Princess.*

The most closely related of the early stories, however, centered on the French navy lieutenant Julien Viaud. Under his pen name, Pierre Loti, he published a wide range of exotic travel accounts. His 1887 *Madame Chrysanthème* describes his visit to Nagasaki two years earlier. The main character means to contract a temporary marriage to "a little yellow-skinned woman with black hair and cat's eyes," turns to "a confidential agent for the intercourse of races," rejects a fifteen-year-old and chooses an eighteen-year-old, but as "a mere plaything" and for twenty dollars per month. The child in the story still has the form of her baby brother, Bambou. The book apparently appealed to the fantasies of European men, because it had no fewer than twenty-five editions in five years, with translations into English and other languages. In real life, Viaud/Loti's "geisha" was a seventeen-year-old by the name of O-Kane-san, and there still exists a photo of them. Five years later, the French composer André Messager wrote an opera based on the story during a stay in an Italian country residence, where his Italian colleague Giacomo Puccini was at the same time working on his *Manon Lescaut*. That may have provided the first spark.

The most widely believed hypothesis, by contrast, centers on the Scottish merchant Thomas Glover and his Japanese wife, Tsuru, who had a son called Tomasiburu. Their former residence is now a foreign tourist attraction in Nagasaki, and a statue of Madame Butterfly looking out over the sea was placed nearby. Yet this version lacks the key dramatic element of abandonment. Former Dutch diplomat Jan van Rij, however, recently published a fascinating book with further details on the various aforementioned hypotheses. He claims that Tomasiburu was not their natural son and was in fact adopted by them. According to van Rij, he was in reality an illegitimate son of Thomas's brother—with a "pleasure girl" by the name of Kaga Maki. This seems to make more sense, even if some other Butterfly scholars stick to their own versions.

A rumor about this or another such abandonment, followed by an attempted suicide by one Cho-san, was reportedly heard by a couple of American missionaries in Nagasaki. The wife, Jenny Correll, passed it on to her brother John Luther Long in Philadelphia, a lawyer with literary aspirations. He then published the short story *Madame Butterfly* in an illustrated magazine. He also reintroduced a number of elements—such as the callous marine lieutenant—from Pierre Loti's *Madame Chrysanthème* about the same theme. One of the most famous playwrights and innovative producers of the day, David Belasco, then turned it into a one-act play ending in suicide. It was performed both in New York and London at the turn of the century. Puccini, in London to supervise his opera *Tosca*, saw the play and immediately asked Belasco "with tears in his eyes" whether he could develop it into an opera.

Puccini then began to do further research and was elated when it turned out that one of Japan's most beautiful and leading geishas had turned actress at twenty-eight, had formed her own theatre company, and had just gone on a tour of America and Europe. Lesley Downer's recent biography of "the geisha who bewitched the West" noted that she had previously had "a tempestuous love life involving some of the most powerful, charismatic, and wealthy men in the country" (2003, p.

3), and one review therefore likened it to "a real-life *Memoirs of a Geisha.*" Her emotional acting caused a sensation abroad, the *New York Times* noted at the time, because "it is difficult to think of Japanese women of any age, rank, or character as anything but a pretty, dainty little creature, sitting in her toy house."

Yet the biography notes on its cover that "from San Francisco to New York, Paris, and Berlin, audiences thrilled to her mesmeric acting and exquisite dancing. She performed for the American president and for the Prince of Wales in London [and was received by the czar of Russia as well]. Picasso painted her, Gide, Debussy, Degas, and Rodin were among her devoted fans." Puccini was disappointed to have missed her performance in Rome but then traveled to Milan to see her in *The Geisha and the Knight.* One local reviewer wrote that it proceeded with "such terrible efficacy as to make a shudder run down the spines of the audience." Another said it had "that type of insane and uncontrollable intoxication characteristic of primitive peoples." But still another said that "the emotion she arouses in us at moments of furor and at death is the same as that aroused by a little domestic animal" (Downer 2003, p. 200). Puccini immediately copied this fateful rhythm and even incorporated one of the *kota* or zither melodies into his opera.

Yet, Downer noted, he also transformed the character to make it fit the same old mold of the naive Asian woman eager to please more powerful men. "The stage directions call for her to behave with 'infantile coquettishness' and 'infantile grace.' She smiles 'like a child,' and when she weeps it is 'infantile crying.' It is all the more shocking when this childlike creature breaks into 'savage' rage. Lieutenant Pinkerton, her faithless husband, is not portrayed as a 'typical American' but a complex, rather unpleasant individual. Butterfly, conversely, is not an individual. This sweet, submissive child-woman . . . was the ultimate Westerner's stereotype of the Japanese female. . . . The irony was, of course, that she [the actress] herself was not remotely like this sweet, helpless little creature" (2003, pp. 200–201).

Puccini finally presented the opera in Italy in1904 but revised it in 1905, when it was also performed in London and Paris. There was also an early partial representation in Tokyo. But even without the tragic ending, the big newspaper *Asahi Shimbun* resented its "contemptuous glance at the customs and habits of loose women" in Japan, according to van Rij (2001, p. 141). It took decades before a full-blown version was staged, but even today it is not very popular in Japan—in contrast to much of the Western world. By 1919, there already was a first movie (albeit silent) about Madame Butterfly, starring Mary Pickford, and this was followed by countless other stagings.

There is a final and sad epilogue pertaining to Madame Butterfly's or Kaga Maki's real-life Eurasian son, Tomasiburu. Throughout his life, he had been torn between the Japanese and Anglo-Saxon cultures of his mother and father (and he even spent some time in the United States), but he felt fully accepted by neither. When an American G.I. entered his Japanese house after the second atomic bomb had devastated Nagasaki, he found that Tomasiburu had just hanged himself. In 2004 there was a news item in the press referring to a huge stir caused in Tokyo by the new opera *Jr. Butterfly*, with a libretto by Masahiko Shimada and music by Shigeaki Saegusa, about his fate.[11] According to some, it should be placed in the context of the current Japanese reappraisal of the history of its relations with the United States—ever since American flotillas forced the opening of the country to outside influence.

Meanwhile, the original *Madame Butterfly* spawned endless imitations and variations. The most famous present-day adaptation of the theme is of course the blockbuster musical *Miss Saigon*, in which French librettist Alain Boublil and composer Claude-Michel Schönberg (of *Les Misérables*) reset the story in the framework of the later ill-fated American intervention in Vietnam and its aftermath.

Boublil and Schönberg were in fact inspired by a 1985 photograph in the popular daily *France Soir*. It showed the emotional goodbye of a Vietnamese mother to her ten-year-old daughter, sent to the United States to get "a better life" with the American father she had never seen. In the musical, the authors made the mother an orphan promised to a Vietnamese man who turns into a treacherous Communist who abuses his position. She ends up in a sleazy nightclub but obviously falls in love when she has to turn her very first trick with a kind American G.I. She is surrounded by more experienced colleagues, all out to catch such a G.I. prize—for money or a getaway ("Tell yourself your passport's standing at the bar"). She later turns out to be pregnant but loses track of the man in the chaos of the collapse of the regime. Back home, he marries an American woman, white and blonde.

On the one hand, the story is a fairly realistic social drama. A well-known Dutch medical professor doing research on prostitution, venereal disease, and AIDS in Southeast Asia noted that not only were there hundreds of thousands of local prostitutes catering to local and Western men in the region, but also that at least fifty thousand of such "half-blood" Bui Doi children had been left behind in Vietnam, of which only

1 percent had been able to trace their biological fathers. On the other hand, he said, the causes and consequences of these ongoing dramas were presented in a rather one-sided way in the musical, with the usual focus on "universal human themes" and not on concrete power relations. The musical was full of clichés and stereotypes about development and migration, about the men and women of East and West, he said.[12] Marina Heung analyzed "the family romance of Orientalism" in a detailed essay (reprinted in Bernstein & Studlar 1997), on how *Madame Butterfly* and *Miss Saigon* (as well as the French movie *Indochine*) reworked conflict traumas in gender terms, featuring the young, insecure Asian woman and the adult Euro-American male rescuer.

A WHITE VIRGIN IN THE TROPICS

There exists a very interesting variation and reversal of the theme of the prudish white lady and the lecherous nonwhite one in the subgenre of steamy romance and soft porn, where a reticent young white virgin is initiated into the wonders of love and lust and sex by being cast into an overseas world of eager white and nonwhite, older and younger men and women. At the outset, there often are some scenes of real or imagined rape or near-rape. In the somewhat sexist jargon of Sigmund Freud, this is a fantasy of "Lust ohne Schuld," of pleasure without guilt. But gradually she gives herself over to these new experiences, increasingly baring both her body and her soul.

An early forerunner of this genre is to some extent the French *Angélique* series. Originally, it was a series of very popular novels, written from the mid-1950s on by husband-and-wife authors Anne and Serge Golon. All together, they published thirteen titles, translated into forty-five languages and selling more than 100 million copies. From the mid-1960s on there were five theatrical movies based on the series, directed by Bernard Borderie and featuring red-blonde Michèle Mercier in the title role, always baring some flesh, and the scarred, darker Robert Hossein as her adventurous lover. Every few years, the films were repeated on television (at least ten times until the turn of the twenty-first century)—an example of an early French blockbuster.

In the series, Angélique is a beautiful seventeenth-century girl who falls in love with an early rebel against the repressive ancien régime of the Roi Soleil, well before the French Revolution. Her beauty soon captures the attention of the monarch and of high aristocrats, but she also encounters a long series of exotic charmers and brutes: the ambassador of Persia, the bey, the sultan, a eunuch, Mediterranean pirates from the opposite Barbarian (Berber) shores, and Arab and African potentates.

One of my favorite scenes I always showed to my students for analysis and discussion is the one in part 4, *Indomptable Angélique*, where she is sold on the slave market in Algiers. Her robe is ripped away, she stands totally nude, desperately covering herself with her hands, so that we do not get to see anything untoward. Opposite her in the amphitheatre is a crowd of beige and brown and black faces, visibly lusting after this unique white prize and bidding inane amounts of precious metals and stones to possess her. In the end she is bought by the ugliest man around. (Be reassured: he turns out to have acted for her lover). This is one instance where the shots and countershots, their rhythm and focus, carry a clearly racist message of revulsion. Note that at the time the books were released France was battling the Arab independence movement in Algeria, and many subsequent moviegoers were draft-age boys, alternately attracted to and repelled by this Oriental culture.

A second example on this same theme was the much more libertine *Emmanuelle* movie, after a novel by Emmanuelle Arsan. The film turned into the best-selling picture of the year and was followed by *The Anti-virgin* and others. It was initially directed by Just Jaeckin and starred novice Dutch actress Sylvia Kristel, but they were later replaced by others. The original plot featured a young, naive girl married to an old and experienced French gentleman, vaguely moving in diplomatic and expat circles in Bangkok. He encouraged her to discover a wide range of erotic pleasures, with rapidly changing partners. It became a reference for soft porn, with its "dosage léché d'exotisme," according to one French film dictionary (Horvilleur 1988, p. 142).

Note that the first installment came out just after the end of the Vietnam War, when the "R&R" of masses of American G.I.'s had greatly boosted nightlife in Thailand and the Philippines, as well as the number of brothels there (some later named after the movie). This then in turn became a major tourist attraction. The sex trade became a major occupation all over Southeast Asia, the third world in general, and for temporary emigrants to Western countries. In order to counter that image, a Swiss ad campaign later asked the question: "What do Thai women do after night falls?" Answer: "They turn on the light, just like most of the Swiss!"

In a recent television appearance, Sylvia Kristel estimated that at least 400 million people had seen her (and her exotic partners) in the nude, on film and television.[13] Later installments with new actresses brought the character to Hong Kong, Brazil, and other similar exotic/erotic locations.[14] The series perfectly fit into the emerging trends of sexual liberation and neocolonial nostalgia, not only visible in pictures of authentic buildings and landscapes in glossy travel magazines but also concerning original fashion and furniture in posh Western department stores.

A final example along these same lines is an American series of soft porn B-films around the *Justine* character, directed by L. L. Shapira and starring Daneen Boone. In Europe the series has also been widely broadcast on late-night television. Justine is the besotted student of a young archeology professor at a traditional university, modeled after Indiana Jones. First she daydreams about accompanying him on his travels and then does so under various pretexts. Here again, she is initiated into the wonders of love and lust and sex by various assorted exotic characters. She is abducted, imprisoned, abused, and sacrificed in all kind of different cultures. The subtext is that she and her mentor are clean and straightforward but their tormentors are dirty and perverted. It is presented as a campy spoof, however, so that the recurring stereotypes are made to seem "just funny."

Helpers and Helpless: Colonial Adventure

How did the forebears of present-day Europeans see their interaction with exotic others in colonial days? Did they embellish their own roles by denigrating non-Europeans in their reports? Does some of this survive more recent, more polished versions? What about the imperial fantasies of those days; what about fictional heroes? Do some of these pop-cult characters survive, in some disguised form, in current Hollywood blockbusters?

Think of premodern times overseas, in Africa, Arabia, Asia, the Americas. What do you see? Half-naked black tribes in the jungle, drumming and dancing in front of their huts; bedouins crossing the desert on camelback, covered from head to toe, to go haggle in some open-air market or covered suq; robed monks in temples, lighting candles and incense before huge statues of strange deities; painted Native Americans with feathers, hunting in the jungle or the prairie—with maybe a lone white visitor or a pair, possibly accompanied by animals or locals carrying their luggage.

To some extent, these are again "true" images: some reality looked like that. At the same time, they have been subject to what I termed "selective articulation" in a previous study of intercultural news. Due to a number of psychological, sociological, economical, political, historical, geographic, and other mechanisms, certain aspects of those situations have been overemphasized in our written reports and images, whereas others—which may be considered just as (or even more) important—have been underemphasized. The collective ego of certain groups is spared in this operation; that of others is disregarded.

In a world where Anglo-Saxon language and culture have triumphed along-side liberal democracy and the market economy, a certain vision of the past has come to prevail. The United States is the largest and richest market for media products, alongside the other English-speaking settler states and Great Britain. Their role in history is ennobled and glorified—not always, but often—even though their democracy long excluded nonwhite peoples at home and abroad, and free trade was embraced only after they had become strong enough to be sure to prevail over others. Of course similar observations hold, to a lesser extent, for the runners-up of history, such as France and others.

In dominant mainstream popular culture, the colonial and imperial past of these states is not systematically seen as problematic. It is usually depicted as a well-intentioned but unfortunately failed attempt to spread civilization and wealth to others, and of little consequence, at that, either for the Western lead or for the non-Western lag in development. Colonial-era famines and epidemics, exploitation and repression, are often painted as "naturally given" background, not as a consequence or responsibility of British or French rule. By contrast, their antagonists—the Germans and the Russians and the Japanese—are depicted as the eternal bad guys, and their expansion abroad is in turn depicted as illegitimate and guilty.

This is the metanarrative and subtext underlying an old but very persistent and appealing genre in popular culture: the exotic adventure story in a colonial or imperial era setting. Since Great Britain was the first and largest empire of modern days, the genre was particularly highly and widely developed there. But since the United States informally took over that role, and is the home of the richest and most influential popular culture industry in modern times, its adaptation of that linguistic heritage to latter-day comic books and theatrical movies, to television programs and video games, is of particular interest.

There are two kinds of colonial-era adventure stories. On the one hand are those that claim to have a basis in fact. Very often these are based on autobiographies of people who became popular culture icons for one reason or another, usually long after the original events themselves had supposedly taken place, and after decades of mythmaking. Examples of such stories and films are *Lawrence of Arabia* and *Anna and the King of Siam*. On the other hand are those stories that make no such claims but are instead variations on similar grandiose themes, even less restrained by reality—for example, such heroes as Allan Quatermain and Indiana Jones. The latter is usually presented and seen as a "stand-alone" fantasy but is in fact largely a direct descendant of the same colonial and imperial family.

Both the supposedly factual and openly fictional subgenres offer a vast screen for psychological projection, for embellishment and denigration at will. But usually neither present-day producers nor present-day consumers are aware of these distortions. They are not equipped to recognize the bias and slant; they simply see the overseas past as a picturesque historical playground for a white adventurer and for great cinematic fun, like a present-day tourist admiring the natural beauty and impressive monuments, strange people, and funny habits of faraway places.

The colonial or imperial adventure hero basically has to confront the odds alone. He is usually a white male, on occasion joined by a white female, which creates a more complex struggle over dominance or subordination (i.e., with nonwhite males). If they are a pair, romance and sex are of only marginal interest to most of these stories. He may or may not bring a comrade or side-kick, somewhat older or somewhat younger, the latter particularly if the story is aimed at a family audience.

What is surprising—and what the audience is eager to identify with—is that the simple act of travelling overseas automatically implies a dramatic leap of social promotion. The white protagonist is suddenly shown as an obvious equal to nonwhite monarchs and aristocrats, presidents and prime ministers, military commanders and police commissioners. Of course, this desire for social promotion is at the heart of the entire imperial enterprise—and of its enduring popularity (also in the related genre of quasi-historical colonial nostalgia movies, not discussed here).

The colonial adventure story usually also has a strong moral dimension. Both the whites and the nonwhites are divided into good guys and bad guys. The good whites usually belong to the same class and/or nation; the bad whites to a different class (e.g., merchants or crooks) or nation (e.g., French or Germans). The good nonwhites are originally a minority of one or a hand-ful: usually rather young, more modern, pro-Western, and therefore sympathetic. The bad nonwhites are a few older traditional authorities (exotic priests, medicine men, tribal leaders) initially tolerated or followed by a large majority. The plot often consists of the protagonist tipping the balance to enlightenment, justice, and development. In the process, this may bring huge rewards (a cultural artifact, a precious treasure), but this is never the prime motive of the hero, only a mere side effect of his actions.

The exotic location, of course, offers great potential for a wide variety of mysteries and threats. But surprisingly, the same dozen or few dozen specific scenes recur time and again in most individual adventure stories: majestic sunrises and sunsets, or even high noon, over vast "virgin" territories; mountain ranges and passes leading to secret valleys; dry deserts with dust storms; thick jungles with strange sounds; palm trees, lianas, and cactus plants; swamps and rivers with aggressive crocodiles, brush land, and savannahs with aggressive lions and tigers, dark grottoes with bats, spiders, bugs and other creepy animals; camels, always in a caravan; elephants, always in a stampede; snakes and snake charmers.

Sorcerers and monks. A temple with ingenious ancient traps. A sarcophagus with a recent victim, dead or alive. A colourful tropical market with orderly stalls overturned by the chase. A body rolled in a carpet. A high fall broken by the convenient sunshade. Vintage automobiles and trains. A chase over, through, and under a running train, with people hanging outside, at the approach of a tunnel. Firearms against swords and spears. The escape by the improvised stealing of a biplane. Gems as big as tennis balls. These are all classic elements in the colonial adventure genre.

Take a closer look at them: the "fantasy" scenes have turned into fade clichés, reproduced time and again. But the real problem lies elsewhere: Whether the stories claim to be true or invented, it is always the same group or civilization that is hailed and the others who are denigrated in a thousand direct and indirect ways. The stories are always about moral superiority and inferiority, behind a dazzling facade of exotic fireworks. Let us dissect a few of the best-known examples.

IMPERIAL HEROES IN REAL LIFE

During the 1990s, there was a sudden revival of an Orientalist story that had fascinated Anglo-American, Western, and therefore global media audiences for well over a century. It began with a new recording of *The King and I* by Ben Kingsley and Julie Andrews, followed by new stagings of the musical in New York and London. The major Hollywood studio 20th Century Fox announced an ambitious new film version starring Jodie Foster and Chinese actor Chow Yun-Fat, accompanied by a widely distributed children's book. At the same time Warner Brothers, part of the largest media conglomerate in the world, prepared an animated cartoon version.

The official website for the Fox movie said: "Set in nineteenth-century Thailand, *Anna and the King* is the true story of British governess Anna Leonowens, who is employed by the king to look after his many children. Soon after she arrives in this exotic country, Anna finds herself engaged in a battle of wits with the strong-willed ruler." Although the traditional claim that it was a "true story" was alternately toned down and then reinstated in the film's promotion, it was blindly accepted in later announcements worldwide—even in some of the upscale television program guides.[1] As it turns out, however, the story may well be said to have only a small basis in fact, with most added in successive layers of ethnocentrist fantasy.

In order to understand the true nature of this story, we have to place it in the wider context of its genre, which is the account of the supposedly "true" experiences of white individuals in the exotic lands of those days. They were published in Europe and America, and the exotic people discussed in these accounts were usually long unaware of this version of events and unable or unwilling to challenge it for a wide range of reasons. So after some time, the accounts often came to be looked upon as the plain historical truth, without further embellishments. Of course, they were not—although it often took academic scholars many decades or a full century to develop critical commentaries. By that time, however, the stories had already taken on a life of their own, had entered into Western consciousness and mythology, and were further popularized and dramatized on that basis.

Great Britain had initially contented itself with gaining mere colonial footholds to support "free" trade. But as the Industrial Revolution at home progressed in the course of the nineteenth century, the nation felt forced to expand and transform these into a huge self-sufficient empire upon which "the sun never set." People and money were sent abroad to reconnoiter and subject vast territories and populations, recruit cheap labor to produce raw materials, destroy local manufacturing by imposing new rules and regulations (e.g., in India), and make markets ready to absorb British industrial goods.

Britain had not only become the greatest naval power in the world, according to the maxim "Britannia rules the waves"; it also spent more on its armed forces than any other nation in the world, and Lord Wolseley conceded at the time that "without doubt we are the most warlike people on earth." The Great McDermott sang at the London Palladium: "We don't want to fight; but, by jingo, if we do/We've got the men . . . we've got the money too" (Read 1983, pp. 199, 205–206). Imperial enthusiasm spread also among the lower middle class and white-collar workers.

At its height between 1871 and 1901, the empire expanded to cover one-fifth of the globe's land surface and 400 million of its population (only one-eighth of which had "white" skin). But signs of some imperial "overstretch" became gradually visible. From the European continent, new powers had joined the race, in shifting alliances. So on the one hand, Great Britain increasingly encouraged the colonies dominated by white settlers to take their own responsibilities, from Canada to Australia and New Zealand. On the other hand, more British emigrants still went to the United States than anywhere else, and it became gradually clear to many that a "special relationship" with that country was the best hope for the long-term preservation of a major role in world affairs.

The heroic feats of imperial adventurers were widely celebrated in British popular culture. The projected image of exceptional opportunity proved particularly appealing to a broad range of citizens. Improvements of the telegraph and press agencies facilitated rapid newsgathering for such purposes; improvements in printing and typesetting facilitated the rise of a true mass press within the larger conurbations. The *Daily Telegraph* already had a circulation of almost two hundred thousand when (in association with the *New York Herald*) it sent Stanley to find Livingstone (more on this below).

Alfred Harmsworth founded the *Daily Mail* at the end of this period, and it soon passed the million-copy mark during the South African Boer War excitement. After he founded the *Daily Mirror*, it soon sold a million copies as well. A jibe said that the former was for those who could not think and the latter for those who could not read, but Harmsworth soon bought the elite *Times* and the Sunday *Observer* as well, to reach those who supposedly could. This mass press contributed decisively to creating and expanding a true pantheon of imperial heroes. Let us review a few.

Imperial Heroes in Nineteenth-Century Asia

The "brightest jewel" in Victoria's crown of course became the Indian subcontinent, with three-quarters of the empire's population, already absorbing one-fifth of British exports. Heroic reports concerning India itself centered on the putting down of rebellions and the dismantling of mysterious indigenous sects, with an emphasis on the riches of the maharajas and the poverty of others. But great adventures were also reported from the west and Afghanistan, where Britain tried to counter Russia; from the north and the Himalayas, where it tried to counter China; and from the East, where it tried to counter competing colonial powers such as France and the Netherlands.

One particularly fascinating episode was that involving British adventurer James Brooke. He quelled local rebellions in Sarawak and Sabah for the sultan of the mini-state of Brunei (located in between, on the northern half of the huge island of Borneo) and was proclaimed raja as a reward in 1842. The dynasty was continued by his nephew, and Britain proclaimed the states "protectorates" in 1888. During World War I, the nephew was in turn succeeded by his son, who felt forced to hand it over to Britain as a full "crown colony" only much later, after World War II. One recent tourist guide observes that the "colorful history might have come straight out of a romantic Victorian novel" (Oon 2004, p. 97)—and indeed the theme was widely picked up by them, in fictional fantasies variously relocated in Africa (Haggard's Allan Quatermain novels) or Afghanistan (Kipling's story "The Man Who Would Be King"), to which we will return later in this chapter.

Imperial Heroes in Turn-of-the-Century Africa

With the abolition of slavery, West Africa had lost much of its initial interest, and emphasis shifted to Central Africa and its useful natural resources. The lost Scottish missionary David Livingstone was dramatically traced there in 1871 by journalist Henry Morton Stanley. Stanley then became involved in the further exploration of the area and in the 1885 founding of the so-called Congo Free State, sponsored by Belgium's King Leopold II. Stanley became an imperial hero through his newspaper reports and popular books like *Through the Dark Continent* (1878) and *In Darkest Africa* (1890). He denigrated blacks as irretrievably primitive and praised the newly invented machine gun as "invaluable for subduing the heathen" (Read 1983, p. 190).

The Congo Free State was supposedly Leopold's "private property," not a Belgian colony. For a decade, it had a near-monopoly on the production of rubber, for which world demand surged after the introduction of tires for bicycles and cars. White supervisors imposed high delivery quotas on the local blacks, a tactic copied from the Dutch in Indonesia. Whoever did not comply had his hand cut off or his kin taken hostage. Protesting groups were machine-gunned, and their villages were burned. According to a recent American study, the population fell from 20 million to only half that number in just a few decades (Hochschild 1998). It was mostly British missionaries and traders who informed the outside world; the king immediately had his private archives destroyed, but some papers and testimonies resurfaced a century later.[2]

But further imperial heroes of the turn of the century emerged during the escalating confrontation with the "free states" of the Dutch settlers over the control of the best farmland, the native population, and South Africa itself, which was also proving rich in mineral resources such as gold and diamonds. British army officer Robert Stephenson Smyth Baden-Powell was acclaimed for holding out during the turn-of-the-century guerrilla siege of Mafeking, a decisive turning point in the Boer Wars. He had earlier written a military textbook for wilderness survival and scouting, which he later developed into an activity for boys (and later girls) and then into an imperial youth movement, the formula of which was then adopted worldwide. (I was a member during my primary school days.)

Imperial Heroes in Twentieth-Century Arabia

With the advent of the Suez Canal, interest in Egypt meanwhile picked up further, as well as in the whole Arab region between the Mediterranean and the Persian Gulf. This was accelerated by the growing importance of petrol during World War I. A large part of the entire area had been dominated by

Turkey and the great Ottoman Empire, which became an ally of Germany. So it was of major importance to stir Arab resistance.

A key role was played by imperial hero Thomas Edward Lawrence ("Lawrence of Arabia"). Lawrence's work as an archaeologist in Arab lands became a source of intelligence, and during World War I he became a kind of British liaison officer to try to unite Arab tribes. He was later lionized as the "true leader" of Arab independence in the U.K. and U.S. media and in his 1926 autobiographical *Seven Pillars of Wisdom*. This myth has since been challenged by Arab scholars.[3]

But the myth was further enshrined in David Lean's 1962 film *Lawrence of Arabia*, a model for many subsequent exotic adventure movies. Lawrence was played by Peter O'Toole, whose light blue eyes and light blond hair were emphatically stressed. Faisal was played by Alec Guinness, with the eternal Anthony Quinn and Omar Sharif in other "ethnic" roles. In one famous key scene Lawrence, dressed in immaculate white headgear and long robe—an obvious Messiah figure—leads a guerrilla ambush and charge of hundreds of dark Arabs against a Turkish train and has great trouble restraining their bloodthirst. The virgin desert is used as an effective backdrop. A more recent television documentary again celebrated the myth.[4]

Many similar accounts of Anglo-Saxon imperial heroes have inspired other major movies, both in Great Britain and in the United States. The scriptwriters have often copied the original belittling of the representatives of other cultures involved in these very same events—either as bullies or as victims. In more recent decades, there have been superficial attempts to make such stories more "politically correct," but they don't come close to doing real justice to the "others" because critical research would kill the very aspects that gave the story its original larger-than-life proportions in the first place. Non-English-speaking and nonwhite viewers were long of marginal concern anyway, for reasons of purchasing power.

Case Study: Dapper Anna and the King of Siam

So how did all this work out in the case of the 1999 production of *Anna and the King*? In the studio's own view, a long series of experienced scriptwriters had bent over backwards to avoid offending the Thais, their traditions, or their king. Apart from that, its defenders said, it had only a few minor and completely innocent embellishments.

Officials in Bangkok nonetheless felt the concessions were insufficient to warrant their cooperation. Not only were much of the language, accents, expressions and ceremonies plain wrong, they said, but critics also felt the dialogue and the scenes conflicted with the

known historical truth, consistently reflecting Western disdain. Therefore, the local authorities refused access, and the movie was ultimately
shot in neighboring Malaysia. Release in Thailand was forbidden, although many citizens have since seen copies of the videotape or DVD.
There was a protracted debate in Thai newspapers, including in local
English-language dailies such as the *Bangkok Post* and the *Nation*, and
some of it can still be found on their websites.

Some of the discussion even spilled over into the American quality
press, such as the *New York Times* and the *Washington Post.* The overseas *International Herald Tribune* carried an early comment by its "old
Asia hand" Philip Bowring, who observed that "Hollywood and history
seldom make comfortable bedfellows. . . . The king [in earlier versions]
is not evil. But the overall impression is of an exotic, ruthless, semi-
civilized figure. Splendor, concubines, and cruelty are there in abundance. The no-nonsense, very British Anna is made to appear wise,
brave, and beautiful, and also as a key figure at the court, which is far
from reality."[5] So what is the story behind this story? One of my students looked into it for a thesis (Gustavii 2004), and I further delved into
the issue myself.

The kingdom of Siam, today Thailand, was the only country in the
Southeast Asian region that was able to maintain its independence and
was never occupied by an outside power during the modern age, in
spite of the fact that Britain pressured it from the West through the Indian subcontinent and neighboring Burma, whereas France pressured
it from Indochina and neighboring Cambodia. King Mongkut, who
reigned throughout most of the 1850s and 1860s, was keenly interested
in the outside world. He accepted the offer of wives of American
Protestant missionaries to teach some of his women and children English and the ways of the West but felt they were secretly trying to convert them to Christianity. In 1862 he hired a British widow with a young
son as a schoolteacher, on the express condition that she refrain from
indoctrinating them. Yet this Anna Leonowens later claimed to have
propagated Western values at the court. She may also have helped
with an occasional English letter but was far from the "private secretary" that some later made her. After five years she left, reportedly also
in a dispute over her role and pay. The aging king died a year later and
was first succeeded by a regent, then by one of her former pupils,
young Prince Chulalongkorn, who embarked on a series of reforms, including the abolition of slavery.

Leonowens returned to England, left her son in a boarding school in
Ireland, and traveled to the United States, later settling in Canada.

Since she had no income, she set herself to writing her experiences down. This first led to the 1870 book *An English Governess at the Siamese Court*, which was still more or less factual and was serialized in the *Atlantic Monthly*. This was then followed by the 1872–1873 book *The Romance of the Harem*, later also called *Siamese Harem Life*, which was heavily dramatized. It focused on the tragic story of a slave concubine, whom she had not previously mentioned. It made Leonowens a celebrity among abolitionists; she was even presented to Harriet Beecher Stowe, the famous author of *Uncle Tom's Cabin*.

The United States had no consul in Bangkok when she arrived and had accumulated little information about the country. Her accounts were received enthusiastically. The *New York Times* wrote about the *Romance*: "This tropical book disarms criticism." *Appleton's Journal* said it proved that "human nature in a pagan palace, burdened though it may be with a royal ceremonial and covered with jewel and silk attire, is a few shades weaker than elsewhere," since it had "as much lying, hypocrisy, vice, and tyranny as may have been found in the palaces of *Le Grand Monarque*" (e.g., France's Louis XIV, *Le Roi Soleil*). And the *Princeton Review* wrote: "The secrets of an oriental harem are exposed with fidelity, and they reveal wonderful incidents of passion and intrigue, of treachery and cruelty, and also of heroic love and martyr-like endurance under most inhuman tortures." Great Britain had, by contrast, had a diplomatic mission in Bangkok for some time and was better informed. Reviews were much more critical. *Atheneum* was even outright hostile and claimed both books were full of factual errors (Morgan 1991, pp. ix–x; Gustavii 2004, pp. 46–47).

A further step was made when both books were brought to the attention of Margaret Landon. She and her husband were Protestant American missionaries to Thailand during the interwar years, trying to convert local Buddhists. She decided to integrate Anna Leonowens's accounts into one smaller book, add her own further fictional embellishments, and turn it into a novel. To make it even more appealing, she added the suggestion that there must have been something of an impossible romantic attraction between the British widow and the Thai king, and also that she became a major informal adviser on diplomatic affairs. The book *Anna and the King of Siam* came out in 1944, at a time when the United States had become heavily involved in the Pacific war against imperial Japan. Its portrayal of an Oriental despot, his many beautiful women, and their strange ways proved an immediate hit.

Hollywood immediately made it into a film script for a successful movie released in 1946, starring Irene Dunne opposite Rex Harrison.

Richard Rodgers and Oscar Hammerstein in turn decided to turn it into the Broadway musical *The King and I,* which premiered in 1951. The entertainment format brought several further changes. The sixty-year-old monarch was turned into a young fool, with funny habits and strange expressions. His female subjects were made submissive and childish. Song and dance further organized them into homogeneous groups of similar-looking people. All this was in line with contemporaneous stereotypes about Asia. The musical was turned into another movie, released in 1956, starring Yul Brynner in one of his eternal ethnic tyrant roles (all played in similar ways), opposite Deborah Kerr, written by Ernest Lehman and directed by Walter Lang. In 1972 it was also turned into a similar TV series with Yul Brynner opposite Samantha Eggar.

By this time, the few historical facts had been embellished by so many layers of ethnocentric fantasy (Leonowens herself, Landon, Hammerstein, Lehman, and Lang) that it had become mostly fiction. During the 1960s and 1970s, commentators and scholars tried to trace other information about that place and time to verify some of the original account. Very little of it turned out to hold up to critical scrutiny.

Leonowens had always been presented and seen as a typical respectable, white, upper-middle-class Victorian widow. When writing a book about her son, Louis, William Syer Bristowe checked some of the family backgrounds as she had presented them and as they were widely accepted. He found that she had willingly changed almost every single detail of her background, for reasons that are both understandable and excusable (1976, pp. 26–31). She was born three years earlier than she had claimed, not in Wales but in India. There is reason to believe that her grandmother was either Indian or Eurasian, which is interesting in view of her entire attitude.

Her father was not a captain but a sergeant, who did not leave her a small fortune, as she claimed, but absolutely nothing. When she was fourteen years old, she left the home of her mother and stepfather and accompanied a thirty-three-year-old minister on a long trip through the Middle East; he was not married, as she had claimed. When Anne herself did marry, it was to a Mr. Leon Owens, not Captain or even Major Leonowens. He did not leave her a penny, either—and that is how she had become a schoolteacher in Singapore. So she already had a strong tendency to embellish her stories, even before she went to Bangkok as a very minor employee. What did she find there?

It is true that King Mongkut was still an autocratic monarch, but he had already started out on the long path to reform that was continued by his son. Sir John Bowring, the British governor of Hong Kong who negotiated a trade agreement with him, even called him "one of the noblest and most enlightened patriots the Oriental world has ever seen."[6] A foreign monograph on Mongkut says that Leonowens instead "did make him out to be a sort of half-educated savage, likeable perhaps, but capable of quite fiendish cruelty." It adds that he only once mentioned her as "audacious, naughty, and meddlesome," but that "her importance in the life of the king and even in the history of Siam has been grossly exaggerated." It also quotes a ten-year adviser to his son Chulalongkorn, who said he "had never once mentioned Anna in his hearing" (Griswold 1961, pp. 68–69).

It is true that a large area of the walled palace grounds called Nang Harm was reserved for women and children. After twenty-six years as a Buddhist monk, King Mongkut accumulated some one hundred partners in later life. Thirty-five wives and concubines provided him with a total of eighty-two children. This gave all noble families a stake in the monarchy and provided for a range of young princes. Anna taught just a few of these at a time. Morgan reports that a few years before her arrival, there had been one reported incident "in which a nobleman who had tried to win one of the king's concubines was executed, along with his wife" (1991, p. xxxiv).

But that is not the story of Tuptim, the most dramatic and most central story in *The Romance of the Harem*, about a beautiful young concubine who elopes to see a monk with whom she is in love. According to Leonowens, they had been captured, tortured, and burned to death in a grisly manner. Griswold's monograph on Mongkut claims this was a "malicious fabrication" and "lifted almost word for word from old periodicals referring to a time many decades or centuries before" (1961, pp. 68–69). The same held for the "sacrificial murder" of an innocent woman and "underground dungeons" for erring women under the palace—also implausible because of the notoriously high groundwater level in Bangkok.

In 1991 the University Press of Virginia published a reprint of Anna's second book, with a scholarly introduction by Susan Morgan, professor of English. She said that there had been absolutism, polygamy, slavery, and cruelty at the Thai court in those days, that Leonowens was right in criticizing them, and that one should not in any way belittle them. At the same time, Leonowens caricatured them and added pure inventions: "Leonowens's fictional instances of Mongkut's cruelty are unjustified, maybe even slanderous, in attributing to him specific instances of cruelty that I have trouble believing happened quite as she says. . . . The more extreme specifics of Leonowens's tales are melo-dramatic and surely false . . . The tales in the *Romance of the Harem* are all preposterous. But they speak for the women of the harem as no other writing about Nang Harm has." So she concludes: "Are the por-trayals of the Siamese in the two films and the play racist? Absolutely. But is this true of Leonowens's books? Yes again, but neither so sim-plistically and unredemptively" (pp. xxvi–xxxvii).

Mongkut's son, King Chulalongkorn, is reported to have briefly spo-ken again to his former teacher during a late-nineteenth-century visit to London and to have asked her why she had written about his father in this way. One of the other sons, Prince Damrong, gave a charitable an-swer to this question, according to Bristowe: "Mrs. Leonowens added drama to her story in order to make money from her books for the sup-port of her children." He added, "As a governess, she carried far less influence with the king than she claimed" (1976, p. 23). Yet in his book about the Thai monarchy, Prince Chula Chakrabongse still deplored the effect of *The King and I* on Western views: "It is almost as fictional as *The Mikado* by Gilbert and Sullivan, but in its case it was advertised as a documentary" (Morgan 1991, p. XXVI). The 1999 remake, which wil-fully ignored all the new information, was presented in the same way. (One Thai school still maintains a website on the controversy, at www.thaistudents.com).

IMPERIAL HEROES IN FICTION

Around the time this book was being completed, Hollywood was eagerly awaiting a long-postponed new instalment of the blockbuster Indiana Jones series by George Lucas and Steven Spielberg. Indiana Jones is one of the most successful movie characters of all time. The first film, *Raiders of the Lost Ark* (1981), had cost only $23 million to make but had made $384 million at the box office. The 1984 *Temple of Doom* had cost only $28 million but grossed $333 million; the 1989 *Last Crusade* cost $44 million but made almost $500 million at the box office. This brought the total revenue for the trilogy to a $1.23 billion, and the films sat in fifth, eleventh, and sixteenth place on the list of the highest-grossing movies up to that day (with five Lucas and Spielberg movies sharing the other half dozen top spots among themselves).

There can be no doubt, then, that Indiana Jones was indeed a very appeal-ing character, to English-language audiences, but to others as well. But was he a completely new character, or a clever variation on a much older theme that had already proven its appeal in novels and movies long before? And if so, on whom was he based? The trilogy was set during the interwar years, and the larger part was set somewhere within the British Empire: from Egypt and Palestine to India and the Chinese concessions, with occasional excursions to Europe and the Americas. So if we cannot find the model in the United States itself, perhaps we should take a closer look at the prewar popular culture of the British Empire.

The development of literacy and education after the Industrial Revolution had contributed greatly to book production and reading in Great Britain. In 1871, some 94,000 people were employed in the paper and printing trades; by 1901, this had more than doubled to 212,000. The annual output of books also more than doubled, from some forty-six hundred per year to ten thousand per year, over the same three decades, and the emphasis increasingly shifted from moralizing literature to light entertainment. In the end, the Victorians were estimated to have published more than forty thousand novels (Read 1983).

Low-priced "penny" novels made them accessible to all, as did new public libraries and private circulating libraries. The number of registered "writers and journalists" almost quadrupled, from 3,400 to nearly 13,800 over the three decades from 1881 to 1911. Meanwhile, international copyright laws had considerably expanded their potential market, not only in the empire but also in the United States. One of the major new light-entertainment genres was the colonial or imperial adventure novel, which further lionized the exploits of white discoverers, pioneers, and settlers and "naturalized" their domination of foreign lands and peoples.

One favorite format was to set these adventurers on the trails of forerunners of Western civilization: the Roman Legions, the Greek (Macedonian) Alexander, ancient Egypt, the Jewish King Solomon, and the Queen of Sheba, whose empire was thought to have spanned the southern entrance to the Red Sea, somewhere in current Yemen and/or Ethiopia. This was supposedly also where some trading routes led from deep inside the African interior. The rediscovery of lost empires, civilizations, and races (white, brown, or black), their remnants somehow surviving deep inside some valley or jungle, was a major theme.

Three of the major novelists of these days were H. Rider Haggard, Joseph Conrad, and Rudyard Kipling.

Haggard was the first and foremost among them all, although he had been largely forgotten by the general public when Indiana Jones came along during the 1980s. His father had been a missionary, but the son felt conversions made no sense. He became a landowner and lawyer, as well as an early advocate of a military showdown with the Dutch Boers over the control of South Africa, since it had a moderate climate similar to that of Europe and was proving rich in agricultural land and mineral deposits. He turned to book writing by the mid-1880s; his exotic adventure novels were an immediate success and a major boon to the imperial enterprise.

As one reviewer of his autobiography later wrote: "It is not to be doubted that [his] South African romances filled many a young fellow with longing to go into the wide spaces of those lands . . . and have thus aided far more than we can ever know in bringing British settlers and influence into the new country" (Katz 1987, p. 1). In that same autobiography, Haggard admitted that the swashbuckling hero Allan Quatermain was "only myself set in a variety of imagined situations" (p. 32). In his memoirs, novelist Graham Greene confessed in turn that he had almost signed up for colonial service, just because of the engaging Quatermain tales, as Wendy Katz noted in the first major study about Haggard, titled *Rider Haggard and the Fiction of Empire* (p. 1).

Quatermain was "once Britannia's greatest hero." A website for Steven Spielberg's blockbuster movie *Raiders of the Lost Ark* also observes that "Allan Quatermain is arguably the first Indiana Jones–type adventurer, with his khaki clothes and his broad-rim hat." The fictional character's life supposedly ran from 1815 to 1886. The first and most famous novel of the series was *King Solomon's Mines* (1885), in which a prim English woman hires the "great white hunter" Allan Quatermain[7] to help her trace her husband, who has vanished in darkest Africa while searching for remnants of the ancient mines that reportedly provided the mythical sovereign with an endless supply of gold and diamonds.

It is thus a romantic variation on the archetypical Stanley and Livingstone theme, pairing a man and a woman to make it more interesting. There are at least four successive film versions of the story (of 1937, 1950, 1977, and 1985; see below) and many more imitations and variations. The next novel, *Allan Quatermain* (1887), had his comrade Henry marry a native queen and thus become the ruler of a forgotten kingdom hidden deep inside a closed valley. Quatermain appeared to die there but was later revived in a long series of prequels.

The Who2 website with profiles says that "Allan Quatermain was the rifle-toting, native-befriending, treasure-seeking hero . . . [who] struggled to keep a proper Englishman's stiff upper lip while hunting elephants, battling or befriending Zulus, chasing diamonds, discovering lost civilizations, and facing other thrills and terrors of the mysterious 'Dark Continent.'" It adds: "Rider's stories are considered racist, sexist, or just plain inappropriate by some modern readers."[8] A website on British Empire literature adds that "This is one of the best Victorian novels that you could ever want to read. Why? Because it is fun!" It also adds: "Of course, the racism and the sexism can grate against the modern ear, but this is what Victorians were like."[9]

Haggard admired the Zulus as "noble savages" and sometimes saw the relativity of European civilization. But in his last years, he also stated his "conviction that the future safety and greatness of the British Empire depended upon the re-distribution of Empire population" of white origin, and also that "the great ul-timate war ... will be that between the white and the coloured races" (Katz 1987, p. 148). Katz concludes: "Throughout his prewar life, Haggard's nationalism, vulgar heroism, and authoritarianism were never far from anti-Semitism, xeno-phobia, and other reactionary sentiments. Following the [First World] war, however, these views combined with his vehement antitrade unionism and anti-Bolshevism, among other aversions, to yield a frighteningly protofascist men-tality" (p. 149).

A second author who emphasized the tragic rather than the heroic side of the imperial adventure was Joseph Conrad (born Teodor Josef Conrad Ko-rzeniowski). Conrad was a seafarer of Polish origin who settled in Britain af-ter twenty years of travels. At least a dozen of his stories were made into films. One of his trips had brought him up the African Congo River for four months, into what he called "the vilest scramble for loot that ever disfigured the history of the human conscience"—that is, the aforementioned "free state" considered as "private property" by the Belgian King Leopold II. Conrad's fa-mous *Heart of Darkness* (1902) tells the story of an ivory trader deep in the in-terior who has fallen to the primitive level of the local population and engages in human sacrifice as their purported god. It inspired part of Francis Ford Coppola's award-winning Vietnam movie *Apocalypse Now* (1979) and was also turned into a television film in 1994.

A third author is still considered the British imperial author par excellence: Joseph Rudyard Kipling, who wrote the turn-of-the-century poem with the famous lines "Take up the White Man's burden and reap his old reward: The blame of those ye better, the hate of those ye guard"—which was "in its im-mediate context an appeal to the United States" to take over some overseas re-sponsibilities, for instance from colonial Spain (Read 1983, p. 483). Kipling often collaborated with Haggard, and both were admirers of the aforemen-tioned imperial hero Baden-Powell. At least ten of Kipling's stories have been made into films, some (like *The Jungle Book)* even more than once.

One typical example of Kipling's work is the story *The Man Who Would Be King* (1888), about two British army officers who want to set themselves up as rulers along today's frontier between Afghanistan and Pakistan. After this fails, they trek through the Khyber Pass, and one of them is mistaken for a God and is indeed recognized as a king and handed huge treasures, although things turn sour thereafter. (The story was also inspired by James Brooke's afore-mentioned feat in setting himself up as ruler of North Borneo). The story was made into a film in 1975, directed by John Huston and starring Sean Connery and Michael Caine. The ten-minute sequence in which they discover a valley with a lost city founded by Alexander, are almost killed by the local monks, then saved by an ancient Freemason symbol, recognized as heavenly rulers, and then led to a huge chamber bursting with precious metals and gems embodies the archetypical "imperial adventure" dream in a nutshell.

Another example is Kipling's poem "Gunga Din," which inspired the famous 1939 movie with the same title. It was directed by George Stevens and starred Cary Grant, Victor McLaglen, and Douglas Fairbanks Jr. as "three musketeer" British army sergeants, sent to a remote mountainous outpost to confront a notorious group of native Indian rebels, the "Thugs" (the British inserted the term into English vernacular as a generic name). The quest for an exotic treasure is again a major theme. The Virgin *Film Guide* notes that the film "has a bit of everything—humour, suspense, spectacle, and a heavy dose of racism, imperialism, and xenophobia" (2001, p. 316). Spielberg conceded that *Gunga Din* was one of the major sources of inspiration for the second Indiana Jones movie, and it does indeed contain many of the same elements.

So the popular adventure novels had gradually been turned into popular adventure movies. Shohat and Stam (1994) have already pointed out that the press photo and then the film newsreel, but most of all the silent features in black and white and then the sound features in color, became the vehicles par excellence for enlisting popular audiences to the overseas enterprise. Exotic lands and peoples were picturesque: Not merely describing but actually showing them further piqued the audience's curiosity, alternately provoking marvel and horror.

At the beginning of World War I, there were already thirty-five hundred cinemas in existence in Britain; by the beginning of World War II that figure had further exploded. Many imperial adventure movies were coproduced with, or exported to, the United States. That is where young Steven Spielberg admittedly saw and admired them.

Case Study: Indiana Jones as an Imperial Hero

We have already noted that Indiana Jones is one of the most successful Hollywood blockbuster series of all time. It resulted from the collaboration between George Lucas as producer/storywriter and Steven Spielberg as director; the two had met during their student days in California. Lucas had previously studied anthropology and comparative religion, among other subjects, at Modesto Junior College, and Spielberg had studied English at Long Beach State before venturing into filmmaking. These specific backgrounds would be of considerable importance to their future collaboration.

While doing research during the early 1970s, Lucas had become interested in comparative mythology (we will return to its significance with the discussion of the Star Wars series in chapter 10). Already in 1973 this had spawned the first ideas for a film or series about an archaeologist whose adventures would connect him to the quest for cultural artifacts and megamyths, and he subsequently recruited a colleague to work on possible storylines.

Lucas later escaped the hype surrounding the 1977 release of the first *Star Wars* film by joining another couple on vacation to Hawaii with his wife. Spielberg had just completed *Encounters of the Third Kind* and also went there to vacation with his wife. When Spielberg told Lucas he would love to do some kind of James Bond series, the latter pitched the archaeologist-adventurer character to him. Spielberg wanted to revive the B-films and popular adventure serials of his youth, and the final products were indeed full of—often literal—references to scenes and dialogues, characters and props, of such predecessors, in an early postmodern game of intertextuality. The character would be promoted as "Indiana Jones—The new hero from the creators of *Jaws* and *Star Wars.*"

The duo at first envisaged Tom Selleck, who had become an icon as an ad model for the paradigmatic "Marlboro man," as their hero, but he was tied up as an actor in the TV series *Magnum, P. I.* Spielberg then met Lucas's *Star Wars* hero Harrison Ford and chose him to play the role (although Lucas was at first reluctant to let him go). Gradually, the hero was made less physically glamorous and more psychologically vulnerable than other action heroes, whereas humor was brought in to provide more complexity to the script (and mask the stereotypes). Over the years, furthermore, the hero evolved from just another immature, wandering adult with vague love interests into a kind of father figure to a younger sidekick and son figure: a proven recipe for an adolescent audience.

Indiana Jones was made into an icon by giving him the idiosyncratic fedora hat (which derived from Allan Quatermain's South African settler hat, was reminiscent of the American cowboy hat, and has since been adopted by would-be archaeologists around the world) as well as the whip of Zorro, rather than more contemporary firearms. As for storylines, they may also have been inspired by the rather similar comic strip series *Tintin*, created by Belgian author Hergé, famous on the European continent. The main character of *Tintin* was initially a Boy Scout but evolved into a roving reporter, crisscrossing the world. After the first Indiana Jones film, Spielberg even took an option on the *Tintin* stories then let it expire, renewing it only recently.

During the 1980s, there were three separate installments of the Indiana Jones series, at three- or four-year intervals. A fourth installment has often and long been postponed but is now scheduled for release in 2008. The first installment was *Raiders of the Lost Ark* in 1981. It brought Indy to the British colony of Egypt, where Arabs, under Nazi guidance, had just made a discovery of the utmost ideological and military importance (i.e., access to a new weapon of mass destruction). One famous street scene shows a series of confrontations and chases, like the (improvised) one in which a frightful Arab dressed in a black robe juggles threateningly with the archetypical scimitar sword, and Indy laconically shoots him. This invariably provokes loud cheers and laughter in an adolescent audience (and has since been said to aptly sum up American endeavours in the Middle East).

The second installment, *The Temple of Doom* (1984), was inspired by the aforementioned colonial-era movie *Gunga Din*, and the opening scene was inspired by the colonial-era villain Fu Manchu. In the movie, Indy rescues both a precious altar stone and the children of a starving village. They are kept as slaves in the splendid palace of a maharaja—or rather, in a mine under it—by the ancient secret society of stranglers or Thugs (from the Sanskrit *sthag*, meaning "conceal"), who are venerating Kali (the dark or destructive incarnation of a Hindu goddess) and who chant: "The British in India will be slaughtered." The human sacrifice scenes (ripping out a throbbing heart by hand, slowly lowering people into a flaming inferno, using drugs and voodoo) were particularly horrifying.[10]

The third installment was *The Last Crusade* in 1988. It once again brought Indy to the Middle East, with references to Byzantium/Istanbul and Alexandreta/Iskenderun, in a principality that looks like a mixture of Turkish and Arab lands under British control at the time. In order to search for the enigmatic chalice of Jesus's Last Supper, in which Christ's blood was also reportedly collected during the Crucifixion, the Nazis buy the cooperation of the local ruler with a trunk full of treasures stolen from Nazi victims and (even more) by a real Rolls-Royce car. Most Turks and Arabs (also marked by iconic headgear such as fezzes and turbans) are once again allied with the Germans, and a significant portion of the film is a comic-book version of Nazi rallies and book burnings in Berlin, featuring Indy requesting an autograph of Adolf Hitler in order to be able to escape.

The last theatrical movie carried an introductory scene with the young Indiana Jones as a Boy Scout, played by River Phoenix. This inspired George Lucas to do three seasons of a thirty-two-part television series, *The Young Indiana Jones Chronicles* (1992–1996). The first installment once again brought him to Egypt to meet the aforementioned Lawrence of Arabia, one of his original role models. Subsequent installments showed him meeting a wide range of other Western luminaries in historical settings, through World War I and the interwar period. The show's ratings were initially high but dropped off quickly as the series proved disappointing, and it was moved from the ABC network to the Family Channel in the United States.

What was the recipe for all these stories: what are the metanarratives and subtexts? Of course, we again find the familiar themes of holy temples, secret underground rooms, and overflowing treasure troves, booby-trapped centuries or millennia ago with falling stone doors and giant rolling balls, with wooden spikes and poisoned arrows. And of course there are the eternal masses of creepy animals from bugs and spiders to snakes and bats in the dark, and wild animals such as lions and elephants outside; the repulsive dishes with fried beetles, sheep eyeballs, live monkey brains, and live baby snakes. This is the standard fare of scary situations in the colonial exotic adventure story, as are the perpetual shootouts and obligatory chases on horseback and camelback, on motorcycles and in cars, in speedboats and biplanes, with submarines and Zeppelins thrown in for good measure.

Apart from Indy's immediate companions, these five to six hours of theatrical film hardly show *any* normal foreigners *at all*, whether French or German, Latino or Native American, Turk or Arab, Indian or Chinese. They are almost all sinister or inert, as villains or traitors or as passive victims unable to take any initiative of their own to change their exploitation or repression by the local potentates and their overseas German allies, never by the British (or Americans). Just as in the 1885 *Allan Quatermain* and similarly jingoistic novels of one hundred years earlier, the Anglo-Saxon liberator naturally has light blue eyes and dark blond hair.

The ideologies in the films go much further, however, because they are tied in with other Western megamyths. This is obscured by the prologue of every movie, which invariably sets us on the wrong track (South America/Portugal, China/Nepal, Utah/Venice). But the main stories form a coherent trilogy about the origins of good and evil, conveniently placed on the eve of World War II, between 1933 and 1939. The treasure hunt is always a quest for a mythical object invested with supernatural power: the Ark, the Grail, the holy stone. The bad guys (Nazis and thugs) are after it for money and power, but the good guys (Indiana Jones and his friends) only want to rescue it for its great symbolic and cultural value. The stories thus acquire a semblance of depth as they happen to derive from the three major stages of Western civilization and its spread abroad.

The Ark and the stone tablets with the Ten Commandments are linked to the origins of Judeo-Christian religion itself (and the obsession with them was a major factor in the recurrent derailment of the Middle Eastern "peace process").[11] The Grail and the Crusades refer to the Passion of the Christ as described in the Gospels; they are also directly linked to the next phase, in which Christianity was forced to confront the third major monotheistic religion, Islam, in the battle for Jerusalem and the ancient Jewish Holy Land. The holy stone is linked to the third phase, where Western civilization has moved beyond Europe and the Mediterranean and is thus forced to confront other indigenous religions such as Hinduism within its colonial empire.

The metanarrative and subtext in these American blockbuster movies is thus quite similar to the British popular novels recruiting the public for colonial and imperial adventure. The white hero may be considered an ordinary guy at home, but once he moves abroad he is automatically accepted by the local people as a smart, courageous, and benevolent leader. The locals are unable to manage their own affairs and must confront local leaders who are proverbially cruel and corrupt, and who find overseas allies in the duplicitous French or the brutish Germans. The Turks and Arabs are presented time and again as the natural allies of the Nazis; the British colonial presence in Egypt and India, by contrast, is consistently naturalized.

Lucas and Spielberg most likely did not consciously choose this ideological framework. They felt they had just thought up some innocuous Californian stories by borrowing familiar elements from older British stories and films. They were unaware of, and perhaps ill equipped to see through, the hidden implications of this whole approach—and they did not care very much either. (Spielberg later publicly expressed regret at the caricature of the Nazis, but not that of Arabs or Indians). Yet many outsiders abroad did immediately see and recognize what Lucas and Spielberg had not. The Indian government, for one, refused to loan the Rose Palace of Jaipur in Rajasthan after reading the *Temple of Doom* script, and shooting therefore had to be moved to the neighbouring country of Sri Lanka (formerly Ceylon).

Ian Freer's monograph on Spielberg's work notes that "*Raiders* came under criticism for perpetuating racial stereotypes and reinforcing old prejudices: be it filling up the bad-guy roster with spineless South Americans, vicious Arabs, and Caribbean pirates or transforming Nazis into cartoony relief" (2001, p. 105). James Clarke's monograph on Spielberg's work also noted criticism about the "possibly unthinking racism toward nonwhite cultures" of the Indiana Jones films (2001, p. 33). Shohat and Stam's overview also discusses the *Temple of Doom*: "In the world of *Indiana Jones*, third-world cultures are synopsized as theme-park clichés drawn from the Orientalist repertoire: India is all dreamy spirituality . . . ; Shanghai is all gongs and rickshaws," adding: "In a classic splitting operation, the third world is both demonized and infantilized: non-Western adult characters are evil; children are eager, innocent, and pro-Western" (1994, pp. 124–25).

In spite (or maybe because) of all this, the Indiana Jones series became a very popular classic, spawning several spoofs, imitations, and variations. The Justine series of low-budget features (discussed in chapter 6) was inspired by a famous scene in *Raiders of the Lost Ark* (and again hinted at in the *The Last Crusade*): "As Indy teaches his archaeology class, a besotted student bats her eyes revealing 'I love you' scrawled on the lids" (Freer 2001, p. 100).

But Indiana Jones also had a number of mainstream imitations and variations, just as frequently repeated on prime-time television. One series, starring Michael Douglas, Kathleen Turner, and Danny DeVito, is often repeated on mainstream television. The first installment was *Romancing the Stone* (1984), with an intrigue also built around a treasure map and the quest for a precious gem in the South American jungle. Its sequel was *The Jewel of the Nile* (1985), built around a popular Bedouin revolt against a rich sheikh potentate, in a mixture of Egypt and Yemen as well as Saudi Arabia and Kuwait. But according to the Virgin *Film Guide*, in the latter movie "it's hard to overlook the racist depiction of Arabs, which is markedly less jovial than the stereotypical treatment of Latinos in the first film" (2001, p. 391).

Encouraged by the persistent success of such colonial adventure films, even the original discredited superhero archetype Allan Quatermain made a comeback in a series of films starring Richard Chamberlain opposite Sharon Stone. The series was produced by Menahem Golan, his cousin Yoram Globus, and their Cannon Group. According to Golan's B-film maxim, "If you make an American film with a beginning, a middle, and an end with a budget of less than five million, you must be an idiot to lose money" (Walker 2001, p. 192–93).

The first installment was the centenary remake of *King Solomon's Mines* (1985), with all the original racist stereotypes about Germans and Turks and Arabs and blacks, and even cannibals dancing around a proverbial huge cooking pot with the white protagonists in it. It is meant to be funny, but it is not. The second installment was *Allan Quatermain and the Lost City of Gold* (1987). There was another ambitious American television version of *Allan Quatermain and the Ancestor's Stone* in 2004. The year before, a film version of *The League of Extraordinary Gentlemen*, which also included the Allan Quatermain character (portrayed by Sean Connery) as one of its main "classical" heroes, was released.

A more recent variation on these same exotic adventure themes is the series around the comic strip hero Lara Croft, which has moved its base from the U.K. to the United States. She originally burst onto the scene as the "daughter of a lord" living in a "huge country estate," with her own butler and gadget designer. The successful 1996 video game *Tomb Raider* was followed by new installments almost every year. In 2001 a feature film with the same title was released, starring Angelina Jolie, and in 2003 a second one, *Cradle of Life*, was released. Both movies combine the archetypical exotic adventure and Indiana Jones format with a past-and-future mix reminiscent of the Stargate films and television series: There is a quest for an enigmatic object (first the All-Seeing Eye in a Triangle of Light, an Illuminati and Freemason symbol, then Pandora's box), which is linked to ancient myths and even cosmic events. The chase brings her to famed archaeological settings, such as the Angkor Temple in Cambodia and the Great Wall in China. Of course, we never learn much about these foreign lands or people or cultures; they are merely inert backdrops to the fast-paced but highly repetitive action: shoot-shriek-run, shoot-shriek-run.

The hero has supposedly become more contemporary and "politically correct" in this case, by making the man a woman and the white protagonist a vaguely café au lait one through the use of heavy makeup, in line with slowly "globalizing" beauty ideals of haute couture shows and fashion magazine covers. Some reviewers considered this "empowerment" for a new generation of emancipated girls, but it also imprisoned them once again in the familiar mold of a Barbie doll with supersize breasts (corrected since), so dear to the commercial media and the fashion and cosmetics industry.

Friends and Foes:
Spy, Action, and War Movies

What about war movies, or, in a wider sense, movies about conflict between countries? Spy movies like the James Bond series, where one of "us" is sent on a dangerous mission to the "other side," to gather information or take action; action movies like the Rambo films, where a one-person commando or a commando unit crosses the border to hit a larger target; war movies like Black Hawk Down, *where a limited military force is sent to intervene in civil strife in a war-torn country such as Somalia; or full-scale war movies such as* Pearl Harbor. *What are the typical characters and storylines, and what is their relation to real or realistic events? Do these polished images in turn influence presidents and commanders, draftees and civilians, in their simplistic approach to complex conflicts such as Iraq?*

Imagine yourself a national hero. You are called upon to defend your country, your alliance, your civilization. You are backed up by all its military might, its technological superiority, its endless supply of sophisticated weaponry and explosives. You are courageous, resourceful, persistent. You use legitimate violence; you have a "license to kill." Your adversaries are despicable tyrants, anyway, repressing and exploiting their own people. Crowds welcome their liberators, acclaim you in the street, wave your flag, throw flowers at you. It is a great feeling—one conveyed by most movies about armed conflict, whether about spies, commando operations, or military units.

The problem, of course, is that they convey an extremely simplified and polished image. Most armed conflicts are woven into complex and even contradictory international situations, where tactical and strategic interests of the various parties play a decisive role. They entail a long and intermittent history of animosity, over vital areas and resources, minority populations and shifting borders, stirring and entertaining hate. Even today, there is hardly ever a "surgical strike" without "collateral damage," meaning civilians—often the elderly, women, and children—being killed or maimed for life. Every day brings new excesses: abuse, torture, arbitrary killings. But blockbuster movies hardly ever show them—at least done by those on "our" side.

Young males have always been the prime audience for such movies about armed conflict, and for movies *tout court*. They are in the process of transferring their allegiance from the family to the larger community and society and are particularly receptive to such simplistic images of patriotic heroes and enemy threats. At this age, they tend to cultivate the male virtues of courage and strength, but they also have the exact age to be drafted or recruited into the army for real. Usually they do not have wives or children yet, and their loss or maiming at the battlefront are thought to cause less harm. This is one unnamed logic behind armed conflict, and behind films about armed conflict.

Conventional warfare with uniformed soldiers is waged by states, furthermore, at some kind of front line, during a limited period of time. In the course of the modern age, however, even conventional warfare has on the one hand increasingly drawn on civilian support on the home front (also in industrial production) and has on the other hand created ever higher percentages of civilian victims—running well into 90 percent. This is even more true for unconventional warfare, from (counter)insurgency to (counter)terrorism. So, most of the time, there is no such thing as a neat and clean war.

The twentieth century has seen more victims of military and political violence than any other century; some even claim it may have made more victims than all previous conflicts of the modern age put together. That is why media coverage in general, and audiovisual fiction in particular, have become all important for maintaining public morale. And that is what they do. In her brief overview of the war film genre, Susan Hayward concludes that it always "tends to glorify or put forward heroics of a particular triumphant nation. Only rarely do these films look at the horrors of war" (2003, p. 449).

SPY MOVIES AND THE COLD WAR

The spy movie is a particularly attractive genre. The hero is a civilian we can easily identify with, but his actions (and he is usually male) take place in a highly charged military context abroad. Spy movies are about good and bad, life and death. Spy novels developed first and foremost in Great Britain, against the background of the rise and fall of its world empire and the successive challenges by newly emerging continental European powers such as Germany and Russia. Many such spy novels were rather realistic, based on the autobiographical experiences of their authors in intelligence gathering (e.g., the 1928 *Ashenden* by William Somerset Maugham).

Graham Greene also worked as a British agent. He became one of the most prolific writers of his generation, and his works were translated more often onto the screen than those of any other twentieth-century author. Many of his stories deal with the shady side of national and international politics, the power motives behind and the counterproductive effects of imperial meddling abroad. Two of the best-known films about them are set in the late 1950s: *The Quiet American*, about Vietnam, and *Our Man in Havana*, about Cuba. After 9/11, distributor Miramax blocked the release of the worthwhile 2001 remake of the former (with Michael Caine) for more than a year. Miramax chairman Harvey Weinstein commented, "You needed to have your head examined if you thought this was a time for questioning America."[1]

John Le Carré (the pen name of David Cornwell) also worked as a spy before he turned to writing. Cold War novels such as *The Spy Who Came in from the Cold* and *The Looking-Glass War* were turned into successful movies in 1966 and 1970. They were supremely realistic precisely because they highlighted the unheroic aspects of the everyday business: the infighting within bureaucracies, the maneuvering between agencies, the uncertainties surrounding assignments, a world of compromises, with moral ambiguities on both sides. Not surprisingly, he too became a skeptic about imperial meddling abroad, for instance, in the hilarious *The Tailor of Panama* (2001). But—surprisingly or not—producers and the public far preferred the totally unrealistic adventures of the mythical British superspy James Bond.

Case Study: James Bond's License to Kill

James Bond got a new lease on his long pop-cult life just before Christmas 2006. His fifth (or sixth, see below) movie incarnation, Daniel Craig, was dark blond with light blue eyes: more physical and common, less elegant and aloof, than his immediate predecessor, Pierce Brosnan. Most reviews of the film were rather positive, and within just a few weeks, the movie had already made $500 million, surpassing all its predecessors.

The installment harkened back to the first of the James Bond novels, *Casino Royale*, and (falsely) claimed to have remained relatively close to the original story, although it was partly reset into the latest, tiniest, and most backward of the former Yugoslav republics, Montenegro, dressed up for the occasion as a kind of glamorous new Monaco with imaginary classical five-star hotels, impressive motorways, and high-speed rail links.

But the movie also added some other highly topical themes and spectacular scenes. In a post-9/11 world, terrorists had of course become the major bad guys—with even an attempt to blow up a new double-decker super-jumbo airplane at a Miami airport. Private armies in East Africa led to an early money chase in Uganda and along high-rise cranes on the island of Madagascar. And a late money chase in Venice led to an entire antique building sinking into the canal. So Bond remained his good old self.

As noted in the 2006 book, *The Man Who Saved Britain* by Simon Winder, Bond is "like a hamster with his wheel; he performs the same narrow set of functions over and over."[2]

"Gunning down people while sipping fine old brandies, Bond has certainly created a comforting nostalgia for the British, an amusing sardonic role model for Americans, and (with the roots of so many faiths) he comfortably feeds into many countries" preexisting ideas."[3]

By the time of the fortieth anniversary of the series in 2002, the hero had already downed fourteen Martinis ("shaken, not stirred"), fifty girls, and 225 opponents. On that previous occasion, the twentieth James Bond in the main series had also been released to great fanfare: *Die Another Day*. At that point in time, James Bond had already become the most profitable movie character of all time, as the main series had earned $3 to $4 billion. It was estimated that half of the Earth's population has seen at least one James Bond film. There were endless imitations, and spoofs such as Derek Flint and Austin Powers, which ultimately became almost as successful as the Bond films themselves.

Interestingly enough, the oldest spoof had long been based on the very same *Casino Royale*. It was the one book for which the rights had been sold separately at an early stage. So after the main series of spy movies had already taken off, the owners of the rights to this one and only installment had decided to make a buck with a satire filmed by John Huston and four other directors. The film featured David Niven playing a James Bond interrupting his retirement, but also Peter Sellers, Woody Allen, Orson Welles, Ursula Andress, Jacqueline Bisset, Jean Paul Belmondo, and numerous other guest stars. It was ludicrous, hilarious, and totally incoherent.

But what about the famous character? It is not an exaggeration to say that the original James Bond stories provide a typically escapist and compensatory fantasy, not very "politically correct," at that, for a

British Empire in decline after the loss of India (and later even of the crucial link of the Suez Canal), for lower and middle classes in a country with a civil service still heavily dominated by an archaic upper class, and for men challenged by female emancipation and women's lib. What is surprising, however, is that the later film versions were also eagerly adopted by audiences abroad, from North America to western Europe and far beyond, often by the very groups that were implicitly denigrated by the stories and films. Somehow, everyone wanted to identify with the cartoonlike male chauvinist white elite superman.

Author Ian Fleming's personal obsessions partly derived from his family background. His father, Valentine, was the wealthy son of a self-made Scottish banker, conservative member of Parliament, and friend to Winston Churchill. His mother, Evelyn Ste. Croix Rose, claimed a long aristocratic or even royal lineage and was a frivolous socialite. Valentine "died a hero" in World War I, it was said, when Ian was still a child. His elder brother, Peter, was kind of an envied role model: first at the elite schools of Eton and Oxford, then in journalism and intelligence, and finally as a writer.

Ian followed a diplomatic course at the Foreign Office, found work as a journalist, and went to Moscow for Reuters—among other things. After the war he organized the foreign desk at the newspaper group of Lord Kemsley. It has been noted that many of such journalists occasionally doubled for intelligence. During World War II, Fleming worked at the headquarters of the Naval Intelligence Service and became the assistant to its head. It was during these years that he made the observations that later entered into his spy novels. Several real-life spies of those days are mentioned as possible models for James Bond: Fitzroy Maclean, a founding member of the SAS commando organization, who had been parachuted into Yugoslavia and had advised Churchill to support the resistance forces of the Communist Tito rather than those of the royalist Mihailovic there, and Biffy Dunderdale, an MI5 chief in Paris who used to flaunt his secret status by driving around in a Rolls.

Fleming was both a snob and a playboy, maintained a rather expensive lifestyle after the war with fast cars and beautiful women ("just as pets," he told a friend at the time), and planned to supplement his income by writing novels—particularly after his dalliance with Lady Anne Rothermere, the wife of the media mogul, led to her pregnancy and divorce. So he retired to his winter home in Jamaica, then still a British colony, to write a new novel every year (Simpson 2002b). Looking for a strong protagonist name, he came across a book titled *Birds of the West Indies*, written by a Harvard ornithologist who lived nearby: one James

Bond. (The book makes a brief appearance in *Die Another Day*—an inside joke.) Fleming looked up to the sophisticated Noel Coward, who also lived nearby, but the playwright looked down upon the novelist as an upstart poseur: "James Bond was Ian's dream fantasy of what he would [have] liked to be—you know, ruthless and dashing—it's got a schoolboy quality."[4]

The first Bond novel to come out, in 1953, was the aforementioned *Casino Royale*, followed at annual intervals by others. With initial sales of forty to sixty thousand copies apiece, the books did reasonably well, but were no million-sellers yet. Real popularity came only after the *Daily Express* began serializing them and published a comic strip version shortly thereafter—even if its sister publication, the *Sunday Express*, later defined Bond as an "arch exponent of pop fascism" (Smith & Lavington 2002, p. 37). Sales were further boosted when the American magazine *Playboy* began serializing the later novels.

But what about the nature of the stories? Fleming once said that the James Bond books were just "fairy tales for adults." But Russian semiologist Vladimir Propp had previously observed that "all fairy tales are of one type in regard to their structure," and Italian semiologist Umberto Eco had said that the same held for 007. He identified nine elements (not always appearing in the same order): "A: M [his boss] gives a task to Bond. B: The villain appears to Bond (perhaps in a vicarious form). C: Bond gives a first check to the villain, or the villain gives a first check to Bond. D: 'The girl' shows herself to Bond. E: Bond possesses 'the girl' or begins her seduction. F: The villain captures Bond and—either simultaneously or at different moments—'the girl.' G: The villain tortures Bond and, sometimes, 'the girl.' H: Bond beats the villain, killing him or his representatives, or helping in their killing. I: Bond, convalescing, possesses 'the girl,' whom he then loses; she either leaves him or is killed by the villain" (Bennett & Woollacott 1987, pp. 70–71). Larry Tritten developed an even more elaborate formula on how to "make your own James Bond movie" (Berger 1992, pp. 120–23).

But real international notoriety and wealth were only to be found in the United States and in television series by that time, even if progress on that score was limited and halting. It is true that rights for the first novel, *Casino Royale*, had been sold for a thousand pounds, ultimately resulting in a teleplay broadcast by the American network CBS in the framework of its *Chrysler Climax Mystery Theatre*. But it was no great success, and the plan for a further series of thirty-two was quickly shelved. In *From Russia with Love*, then, Fleming seemed to kill his ultra-British hero, and he shifted his attention to developing a more

Americanized hero for New York media mogul Henry Morgenthau, who had designs for a pan-Caribbean television network and also had contacts at NBC. The title was *James Gunn, Secret Agent*, also known as *Commander Jamaica*. The project stalled, but the script for the pilot later evolved into the outline of a sixth James Bond novel and the first theatrical film of the main series, *Dr. No*.

Meanwhile, Canadian producer Harry Saltzman had taken an option for film rights to the Bond novels for a mere thousand dollars. He scoured the United States to find a partner but encountered little enthusiasm until he met Albert Broccoli, who had just set up in the film business, after a lucky win at the races. Together, they founded Eon Productions and persuaded the major studio United Artists to give Bond a try. The financial backers seriously doubted whether even the budget of less than a million dollars would be easily earned back at the box office. Yet it was at this point in time that the James Bond phenomenon as we know it finally took off.

The film series started in 1961–1962, with new installments every other year on average. Note that maintaining the hawkish tone of the original Bond novels was considered risky for these movies, as the Cold War had already begun to thaw. So Fleming adapted both the format and the villains of the novels, whereas Saltzman and Broccoli did even more so in the movies, by making them more ambiguous and campy. This is how James Bond was turned into a worldwide and lasting success, appealing to a wider audience. The novels had now become available in pocket editions and overseas translations, and sales began to soar. After Fleming's untimely death, the publishers even invited other authors to continue the now-profitable series.

By that time James Bond had become more than just a series of books and films: He had become one of the first true multimedia phenomena. Real-life tidbits about his first incarnation, Sean Connery, filled the gossip columns and popular magazines—even though Fleming had first dismissed him as "that great snorting lorry driver" according to one screenwriter (in the aforementioned documentary). Images of the "Bond girls" filled the lifestyle pages and men's magazines. The theme songs filled the hit parades and video charts. Bond became a complex phenomenon, and every new release added a new layer. Postmodernists later pointed out that part of the fun was the way these elements resonated with each other in a never-ending game of cross-references and intertextuality. Yet certain underlying themes remained relatively stable, even if they were alternately questioned and reaffirmed.

In the eyes of the outside world, James Bond was a typically British hero with a stiff upper lip: uniquely phlegmatic and laconic, with a dry sense of humor. His values were also apparently British, but as soon as television and film came along, he broadened his base to become a truly Anglo-American hero, a Euro-American hero, a Plato-to-NATO hero—that is to say, a hero of Western civilization as a whole, "one of the seven greatest legendary champions of Christendom," according to Anne Boyd, on a par with Saint George the dragon slayer (Bennett & Woollacott 1987, p. 255–56).

When he was conceived, Great Britain and its rulers were still at the pinnacle of the international class system. So James Bond was given all the trappings of an overly confident, elite white playboy, a connoisseur of the high life, but in such a way that working-class boys (and girls) would love to look up to him, too—as would even minorities and foreigners. Hence the elaborate film scenes in jet-set playgrounds: from the French Côte d'Azur to the Swiss Alps, from the Caribbean islands to Las Vegas; the emphatic display of expensive cars and suits, food and drinks, and other signifiers of "good taste," always eagerly copied by nouveaux riches around the world; and, of course, gadgets and other toys for boys reluctant to grow up. In the films, they are meant to stir feelings of "wanna go" and "wanna have," so that corporate sponsors came to be eager to participate in the movie budgets—ultimately for a $100 million apiece or more.

In order to justify 007's "license to kill," the villains had to be uniquely evil, powerful, and dangerous. So Fleming invented near-omnipotent organizations and leaders, always bent on destroying the world civilization in its entirety—nothing less. At first the emphasis was an ideological one: on SMERSH, or *Smiert Spionam*, a Russian state counterintelligence agency. Later the emphasis became a criminal one: on SPECTRE, or the Special Executive of an international network—not only for counterintelligence, but also for "terror, revenge, and extortion." Madman moguls mingled with mafiosi there, to chase huge treasures of nuclear material or explosives, gold or diamonds, or drugs. Depending on the East-West atmosphere of crisis or détente, the emphasis could thus be shifted back and forth.

Fleming believed in "innate characteristics" of races. His villains were, to varying degrees, un-Anglo-Saxon: first un-British and later un-American. They mostly originated from larger central and eastern European nations such as Germany and Russia, and had exaggerated Aryan traits, or they originated from larger East Asian countries such as Japan and China, and had emphatically Asian traits. Finally they came to cover the usual range, from Latino guerrillas and drug barons, to Arab sheikhs and terrorists, black bullies and criminals. The stereotypes were, of course, exaggerated and supposed to be funny. The villain was often bald, ugly, or handicapped (one-eyed, one-armed, one-legged, etc.). His psychopathology also seemed to be related to some kind of sexual abnormality or perversity: he (or she) hardly ever seemed to be a "straight" heterosexual (this is also the case in the 2006 version of *Casino Royale*).

The Bond girls often radiated exoticism, as seen from a British perspective. Some were first more or less northern European, then eastern and southern European. Only later is there a clear preference for "nonwhite" belles: Asians associated with "sensual massage" and blacks associated with "physical prowess"—clichés recurring in *Die Another Day*. The Bond girls always fall for James Bond's charms—even if this means changing sides. They are sexually eager, but there are of course never contraceptives or pregnancy, or commitment or guilt, in sight. If there is even the slightest suggestion that 007 might be willing to tie up with a Bond girl, this is a sure death warrant, and she will soon be killed off. Apart from that, they did indeed get stronger and more emancipated over the years—at least in the movies.

Meanwhile, James Bond not only reflected Cold War realities, albeit in a distorted form, but he also influenced them. President John F. Kennedy and Ian Fleming shared similar elite backgrounds and family constellations; like James Bond, they were both voracious womanizers as well. Kennedy and his CIA chief, Allan Dulles, read Ian Fleming's novels and went to see some of the films—to the dismay of more serious spy novel writers like Graham Greene. In public, Kennedy, Dulles, and Fleming exchanged compliments. In private, they met and discussed ways to take Fidel Castro's charisma away, among other things by causing his beard to fall out.

It has been well-documented that Kennedy's supposed killer Lee Harvey Oswald had been a double spy first prepared to infiltrate the Soviet Union, then Cuba and pro-Castro groups. Oliver Stone's film *JFK* suggests that Kennedy was assassinated on behalf of such anti-Communist intelligence networks, disappointed in his reticence, but that Oswald may have been set up. Too fictional? According to one biographer, both Kennedy and Oswald were in the midst of reading a Bond novel at the time of Kennedy's death (Simpson 2002b). But what about Kennedy's successors, Johnson, Nixon, and Ford, and the fateful further American slide into the Vietnam War? How did they affect Hollywood films?

COMMANDO MOVIES AFTER VIETNAM

The Vietnam War was the first major U.S. "living room" war—that is to say, reported on television every day—and also the first overseas war the United States unambiguously lost. But it is a myth that it was lost because of media coverage and critical movies. The one successful major movie of those days highlighting the absurdity of the war was *MASH* (1970). But director Robert Altman later said that the studio had forced him at the eleventh hour to emphatically change the setting from the Vietnam War to the Korean War, in order to make it less topical and more timeless.[5] It was later followed by a long-running television sitcom that further diluted the original message.

Influential media people long continued to support the war, even after it had become apparent that it could not possibly be won and images about escalating atrocities on both sides became increasingly unsettling. Between the mid-1960s and mid-1970s, some one hundred movies dealt with the war in one way or another, and another two hundred did so immediately after the war was lost (Kleinen 2004, p. 13), but only a limited number focused entirely on the war itself and reached broad audiences as well.

One early example was *The Green Berets* (1968), heavily supported by the Pentagon and starring John Wayne, which still approached the war as a simple cowboys-versus-Indians fight. Thereafter, when the tide began to turn, major productions somehow shunned the subject and tended to look away (see the 1975 study by Julian Smith). It was only after the war had already been lost that somewhat more critical mainstream films were released (for which the Pentagon now refused its support)—to some acclaim and Oscar nominations. They did not in any way, however, focus on the tragedy of the Vietnamese, who lost more than 3 million lives (mostly civilians). Instead, they focused almost exclusively on the tragedy of Americans, who lost fifty-eight thousand soldiers, a disproportionately high number from ethnic minorities. Five times as many were wounded: some 10 percent of the total that went on a "tour of duty" there.

Hal Ashby's worthwhile *Coming Home* (1978) emphasized the plight of the returning veterans. But Michael Cimino's *The Deer Hunter* (1978) took the major American atrocities that had been registered in words and images—the small "tiger cages" in which prisoners were held, prisoners executed by putting a pistol to their heads, the torching of a mother and child, the indiscriminate massacre of an entire village (as in My Lai)—and turned them on their head: It restaged them but ascribed them to the adversary. *Apocalypse Now* (1979) was partly transposed from Joseph Conrad's African novel *Heart of Darkness* (discussed in chapter 7). It was an impressive piece of work but tended to aestheticize the violence and turn the whole experience into a timeless literary-artistic tragedy.

Only *Platoon* (1986) and *Born on the Fourth of July* (1989) by Vietnam vet Oliver Stone and *Full Metal Jacket* (1987) by British director Stanley Kubrick painted somewhat more realistic pictures of the war. But even the former, too, rewrote certain archetypical scenes to spare the sensibilities of American audiences (Walsh & Aulich 1989, p. 4). By that time, ten to twenty years onward, an entirely new generation of youngsters had grown up with little direct knowledge of the original events. *Time* magazine reported that "many students cannot say whether the U.S. was allied with the South Vietnamese or the North Vietnamese" (Jeffords 1984, p. 188). Meanwhile, conservatives began to peddle the idea that the war could easily have been won if only the United States had helped South Vietnam to "counterinvade" North Vietnam, risking a direct confrontation with China and Russia.

The Vietnam War changed movie history, as it spurred entire genres with various degrees of politicization: action movies, with body-builder heroes such as Arnold Schwarzenegger, who later became governor of California; martial arts movies, produced in the British "crown colony" Hong Kong and inspired by mainland theatrical traditions, with Chinese actors such as Bruce Lee and Jackie Chan (the first non-Western films to become international blockbusters); but also paranoia films about the American security apparatus running amok, like those with Robert Redford. These three traditions continue to produce successes to this very day.

But the disappointments of the Vietnam War had also generated dissent within governing circles from the publication of *The Pentagon Papers* to the exposure of the Watergate scandal (portrayed in the 1976 film *All the President's Men*). Republican president Richard Nixon had been forced to step down and was succeeded (and absolved) by his vice president, Gerald Ford. Democratic president Jimmy Carter had been faced with the overthrow of the pro-American shah of Iran, the protracted hostage taking of embassy personnel in Tehran, and a helicopter rescue attempt turned disaster.

There seemed to be no end to U.S. humiliation until conservatives in the Republican Party decided to back Ronald Reagan for president: a minor actor sponsored by movie moguls to become an industry lobbyist and then a Republican politician. He had played alongside macho stars such as John Wayne and Clint Eastwood, and political scientists noted that he made a point of incorporating famous movie lines into his political rhetoric.[6] His election and reelection as president during the early 1980s, along with American successes at the Los Angeles Olympic Games and other similar events, marked a nationalist revival. (This is discussed in detail in a 1984 monograph by psycho-historian Lloyd DeMause). One particular blockbuster character captured the changing mood particularly well: John Rambo, who would be portrayed in film by Sylvester Stallone.

Case Study: Rambo the Rebel

Sylvester Stallone was a son of Sicilian immigrants, a body builder and porn star nicknamed "the Italian Stallion." When his career failed to take off, he wrote the script for *Rocky* (1976), inspired by a boxing match between Chuck Wepner and Muhammed Ali, sold it on condition that he could play the title role, and scored a major success and even some Academy Awards. It was followed by three sequels. *Rocky IV* achieved additional emotional resonance by placing the fight plainly in the context of the Cold War and having the all-American hero defeat a despicable Russian competitor.

But Stallone scored an even bigger series of successes in the role of Vietnam veteran John Rambo. Movies like *Taxi Driver* (1976) had depicted Vietnam vets as alienated loners, although popular TV series like *The A-Team, Magnum, P. I.*, and *Mickey Spillane's Mike Hammer* had put them in a more positive light. The film *First Blood* (1982) was the story of a Vietnam vet's return to middle America to look for an old comrade, where he gets into a fight with a redneck sheriff and then raises total hell. Its twisted message somehow hit a nerve; it became a major box office hit and begged for a sequel. The ground for it had been further prepared by B-films such as *Uncommon Valor* (1983).

A major ideological reversal was achieved by turning veterans into pop-cult victims, rescuers, and avengers. Ideologues had successfully peddled the fable that the more than two thousand American soldiers who had been reported MIA or "missing in action" in Vietnam, were in fact still secretly held prisoners of war in concentration camps, completely forgotten and betrayed by successive U.S. administrations. This paranoid theme was successfully exploited in B-movies such as *Missing in Action* I and II (1984, 1985), where a commando went in to locate and liberate them. The films were shot in the Philippines and Mexico, for the originally Israeli Cannon group of the Globus cousins, one of whom had renamed himself after the contested Golan Heights (Jeffords 1984, p. 187). The same theme was also adopted for *Rambo: First Blood II* (1985), which broke all previous action hero and war film records.

The film release had been smartly planned for the spring of 1985, just two weeks after the sad commemoration of the tenth anniversary of the humiliating fall of Saigon, and openly catered to a desire for revenge and victory. It was simultaneously released in a then-unprecedented number of more than two thousand cinemas, immediately shot into the top ten of the all-time charts, and ultimately made more than $300 million. The news agency Reuters reported: "Young enthusiasts have jumped to their feet chanting 'USA! USA!' as Johnny Rambo blasts yet another batch of the enemy. . . . Forty-four persons, an average of one every 2.1 minutes, are slain in the film, not counting the hordes sent asunder in more than seventy explosions."[7]

Reuters also reported that bumper stickers exalted America's latest weapon and one-person army and that "Rambo knives . . . are selling for $760 each. A Los Angeles firm claims to have sold more than 150,000 aluminum replicas of Rambo's bow . . . at $150 apiece." Two hundred fifty thousand Rambo T-shirts were sold that spring (replacing the relativist *MASH* as number one). Three hundred thousand buttons and six hundred thousand posters were sold, and "the U.S. Army . . . started hanging Rambo posters outside its recruitment offices, hoping to lure enlistees." A novel based on the film sold eight hundred thousand copies. A true Rambo-mania gripped millions of Americans and also appealed to all kinds of foreigners with a grudge.[8]

The film is based on the notorious theme familiar to Germans as the *Dolchstoss Legende*: the idea that a lost war could have been won, if only the courageous soldiers at the front had not been "stabbed in the back" and betrayed by cowardly civilians at home. (The legend had played a key role in the rise of Hitler and the Nazi party after World War I and directly led to World War II). In the new Rambo story, a veteran was approached to infiltrate Vietnam and verify the existence of POW/MIA camps. Asked why he left the army, he said: "I, er, came back to the States and found another war going on." Question: "What war?" Answer: "A war against the soldiers returning" (i.e., the veterans). Queried whether he still loved his country, he confirmed that he did but added that he wanted it "to love us as much." He countered: "Do we get to win this time?" His commander said: "This time it's up to you."

But of course the military were again overruled by civilians in the film, so when Rambo decided to go ahead and liberate his old comrades anyway, he did so against express orders from the top. The comic-book fantasy subtly transformed lingering feelings of resentment into a desire for revenge. An editorial writer for the *Miami Herald* wrote: "The film is about being fed up with the smug bureaucrats, the prep-school boys who would use a decent working-class man . . . and then discard the remains." And *People* magazine reported, "Rambo has touched a raw nerve in America, a feeling that we should, in the words of Ronald Reagan, stand tall again" (Kellner 1995, p. 70–71). The film was much more than a mere action movie, then—it was one of the most ingenious pieces of political propaganda of all time. It achieved its goals by turning every key aspect of the Vietnam War on its head: turning the mighty U.S. Army, the Goliath, for instance, into an isolated U.S. soldier, a courageous David figure. Let us take a closer look at the many subtle ways in which this is achieved.

The close-shorn soldier look had become less popular, and the long-haired hippie protester look had taken its place. So Rambo is given a quasi-pacifist makeover. The antiauthoritarian counterculture of the 1960s and 1970s had helped stop the war at home, furthermore, but Rambo single-handedly resumes it in the name of a revolt against authority. He is close to nature and eats only healthy food. The Vietnamese had also won the war because they were more familiar with the terrain, the country, and the people, so Rambo sheds his uniform and just wears a headband over a half-naked torso. This turns him into a better native than the natives: a jungle-fighter—half Tarzan, half Indian.

The United States had tried to win the war through its superior fire-power. Its B-52 bombers had dropped more explosives on Vietnam than the 2.1 million tons dropped during World War II, not to mention huge clouds of napalm and Agent Orange poison (which led to wide-spread genetic defects). The Vietnamese guerrillas had instead relied on primitive means, such as traps with pointed bamboo sticks. So even if Rambo extensively uses firearms and explosives, he has a preference for iconic knives and bows and arrows. He turns into the resourceful frontier man familiar from Western movies.

Images of American soldiers being drunk, hanging out in sleazy bars and brothels in Saigon and elsewhere, had become overly familiar. The movie places puritan Vietcong in that same familiar environment, however. It takes great care to dress the Vietnamese soldiers like the Japanese familiar from World War II movies, giving them similar traits. The prison camp set is partly copied from the Japanese prison camp sets in *The Bridge on the River Kwai*, for instance. The movie also takes great care to dress the Russians advisers like German S.S. officers and to give them similarly exaggerated Aryan traits. In a torture scene, one of them gives Rambo a typical German *Schmiess*: a big, highly visible scar on the cheek.

Rambo is also surrounded by arch-images of martyrdom and victimhood. In the torture scene, he is emphatically placed in the position of the Crucified, the suffering Christ himself—the Messiah. When he is beaten, there is briefly and marginally a text in sight, almost subliminally. It is a sack with food aid, marked as a humanitarian gift from the American people. Everything is thus done to further stir a sense of outrage, and a cry for revenge. Rambo falls in love with a Vietnamese girl-helper, but seconds after he has promised to take her with him to

America, she is ambushed and shot. (This familiar theme of the expendable exotic beauty is discussed in chapter 8).

The Rambo triumph was one of the factors that helped restore public support for renewed military action abroad. When preparing for a speech on the liberation of hostages from a hijacked TWA plane held in Beirut, Reagan said in a microphone test: "Boy, after seeing *Rambo* last night, I know what to do next time."[9] When Reagan had the private residence of Lybian leader Mu'ammar Gadhafi in Tripoli bombed (killing his adopted child), Europeans feared possible counterattacks on their Mediterranean shores. So American action heroes cancelled their attendance of the Cannes Film Festival—including Stallone as Rambo.

Meanwhile, the United States had reaffirmed its military might by invading one of the smallest islands in the Caribbean, Grenada. Susan Jeffords reports that the landing was accompanied by the playing of Wagner's *Valkyrie*, in direct imitation of a similar scene in Coppola's *Apocalypse Now* (p. 188). Washington invoked a Cuban and Soviet military presence, mass kidnappings, and mass graves—which all turned out to be inventions. (The invasion later became the subject of Clint Eastwood's film *Heartbreak Ridge*). Congress interdictions of undeclared wars were further dodged by simply "privatizing" them, for instance, in Central America. When the pro-American dictator Anastasio Somoza Debayle was overthrown by Sandinista radicals in Nicaragua, a contrarevolutionary army was financed by shady arms deals in the Middle East. One installment of a sixty-five-part *Rambo* television series had the hero join them (Walsh & Aulich 1989, p. 185). And when the aide responsible for the real-life illegal covert operation, Colonel Oliver North, was finally interrogated by Congress, press articles frequently likened him to the heroic John Rambo.

Increasingly, however, the mood in the Pentagon and in Washington changed. Infantry should only be sent into hostile lands when there really were no other options—only exceptionally, briefly, and massively—but the emphasis should be on high-tech weapons backed up by superior air power and linked in sophisticated electronic networks. The paradigm shifted from body-builder foot soldiers in the mud to elegant high-flying pilots in the air.

The new paradigm was captured by the movie *Top Gun* (1986), produced by Jerry Bruckheimer and Don Simpson, with heavy Pentagon support. It was directed by Tony Scott and starred Tom Cruise as the son of a Vietnam veteran turned super-pilot. The Pentagon rented out an entire naval base for a modest sum, with aircraft carriers and as

many planes as could be handled. It also posted army recruiters outside cinemas showing the movie.

Reagan's agenda was further carried out by his Republican successors: the Bushes, father and son. After the 2003 invasion of Iraq, the latter (whose military and Vietnam War credentials had been repeatedly
challenged) dressed up as a Top Gun–style pilot, landing on a diverted
air carrier to (prematurely) announce the end of the hostilities for the
television cameras in front of a big banner declaring "Mission Accomplished," which he long maintained was spontaneously improvised by
the ships crew but later turned out to have been produced by the White
House communication office.[10] Hollywood fantasy and Washington
politics thus became ever more closely intertwined.

WAR MOVIES AND ISLAM

A study by James William Gibson reports that between 1945 and 1965 alone,
some five thousand war movies were made. Almost a quarter received major
assistance from the Defense Department, which originally required only that
they be "realistic" but after the Vietnam disaster came to demand that they be
"favorable." Most American war movies share the same characteristics, he adds.
They "show the United States always fighting on the morally correct side. . . .
U.S. soldiers win almost all battles and always win the war . . . war movies show
good guys and bad guys, but few innocents." Furthermore "war does not appear dangerous" as the "heroes survive battle" and their service is "a crucial ritual transition from male adolescence into manhood" (Walsh & Aulich 1989,
pp. 17–18). Robert J. McKeever links this to "the myths of American innocence,
uniqueness, and superiority" (Walsh & Aulich 1989, pp. 44–46).

The Defense Department usually trades its cooperation at a nominal "cost
price" for influence over the script and final cut. It has an elaborate PR liaison
office for army, navy, and air force in Los Angeles, which suggests dozens upon
dozens of minor changes. Hiring ships, planes, tanks, personnel, and consultants may otherwise cost millions, eating into Hollywood profits, so most producers silently submit to censorship and self-censorship. But since some have
tried to outwit their supervisors, the Pentagon now favors "trusted" partners,
such as Jerry Bruckheimer of *Pearl Harbor* and many predecessors.

The latter is a simple romance *cum* action movie, with little historical or
military realism. But Philip Strub, a senior PR man with the liaison office, says
that Disney research showed that the film generated *three times* as much publicity for the subject than the fiftieth anniversary of the event itself. He also
notes: "We have seen recently in surveys that large numbers of Americans base

their impressions of the U.S. military from [on] entertainment movies and television shows."[11] The same holds for combat and war. So this method is much cheaper and more effective than advertising campaigns to make military-age boys sign up for an "exciting career" using high-tech weapons systems.

The Pentagon also sponsored a $50-million initiative to set up the Institute of Creative Technologies in Los Angeles, to improve combat simulation and video games—further bridging the gap between the two. The CIA, FBI, and other federal security agencies have since learned to take similar initiatives, as is reflected in a recent spate of new films and television series.[12] Earlier, the major film studios had poured $150,000 into renovating the forty-seat White House movie theater. In a later documentary the projectionist revealed that the presidents and their staffs preferred all kinds of action movies and that the all-time favorite was the Western *High Noon*, with its cartoonlike standoff and shootout between the good guy and the bad guy. Personal favorites were gung-ho movies such as *Patton* (for Nixon, at the time of Vietnam) and *Black Hawk Down* (for Bush the younger, at the time of Iraq). Food for thought.[13]

The Cold War had ended with the fall of the Berlin Wall and the reunification of Germany, the disintegration of the Soviet Union and of the Warsaw Pact. Yet another major conflict was already looming on the horizon. One of its triggers had been the defeat of the Soviets in Afghanistan, where the United States and Saudi Arabia had secretly poured billions into financing, arming, and training an international network of Sunni Islamic fundamentalist fighters, from which the local Taliban faction (and their Saudi ally Osama bin Laden) emerged victoriously. But the United States had also secretly helped Saddam Hussein of Iraq to hold his ground in his war against the Shiite Islamic fundamentalist regime of the Ayatollah Khomeini in Iran. When Saddam invaded Kuwait and the Western allies evicted him in 1991, American troops were stationed in the Islamic Holy Land of Saudi Arabia and turned the entire fundamentalist network against the United States.

The first terrorist attack against the World Trade Center in New York took place in 1993, but it largely failed and caused only limited death and damage. From then on, however, the new enemy became increasingly obvious. Whereas Francis Fukuyama's famous book had prematurely proclaimed *The End of History*, Samuel Huntington's equally famous book now predicted *The Clash of Civilizations*. Hollywood immediately subscribed to the new trend.

The terrorist attacks of September 11, 2001, whereby hijacked airplanes where flown into the World Trade Center and the Pentagon, were obviously planned for their dramatic effect. Commentators pointed out that they might have been coinspired by recent popular novels (e.g., those of Tom Clancy) and movies. *Air Force One* (1997) already featured a hijacked plane in relation to the

White House; *Independence Day* (1996) featured landmark buildings blown up by aliens; *The Towering Inferno* (1974) featured a skyscraper in flames; *Deep Impact* (1998) featured a major disaster followed by a mass panic.

The Hollywood blockbuster industry took a pause to reflect. It reconsidered its current portfolio for possibly objectionable material. *Swordfish*, with John Travolta, was retired from its run in some overseas countries. The upcoming release of action movies such as *Collateral Damage* with Arnold Schwarzenegger was postponed. The landmark Twin Towers were edited out of *Spider-Man* and *Men in Black 2* and from a number of running television series. Film posters, like those for *The Last Castle* with Robert Redford (showing an American flag upside down), were destroyed. Yet the fears of a backlash against action movies soon proved to be premature.[14]

The most-rented videos in the week after the attack were the Die Hard and Rambo series. The producer Jerry Bruckheimer later said there turned out to be a new trend toward "revenge movies": "We were all proved wrong. The pictures that were held, when they did come out, they did very well." Over the entire year, there even was a modest rise in movie attendance, bringing it back to the high levels of the end of World War II.[15]

Case Study: The Absent "Other" in *Black Hawk Down*

Jerry Bruckheimer was one of the few to recognize the new trend right away. His director, Ridley Scott, later said, "We concluded that this was a good time."[16] So they scrambled to move the release of their commando movie *Black Hawk Down* forward by almost a full quarter. It recycled a "real-life" Rambo-like story of heroic rescue abroad, in order to "leave no MIA/POW behind." It was accompanied by the repetition of a November 14, 1993, CNN special on *Larry King Live*. The film was released immediately after Christmas 2001, garnered $75 million at the U.S. box office within five weeks, and was nominated for four Oscars. According to the White House film projectionist quoted earlier, it also was one of the favorite movies of President George W. Bush during the invasions of Afghanistan and Iraq: another good reason to take a closer look at it.

Although it was indeed "based on an actual event," it turned a forgotten defeat of eight years earlier into a heroic accomplishment. The makers even considered adding a topical epilogue claiming that the retreat in that case had emboldened America's enemies and thus contributed to the present disaster. "It goes to show you how context is everything," the original author of the story said. "If tomorrow you read that we captured two of Osama bin Laden's key advisers and killed and wounded one thousand of Al Qaeda, and in the process lost eighteen men, you'd think they'd done a helluva job." But the comparison of the prime international terrorist mastermind with a minor stubborn regional warlord was rather a stretch.[17]

Only a series of titles at the beginning tell us anything about the history and context of the original events, but the film itself does not and thereby succeeds in reducing them once again into a simple struggle of the good guys versus the bad guys. Yet the true story was much more ambiguous. Some years after the independence of the minor country of Somalia (on the Eastern Horn of Africa), General Mohammed Siad Barre had seized power in a coup d'état. The dictator had at first allied himself with the Soviet Union but then changed sides to the United States, thus providing it with another invisible rearguard base for operations throughout the Middle East. In 1991, however, his minister Mohammed Farah Aidid had in turn seized power in another coup d'état. He was a Soviet-trained officer and was seen as anti-American: a potential sponsor of terrorism.

His Somali National Movement (SNM) met with fierce resistance from other political and regional factions. The resulting protracted civil war created chaos and famine. The United States then got a UN mandate for a humanitarian intervention. In late 1992, U.S. television networks filmed the dramatic landing of twenty thousand marines. But the marines proved unable to sort things out, and most left half a year later. In the summer of 1993 things got worse: Commandos burst into a meeting of clan elders, and several journalists were stoned in the streets. The United States got a UN mandate to apprehend Aidid, and that autumn it stepped up its operations.

Sunday, October 3, was the fateful day. The U.S. command had planned a "shock and awe" strike to apprehend two of Aidid's closest lieutenants in a building and neighborhood controlled by them. An advance force of several helicopters would drop off a commando unit to carry out the surprise arrests; a column of Humvee vehicles would then join them and return safely within the hour. The progress of the surgical operation was filmed from the air and followed in real time by the commanders on the base—like in a shooter video game. But the enemy had been severely underestimated, and things quickly began to turn sour.

A first Blackhawk helicopter was downed by a rocket-propelled grenade, and later a second helicopter. The Humvees encountered resistance at one point and had to turn back; it took nine hours to gather an alternative force of armored vehicles. Altogether, the commandos had to hold out for fifteen hours against armed rebels and aggressive crowds. The mob got hold of the corpses of fallen commandos and triumphantly dragged them through the streets.

Somalis videotaped the whole affair and sold the material to journalists even before Washington officials had acknowledged the defeat. There were few reporters in Somalia itself; the *New York Times*, for one, covered the disaster from afar—in Kenya. One pilot had been taken prisoner, eighteen soldiers died, and seventy-five were wounded in what was the worst ground fight since the Vietnam War. Interestingly enough, international media coverage devoted hardly any attention to Malaysian, Pakistani, and Nigerian victims that were also involved in the larger episode. The American expeditionary force was retired, and ten years later the standoff between Somali factions persisted, and an Islamist faction briefly took over the country in late 2006 and early 2007.

But what went wrong at the time, and how? Journalist Mark Bowden of the *Philadelphia Inquirer* made a detailed reconstruction in a long series of newspaper articles published four years later. One telling detail in the first article: "Many of the men had left at the base their night vision goggles, canteens, and food rations and had with them a limited supply of ammunition—thinking about a quick operation and then of an afternoon relaxing on the beach" (November 16, 1997; Cittati 2003, p. 5). Bowden's website, a CD-ROM, and a documentary became the subject of cult fascination. The proofs of the book were immediately bought by Bruckheimer. The original account had been more or less factual, although largely based on American eyewitnesses and points of view, with only a few Somali voices added as an afterthought. But the film scenario reworked this material into an epic tale of courage and solidarity around the familiar theme of "no one gets left behind" (an implicit reference to the Rambo myth).

The scenario was submitted to the Pentagon. It demanded a number of changes: about a reported exchange of "friendly fire," about tensions between the units, about the real name of a hero soldier who later got into serious trouble with the law. But it then supplied Blackhawks helicopters, eight in all, and 135 men. At the time of release, the director claimed, "This isn't a movie movie. It's as near to the edge of a documentary as I could make it"[18]—a claim quickly copied by the media. But the problem, of course, is that it makes the viewers identify and sympathize exclusively with one side; the perspective of others is entirely left out. This is underlined by the music: American pop songs when their team spirit is shown, Western quasi-classical pieces when their tragedies are shown, vaguely Arab or African music (but not really very Somali) when the other side is shown (Kroes 2002, p. 7). Let us look at some further details.

The American protagonists are shown as individuals, and their names are written on their helmets. Their bodies are filmed from nearby, their faces in close-up, particularly when they are suffering. When they are injured, we also see some of the gruesome details and feel sorry for them. They do most of the understandable speaking, explaining and therefore "framing" the action. When one of them is forced to flee into a house in panic, he nevertheless manages to treat the woman and children there in a calm and friendly way. But the commandos among themselves derogatively call the capital Mogadishu "Mogh" and the Somali people "skinnies."

The urban scenes are shot in a bluish or greenish night-vision light, which actively alienates the houses and the people from the viewer. The Somalis are just fleeting shadows: they are hardly ever identified by name, and we hardly ever see the same face more than once. Most of what they say or shout remains untranslated, only a few have English lines (when speaking to Americans), and only two say anything about the local situation at all—like the sarcastic, "Do you really think that if you get general Aidid we would simply put down our weapons and adopt American democracy?"

The Somalis thus remain anonymous for the most part. They are played by black Africans with an entirely different morphology, even flagrant to a European eye, in scenes that seem rather copied from the entirely different Liberia or Sierra Leone civil wars. The front rows of the crowds are consistently portrayed as very heavily armed (whereas the real-life videos shown on CNN instead show large groups of mostly unarmed civilians). When Somalis get shot at (or mowed down) by Americans, they simply drop like bowling pins. They do not move; they do not seem to suffer at all. Sometimes they even kill each other, as in an inserted scene of a child shooting his father in error.

Of course this remains one of the major controversies to this very day. Did the American commandos keep their cool, shooting only at hostile and/or armed men, as the Pentagon claimed? Or did they panic, shooting at "everything that moved," as some of the soldiers later admitted? Whereas eighteen Americans died, early estimates were that three hundred Somalis did. Later estimates rose from five hundred to one thousand, with many more wounded. The *New York*

Times on October 14, 1993, quoted Red Cross sources saying that that *one-third* of the wounded were women and children, but the Pentagon countered by saying that the enemy fighters did not wear proper uniforms and frequently dressed like women, or used women and children as decoys (Cittati 2003, p. 10).

THE FICTIONALIZATION OF WAR REPORTS

During subsequent years, the Pentagon increasingly began to match such "quasi-documentary" war films with "quasi-fictional" war reports on interventions overseas. The Rambo/Black Hawk theme of heroic rescue, to leave no man or woman behind, was given an increasingly prominent role. Under President Bush the elder, Washington neoconservatives regretted that the first intervention against Iraq did not result in the toppling of Saddam and the takeover of the country. Under President Bush the younger, they therefore pushed hard to "finish the job." Secretary of State Colin Powell presented a video to the UN Security Council in an attempt to persuade it that Saddam still had weapons of mass destruction and was planning to use them against the West (van der Heide 2005). One of my students did exemplary thesis research by interviewing many key U.S. journalists about why they had believed the dubious WMD story; many claimed that they were only allowed to quote "credible, authoritative, on-record Washington" sources—meaning the White House, the Pentagon, and the State Department. This excluded vocal critics, weapons inspectors, the UN, European officials, and the like (Verkaik 2007). Although the UN refused to give them a mandate for military action, the United States and the U.K. went ahead anyway, attacking on March 20, 2003, and beginning a blitzkrieg that lasted three weeks.

The Pentagon also experimented with even subtler methods of news and issues management, and a confidential strategy paper spoke of the necessity of "shaping world public opinion." On the one hand, an unprecedented number of six hundred allied reporters were "embedded" with the troops. This made many identify with their units and gave the illusion that they were eyewitness to the events taking place. On the other hand, another seven hundred reporters were stationed at a media center and fed daily briefings. This center was not in neighboring Kuwait but in distant Qatar, far away across the Persian Gulf, so that they could not possibly be tempted to go out to try and collect information on their own in the border area. Whenever bad news trickled out anyway, spokesmen immediately tried to put a positive spin on it.

One such incident was when a convoy of the 507th Maintenance Company was reportedly ambushed: eleven died and five were captured. The heroics of one particular soldier were highlighted. A modest young woman from a small town in West Virginia, in the county with the lowest population (and the highest unemployment rate) of that entire state, Jessica Lynch was a frail nineteen-year-old, once elected Miss Congeniality at the local fair, with light blonde hair and light blue eyes. The Pentagon later released a picture in which she was shown smiling broadly, posed in front of an American flag.

Authoritative newspapers, such as the *Washington Post*, reported that she had been "fighting to the death," "fought fiercely and shot several enemy soldiers," "continued firing . . . even after she sustained multiple gunshot wounds" and "stab wounds," "firing her weapon until she ran out of ammunition," as "she did not want to be taken alive"—even though the article noted further down that these were merely rumors, provided by "unidentified officials" (Jessen 2003, pp. 1–4). The only thing that was certain was that she had been wounded and was carried away. The story that follows is based on reporting from the *New York Times* and the Associated Press as carried by the *International Herald Tribune*, unless otherwise indicated.[19]

A week later, on April 1, reporters at the Qatar Media Center were woken up in the middle of the night and summoned to an urgent extra press conference with important news. (This precise timing was crucial in view of breakfast broadcasting news in the United States, although this of course made any checking of the presented facts impossible). The general reported good news at a bad time, because the main offensive seemed to be bogged down by sandstorms that temporarily impaired U.S. electronic superiority, as a "successful rescue mission" had been carried out "by our nations finest warriors" to liberate the prisoner of war. The entire operation had been filmed live by an army camera crew and had been followed in real time by the supreme commander of the allied forces and his senior officers at the base. A small part of the videotape was made available: the gritty images and the greenish light (because of night-vision exposure) further helped giving it the character of a realistic commando movie.

Jessica Lynch had been held in a local hospital in Nasirya. The U.S. spokesman added that "the troops had found no evidence that the hospital was used to torture American prisoners or opponents of the regime." A nurse and her husband had seen her there and had directed the commandos to the spot. (Out of fear for reprisals, the family in question was immediately flown out to the United States, given political asylum, and helped to find jobs—and a book contract). The "classic special operations raid" then reportedly "fought its way in" under a "barrage of hostile gunfire." As the entire affair had been planned for the middle of the week, the Rambo/Black Hawk–type story was updated every day thereafter, with broad and emotional media play until well after the weekend. A week later, Baghdad was liberated, followed by the top-pling of the Saddam statue—a supposedly spontaneous popular initiative that later turned out to have also been carefully planned and orchestrated by the Pentagon as long as months before, to be covered by the journalists and cam-eras from the major media hotel near the same square.

Since the situation now seemed to be settling down, newspaper reporters and a BBC television crew traveled to Nasirya to follow up with a further "hu-man interest" story on the heroic rescue. But it was gradually revealed that the whole story of capture and liberation had been a hoax from the start.[20] Lynch's unit had been extremely tired, and communications were bad. The convoy had taken a wrong turn and got lost before it ran into enemy fire. Lynch had been praying for survival when her Humvee plowed into the tractor-trailer in front of them, and she was wounded. Her wounds were subsequently classi-fied as "RTA," or a road traffic accident.

She had not been able to fire a shot because her M-16 had jammed, as did the weapons of many of her colleagues. She passed out, and the Iraqis brought her to a hospital. The doctors said they had liberated the one special bed they had, gave their own blood, and assigned her one of the two nurses available. When she risked being transferred to another hospital, a friendly doctor in-structed the ambulance to bring her to an American control post instead, but they were fired at and chased away. The whole later "rescue operation" was a Sinbad the Sailor–type fairy tale, the doctor said. There had been no fighters or fighting in the hospital at all. Another doctor confirmed that it had been "like a Hollywood film. They shouted 'Go, go, go.' With pistols and blank car-tridges and the sound of explosives. They made it a show, an action movie, like those of Sylvester Stallone or Jackie Chan."[21] As the ancients said: life im-itates art.

Yet the Pentagon awarded Jessica a Purple Heart and a Bronze Star for un-common valor. That same summer, it staged a spectacular hero's welcome, with a Blackhawk helicopter bringing her back to her small town, where she "was enthusiastically greeted by thousands of local residents and well-wishers from other parts of the United States." The publisher Knopf gave her $1-mil-lion book deal and a Pulitzer Prize–winning ghostwriter. By the time the book hit the bookstores, the television networks were fighting to be first to have her as a talk show guest. "I've never seen anything like this," the publicity director said. "It was like blood sport, the competition for this story."[22]

Advance publicity was further heightened when newspapers reported that her ghostwriter quoted "some intelligence reports" that the blonde girl must somehow have been raped/sodomized by the Arabs while she was uncon-scious, although she herself said she could not confirm anything of the kind. He said graphically: "Jessie lost three hours. . . . She lost them in the snapping bones, in the crash of the Humvee, in the torment her enemies inflicted on her. . . . The records do not tell whether her captors assaulted her almost life-less, broken body after she was lifted from the wreckage, or if they assaulted her and then broke her bones into splinters until she was almost dead." But he gave no hard facts to back up these conjectures.

Soon thereafter, the filming of a first movie on *Saving Jessica Lynch* began at a Nasirya set specially built in Dallas. The Pentagon once again provided aid in return for its say. Producer Dan Paulson said: "It's cheaper than going to [the car rental agencies] Hertz or Avis." The Pentagon had found the ideal symbol—hero and victim—for the war. Some time later, the Pentagon in-vented a similar story about the death of American sports star Pat Tillman in Afghanistan (Rich 2005).[23] The Iraq and Afghanistan wars also spurned a range of feature films, television series, and video games, often based on a slick alternation of real-life combat videos and fictional embellishments. From now on, the distinction between the two had totally blurred.

9

Believers and Heathens: Religious Films

What are the characters and stories that are most sacred to us, as individuals and as a group? Can we accept radically different views of God, his incarnation, his prophets? Or would they be considered blasphemous, breaking a taboo? Have the stories about the saints been embellished, and have their heathen challengers further been vilified? In what ways is this still reflected in today's blockbusters? Or have Hollywood directors even gone so far as to correct the holy books and their current interpretations—just for further dramatic effect and to please their Western audiences?

Do you come from a Christian background? Think of God. Think of Jesus, Moses, and the other prophets. What do you see: what is the prime representation in your mind? Is it a text or is it an image? It is likely the latter and therefore far removed from the Holy Scriptures. If it is a still picture, it is probably a "classical" work of art, often dating from the Middle Ages or the Renaissance, or a more "popular" version deriving from it.

Now try to imagine a lively biblical scene—any one will do, from the Old Testament or the New Testament, it does not matter. Once again: What do you see: what is the prime representation in your mind? If it is a moving image, it probably comes from your cinematic experience. It may derive from an art film, but it more likely derives from a popular film,[1] such as *The Passion of the Christ, The Prince of Egypt,* or *The Ten Commandments.* The problem with such religious movies is, of course, twofold. On the one hand, they were mostly imagined by American or European scriptwriters and directors, crews, and producers. On the other hand, they were commercial ventures primarily aimed at American and European audiences. That is to say, that the original stories were primarily adapted (and embellished) to suit mainstream Western tastes, identities, and orientations. Even though the filmmakers often claimed to have been sensitive to the concerns of other ethnic and/or cultural groups (for instance, by consulting a few well-chosen and nonvocal minority representatives), they are often shown to have taken a cavalier attitude on this score, mostly by taking a naive and conventional approach for granted, but sometimes also by willingly catering to audience blind spots.

So what are the hidden traps of such religious movies from an intercultural perspective? More than any other genre, religion and therefore religious movies are directly related to the ultimate dimension of moral superiority and inferiority, of "us" versus "them." The believers embody the highest pinnacle of civilization; the heathens represent the lowest level of barbarity. *We* can tell right from wrong, *they* cannot—or not correctly. *We* respect what is sacred, *they* break taboos all the time, are sinful and impure, sometimes without even knowing or acknowledging it. The Jewish high priests who conspired and the crowd that called for the killing of Jesus in *The Passion of the Christ* were vicious, and so were the Egyptians who enslaved Moses and his people in *The Prince of Egypt* and *The Ten Commandments* and who stubbornly refused to let them go.

But these films are faithful to the historical record, one might object. The problem is that this is not the case—nor can it be, for a number of obvious reasons. First, these books date from a time when historical records were scattered and writing had only recently begun to appear. Second, the present-day "official" version is based on a narrow selection of the source material available, made in a specific context and with a very specific goal. Third, these accepted versions were usually written down long after the events had occurred and were largely based on an oral tradition spanning one or many intermediary generations, most often not on immediate eyewitness accounts. Fourth, like all hearsay, these accounts were obviously embellished to support only one side of the story, that of the "heroes"; the other side, of the supposed "villains," is not heard. Fifth, these texts were translated from an earlier form of a host of foreign languages, with which we are not completely familiar today. Sixth, these translations were repeatedly reinterpreted and subtly changed to suit the changing spirit of the times. Seventh and finally, the standard interpretations widely accepted today are often at odds with the historical and archaeological record.

Slightly revising the accepted "literal" interpretation of the holy texts is often presented as blasphemy, yet blockbuster scriptwriters and directors have always felt free to fill in these incomplete stories with additional details in order to give them more emotional resonance, or even to alter the story on key points if this better suited their dramatic purpose, but almost always with a keen eye on what mainstream audiences in America and Europe wanted to see.

It is important to recognize, furthermore, that such Hollywood productions often depended on acceptance or even endorsement from spokesmen of major Christian denominations in the United States, with conservatives and fundamentalists often playing a dominant role, in order to maintain potential access to mainstream audiences, but also to television and commercial sponsors. At the same time, clerics and churches usually welcomed such mainstream new Bible films because they helped bring an otherwise textual and abstract creed to vivid life. Salient emotions such as loathing or shame, fear or guilt, provoked by such films helped reinvigorate these churches. Thus, there was psychological cross-fertilization.

Meanwhile, the question of course remains if (and how) such major recent Bible films can legitimately be called ethnocentric. The Christian faith has universal pretensions and even missionary zeal: It does not see itself as a priori limited to one geographic area or ethnic group, even if its current distribution and previous history are primarily limited to the Americas and Europe. But this is forgetting that the arch-stories in Christianity's Holy Book insert it into very specific sets of historical and geographic circumstances. In the Old Testament these circumstances are the emergence of the Hebrew nation and faith out of successive confrontations with Arab civilizations and creeds to its northeast and southwest. In the New Testament these circumstances are the emergence of the Jesus movement and the Christian faith out of a confrontation with the dominant strand of Judaism, within the wider framework of the Roman Empire.

Put in this perspective, it is immediately clear why and how so many mainstream presentations of biblical material are full of vivid enemy images and ethnic stereotypes, even if they are often not recognized as such and adopted only subliminally. Let us therefore take a closer look at some of those recent blockbuster movies, built around the most dramatic arch-stories in the Old and the New Testaments—namely, the Exodus and the Passion. It turns out they are indeed told in rather ethnocentric ways, even in this supposedly "enlightened and cosmopolitan" day and age.

OLD TESTAMENT MOVIES

One of the most impressive stories of the sacred world literature is indeed that of Moses and the Exodus of the Jews from Egypt. Over the years, at least eight different major film versions have been made of it.

Cecil B. DeMille alone made two successive versions of *The Ten Commandments*. The later version came to be considered one of the most impressive

Hollywood productions of all time and one of the great landmarks of Western civilization. After its release, DeMille was received by the pope and the British queen, by Winston Churchill and the West German president. No other Western director dared to touch the subject for several decades.

Since it would be impossible to trump this Cecil B. DeMille production in live action, Jeffrey Katzenberg's *The Prince of Egypt* tried to do so in an animated cartoon, much later. It was released simultaneously in forty countries, just before Christmas 1998. Whereas DeMille's productions had cost a mere $1.5 and $13.5 million, respectively, Katzenberg's cost $75 million, plus an estimated $40 million spent on publicity. So what about these movies?

The Old Testament relates events supposedly going back to several millennia before our era. According to archaeological and philological research, the text took shape during the seventh century BCE, and the final selection of thirty-nine Hebraic texts (out of some two hundred candidates) took place during the first centuries CE (Finkelstein & Silberman 2002, pp. 10–24; Ehrman 2003, p. 232). The Pentateuch, or five books of Moses, form the most important part, particularly the book of Exodus.

The Exodus has always been understood as relating the true origins of the Jewish religion and culture, and thereby also of the subsequent Christian religion and culture (even Islam also shares some of the same material). More than the texts themselves, Hollywood movies have brought these ancient roots of our civilization to life, filling them with recognizable characters. They had a major emotional impact on people in the West and beyond, and they still guide many of the ways in which we approach the lands and peoples discussed there. But to what extent do they square with the results of current archaeological and historical research?

Since half a century or so, the scientific gap between believers and nonbelievers has gradually widened rather than narrowed. Believers maintain that postwar archaeological finds in the Middle East fit and confirm the major Old Testament stories. Nonbelievers maintain that on many important scores this is not the case. Noteworthy nonbelievers even maintain that, so far, no material proof of an ancient unitary, powerful, and flourishing biblical kingdom has been found yet; evidence supports the existence of only two smaller ministates, Israel and Judah. At the time supposedly described in the book of Kings, Jerusalem was but a small town, and the First Temple must have been a very minor building indeed.

A 2002 book followed by a four-part television documentary[2] by Tel Aviv University archaeologist Israel Finkelstein and Neil Asher Silberman of the Ename Center for Public Archeology in Belgium concludes that the Old Testament may have been a saga written to serve territorial ambitions of the south in the north, because to the farther northeast the Jews confronted successive well-documented Assyrian and Babylonian empires stretching to Asian Mesopotamia, around the Euphrates and Tigris rivers, and to the southwest they confronted successive well-documented pharaoh empires based in African Egypt, around the Nile River. The lands of Canaan were alternately invaded from either side, but also by "Philistines," who came to its shores from the Mediterranean Sea.

Egyptian records, however, contain no reference to the massive enslavement of the Jewish people during this epoch, or to any of the key events mentioned in Exodus. In fact the massive return from slavery abroad may have been related not to Egypt in earlier days, it is now widely thought, but to Babylon in later days. Yet that story may have been less convenient and also less heroic, as the leaders and the people did not liberate themselves at that point in time.

Derek Elley's overview of relevant movies summarizes: "Much of the Old Testament is [now] thought to have been written (or reworked during the experience of bondage) in the two centuries the Hebrews spent in Babylon— hence the 'let my people go' theme of long-suffering innocence . . . designed as both a record of the past and an inspiration for the future, conceived at a time when the Hebrews lacked identity" (1984, pp. 25–26). It was only some time after Babylon fell to the Persians in 539 that their King Cyrus allowed the tribes to return.

It might therefore be considered a typical founding myth, like so many, a convenient mixture of fact and fiction, drawing on a wide range of other founding myths from the Middle East and beyond. The story of the Great Flood can also be found in major epics from all neighboring cultures, including the much older Gilgamesh from Babylonia. Mythical stories of mass baby killings, and of a great trek preceding the founding of a new nation, recur periodically to this very day.[3] In his famous study *The Myth of the Birth of the Hero* early psychoanalyst Otto Rank compared the Moses story to a dozen or so similar stories from the entire region, to conclude that they all shared the same dozen or so elements. He attributed this to "universal fantasies which . . . have their source in the infantile psyche" (1964, p. 11).

The characteristic elements of the Moses story can be dated as far back as the origins of Babylonia, three millennia BCE, Rank said, because its first king, Sargon, had already reported about his mother: "In a hidden place she brought me forth. She laid me in a vessel made of reeds . . . and dropped me down into the river . . . [and] carried me to Akki . . . [who] raised me as his own son. . . . In my work as a gardener I was beloved by Ishtar, I became the king, and for forty-five years I held kingly sway."[4] Sigmund Freud himself spent the last years of his life trying to unravel the Moses myth and closely identified with it.[5]

Finkelstein and Silberman are not alone in claiming that archaeological research since World War II has turned up very little material proof for the Exodus story, as is also evident from an extensive overview in a 1999 documentary *Moses*, made by Jean-Claude Bragard for BBC television.[6] Meanwhile, even official Christian Bible societies and mainstream Bible translations have begun to acknowledge that translation and interpretation errors tended to further embellish and overdramatize the Exodus story in the past. Let us look at a few examples relevant to the Hollywood vision of the events.

The stay in Egypt referred to in the Exodus story may have been somewhere between 80 and 175 years, rather than the previously claimed 430 years, if one takes into account the number of generations and the average length of a generation mentioned elsewhere. Such a quick succession of plagues has not been recorded anywhere else, and these may have been a compilation of common pestilences spread out over a much longer period in time. The Exodus story may mean to refer to six thousand people rather than six hundred thousand people, if one takes into account that the word previously translated as "thousand" is elsewhere taken to mean just "clan" or family. It probably did not claim a crossing of the deep Red Sea in the south but of the much shallower Reed Sea in the north (the mistranslation of the original words, *yam suph*, is now widely acknowledged). The parting of the waters may therefore originally have referred to a simple phenomenon of ebb and flow, later aggrandized in oral tradition and myth of people unfamiliar with it.[7] But accepting all this would of course make the story far less epic, and the stories and Hollywood movies derived from it far less impressive, with many opportunities for great miracles and special effects lost in one stroke.

To sum up: the Exodus and Moses stories, which so many Jews and Christians have learned to take literally, may well be a combination of preexisting and further embellished Middle Eastern myths, put in the service of founding another religion, another culture, another nation. For that very same reason, however, they are also profoundly Manichaean, with "us" and "them" painted in pure white and black. The Hebrew people show unprecedented persistence and courage, inspired by visionary leaders, such as Moses, who are in direct contact with the one and only God. But they are also the recurrent victims of persecution by the evil rulers of surrounding empires, ranging from what is now Iraq in Western Asia to what is now Egypt in North Africa, later superseded by hostile Arab-Islamic culture and regimes. The peoples of these regions, by contrast, are depicted as superstitious heathens and cruel barbarians.

This is the metanarrative of the Old Testament, made concrete and brought to life in many Hollywood Bible films to this very day.

As soon as the movie industry emerged, so did Bible and Exodus films. In his overview *The Epic Film*, Elley observed that the early cinematic attempts very much prolonged the Sunday school tradition, "with its confetti mannah, winged angels, flame streamers, and God with a paper halo." Later directors, like Cecil B. DeMille, "added size, technical virtuosity, and showmanship, but the same theatricality and naivety of vision is there." Yet such projects would always be worthwhile to Hollywood, DeMille later said, because "what else has two thousand years' advance publicity?" (1984, pp. 35, 26).

DeMille further twisted the Bible story, however, for greater effect. In fact, these key revisions of the Old Testament had been initiated by Dorothy Clarke, who was married to Methodist minister Elwin Wilson. In 1949, she published the novel *Prince of Egypt*, which won several prizes and sold no fewer than half a million copies. She introduced a very subtle change in the Moses story, which opened great new dramatic possibilities, as she did did not have him adopted by the *daughter* of the pharaoh, which made him only a minor figure at the margins of the court—she had him adopted by the *wife* of the pharaoh, which made him a key figure at the center of the court—namely, a prince. In the same stroke, she also made him the major architect of the realm. This considerably raises the stakes in DeMille's film.[8]

In his study *The Ancient World in the Cinema*, Jon Solomon in turn recalled how Paramount's Adolph Zukor was initially skeptical about the first *Ten Commandments* project: "Old men wearing tablecloths and beards! Cecil, a picture like this would ruin us!" But DeMille assured him that there would be "plenty of box office–worthy sinning" in addition to the religious message. Solomon added, "In keeping with this promise, DeMille centered his approach to the story around the Golden Calf revelry . . . its one hundred thinly clad women would certainly give it huge mass appeal." After others reproached his spicing up of the Exodus story in this way, DeMille responded coyly: "I wish my accusers would read their Bible more closely, for in those pages are more violence and sex than I could ever portray on the screen" (2001, pp. 143, 134).

Whereas DeMille's 1923 version had still been silent and in black and white, his glorious 1956 remake was in full sound and Technicolor. It was one of those Hollywood spectaculars designed for wide-screen theatres, to trump the small screens of television. This time around, the highly successful director received carte blanche and an almost unlimited budget for those days. He was thus able to shoot the Egyptian and Sinai scenes on location and to increase the number of extras from thirty-five hundred to twenty thousand. Ironically, many of those were drawn from the cavalry corps of the Egyptian army not long before Israel invaded in support of the Franco-British expedition against Gamal Abdel Nasser's nationalization of "their" Suez Canal.

Violence was highlighted right from the famous early scenes, where taskmasters urge thousands of Jewish slaves on and incessantly whip them. This stereotypical image is widely questioned by Egyptologists today. When a taskmaster condones that an old woman (Moses's biological mother) be crushed under a giant moving stone moved forward by slaves (rather than halting its progress), the prophet intervenes. Sex was also highlighted early on, in a scene where the pharaoh holds court and receives visitors. They are continually entertained by ravenous girls and young women clad in transparent dresses with flesh-colored undergarments, if not in the antique equivalent of swimsuits and bikinis: an Orientalist fantasy par excellence.

The influence of this version on Christians' visualization of the Bible stories cannot be overestimated. The plagues and Moses's miracles are of course welcome subjects in Hollywood, always eager for special effects, as is the parting of the waters in the Red Sea, which we already discussed (and which is still part of studio theme park rides today), as well as Moses's retreat to Mount Sinai and his return with the monumental stone tablets. Copies of these tablets were used for the film's promotion, but their presence on state property became the subject of a protracted court battle that persists to this very day.[9]

Of course, DeMille's scenario was made highly political in many other ways. Not only were the opening scenes preceded by an elaborate on-screen speech on "dictators" and "freedom," putting the Bible story plainly in the service of the Cold War with communism, but other choices also resonated with late colonial and racial themes in many different ways. One was casting. As so many times before and after, the Moses figure was inspired by Michelangelo's interpretation and portrayed by an actor otherwise known for his wide variety of noble "blond hair/blue eyes" roles: Charlton Heston. Several poses and scenes also implicitly referred to the much later Christ story.

Only Dathan, a Jewish traitor and collaborator played by Edward G. Robinson, was made to look stereotypically Semitic in appearance. As so many times before and after, the younger pharaoh figure was made incarnate by a Hollywood actor in brown-face, specialized in portraying "exotic barbarian" despots: Yul Brynner. Moses's wife, who reportedly twice saved his life and therefore the survival of the Judeo-Christian tradition, was played by a white actress, although the Bible emphatically reports that she was from the southern kingdom of Kush (present-day Sudan), and dark-skinned or black.[10]

Case Study: The Jewish Prince of Egypt

The 1998 mega-project *The Prince of Egypt* was an animated re-make of *The Ten Commandments.* It had a lot of surplus significance for a lot of people around Hollywood. The film was directed by Jeffrey Katzenberg, who, as studio chief, had revived Disney by supervising *Aladdin, The Lion King*, and similar productions (discussed in greater detail in chapter 2) and felt their overwhelming success had been largely due to his efforts. Yet Disney chairman Michael Eisner refused to elevate him to company president, complaining that he was "overly aggressive." Katzenberg quit, claiming he was still owed 2 percent of company profits, or $250 million. He then endeavored to set up a major competitor—and to lure many major talents away. It was as if the Egyptian pharaoh had refused the crown prince or state architect credit for building the pyramids, whereupon the latter rebelled and led an exodus of his people to found a competing nation.

Katzenberg joined forces with blockbuster director Steven Spielberg and record executive David Geffen to found the popular culture powerhouse DreamWorks in 1994. Spielberg said he intended to continue "retelling history" through feature films, and Katzenberg said he intended to make "serious animation" films. When they brainstormed about what kind of ambitious project they would like to do together, they soon agreed on a remake of DeMille's awesome *The Ten Commandments*—but this time as an animated cartoon. When DreamWorks' *The Prince of Egypt* was released just before Christmas four years later, it competed worldwide with Disney's somewhat similar "ancient civilization" project *Mulan* (also discussed in chapter 2).

Katzenberg later claimed, though, that he had told his animators not to watch DeMille's film, with its slave masses pulling stone colossi under cracking whips, again—but instead to see David Lean's *Lawrence of Arabia* (discussed in chapter 7), a rather curious model from a cultural perspective. He furthermore claimed he had consulted some seven hundred Egyptologists and Bible scholars, but also many religious leaders—including influential Christian conservatives such as Jerry Falwell and Pat Robertson. The producers claimed to have kept an eye on possible Arab and/or Muslim sensitivities, but of course such concerns were much more marginal in their minds.

DreamWorks said it wanted to do better than Disney by focusing on adults as well as children, and therefore on the broadest possible "family audiences." But whereas the initial "newspaper ads for the movie evoked a museum poster—an iconic silhouette of the Moses character, inset with a far-off view of the Great Pyramids," they soon backed down. The ads now "evoked a superheroes cartoon, depicting a chariot race between a youthful, bare-chested Moses and the youthful, bare-chested Pharaoh-in-waiting"[11]—in typical Disney fashion.

The archetypical Hollywood "car chase" at the beginning chipped off the Sphinx' nose, subject to eternal Egyptian tourist guide jokes, but Katzenberg defended himself from trying to do camel jokes like the monkey jokes in *Aladdin* or priest jokes like the genie jokes in *Aladdin*. And although Wal-Mart promoted the musical soundtrack of the film in its stores, and also sold some six hundred thousand advance tickets, DreamWorks "decided against arranging fast-food tie-ins and toy spin-offs, in deference to the subject matter."[12]

At first and superficial sight, the film is just a nice new version of an age-old story, without much stereotype or prejudice. But a closer look reveals some curious changes, based not only on unconscious associations but apparently also on conscious decisions. The tendency of most postwar historical scholarship to tone down the grandiose claims made in the biblical Exodus story somewhat was willingly overlooked, for instance. The scriptwriters not only stuck with the flagrant embellishments in Dorothy Clarke Wilson's book and Cecil B. DeMille's films but further raised the stakes and even went so far as to suggest that the story was registered in the Egyptian hieroglyphs—which it was not. Let us review just a few of the most flagrant embellishments.

In Jeffrey Katzenberg's film, Moses is further elevated to a kind of half-brother of Ramses and actually made an alternate crown prince and even a designated future pharaoh. They start out as natural peers, but of course the former develops into the archetypical good guy and the latter into the archetypical bad guy. Katzenberg further embellishes the Bible account on other scores as well and makes it fit the sugar-sweet Hollywood/Disney mold: Whereas the Old Testament emphatically says that Moses murdered an Egyptian taskmaster and that the pharaoh therefore wanted to have him killed in turn, Katzenberg suggests it was a mere accident and has Moses leave the court of his own free will. The whole orgy around the Golden Calf, less interesting in family fare, is also skipped this in this version.

The film further heightens not only Moses's moral superiority but also his cultural standing. As in Dorothy Clarke Wilson and Cecil B. DeMille's story, Moses is no longer a mere courtier or adviser; he is the chief architect of the realm. Images at the beginning of the Katzenberg film emphasize this even more, showing many of the major buildings and monuments of the ancient civilization with which the average tourist is familiar—at Giza, Luxor, Karnak, and Thebes—with the familiar images of Tutankhamen's splendid funerary mask thrown in for good measure (Bergmans 2002). The dialogue and scenes now clearly suggest that these wonders were in fact designed by Moses or built under his supervision. Thus the glorious Egyptian heritage is further expropriated, confiscated, and reassigned to a different cultural lineage.

Egypt is, of course, made a barren place in typical Eurocentric fashion: the emphasis is not on the fertile Nile and its green-blue colors, but on the dry desert and its beige-brown colors. But even within the framework of this chosen palette, hues and shades are further assigned ideological connotations. Just before the release of the movie, an article in the *New York Times* summed up the choices made: "The contrasts in *The Prince of Egypt* are striking. The pharaoh's palace is splendid and chilly, all white and light pastels, in contrast to the warm, burnished colors of the modest dwellings of the Israelites in Goshen."[13]

In the production notes, the art director said that the world of the Hebrews was made more organic, by contrast: "We gave Goshen more of a rounded, eroded look because the homes were made of mud brick, which is weathered by the rain, the wind, and the sand. The homes are asymmetrical and out of kilter to give them a flow and ebb that the angular Egyptian side does not have. The faces of the Egyptian characters are more sculptured in appearance, with chiseled features; the Israelites are more curved, and their shapes are looser."[14] So the sympathy and identification of the audience were subtly guided.

Most reviews in the general press, such as those already mentioned in the *New York Times*, were rather positive, as were those in the Christian and Jewish press. One interesting example comes from the "largest circulation progressive Jewish magazine" *Tikkun*, which carried unanimous praise by three rabbis. Its head, Rabbi Michael Lerner, said that the film would "shape the understanding of the Torah for generations to come" and had followed Hollywood conventions by not only portraying Moses but "virtually all the Jewish people in this romantically appealing way." Rabbi Dan Goldblatt added that "in the Jewish world, religious school teachers and rabbis should be jumping for joy. . . . Though framed as a universal and paradigmatic story of liberation, the *Prince of Egypt* reminds us of the particularity of the 'Hebrews.'" He concluded: "For the Jewish community, the three 'wise men' of DreamWorks deliver a new and extraordinary Passover story as a Chanukah present on Christmas." And Rabbi Laura Geller referred to Michael Walzer's study *Exodus and Revolution*, which had shown how this Jewish arch-story had permeated the whole of Western civilization for more than two thousand years, in this context.[15] One might add that this was particularly true for Judeo-Christian settler states such as the United States, Canada, Australia, and New Zealand, where the theme of a tragic flight from poverty and oppression to go and build a new life in a "promised land" struck a deep chord. But let us now look at a contrary example, where ethnocentrism may have taken an anti-Jewish twist.

NEW TESTAMENT MOVIES

The greatest religious blockbuster movie of all time so far was *The Passion of the Christ*. The project's originator, Mel Gibson, meant it to become the ultimate movie about Jesus's last twelve hours, more authentic and realistic than any previous one. This carried great risks: Such movies had always proven potentially popular but also potentially controversial. When he could not find a major studio to back him, Gibson invested $25 million or more of his own money. One gimmick in the film was to have the actors speak the "original languages" such as Aramaic and Hebrew. The filming in Rome and Italy was further accompanied by early publicity hype, for instance, about the "coincidence" that the lead role was played by a thirty-three-year-old actor with the initials J. C., or that a real-life thunderbolt supposedly split the skies when the Golgotha scene was being filmed.

Christian opinion leaders and churches had been carefully selected for previews. The pope was reported to have said, "This is how it really was"; the Protestant preacher Billy Graham said, "It was as if I was there." The movie was then released simultaneously in no fewer than two thousand theatres across the United States on a very carefully chosen day: Ash Wednesday, the beginning of the forty-day Christian Lent period of asceticism and reflection that precedes Easter.

The movie immediately proved to be an unprecedented hit: By the very next day it had already broken even. It continued its triumph to become the highest grossing "foreign-language" movie in the United States. Over the next six months, it sold $370 million in tickets in the United States alone; only *Spider-Man* and *Shrek* did better. By that time, 20th Century Fox had taken up video and DVD sales, among other things, by "wooing pastors at 260,000 churches to buy the movie in bulk" in "its most exhaustive Christian marketing effort ever."[16] Yet Gibson had trouble getting the film released in Israel, and it was accompanied by one of the most violent polemics Hollywood or the American media had ever seen on its gratuitous violence—and the accusation that it had a hidden agenda of anti-Semitism.

Around the same time that Gibson's *Passion* was released, the Franco-German "highbrow" channel Arte broadcast one of the most un-Hollywood projects shown on television anywhere, ever. It was a series of ten programs on *The Origins of Christianity,* and it expanded on a similar previous extended series, also by Gérard Mordillat and Jérôme Prieur.[17] It was fascinating material, although it had just "talking heads" in various different languages. But they included dozens of the very finest biblical scholars of the day, from all around the globe: North America, western Europe, and the Middle East; Protestants, Catholics, and Jews. They had an elaborate and state-of-the-art debate about what is known today about the historical Jesus, about the various gospels and the New Testament.

The Arte documentaries concluded that the status of the New Testament as a historical source was highly questionable. The earliest material included in it, the letters of Paul (which rarely mention Jesus' life or sayings), date from around the year 50 or 60 CE. Their writing was soon followed by the Jewish revolt against Roman domination and the destruction of the Temple in the year 70 CE. This provoked a complete redefinition of all religious strands. One branch of Judaism triumphed over all others, but the emphasis necessarily shifted from worship in the Temple to the contemplation of the Torah. The Christian "sect" meanwhile spread to the north—that is to say, to the current area of Lebanon, Syria, and Turkey; it conversed and wrote mostly in Greek.

Biblical scholar Bart Ehrman of the Department of Religious Studies at the University of North Carolina at Chapel Hill made an inventory of no less than forty-seven alternative gospels and Christian texts from the earliest days. Many of these texts are or contain falsifications, he says, produced in order to further the claims of the many early Christian sects struggling for supremacy. The four gospels that were later selected and canonized had been written anonymously and were only much later ascribed to four known prominent members of the early Jesus movement, on grounds that are widely questioned today.

We have no originals but only handwritten "copies made from copies of the copies of the copies of the originals." The earliest ones date from around the year 200 CE; the first complete manuscripts date from the fourth century. There are nearly fifty-four hundred later Greek copies in existence, and no two copies agree in all of their wording. The number of differences is estimated at several hundred thousand: more than there are words in the entire New Testament (Ehrman 2003, pp. 217–19). Keith Hopkins, professor of ancient history at the University of Cambridge, has in turn demonstrated how the texts were made to fit preexisting or preferred moulds.

None of the authors was an eyewitness to the events they described. Often they had not even based their accounts on direct eyewitness reports but rather on an elaborate oral tradition of embellished hearsay. It is not surprising, then, that "Mark," "Matthew," and "Luke" often gave somewhat contradictory accounts of the same events and comments. The last and fourth gospel by "John," furthermore, is rather different in emphasis and tone but has nevertheless become the prism through which the others are read today. The four are often harmonized into one linear story, furthermore, which takes a lot of leveling and sharpening of details.

At that time, there were still dozens of Christian sects, all adhering to their own versions of the historical truth. It was only after the Roman emperor decided to tolerate Christianity during the early fourth century that the articles of faith were codified. This contributed to the acceptance of Christianity and its integration with other and older traditions into the more or less official religion of Rome [18]

Another recent ambitious European television documentary, *Son of God* (2003), with the talking heads of another host of famous Bible scholars went one step further than the Arte series.[19] This documentary focused more on the postwar archaeological finds of new documents dating back to the earliest days of Christianity, such as the eighty thousand pieces of the Dead Sea Scrolls, the Gospel of Thomas, the new Gospel of Judas (released by the National Geographic Society in 2006), and a number of others.

This analysis revealed that many made *no reference at all* to some of the most characteristic elements of the Jesus story as it had become codified—including his supposed claim to be the literal "Son of God" and the subsequent hostility of the Pharisees. God impregnating an earthly woman and Virgin Birth, the birth on Christmas day and a resurrection in spring (both related to sun worship and the solstices), the crucifix as a symbol and the crucifixion as a sacrifice to save the people, an afterlife and paradise, and so on—often none of these were mentioned. Even more surprisingly, many of these precise elements were already present in much older religions and cults, such as those surrounding the Egyptian Osiris, the Persian Mithras, the Greek Dionysos, and others—well before Christ's days.

A final element about the "image" of the Passion is the following: The earlier Jewish religion had maintained its ban on visual representations, and the later Islamic religion adhered to it as well. It was only after the spread and challenge of the latter during the eighth century that another council decided to give up the Christian ban on idols and thus to widen its popular appeal to the illiterate masses, two centuries before the first Crusades. This spurred the famous pious European art of early medieval times, which centered around Jesus and a "blood theology" of torture and suffering. The paintings of the late

Middle Ages and the Renaissance, the stations inside and decorations outside the cathedrals, became the first elaborate nontextual *representations* of the Passion.[20] From then on, they also came to be confused with some kind of original rendering, even though they were produced a full millennium or even more after the supposed events themselves.

It was also from those same days on that the Passion came to be reproduced in European plays and musical works. When photography and film were introduced during the nineteenth century, these arbitrary iconographic conventions in turn became further frozen in time. Over the first century of cinematography, there have been at least a hundred major films about Jesus Christ—that is to say, on average a new version every single year. They differ in many respects, but they also have much in common. W. Barnes Tatum has compared and analyzed a dozen of the most influential productions in his illuminating overview *Jesus at the Movies: A Guide to the First Hundred Years* (1997), which in turn inspired at least one television documentary with extracts from these films.[21]

Tatum reports that the first three were filmed Passion plays. The third claimed to be a faithful registration of the famous Passion play of Oberammergau, which had been staged every decade in Bavaria since 1634 but was in fact filmed on the roof of a building in New York.[22] Tatum distinguishes between embellished Christ stories variously placed in Roman or present times and more literal Jesus stories focusing on episodes from his life and death as reported in the four canonical gospels. The successful novels *Barabbas, Ben-Hur, Quo Vadis,* and *The Robe,* for instance, did inspire repeated scripts and productions in the former category.

They were rather profitable projects, too. Tatum notes that "*Quo Vadis* brought in more than $11 million, the second highest box office total for 1952, against a production cost of some $6 million. *The Robe* produced $17 million in the last few months of 1953, against a production cost of only $4 million, on the way to becoming one of the top box office draws of the decade. . . . William Wyler's *Ben-Hur* (1959) represents one of the most successful films in the history of cinema. The biggest box-office draw of the decade 1951–1960" (pp. 69–70). Samuel Bronston's *King of Kings* (1961) and George Stevens *The Greatest Story Ever Told* (1965) come closer to the latter category. They wrestled even more with questions of truth and representation.

From the early 1960s on, and throughout the 1970s, there was a widespread reaction to the embellished "Sunday school" approach and a call for more authenticity. Two Italian films that made it to the United States set an example. Pier-Paolo Pasolini's *The Gospel According to Saint Matthew* (1964) was filmed in black and white in the desolate landscapes of southern Italy. It was dedicated to the reformist Pope John XXIII, who had died during the Second Vatican Council. It made the Jesus of the Sermon of the Mount somewhat further a rebel and a revolutionary (in line with the emerging liberation theology and Marxist liberation movements of Latin America), yet it became popular among the faithful for its sober and ascetic approach. Pasolini later explained: "I, a nonbeliever, was telling the story through the eyes of a believer" (Tatum 1997, p. 105).

Franco Zeffirelli's six-hour TV series *Jesus of Nazareth* (1977), based on all four gospels, was initially made for the Italian RAI and British ATV, after which NBC acquired the U.S. broadcasting rights for $15 million. Both Pasolini and Zeffirelli earnestly wrestled with questions of authenticity, but they stirred considerable controversy anyway, both at home and abroad. Fundamentalist Christians tried to control the images that were allowed onto the screens. In the latter case, General Motors dropped its television sponsorship after receiving eighteen thousand angry letters, only to be replaced by Procter & Gamble, which would soon have a similar problem.[23]

But there were Anglo-American productions striving for more liveliness and authenticity as well. In the late 1960s the strict Hollywood Production Code was replaced by a more liberal rating system, which opened the way to further experiments. After the single "Jesus Christ Superstar" turned out a major success, Tim Rice and Andrew Lloyd Webber wrote a "rock opera" by that name, which was staged in New York in 1971 and then filmed by Norman Jewison in 1973. In line with the countercultural spirit of the times, the historical Jesus was further transformed—not into a Marxist revolutionary this time, but into a hippie pop singer.

It was also around the mid-1970s that the young New Hollywood "movie brat" director Martin Scorsese decided to make *The Last Temptation of Christ*, but he inevitably ran into huge resistance and delays, and the movie was only released much later, in 1988. It was based on a controversial novel by Nobel Prize–winning author Nikos Kazantzakis (whose work had also inspired the 1964 movie *Zorba the Greek*). The story imagined Jesus on the cross as a true man, contemplating what it would have been like to marry Mary Magdalene and found a family.

Here again, GM soon dropped its intended television sponsorship and Paramount Pictures dropped the entire project. Universal then turned it into a low-budget movie, although a fundamentalist Christian offered to buy the original—to destroy it for all time. Others staged protests and pickets outside the theatres, whereas Jerry Falwell and his Moral Majority movement called for a full-scale boycott. The provocative movie received good reviews but was prevented from becoming a commercial success.

There are several lines running through this entire long tradition. Many films try to get closer to the "real" Jesus, literally or figuratively, in a way that is appealing to mass audiences in the West. How do they try to solve this problem, and how does that relate to the subject of this book—that is to say, to the depiction of ethnic or cultural "others" on the screen, in Hollywood blockbusters or other very popular movies? The problem has various obvious aspects.

We have seen that there is little we know with complete certainty about the "true" Jesus from a secular point of view, even though there are no historical figures about whom so much research has been done and so many studies have been written. The only thing we know for sure is that around that time there were several strands of Judaism. One of the many emerging movements was led by a man called Jesus, who criticized decadence, warned that the world might be coming to an end, and was possibly executed at the instigation of his enemies.

The story turned into one about the Son of God incarnate. But what type of actor looks like God? What kind of wig and makeup should he wear? We do not know. One way around this is to film the principal character only from a respectful distance, and/or never to show his face, as is done in some of the older movies, even though from the first medieval representations on there is near-unanimity on his appearance. He is usually depicted as relatively tall, self-assured, and easily accepted by others as a leader. But he also became lighter, as the center of the Christian religion moved further from the southeast to the northwest.

A day after Christmas 2004, Italian television had forensic scientists in Rome produce a computer portrait of the young Jesus, based on the controversial Shroud of Turin. The image showed "an angelic face reminiscent of the prayer cards sold in Vatican souvenir shops . . . with fair hair, smooth skin, glassy blue eyes, fleshy lips, and waves of dirty blond hair."[24] As an adult, Jesus is usually given long, straight hair, a moustache, and a beard. This is the image that has been codified in Hollywood films. A classic example is the Jesus in Cecil B. DeMille's *King of Kings*. Yet a much more serious scientific reconstruction done in 2001 for a BBC television documentary depicted him much smaller, with a typically Middle Eastern face, darker skin, frizzy hair, and brown eyes.[25]

We know more or less what the biblical landscape looked like, but should the entire crew and cast of Bible films necessarily be made to travel to Israel and Palestine for veracity? Are Tunisia and Morocco just as good, or even Italy or California? This also has implications for the extras hired on the spot, to represent "the people" and "the crowd" in key scenes of the film. Should they be Jewish or Arab looking? Or can they just as well be Europeans or Americans? Zeffirelli decided to shoot his film in Tunisia but to hire many extras from the Jewish community on the coastal island of Djerba. Throughout many of these movies, there is a noteworthy tendency not only to make Jesus and some of his apostles (their skin, hair, eyes, etc.) lighter, but also to make the Jewish people and crowd darker by contrast. This held for Judas "the traitor" in particular, often depicted as the exponent of Judaism par excellence. All this is, of course, significant in view of what follows.

We have seen that even the four canonical gospels do not agree on the words spoken (for instance, the famous last words in the cross) or on the events themselves (for instance, the exact circumstances of the resurrection). But in what language should they be rendered, and in what language were they spoken originally? Not only do the main characters usually speak fluent English in Hollywood Jesus films, there is even a tendency for them to speak more with a civilized or even upper-class accent if they are higher in the movement's hierarchy.

Gibson had it right that they probably spoke Aramaic (but also Hebrew) in everyday life, but Greek (and not Latin) was the administrative language. But when he explained after a preview that he adopted those because they sounded stranger, some called it xenophobic. If he had made a movie, he insisted, "about horrible cruel Vikings, landing with their boats and atrocious arms, ready to commit massacres, it would not have been menacing enough to have them speak English."[26]

But what about the charges of anti-Semitism in the official gospels and their successive translations, in various movie scripts based on them and in Gibson's *Passion*? Here again it is important to look at the original context. There were several major currents in Judaism: the Pharisees, the Sadduceans, the Essenes, and, later, the Zealots. The former controlled the center in Jerusalem; Galilee was seen as a distant and marginal region with too many outside influences. Furthermore, Jesus and his followers somehow belonged to an oppositional branch criticizing the dominant branch. This was one reason why some writers of the Christian gospels alternately praised and scorned "the Jews," often meaning "the other Jews."

One central question has always been to what extent this process also provoked the hostility of the dominant branch, to what extent they twisted the truth and the rules on Jesus's guilt, to what extent they were responsible for his ultimate execution. Tatum explains that the political and legal situation in the Judea of those days was extremely complex and ambiguous. Pontius Pilate was the Roman governor and prefect. The Romans had previously appointed Herod "king of the Jews," although he was a bit of a stranger. After his death, however, none of his sons inherited the title of king; all three were merely made rulers of marginal districts. High priest Joseph Caiaphas presided over the Jewish Temple and over the Sanhedrin, the chief judicial body, but its exact role at the time is somewhat unclear (1997, pp. 158–59).

There is also confusion over the nature of the interrogation of Jesus by Caiaphas and the referral to Pilate. The key scene is that in which Pilate asks the Jewish crowd what to do with Jesus. According to John, they shout: "Crucify him, crucify him!" (19:15). According to Matthew they add (in the traditional King James translation): "His blood be on us and on our children!" (27: 24–25). But the latter crucial phrase may have been inserted later, into the earlier account by Mark, so it is subject to questions. In Gibson's version, the crucial phrase was uttered in Aramaic, but at the very last moment it was decided to skip the subtitle translation in English, because a huge controversy was already brewing over it. Why is this so important?

This key scene in the New Testament has been subject to complete reappraisal and reinterpretation during the decades after World War II. Before the war, the scene was presented and read by many mainstream Catholic and Protestant leaders both as a justification for anti-Semitism and as a naturalization of its consequences: from the destruction of the Temple to the European pogroms. After the Holocaust, however, there was a complete reversal—even though it took several decades to feel its full effect.

The Second Vatican Council of the mid-1960s, for instance, now condemned these abuses. In newer translations of the New Testament the word "Jew" is therefore translated using rather different terms, such as "Jewish authorities," whenever a remark might otherwise be read as anti-Semitic. Biblical scholars have since suggested that Matthew chose to blame Jesus's execution more on the Jews, and less on the Romans, in order to be less threatening and more acceptable to them. Suddenly, theologians no longer spoke of Judaism and Christianity as conflicting creeds but came to speak of a common Judeo-Christian religion. But not everybody was equally happy with this.

Case Study: The Passion about *The Passion*
     It is clear now why many of the older Passion plays and movie scripts highlighted the controversial scene ("his blood be upon us and on our children") and also why many of the newer ones toned it down or left it out altogether. So the question became: Why did Gibson emphatically reinstate an earlier version, reinforcing its emphases throughout the whole movie rather than toning them down? In his film, Pilate and the Roman authorities are shown as extremely reluctant at every single

turn; by contrast, Caiaphas and the Jewish high priests are shown as the driving forces.

They are also cheered on by most of the Jewish people and crowds, and the movie goes really out of its way to insist in image and sound on the goriest details of Jesus's resulting torture and death. The suggestion of the film is therefore emphatic and clear. Many Jewish commentators, media, and antiracist groups in the United States were alarmed when they first heard about early versions of the script. The prestigious *New York Times* subsequently devoted dozens upon dozens of pages to the controversy, and even the slim overseas *International Herald Tribune* carried an unprecedented number of articles on it. One example was "a Jewish view" titled "Mel Gibson Revives an Old Message of Hate" by Rabbi Michael Lerner, head of the Tikkun interfaith group.[27]

But what had stirred suspicions of his true intentions and motivation? Mel Gibson's career had been very much built on archetypical myths, about the future as well as the past. He had become a successful actor through rather violent action films such as as *Mad Max* and *Lethal Weapon* and a successful director with *Braveheart*. He was a typical macho Hollywood sex symbol and at one point confessed to the usual substance abuse and other carnal sins. But he had since turned a born-again Christian and very conservative Catholic. He had seven children and reportedly spent several million dollars of his own money to help build a new church in the hills of Malibu, where mass would be celebrated every Sunday in the traditional Latin. He adhered to the "traditionalist" branch of Catholicism and a dissenting group advocated by his father.

This group rejected the Catholic reforms of the early 1960s as a serious deviation and consequently also rejected the authority of the pope in Rome. Gibson had always conceived his film project on *The Passion of the Christ* as a vehicle for the spread of this "traditionalist" version of the faith. The filming took place in Rome and around the same southern village where Pasolini had worked. He later claimed in an interview that, as a director, he had been guided by the Holy Spirit himself. But since traditionalists like him had a troubled relationship with the Vatican, he chose to send his lead actor to give a preview of the film to the ailing pope.

Meanwhile, it had also turned out that a series of precise details in Gibson's original script and final film about Jesus's last hours (in Gethsemane, before Herod, with Mary, as well as the crumbling of the Temple on the Jewish high priests) derived from a rather curious source:

Anna Katharina Emmerich, an early nineteenth-century nun who claimed to have received not only stigmata but also extremely precise visions of the events of his last few hours. These accounts were taken down in sixteen thousand pages of notes by the romantic poet Clemens Brentano, also the founder of a Christian-German society. When the first volume was published it became a huge best seller, and five large volumes were ultimately published. The problem is that both coauthors were virulent anti-Semites and were frequently quoted by virulent anti-Semites for their (oriented) visions of the Passion.[28]

But there was more to the pattern. Hutton Gibson, the father of the director, had proven not only a traditionalist Catholic polemicist in his past writings but also a consistent anti-Semite and even a revisionist denier of the Holocaust. A week before the movie was to be released, the Jewish radio talk show host Steve Feuerstein called him under a pretext and taped an interview. Feuerstein asked, "What was this event called the Holocaust?" Gibson's reply: "They claimed that there were 6.2 million [Jews] in Poland before the war. And after the war there were 200,000. Therefore he [Hitler] must have killed six million of them. [But] they simply got up and left! They were all over the Bronx and Brooklyn, and Sydney and Los Angeles. . . . I've known a lot of Germans. . . . They were efficient, and they know how to do things. If they had set out to kill six million Jews, they would have done it. But all we hear about are Holocaust survivors. . . . This is absolutely ridiculous. And [the Holocaust] it's all—maybe not all fiction—but most of it is. . . . Guess who owned the railroads? The Jews. IG Farben industries was never touched. . . . They were owned by the Jews. They owned the banking system. Hitler's big crime was operating without the big banks (and the Jews)."

He continued to say that today's Holocaust museums are "just a gimmick to collect money." Roosevelt tricked the United States into the war. "They killed several generations of us Americans. The Jews weren't in the army much." All this continued today, he said. The banker Greenspan should be "taken out" and hanged. "They're after one world religion and one world government." Jews are anti-Christian and "anti–everyone else." Asked by Feuerstein, "Why did the [Jewish] Anti-Defamation League oppose the film [of his son]?" Gibson answered, "This is part of their deal. . . . Mel says he absolutely couldn't buy PR like this. And (thanks to the A.D.L.) everybody knows the line now: Let the blood be upon us and on our children."[29] Such statements raised further questions about Mel Gibson's sources of inspiration.

This radio interview was not an isolated outburst but had been preceded by a long series of similar well-documented statements. Yet Mel

Gibson suggested that journalists had abused his father's very old age and deteriorating sense of judgment. At the same time, he distanced himself somewhat halfheartedly. Peggy Noonan, a former speech-writer for conservative president Ronald Reagan, later wrote an enthu-siastic piece about the film for the *Wall Street Journal*, posted on its website, saying that the pope had given *The Passion* a "five-star rat-ing." So it was as a friendly journalist that she in turn interviewed Mel Gibson for *Reader's Digest* at the time of the film's release. Question: "The Holocaust happened, right?" Answer: "Yes, of course. Atrocities happened. War is horrible. The Second World War killed tens of mil-lions of people. Some of them were Jews in concentration camps."

The influential *New York Times* critic Frank Rich called this less than straightforward. He was one of those to lead the charge before, during, and after the release of the film, even though he later denied he had ei-ther called the movie anti-Semitic or called for its suppression. But he wrote acerbicly: "With its laborious build-up to its orgasmic spurtings of blood and other bodily fluids, the film is constructed like nothing so much as a porn movie, replete with slo-mo climaxes and pounding mu-sic. . . . Does that make it bad for the Jews? Not necessarily. As a di-rector, Gibson is no Leni Riefenstahl [Hitler's preferred filmmaker]. His movie is just too ponderous to spark a pogrom on its own—in America anyway." In typical Hollywood macho style, Gibson had earlier replied to Rich's attempts to discredit the movie: "I want his intestines on a stick. . . . I want to kill this dog."[30]

At the time of the premiere, the *New York Times* also reported from Los Angeles that the charges of a hidden agenda had greatly upset the movie world, because "many of Hollywood's most prominent figures are also Jewish. . . . Jeffrey Katzenberg and David Geffen, the principals of DreamWorks, have privately expressed anger over the film. . . . The chairmen of two other major studios said they would avoid working with Gibson. . . . [O]ne explained: 'It doesn't matter what I say. It'll matter what I do. . . . I won't support anything he's part of.'" But others disagreed. "I don't think it will hurt him," said John Lesher, an agent with Endeavor. "People will work with the Antichrist, if he'll put butts in seats." Two weeks later, Rich reported that Gibson was "hotter than ever in Holly-wood" and that "one Jewish movie mogul" had cynically told him, "If Hitler did a movie with these numbers, we'd give him his next deal."[31]

Meanwhile, the media's skepticism provoked a major backlash from conservative Christians, Catholics, and Protestants alike. Rich's *Times* colleague A. O. Scott reported, "After my review, I received, not sur-prisingly, an unusually large number of phone calls and e-mail messages from readers. Most of them took issue with my criticisms of what I took to be the film's excessive violence and its vengeful, angry spirit. Some were abusive (and startlingly foul-mouthed) rants about the 'left-wing' media (and also in some cases, predictably enough, the 'Jewish media'), while others, repeating certain key words and phrases almost verbatim, looked like an orchestrated e-mail campaign."[32] According to a poll in the subsequent Christmas issue of *Newsweek* "85 percent of American adults call themselves Christian, 82 percent see Jesus as the son of God, and 79 percent believe in the virgin birth."[33]

Although Gibson was nervous on the eve of the release of *The Passion*, the attacks on it did indeed prove completely counterproductive. They drew a huge amount of additional public attention to a relatively modest production and mobilized believers all around the world. Even the merchandising around the film proved highly successful, although Gibson had joked that there would not be a *Passion* Happy Meal at McDonald's. The Christian Publications Bookstore in New York, for one, reportedly sold a wide range of *Passion* T-shirts and *Passion* coffee mugs and even an "original" crown of thorns for only $14.95. A shop assistant estimated that after six weeks there were also already a hundred thousand copies in circulation of a nail chain, which a jewel designer had created especially for the occasion.[34]

By early April, 19 percent of Americans reported they had already seen the movie, and a further 49 percent planned to go and see it. But according to an opinion poll taken by the authoritative Pew Research Centre, the movie did indeed provoke a significant rise in age-old anti-Semitic sentiments in the United States. Since a previous poll, it said, the number of people who felt that "the Jews" were responsible for the death of Jesus had suddenly risen from 19 to 25 percent. Among those under thirty it had risen from 10 to 34 percent, and among blacks from 21 to 42 percent.[35] The movie indeed contributed to a significant revival of Christian anti-Semitism, whether Gibson consciously meant to do so or not.

The controversy over the movie was reviewed in a collection of essays, pro and con, edited by S. Brent Plate, an assistant professor of religion and the visual arts at Texas Christian University. A year and a half later, the *New York Times* reported that Gibson wanted to "come clean" on the Holocaust and was considering making a television miniseries on Flory van Beek—an Anne Frank kind of character who had survived the war.[36] But the controversy was revived and intensified after Gibson was reported to have launched into an anti-Semitic rant after a drunk-driving arrest in California in the summer of 2006.

So mainstream blockbuster movies naively based on traditional readings of the Bible, or even on further embellishments in the same direction in order to heighten religious feelings, do of necessity risk being ethnocentric in one way or another, as the Old Testament closely identifies with a Jewish point of view in its confrontation with the "Arab" civilizations to its northeast and southwest and the New Testament closely identifies with a Christian point of view in its confrontation with the Jewish civilization. Even though the details themselves concerning these traditional "others" may at first be marginal, their sacralization may further build their significance and insidiousness.

The Advanced and the Backward: Science Fiction and Space Adventure

What about the future? Will it entail ever easier living or hard times on Earth? Will science and technology foster exchanges with the moon or Mars, other solar systems—or even other galaxies? How do we imagine aliens from outer space, based on recent Hollywood blockbusters? Is it possible they may already be among us, in some invisible or disguised form? Or will we make "first contact" when traveling to distant planets and stars ourselves? Could this result in military confrontations on an unprecedented scale—even without human involvement, just between distant cultures in space? How do we tell the good guys from the bad guys? Or would these apparent "free fantasies" remain tainted by current-day ideologies and states of affairs, with exactly the same stereotypes and prejudices, just dressed up in strange gear and projected into the far skies?

Would you be able to imagine fundamentally different creatures in fundamentally different situations? They are the fare of fairy tales and fantasy, but also of horror and disaster movies. They too employ archetypical images of "us" versus "them," of reassuring versus scary characters. One particularly interesting genre is that of science fiction and fantasies of the future. These are usually based on a mere extrapolation from the present, but this usually misses the nonlinear shifts that have proven all too common in the recent past in the technological, economic, social, political, and military fields (Schnaars 1989; Sherden 1998).

So, how do you imagine the future? Do you believe that the current Western model of development will simply continue to spread and grow for many centuries to come, with ever more energy consumption, sophisticated automation, high technology, and data processing? Or do you feel that sooner or later it will slide into a major crisis, which may prove extremely hard to overcome, over resources or pollution, wealth distribution or power sharing, or simply related to climate changes or astronomical events? These are subjects of science fiction.

Science fiction seems to be a paradoxical term, one overview notes, as it combines fact and fabrication. It plays "what if" games (Telotte 2001, pp. 3–4). The genre already had predecessors in premodern society, but it only flourished widely with the industrial and postindustrial, the electronic and information age. The British sci-fi author J. G. Ballard famously quipped, "Sooner or later all science fiction comes true." But sci-fi always capitalizes on the hopes and fears of *contemporary* man. Although there seem to be no limits to these visions, they must somehow be rooted in current affairs—if only to remain both recognizable and topical. Paradoxically, then, few genres age as quickly as precisely this futurist one. Even only a few years later, it is relatively easy to recognize the signature of the exact era of a sci-fi work's creation.

The future state of affairs in such stories is often valued as highly desirable or highly undesirable, as a utopia or a dystopia, or a mixture of both. Sometimes the dystopian elements are highlighted (a threat to our current way of life and beliefs), whereas the utopian elements remain backgrounded (a high-tech future in which no one will have to work hard or even clean up after themselves). Not surprisingly, the United States, with New York and Los Angeles as its most notable eastern and western poles, has today become the most influential breeding ground as well as future terrestrial setting for sci-fi. But today's international situation and intercultural tensions do inevitably continue to shine through.

Utopian elements prevailed in the work of the pioneer nineteenth-century French novelist Jules Verne, for instance, in his *Voyages Extraordinaires*, where new vehicles opened up new realms for adventurous travel: the train, submarine, balloon, and so on. Most of his many books have been made into films, both in France and abroad. The work of the pioneer turn-of-the-century British novelist H. G. Wells was more reserved in tone. Most of his many books have also been made into films, both in England and abroad. But his concepts have been copied and varied even more frequently: the invisible man, the time machine, the invasion from space. The most famous dystopian visions of the future were outlined by the twentieth-century British novelists George Orwell with *1984* and Aldous Huxley with *Brave New World*, both made into films. Although they are usually linked to faraway totalitarian societies, they also apply to nearby democratic societies—for instance, to growing electronic surveillance and media consumerism (for the latter see Postman's 1985 critique).

Early dystopian films about rampant urbanism, industrialism, and class are *Metropolis* (1927) by the German (later American) director Fritz Lang and *Modern Times* (1936) by the British (later American) actor/director/producer Charlie Chaplin. Small-scale arty films in this same dystopian tradition were *Alphaville* (1965) by Jean-Luc Godard and *Fahrenheit 451* (1967) by François Truffaut—both French nouvelle vague directors. Later famous films in the same line are *Blade Runner* (1982) by director Ridley Scott (who moved from Britain to America) and *Brazil* (1985) by director Terry Gilliam (who moved from America to Britain, and back). Somehow, they all imply an intercultural perspective, as they imply a very critical look at everything that is normally taken for granted. Some disaster films might also be placed under the same heading, from resources running out in *Soylent Green* (1973) to climate change in *The Day After Tomorrow* (2004). Most such films are warnings about where we could be heading, one or two generations down the road.

One theme that is particularly prominent in sci-fi movies is that of man-made and man-imitating inventions, smart or strong, or both. It necessarily implies a reflection upon the nature of the human mind and human cooperation, conformity and individuality, determination and "freedom." The theme harkens back to older literary traditions about the Golem and Frankenstein. In sci-fi film it came to cover the whole ground from machines or computers taking over and running wild (e.g., "HAL" in *2001: A Space Odyssey*), to android robots and cyborg hybrids (*The Six Million Dollar Man* of 1970s television fame), to present-day replicants and clones (prominent in *Star Trek* and *Star Wars*, as discussed below). Blockbusters entirely built around the cyborg/robot theme were *Terminator* (1984) with Austrian-American actor Arnold Schwarzenegger, its sequel, *Robocop* (1987) by Dutch-American director Paul Verhoeven, and its sequels. Also think of the later *Matrix* trilogy, with its parallel virtual and programmed universes. But what about living creatures from outer space?

VISITORS FROM OUTER SPACE

As knowledge of evolution and the universe progressed, so did the realization that other living creatures might somehow be inhabiting distant planets. Nineteenth-century observers had been fascinated by a landscape on Mars that seemed to look like a human face and by a number of straight lines and geometric figures many felt were canals, pointing to a highly developed civilization. Would the Martians be able to come to Earth before we would be able to visit them?

After World War II, there was a rumor that a space ship had crashed in the United States near Roswell, New Mexico. Skeptics maintained that a piece of

black-and-white film that turned up later (and claimed to show the secret dis-
section of alien bodies by experts) was an easily discernible hoax, yet some
150,000 people flocked to the fiftieth anniversary of the supposed event in
1997. On the occasion of the landing of the first Pathfinder mission that same
year, BBC television aired "A Weekend on Mars." A documentary on the cold
war *Fear of a Red Planet*, directed by Michael Wadding, showed the emerging
consensus about Martians in feature films: often greenish, with protruding
brains, oval heads with feelers on top, only four or three long fingers on each
hand, and so on.[1] In it, black scholar Paul Goodwin observed they embodied
a fear of foreign races.

Throughout these decades, huge numbers of people claimed to have spot-
ted unidentified flying objects (UFOs)—or merely fast-moving lights—in
the sky. Smaller numbers claimed to have seen low flying saucers or even
landing ones. Some research suggests that millions of Americans believe they
have been abducted by aliens in their sleep or might even have been sexually
abused to produce hybrid experimental offspring (details in Showalter 1997).
Many scientists supported the serious Search for Extra-Terrestrial Intelligence (SETI) project, and today many computer buffs are helping to filter
possible alien signals out of noise from outer space. But the most frightening
idea is that "they" could somehow already be among "us"—in some invisible
form.

Around the mid-1950s, the United States was afraid of subversion from
within. Joseph McCarthy and his Committee on Un-American Activities
claimed that many government departments (State or Foreign Affairs, the
Pentagon or Defense) and outside sectors had been infiltrated by liberals, former radicals, and Communists—who were in fact Russian agents. Prime sus-
pects were key media and those in the Hollywood film industry, where
luminaries such as studio boss Walt Disney and actor Ronald Reagan con-
curred in blacklisting and chasing people who had held leftist sympathies during the Depression years, causing even stars like Charles Chaplin and others to
flee abroad (see Schwartz 1982). This Red Scare paranoia about a silently advancing Fifth Column was metaphorically reflected in many movies of the
1950s, including science fiction (see Sayre 1982, chap. 7).

As the country was preoccupied with a totalitarian ideology silently infect-
ing ordinary citizens and turning them around, some of the most scary sci-fi
films were similarly preoccupied with aliens invisibly capturing the minds and
bodies of everyday Americans, one after the other, until the vast majority
would have unnoticeably changed. It was impossible to distinguish them, except for their lack of proper expression and emotion. This is the central theme
of the compelling 1956 film *Invasion of the Body Snatchers*, with a worthwhile

remake in 1978. The theme became standard fare of the genre, with creepy insects or slimy reptiles from outer space nestling themselves somewhere between our shoulder blades or deep inside our stomachs, and taking control. Another harrowing example was the television series *V*, broadcast by NBC from 1983 to 1985. The 1997 blockbuster *Men in Black* and its 2002 sequel were spoofish variations on this familiar theme.

In most such thrillers, the invading aliens are quintessential "others." They may be technologically more backward or more advanced, but they want to take over our world and destroy our civilization. Therefore they are ruthless barbarians that must be confronted with all means at our disposal, ranging from laser beams to atomic, biological, and chemical weapons of mass destruction that would otherwise be frowned upon. A few such sci-fi movies have an opposite agenda, however: They posit that alien civilizations from far away may also be more morally advanced—that is to say, peaceful and wise. They may come to teach us a lesson or even decide to leave us alone.

This contrasting perspective is particularly prominent in two of the earliest and best films directed by Steven Spielberg, who not only made more varied blockbusters than anyone else but also some very subtle ones. He claims his optimistic outlook on life was rooted in a happy childhood. He was born in Ohio and raised in Arizona, but also in California, where he studied English at Long Beach State while dabbling in filmmaking (Clarke 2001; Freer 2001). After the dark *Jaws*, he made the uplifting *Close Encounters of the Third Kind* (1977), about ordinary Americans inexplicably obsessed with a certain shape, which turns out to be that of Devil's Tower National Monument in Wyoming. Once they travel there, it turns out to be the landing site of a huge space ship with benevolent aliens. *E.T.: The Extra-Terrestrial* (1982; reedited in 2002) depicts a benevolent alien lost in suburbia, helped by children to return home. One can also recognize such aliens as more evolved from the fact that they seem to possess various paranormal faculties.

Both films are engaging small-scale dramas about ordinary people, starting in an ordinary family environment and moving from there. The protagonists are open to other realities but find narrow-minded relatives, authorities, experts, and others blocking their way. The two movies were extremely successful, together making well over $1 billion. Some reviewers related the movies to the popularity of gurus and cults and to a "Disneyfied version of religion" (Telotte 2001, p. 147). Others noted that "in Spielberg's cozy home world of cuddly beasts and warm-hearted social relations, liberal ideals thrive of a sort that elsewhere in American society and Hollywood cinematic culture were being shunted aside in favor of a brutish, quasi-fascist cinematic and economic realism" (Ryan & Kellner 1988, p. 258).

SPACE TRAVEL AND EXPLORATION

So far we have discussed only encounters with aliens that came from outer space, either as friends or foes. But a new step is made when humans themselves take up space exploration. Once again related fantasies can be traced back to the premodern world, but it was only with the industrial and transport revolutions of the nineteenth and twentieth centuries that the real possibility came into view. Western authors saw exploration and travel as a necessary corollary to expansion and progress. They involved an exchange with distant ethnic groups, cultures, and nations, either through colonization or "development cooperation." As the American frontier had closed and other continents had also been penetrated in all directions, the realm of the unknown shifted to space.

The French sci-fi writer Jules Verne had already written a story about travel to the moon, and the early French filmmaker George Meliès had already made a very short film about it. American comic strip artists had created futurist space pilots *Buck Rogers* and *Flash Gordon* during the interwar years, leading to radio series and early movies. But the real possibility only came within view after Germany developed the V1 and V2 rockets to bomb London from across the English Channel. Both Russian and American occupation forces later chased and courted Nazi scientists in all fields, guaranteeing them immunity from war crimes charges in exchange for their knowledge and cooperation.

By the late 1950s, both superpowers thus already had space programs up and running: purely civilian on the outside, but of course with a secret military nucleus hidden deep inside. It soon looked as if the Soviet Union had a considerable head start: It was first to put the *Sputnik* satellite into orbit around the Earth in 1957; first to put a *Lunik* satellite in an orbit, to have one land on the moon and send pictures of its other side in 1959; first to launch a spacecraft with two dogs on board and to have it land again; first to launch a man into space and bring him back in 1961, then a woman in 1963; first to have a "cosmonaut" walk in space in 1964.

The United States had meanwhile founded the space agency NASA, and soon after his election in 1960, President John F. Kennedy pledged to catch up with the Russians and surpass them by putting the first man on the moon by the end of the decade. He was assassinated in 1963, but the landing of two American astronauts on the moon in the summer of 1969 became the biggest television and media event in history. (The step was subsequently selected as the most noteworthy and historical event in the space race, albeit in a somewhat arbitrary fashion). NASA learned to devote a considerable share of its attention and budget to the glamorous staging of such spectacular launchings and landings, in order to sustain popular support and Congressional funding.

It is not entirely surprising, then, that the grainy images of the moon landing soon came to be haunted by a pernicious rumor.

One version of the rumor claims that last-minute impediments had raised the specter of a possible failure. President Richard Nixon reportedly feared an international PR defeat and had his staff contact the film genius Stanley Kubrick, a recluse in Britain. He had just completed his sci-f movie *2001: A Space Odyssey* (after a story by Arthur C. Clarke), and the film sets were allegedly still available. So a backup scene of the moon landing was supposedly filmed there, just in case. This version of the rumor was recently told by the worthwhile French documentary filmmaker William Karel. His revelations were seemingly confirmed on camera by half a dozen of the top U.S. national security brass at the time: Henry Kissinger, Alexander Haig, Richard Helms, Lawrence Eagleburger, Donald Rumsfeld, and General Vernon Walters. However, it was a hoax. The hoax, with their manipulated video testimony, was shown all over Europe and will no doubt help to keep the rumor alive.[2]

Another version of the rumor maintained that the landing had in fact never taken place and that the familiar images had indeed been filmed in a studio. This is shown in the sci-fi feature film *Capricorn One* (1977), albeit nominally about Mars. One of the actors playing an astronaut was the popular American football player O. J. Simpson, then still an unknown abroad. But at the time of his later, much-hyped televised trial for murder, opinion polls showed that a significant part of the African American community held that he had been framed for the crime, both for being a black man with a white wife and for having helped reveal the "truth" about the moon landing. The rumor persists to this very day. On September 24, 2002, the *International Herald Tribune* reported that the seventy-two-year-old astronaut Buzz Aldrin had punched a man in the face outside a hotel after the latter had called him "a coward, a liar, and a thief." The man had dared him to swear on the Bible that he had actually been to the moon.

Other fantastic themes emerge, of course, when human astronauts move beyond the moon and Mars to other planets circling distant stars, where they may encounter different life forms. They may be rather similar, and the stories may then take a philosophical turn, as in the successful *Planet of the Apes* (1968, after a French novel), its no fewer than four sequels, and a completely new 2001 remake. But the other life forms may of course also turn out to be radically different, and the stories may veer into horror, as in the successful *Alien* (1979), which also had three sequels. In both cases, however, the depiction of the encounter with the strangers in outer space does inevitably resonate with the encounter among human cultures, ethnicities, and nations. Let us just look somewhat more closely at one particularly successful series.

Case Study: Star Trek—Multiculturalism in Space

The year 2002 saw the release of the tenth Star Trek theatrical feature film, *Nemesis*. The story was based on an interesting splitting of overly familiar characters and a new interplay between them, showing that everyone has two sides. The extraterrestrial Romulans faced a rebellion of the Remans, who they had always suppressed and exploited. The good guy, Captain Picard, had to face a younger bad guy who turned out to be a clone of himself, creating a kind of father-and-son situation. Picard's android assistant, Data, was confronted with an earlier version of himself, B4 (or before), allowing him to sacrifice himself for his boss in order to be resurrected as his older brother. Well done.

The film was no top-two-hundred blockbuster, but it was a reliable money-maker. It had been preceded by four long television series of several seasons each, continually repeated all around the world, to this very day. A dozen years ago, the actor playing Picard proudly noted that the entire franchise had already earned Paramount more than $4 billion. There are not only *Star Trek* videos and DVDs, books and magazines, posters and figurines, models and toys, laser and other guns, but also bumper stickers and buttons, calendars and coffee mugs, and even entire outfits and masks, with pointed ears and wrinkled foreheads.

There are vocabularies and encyclopedias of *Star Trek* terms, Internet sites and chatrooms. There are dozens of national fan clubs, which at one point reported hundreds of thousands of members, holding annual or quarterly conventions, which enthusiasts attend dressed up as extraterrestrials. It is like "one big family," they say, upholding high-minded "interplanetary" ideals. Many of Star Trek's frequent expressions have entered into mainstream language ("Beam me up, Scotty"). According to one overview, the spaceship captain and his crew "have become icons in American popular culture, representing the best of our dreams" (van Hise 1991, p. xi). All this was at the outset invented by one man.

The Star Trek franchise was created by Gene Roddenberry. Born in Texas and raised in California, Roddenberry was the son of a Los Angeles policeman and later became a policeman himself, turning ghostwriter for its commissioner. During World War II he was an air force pilot in the Pacific. After that he crashed in the Middle East and reportedly rescued his crew despite being wounded himself. All this real-life action experience came in handy when he became a technical adviser and then full-fledged scriptwriter for television, contributing to various well-known series. But he wanted a series of his own, with machos and babes—but also with something of a social and philosophical sauce.

Whereas the traditional Western was losing its interest, Rodden-berry wanted to revive the genre by sticking a futurist Western into space, with astronaut cowboys and Indians—situated not in the nine-teenth century but in the twenty-third and twenty-fourth centuries in-stead. Its original working title was *Wagon Train to the Stars*. To make it more easily recognizable, the heroes were put on a U.S. spaceship, initially named after the famous USS *Yorktown*, but then simply *Enter-prise*. It was quite similar to airships and sea ships, with a crew having familiar functions and ranks. This also implied that they themselves necessarily formed a close-knit community in a hard shell: an attack on one automatically implied an attack on all. It was also a typical techno-topia for gadget buffs and nerds.

The whole setup was underlined by the rhetorical announcement about "space—the final frontier" and the Columbus-like mission "to explore strange new worlds, to seek out new life and new civilizations, to boldly go where no man has gone before." Henry Jenkins, author of several books on science fiction and fandom, said it could be seen as "the fantasy of a liberal LAPD cop." But Reverend Richard Boeke of the Unitarian Church, a former army chaplain who held entire services de-riving from the Star Trek themes, compared the *Enterprise* captain to the prophet Moses, calling the stories "a wonderful addition to our an-cient Holy Books" and also likening them to the ancient Greek *Iliad* and *Odyssey*.[3]

The original boss was Captain Kirk, who somewhat resembled Rod-denberry himself. But his fictional initials JTK also strangely resembled Kennedy's JFK. He was purportedly the youngest captain of the fleet, just as Kennedy had been the youngest president. The three of them even had similar hairdos, faces, and physiques: all supposedly charis-matic men, but also inveterate womanizers. Like so many others of his generation, Roddenberry adhered to a naive "politically correct" the-ory about the relations between genders and ranks, nations and races, but the practice often diverged. He even saw the series as his "Trojan horse" in mainstream television, addressing taboos and dodging cen-sors. The series' optimistic and seemingly idealistic outlook on the fu-ture proved its major attraction.

Roddenberry developed the idea in 1964, the year after the assassi-nation of Kennedy. JFK had put the first American astronaut into orbit and had announced his larger space program in proto–Star Trek terms: "We set sail on this new sea . . . for the progress of all people." (NASA called its prototype space shuttle *Enterprise*, after *Star Trek*, and Rod-denberry's ashes were later sent to the stars on the shuttle *Columbia*).

The series was first produced by Lucille Ball's Desilu studio, then by Paramount. It was pitched first to the CBS television network, then to NBC, which accepted it, albeit with much reservation and a scaling-down of the most unusual elements. The first season of the original series was broadcast in 1966–1967. It proved no ratings hit, but when the network wanted to cancel the show, five thousand letters by sci-fi enthusiasts protested the move, and it got a reprieve. The second season did only marginally better, but this time hundreds of thousands of letters by Trekkies saved the day. The third season, on a lower budget, did even worse, and the series was finally shelved—as it seemed, forever.

But by now the series had acquired a loyal cult following. They had their first major convention in 1972. The original series was repeated in syndication, sold well abroad, and also had a few further seasons in an animated version, with the original actor's voices. Somehow, *Star Trek* continued to grow into a major fan phenomenon. The British BBC had already started the *Doctor Who* space series in 1963 and produced a new series as recently as 2005. It also produced hilarious spoofs such as *The Hitchhiker's Guide to the Galaxy* (1981) and *Red Dwarf* (1988). The American ABC network started *Battlestar Galactica* in 1978 and produced a new installment as recently as 2003. But it was only in 1987 that a new *Star Trek* series of seven seasons began in the United States, titled *The Next Generation*, which was more consistently liberal in general outlook.

One additional reason for the series' success was that viewers eager to identify with the story tended to be white, well educated, middle class, and sensitive to techy trends: a very interesting target group for advertisers and marketers. (Of course, there never was a cleaning lady or maintenance worker in sight on the original spaceships, although everything always seemed to be spic and span). Patrick Stewart, a British Shakespearean actor, was selected to play the role of Captain Picard. *The Next Generation* was followed much later by a third and a fourth series (*Deep Space Nine* and *Voyager*). Meanwhile, the success of Spielberg's and Lucas's space adventures had made Paramount embark on a long succession of theatrical features as well, of which the 2003 *Nemesis* was the tenth.

The study of *Star Trek* became a popular subject for university students and scholars, courses and conferences (see, for example, Harrison et al. 1996). Its often implicit and ambiguous ideologies became a major object of study, even if it was soon recognized that these "texts" could be "read" in many different ways—for instance, as a reflection of the American realities of the day, as a critique of them, as neither, or as both. "I'm not a guru, and I don't want to be," Roddenberry said. "It frightens me when I learn of ten thousand people treating a Star Trek script as if it were [holy] scripture" (van Hise 1991, p. 73). The later installments included many campy elements and winks to the initiated. Intertextuality thus came to play a major role. Let us take a somewhat closer look at some of its major themes.

One theme in the original series was women's lib, but from the typical perspective of a male chauvinist. His producer said in an obvious understatement that Roddenberry "had an eye for the ladies." He would always drop all other matters at hand when it came to inspecting the already skimpy outfits of sexy new "space babes" and make the molding shirts and minimal skirts even "more revealing." According to one of his scripts, the actresses were supposed to be "walking with the natural poise of a striptease artist." His hero, Captain Kirk, aboard his giant phallic spaceship, was counted to have flirted with no fewer than twenty-seven different women in the original series alone (Harrison et al. 1996, p. 12). Even though his successor, Picard, claimed that rape did not exist anymore in the civilized society of the future, critics claimed that gender relations seemed to have evolved surprisingly little over all these centuries.

Another theme was civil rights, at a time when Reverend Martin Luther King Jr. and others led the civil rights movement against segregation in the Southern states and when Kennedy's no-nonsense successor Lyndon B. Johnson had finally succeeded in actually getting civil rights laws through Congress. Fans point out that the black female character Uhura (meaning "freedom") held an early staff position as a communications officer, but critics say she was hardly more than a glorified telephone operator who was never allowed to lead. More interesting was that she also gave/received a kiss from a white actor at one point, which was said to have been the first interracial kiss on mainstream American television (even though it was to be many more years before the favor could be returned and a black man was allowed to kiss a white woman—which remains much more taboo). Yet the black actress Whoopi Goldberg later recalled being inspired by it as a kid, and civil rights leader King persuaded the original actress to stay on when she wanted to quit because of the limitations of her role.

But let us take some more time to review the entire framework of the show. The USS Enterprise did indeed have a multicultural crew, with a black character, an Asian character, and so forth. Its American captain was also a commander of the entire Starfleet. It sailed into the unknown but often acted as a self-appointed policeman in outer space.

Peter David, sci-fi writer and Star Trek novelist, said (in the BBC documentary *Fear of a Red Planet*): "They were always right, knew exactly what to do, would go in there with guns blazing. The prime directive—noninterference—was the thing that Kirk always quoted, right before he then ignored it. . . . The show kicked ass and took names." Sounds familiar.

Roddenberry, of course, saw "a new world with new rules," as the fleet had a mandate, not only from the United States, but from the whole Earth and even from the United Federation of Planets, a kind of space UN. This notion resonated with contemporary ideas about the United States as the representative par excellence of "the international community," as these were the years of the so-called Trilateral Commission, a confidential meeting ground for the political and economic elites of North America, western Europe, and Japan (preceded by the similar Bilderberg conferences and followed by the similar Davos economic forums to this very day). Western-style modernity was the undisputed norm for the rest of the Earth, and indeed the universe.

What about "others," then? Critics claim the gender and race relations in the original series betrayed a kind of "species-ism" or "bioessentialism," where ethnic differences between populations almost automatically translate into cultural differences, mentalities, and ideologies that are hard to surmount, even though isolated individuals from such groups might change allegiance. There is, for example, Mr. Spock: half-Vulcan and easily recognized by his devilish pointed ears (first refused by the network, later immensely popular). His successor in the later series is the android Data, a whiter character in the rather black position of a virtual slave, because a "possession" of the fleet: the high-tech equivalent of the Caliban/Friday characters discussed in chapter 4. Spock was a somewhat emotional person trying to remain ultra-rational, furthermore, whereas Data was an ultra-rational robot trying to acquire emotions (Harrison et al. 1996, p. 76), comparable to the wooden puppet Pinocchio desiring to become a real boy.

The most quintessential others and alien enemies, aggressive bullies at that, were the Klingons, at first. If the fleet embodies the civilized and liberal first world, they were a mixture of the barbarous and illiberal second and third worlds—that is to say, of the cold Soviet Union, with its freezing Siberia and its notorious penal colonies, but also of its hotter/darker Marxist proxies at the time: overseas nations such as Cuba, Angola, and Vietnam. Says Data, "There is, of course, a genetic predisposition to hostility among all Klingons." They are unsmiling and impolite, rude and rough. Rather than nicely saying, "How are you?" they would just say, "What do you want?" (Kreetz 1998). Their spaceship at one point is called "Bird of Prey." After the Soviet Union collapsed and made peace, the Klingons did, too (in *The Next Generation*).

Lieutenant Worf, who became a high officer on the USS *Enterprise*, was a liminal or in-between "other": an adopted and more or less assimilated Klingon, played by a six-foot five-inch African American actor (Harrison et al. 1996, pp. 51–68). But such characters and stories always retain their potential for polysemia: Their "reading" can always be inverted. In spite of everything, the exotic Klingons turned into a kind of "noble savages," fascinating the fans. You could put on their face and try to speak the strange language, in their typically mumbling and moody way. Students at the Massachusetts Institute of Technology further developed the Klingon vocabulary and grammar. Some fans claim (with obvious exaggeration) that there must have been some two hundred thousand fans in the world who understood some Klingon, twice the number who understood the idealistic international language Esperanto.

SPACE CONQUEST AND EMPIRE BUILDING

The premise of Star Trek was a peaceful exploration of outer space, the gradual expansion of a federation of planets into a quasi-universal alliance. But it was of course inevitable that some of the newly discovered races would initially be hostile and that there would be armed confrontations leading to full-scale wars. Spielberg's *Close Encounters* and *E.T.* had postulated a benevolent visit from outer space, but *The Body Snatchers* and *V* showed a creeping takeover. The theme of a direct military campaign against Earth was therefore inevitable.

British author H. G. Wells's novel *The War of the Worlds* (1898) had already painted vivid and horrifying scenes of an invasion of England by Martians, a kind of blood-sucking Transylvanian vampire from outer space. The twenty-three-year-old American director Orson Welles then transposed the invasion to New Jersey for a broadcast from New York, in the weekly series *Mercury Theatre on the Air*, on the eve of Halloween 1938. As his network was battling its competitors for ratings and a sponsor, he made the radio play sound like a sensational series of breaking news reports.

The vast majority of American homes at the time (or 27 million families) had a radio, and 6 million listened to CBS that night. But an estimated 4 million of these were late in switching the program on, thus missing the initial announcement that the invasion was fictional—and between 250,000 and 1 million of these took the threat seriously, as there already was a crisis atmos-phere following the harrowing live radio reports on the crash of the *Hinden-burg* airship in New Jersey, the Nazi invasion of the Czech Südetenland, and the narrow Munich compromise. So many people also ran outside and missed the signature of the program as a radio play. They panicked; the switchboard was overburdened, as were police departments and city halls, particularly in the northeastern United States. The director and the network were forced to apologize the next day, but their ratings soared, and they fi-nally acquired a sponsor (the heavy advertiser Campbell's Soup, of later Warhol pop-art fame).

Some claimed the scare showed a general lack of education and a worrying susceptibility to propaganda. But it also triggered one of the first major em-pirical broadcast audience studies, as psychologist Hadley Cantril of the newly founded Office of Radio Research at Princeton University conducted elabo-rate interviews with 135 listeners. He also investigated the further causes and consequences of the impact of the hoax and published *The Invasion from Mars: A Study in the Psychology of Panic* (1940; this is discussed further in Lowery & De Fleur 1983, chap. 3). Later adaptations of the radio play in Chile, Peru, and particularly Ecuador caused similar scares, and even a 1974 adapta-tion in Providence, Rhode Island, repeated the feat to some extent (as dis-cussed in Bulgatz 1992, chap. 4). So did later similar hoaxes on nuclear and other disasters in Europe.

There are several movies on the whole affair. Jim Moore wrote and pre-sented a documentary about the causes and consequences of *The Invasion from Mars*, broadcast in a series Neil Cameron produced for BBC and the Open University (1987). Joseph Sargent (Giuseppe Sargente) later directed a telefilm *The Night That Panicked America*. The 1953 movie based on the same H. G. Wells book, *The War of the Worlds*, was a solid box office hit (for an elab-orate semiological analysis, see Berger 1992, chap. 10). The 2005 remake by di-rector Steven Spielberg (with Scientology adept Tom Cruise in a major role) immediately jumped to the twenty-eighth spot on the all-time blockbuster list, albeit still fifteen places (and several hundred million dollars) behind the even more spectacular 1996 invasion movie *Independence Day*, by German di-rector Roland Emmerich.

But, meanwhile, another blockbuster cycle had popularized the whole con-cept. Although the introductory titles emphatically said it was situated "long, long ago" in a galaxy "far, far away" and it combined humanlike characters with an extremely wide range of invented alien races, however, few sci-fi fan-tasies were so closely intertwined with the political realities of the day.

Case Study: Earth Wars and Star Wars

It was trumpeted as the greatest movie event of all time: the 2005 release of *Revenge of the Sith*, the latest installment in the Star Wars cycle—a near-simultaneous global release, out of fear of the new phenomenon of Internet piracy. Some said that "very little of the new film makes sense, taken as a freestanding narrative." Only those who had seen the earlier five films could connect all the dots. But one *New York Times* reviewer exulted, "This is by far the best film" of the ones that George Lucas had directed.

One reason was a major twist to the familiar story, he wrote, which "cuts sharply against the optimistic grain of blockbuster Hollywood"—as it seemed to criticize the approach of the current U.S. administration to the rest of the world. As the major bad guy at one point hisses to the major good guy: "If you're not with me, you are my enemy"—a fateful unilateralist line once spoken by President George W. Bush, to the great disappointment of traditional U.S. allies, for instance, in Europe.[4]

The film made some $840 million at the box office over the next four and a half months. Together with its five predecessors, the entire cycle had made $4.3 billion at the box office worldwide. Merchandising rights were estimated at far more than that. This made the entire enterprise the most profitable single ongoing story ever told—so far.

It was also mostly invented and realized by one man: George Lucas. He was born in Modesto, California, where his family owned a stationery store and later a walnut farm. He had been an average student in high school, mostly preoccupied with cars and racing. He narrowly survived a major crash just a few weeks before his graduation, which set him thinking. In junior college he took classes in comparative religion and cultural anthropology, which he later invoked to give his great creation an intellectual pretense.

He claimed to have been inspired by the mythologist Joseph Campbell, who later called him his "best student" and became a mentor and older friend. Campbell had not only studied in New York, but also in Paris and Munich, where he had acquainted himself with continental European thought. His 1949 book *The Hero with a Thousand Faces* claimed that all holy books and great epics of world literature basically followed a "mono-myth": a similar pattern of departure, initiation, and return, consisting of five or six elements each (the call, the threshold, the trials, etc.). In the process, the hero also underwent a series of transformations (as warrior, lover, tyrant, redeemer, saint, etc.). The underlying logic had meanwhile been revealed in the study of dreams,

archetypes, and symbols, Campbell claimed, and also by psychoana-
lysts such as Freud and Jung (and one might add Rank). He published
a new collection, *Myths to Live By*, in 1972, just before Lucas embarked on his Star Wars project.

Meanwhile, Lucas had become interested in movies and had enrolled in the Film School of the University of Southern California. His
initial orientation was on camera work and documentaries, but he later
met USC alumnus Francis Ford Coppola, who became another mentor,
and did an internship at Warner Brothers. He made the short sci-fi film
THX, inspired by Godard's dystopian *Alphaville*. After graduation, he
took a closer look at *Flash Gordon* and *Buck Rogers* as possible further
sci-fi movie material but found the rights were not available, although
they seem to have inspired the later character of Han Solo (played by
Harrison Ford) in *Star Wars* and also father and son Skywalker.

After Lucas scored an initial success with *American Graffiti*, based
partly on his own adolescent experiences. He the returned to science
fiction. He wanted to make a super-epos, projected into distant space,
but in fact based on an inventive remix of all of Campbell's megamyths
from the ancient past: the Bible, the Greek myths, Roman history, King
Arthur and the knights of the round table—all that and more. Some recognized pastiches of Wagner and even Riefenstahl as well, with a
heavy dose of Orientalism thrown in for good measure: from the Indian
yogi masters and the Tibetan Zen monks to the Chinese martial arts
fighters and the Japanese samurai as filmed by Kurosawa—a cocktail,
shaken and stirred.

Few understood right away what Lucas was talking about, and the
project was turned down by United Artists and Universal. Critics maintain that he remains a rather bad storyteller and actors' director to this
very day but is very good at the razzle-dazzle of sci-fi character development and special effects. The Industrial Light and Magic (ILM) technique he developed, his new sound technique, and the quality
certification system, or Theatre Alignment Program (TAP), revolution-
ized the industry.

Others felt the "movie brat" should have a chance to prove his
worth, however, and 20th Century Fox ultimately accepted his pitch—
albeit with many reservations. He was given $15,000 to develop a script,
$50,000 to write the entire movie, and $100,000 to direct it. Fox made
twice as much in profit in the quarter after the film's release than it had
previously made in a year, and its share price doubled in just three
weeks. Lucas had been keen enough to reserve most merchandising
rights for himself, however—including (to their great surprise) those to

the faces of his major actors. Carrie Fisher later reminisced in a television documentary, "They had a shampoo where you could screw my head off and pour liquid out of my neck." The resulting millions allowed him to flee the incestuous little world of Hollywood, to become an "independent" with his own studio and postproduction facility, based on a huge farm property near the "cooler" San Francisco.

The first Star Wars film proved a hit. The *New York Times* called it "a knowing critique of various ancient myths and legends." *Time* magazine called it "a subliminal history of the movies, wrapped in a riveting tale of suspense and adventure." Jim Smith's monograph on the director later said: "*Star Wars* is Lucas's personal summary of culture: a blend of pop, literature, and film that borrows brands and motifs and tropes from wherever it chooses. It is one of the first artefacts of cut-and-paste culture, and . . . it functions like Internet hypertext" before its time (Smith 2003, p. 83).

But critics like Robin Wood deplored the entire Hollywood shift to this type of blockbusters, characterized by half a dozen key traits, he said:

1. Childishness: "intellectually undemanding" and catering to "a widespread desire for regression to infantilism."
2. Special effects: "reckless, prodigal extravagance, no expense spared." [The number one in the whole series had two thousand special effects shots, taking up no less than one full hour of screen time].
3. [Facility of] imagination and originality: "window-dressing to conceal . . . the extreme familiarity of the plot" with "make-up and the creation of a range of cute or sinister or grotesque fauna."
4. [The exploitation of] anxieties about a nuclear holocaust or an apocalypse.
5. The simplistic portrayal of totalitarianism: with the older heroes having British accents, the younger heroes having American ones, [and the bad guys being linked to German-Russian stereotypes in various ways—for instance, uniforms].
6. The return to patriarchy and male chauvinism. (1986, pp. 165–172)

Others, like Matt Hills, countered that the taken-for-granted modernist opposition between highbrow and lowbrow, between cult films and blockbusters, had ceased to make sense in a postmodernist world (Stringer 2003, chap. 11).

The entire Star Wars cycle consists of six films, organized in two trilogies. One is the so-called republican trilogy, or prequel, of *The*

Phantom Menace, Attack of the Clones, and *Revenge of the Sith.* It narrates a course of events that take place before the initial trilogy but was made and released later, between 1999 and 2005. The other is the so-called imperial trilogy, or sequel, of *A New Hope, The Empire Strikes Back,* and *Return of the Jedi.* This narrates a later course of events but was made and released almost a full generation earlier, between 1977 and 1983, with an improved reedition in 1997. (It was followed by a spin-off of two major telefilms or television movies made for ABC on the cuddly Ewoks). Although two of the six theatrical movies were directed by others, all the stories were written by Lucas, though he has cancelled plans for a third trilogy.

The six Star Wars stories seem profoundly confusing because of their reversed order and varied characters, ranging from animal-like to myth-like to machine-like extraterrestrials. But, hidden deep underneath, there turns out to be a simple metanarrative familiar from ancient Rome and elsewhere. Somewhere far away in the universe, there is an entire galaxy ruled by a collegial senate. But separatist tendencies and distant adventures on other planets stir political strife and personal ambition. A supreme chancellor grabs power (compare Caesar and Napoleon) and turns the democratic republic into a dictatorial empire, thereby stirring popular resistance. Politicians position and reposition themselves, but they are always assisted or obstructed by two generations of good and bad guys in the wings: both fighting against extinction and for the control of a mysterious life force. That is basically it.

The good guys are an order of knights and mystic warriors with their own honor code, the Jedis. There are Master Yoda, Qui-Gon Ginn, and his apprentice Obi Wan Kenobi. The bad guys are the last survivors of an ancient race, the Siths. There are Lord Darth Sidious, his apprentice Darth Maul, and finally the "dark invader" Darth Vader (his very deep voice done by a black actor). In good old Hollywood tradition, the bad guys are dressed in black, and their faces are often hidden. The "human" heroes are torn between good and bad, between these angel guardians and demonic tempters with Faustian powers.

The simple white and blond slave and farm-boy protagonist Anakin is (in Dalai Lama style) discovered to be "the chosen one" to "bring balance." He is a slave, but when he leaves, he promises to return and liberate others (think of the Moses theme). He possesses paranormal gifts and is first made an apprentice and then a knight. But later he is drawn toward "the dark side" (just as George Lucas began the project with a fight against the almighty corporate CEOs but ultimately became one himself). The son, Luke Skywalker, in turn battles the abominable monster Darth Vader and triumphs over him. This hero was called Luke Starkiller in the earliest versions. This is basically a combination of the names of Saint Luke the gospel writer and Saint George the dragon killer, I would add as a psychologist—or reversed, "George Lucas." Sunset and music, happy end, title roll.

Some critics maintain that in the guise of futurism the series has clear roots in a "sort of nostalgic populism," that it favors strong leaders and elites in the name of individualism and "freedom from state control" (Ryan & Kellner 1988, p. 228). Others say the series, and the perpetual fights with laser beams and other gadgets, implies "a very male bias" and "a great deal of crude cultural stereotyping" (King & Krzywinska 2002, pp. 110–11). The center of the Star Wars universe looks very much like a latter-day New York. Most of the noble Jedi knights and main protagonists have dark blond hair and light blue eyes, and they often wear lighter clothes. Many elements implicitly refer to the Holy Family story also, in the grooming and dress of Christ-like, Mary-like, and Joseph-like figures.

Other critics maintain there is a lot of subtle ethnocentrism. The slaver, with his big bent nose, reminded some viewers of anti-Semitic stereotypes in classical Anglo-Saxon literature (such as Shakespeare's Shylock and Dickens's Fagin). The duplicitous "sand people" are dressed like Arabs, they said, and were placed in a desert environment (filmed in North African Tunisia). The name of the sidekick Jar Jar is similar to the repeated monosyllabic names often ascribed to colonial-era natives. His people, the Gungans, were given a black/Jamaican/Caribbean accent in the American version (and a primitive colonial-era native accent in the French translation). But Lucas and his fans retorted that the slaver was a kind of big blue fly, and Jar Jar an orange lizard—so the accusations were absurd—and that many counterexamples of all-white characters playing bad guys and of nonwhite characters playing good guys in the films could easily be given (Smith 2003, pp. 243–44).

I would say that possible problems lie elsewhere, in the ideological pretensions of the cycle. In an American television documentary *The Mythology of Star Wars*, interviewer Bill Moyers complains that such films have come to replace the Bible but that they have "no strings attached," meaning they do not imply any long-term commitment to a creed or a church. George Lucas responds that they make "old stories new" and also that Star Wars is not religious but "a more modern concept." When pressed, he reluctantly admits believing in some god, but one that transcends traditional religions.[5]

Rather than about the supernatural, however, the films are about Manichaeism. In the Moyers interview, made at the time of the release of the first film in the later trilogy, Lucas said, "We all have good and evil inside of us." But Moyers retorted that in post-Vietnam days, "One of the appeals of *Star Wars* was originally that it satisfied our craving to resolve our ambiguities. The good guys were good guys and the bad guys were bad guys. You used color to suggest some of this philosophy." Whatever Lucas had intended, the early trilogy and the entire series were largely read by audiences to mean that people and racial/ethnic/national groups throughout the universe were either all good or all bad.

This widespread reading was hardly inflected by later more ambiguous hints, where Luke Skywalker finds out there is something of him in Darth Vader and vice versa, and then that his good father, Anakin, has indeed turned into the bad man-machine cyborg Darth Vader. It is interesting (in view of what follows) to note that most of the films came out under Republican administrations with neoconservative leanings and that some of the key notions of the series were adopted by them, whereas the two trilogies had largely been developed under Democratic administrations with liberal leanings instead. This may account for some of the confused readings.

When the earlier-made trilogy was being completed, conservative president Ronald Reagan presented his Strategic Defense Initiative (SDI) for the interception of strategic ballistic missiles from space, which was quickly dubbed "Star Wars." More than $100 billion have been spent on it since, but in an age of suicide bombers such missiles have lost most of their relevance—and their interception can still not be assured. We have already seen that as a former movie actor Reagan, "the great communicator," borrowed much of his political rhetoric from movies. The concept of an aerial shield also came from the movie *Murder in the Air*, in which he had played. He once even claimed that he himself had been a tail gunner on a U.S. bomber, whereas in fact he had merely played one in the movies (Simpson 2002b, pp. 244–46).

After the collapse of the Soviet Union, the concept of an "Evil Empire" was soon replaced by an "Axis of Evil" in political rhetoric, although the countries in question did not form an alliance in any way. After President Bush the younger renounced the thirty-year-old ABM treaty forbidding weapons in space in 2002, he relaunched SDI (under the guise of New Missile Defense NMD), which places every location throughout the entire world within the range of U.S. weapons systems partly based in space. During the same month in which the very last

Star Wars film was released, Bush launched a further sci-fi plan: an ul-
trafast space plane capable of striking anywhere, anytime, within only
forty-five minutes,[6] whereas the United States already spent almost as
much on defense as the rest of the world taken together, particularly after the Iraq intervention, and its deficits continued to grow.

So wishful thinking and superpower politics, Hollywood and Washington, continued to become ever more closely intertwined—to such
an extent that is has become impossible to separate them anymore.

Other People's Dreams

The inner walls and doors of public restrooms often provide an outlet for students' frustrations. One restroom at the University of Amsterdam showed eruptions such as: "Movies are not semiotistic [*sic*] bullshit," and "Communication scientists cannot communicate." Fortunately, this was not close to my own office or lecture room, but it provided a further stimulus to try and write clearly about these matters, and without unexplained jargon. But many still have trouble believing that popular culture may reflect ethnocentrism in a thousand different little ways. A movie production demands repeated choices, made under high pressure and in split seconds. It is reasonable to assume that the results will more often than not subtly reflect the worldview of the filmmakers themselves and of their prime target audiences.

In an earlier book about global news, I labeled this "selective articulation." Certain facts and relationships are emphasized, made plausible and coherent, whereas others are made to look strange and far-fetched, even if they need not necessarily be. This starts with the choice of subjects for which interest and financing can easily be found, the precise stories and viewpoints that will be privileged, and the few sources that will be taken as a point of departure, as well as the experts who will be consulted and the lobbies that will be listened to. Think of the example of Bible films: It is evident that Christian beliefs but also national myths will be respected—most of the time.

The "literary classics" from the age of colonialism and segregation are also shot through with a white perspective. The other side of the story is often largely absent. The *UNESCO Yearbook* provides overviews of the number of books translated from one language into another. Not surprisingly, Anglo-American novels and those from a small number of larger countries on the European continent are translated exponentially more often into other languages than the other way around; it has long been almost a one-way street. There are exceptions, but they are rare. Similar things are true for gender, class, education—and the same holds true for global film. We learn to empathize with the concerns of some groups in the world, but not of others at the bottom of the scale, such as the hundreds of millions of "untouchables" in India or indigenous peoples elsewhere.

For well-off urbanites in major Western countries, those indigenous peoples have even become a kind of antipode and "absolute other." Sometimes this is interpreted in positive ways, as with light-skinned Indian tribes from the Americas, to whom New Age wisdom is often ascribed. But often it is interpreted in negative ways, as with darker natives from the unknown interior of continents and islands ranging from Africa to Melanesia. Over the years, they even seem to have merged into one prototype, which turns up time and again—with a fantasy appearance, fantasy dresses, fantasy dances, fantasy music, and most of all fantasy cannibalism and human sacrifice, or the threat of it.

An interesting counterexample of a supposedly well-researched film about natives is Mel Gibson's *Apocalypto*, released Christmas 2006. In view of its huge budget, the film was expected to be the glorious reconstitution of a fascinating but more or less extinct civilization of five centuries ago, the Maya in Mexico. It was trumpeted as such by special advance editions of color magazines, and impatiently awaited by taste makers and fashion designers as a source of inspiration. Instead it turned out to be a ludicrous story of good Indians versus bad Indians. The good guys loved their family and nature; the bad guys had slaves build pyramids for bloody sacrifices (usually ascribed to their neighbors, the Aztecs). It turned out to be a mere noisy horror movie. It was spoken in the original Yucatan language, all right, but without any explanation of the meaning of the practices transpiring at all.

An American reviewer wrote about Mel Gibson's "apparently limitless appetite for gore," with "plenty of disembowelings, impalings, clubbings, and beheadings. Hearts are torn, still beating, from slashed-open chests." A French reviewer wrote that the story limited itself to a simple chase back and forth, out of the forest and back into forest, strewn with fights and corpses, and that the ambition of his recent work only seemed to be to have people say "ouch" in all the rare or dead languages of the world. A Dutch reviewer said that the protagonists remained "cardboard puppets, which only seemed to matter for the mechanics of an embarrassingly simplistic scenario."[1] Yet some in Hollywood felt its action-style craftsmanship deserved Academy Awards.

Others had meanwhile learned to treat the cinematic myth of wild indigenous tribes more subtly. The latest remake of *King Kong* first reproduced the original stereotype in a Pacific environment but then poked fun at it during a later theatrical presentation in New York—a smart postmodern move. Increasingly, black natives had disappeared from "politically correct" Africa movies—witness Disney's *Tarzan*. They have often been replaced with anthropomorphic animals, made to behave and speak like humans. The distinctions between animal species have often come to "stand in" for the distinctions between human races, although they also seem to "naturalize" the earlier view. Science fiction movies like *Star Trek* and *Star Wars* in turn have aliens, robots, cyborgs, and clones that take over former native and slave roles.

But what cinematic choices play a role in this entire game of "saming and othering," of leveling and sharpening of ethnic difference? Let us review some of the current debates in the press, and four key categories.

LIGHT, COLOR, AND CAMERA MOVEMENTS

In his instructive book on whiteness, Richard Dyer has shown in great detail how and why photography and film resonated closely with skin and hair color, from their earliest days on. Light sensitivity of standard film, as well as the lighting conventions for filming people, were primarily geared to white skin, not to darker skin. This can easily be noted whenever an inexperienced photographer or cameraman shoots dark faces in an overexposed tropical environment: They tend to become mere dark blobs, without detailed expression, unable to elicit empathy. Lighting conventions in feature films often have similar aspects, for instance when the ethereal whiteness or blondeness of Euro-American divas is emphasized, he said. In these respects, the silver screen has long remained a white screen.

All this was particularly obvious in the heyday of the black-and-white movie. But during the age of the color movie, too, light and color have assumed all kinds of collateral meanings of which most filmmakers are not completely aware. This is most flagrant in older animated cartoons (including those of Disney), which not only depict all negroes as pitch black, but also Native Americans as stark red, Chinese as stark yellow, and so on. The ascribed skin color has so emphatically been made the major marker of someone's identity, and we even came to see colors that were never there, rather than a thousand small and insignificant shades from very beige to darker brown—as in the exemplary U.S. children's television series *Little Bill* made by Bill Cosby (De Vroet 2003).

Something similar holds for landscapes, where the distinction between reality and artifice has disappeared in synthetic images that reproduce the same color clichés time and again. The tropical sea is increasingly color-corrected to azure blue, the sandy beach to immaculate white. Beyond it is invariably a row of green palms, contrasted against the light sky, preferably an orange sunset. The design of movies is shot through with seemingly technical choices hiding partly ideological ones. The example of *The Prince of Egypt* showed that designers often mean colors and forms in such films to evoke sympathy or antipathy with relevant groups.

Close-ups, medium shots, and totals (only the face, also part of the upper body, or from head to toes—sometimes with others) are often unevenly distributed among dominant and dominated characters, and therefore also among whites and nonwhites. The former are more often shown as remarkable individuals, the latter as an anonymous mass (for instance in colonial adventure movies such as the Allan Quatermain and Indiana Jones series). Something similar holds for the vertical angle of the camera or tilt: The one from low to high (frog perspective), which suggests dominance, versus the one from high to low (bird perspective), which suggests insignificance. They, too, are seldom used in a culturally neutral way.

A horizontal camera viewpoint at eye level tends to imply some kind of personal relationship. But it can be filled in as one-sided or mutual, as love or as hate—very visible in the older French *Angélique* blockbusters we discussed in chapter 6. The succession or sequence of looks may carry a definite suggestion. A good example is the protracted alternation of close-ups and totals when Angélique is sold to Arabs and Africans in an Algiers slave market. Camera and cutting (that is to say, the precise way in which the images are put together) convey her repulsion and their lust in a forceful manner.

Camera movements, too, may be used in an ideological manner. The travel shot, with an (often fast, linear) movement through a scene, may for instance emphasize the vastness and emptiness of an unknown wide-open space. We earlier discussed the hidden implications of this in Westerns. It is often accompanied by the drawing of a superimposed straight line on a map (for instance in the Indiana Jones films). A horizontal pan(orama) movement along the horizon may carry a similar suggestion. Other examples are the vertical pan along the body of a standing man or woman, which may emphasize physicality or sensuality—particularly in an intercultural context. The latter connects with scopophilia or the lustful gaze, linked to gender and sex (think of the aestheticized images of white and nonwhite girls in the tropics in the *Emmanuelle* movies, discussed in chapter 6).

ACTORS, MAKEUP, AND COSTUMES

Casting is about finding suitable actors for specific roles. Physical appearance plays an important role. For an "overall prime hero," most Hollywood movies still tend to prefer someone with more or less blond hair, more or less blue eyes, a more or less Caucasian appearance, rather white skin (even for Middle Easterners such as Moses in the Exodus and Christ in the *Passion*). Whites are thought to be "universal" and nonwhites "specific"—so the former may (with extra makeup) easily play the latter, but not the other way around.

Someone with a single exotic ancestor, furthermore, is easily seen and cast as completely exotic. Over the last half-century or so, a specialized category of actors and actresses with a few drops of "foreign blood" emerged, who were routinely invited to play a wide range of completely ethnic roles: Yul Brynner, Ben Kingsley, Anthony Quinn, John Rhys-Davies, Omar Sharif, Raquel Welch, and many others. Whether they were to play a Latino or an Arab or an Asian did not matter so much—and they switched continents all the time. Chinese are easily cast as Japanese or Thai characters with completely different looks (*Memoirs of a Geisha, Anna and the King*), and West Africans as East Africans (*Black Hawk Down*). Certain ethnic traits thought to be distinctive are on occasion heavily accented, by contrast, also to regulate antipathy and sympathy (e.g., the emphatically Semitic noses in *Aladdin*).

Whereas white actors were long preferred for ethnic main roles, "real" ethnic extras were often hired for exotic crowds or armies. When filming in overseas locations, these could be hired easily and cheaply (as in *The Ten Commandments*). The overwhelming numbers and uniformity of overseas populations was further staged and emphasized in song-and-dance scenes of musicals (*The King and I*), with only token references to individuality. All this is usually done intuitively, without giving it much thought.

Today, computer-generated imaging (CGI) makes it easy to electronically multiply limited groups of extras to astonishing numbers. It also becomes tempting to make antique and overseas scenes much more massive than they probably were (think of *Troy* and *Alexander*). In the early days of CGI, there also was a tendency to make exotic people and faces unduly uniform (think of animated cartoons such as Disney's *Mulan*), in line with the colonial stereotype: "They come in vast numbers, and they all look alike."

White protagonists often have irreproachable looks, as walking ads for shampoo, toothpaste, and skin lotions (for instance, the antique heroes in *Troy* and *Alexander*). Dark makeup and strange hairdos are occasionally used to make Caucasian actors look "ethnic" or to underline the exoticism of nonwhite actors. A tribe of "natives" is preferably shown half naked: painted in war colors even during peacetime, with funny bones through their noses or large feathers on their heads (as in *King Kong*).

The seminudity of a white male protagonist is often used to underline that his physical strength and basic skills match those of his nonwhite adversaries, because he has very quickly become a better native than the natives themselves

(*Tarzan, Rambo*). The seminudity of nonwhite female protagonists, by contrast, is often used to underline their inborn sensuality and sexual eagerness. Among seminude nonwhite female candidates for extra roles (in South Sea movies such as *Mutiny on the Bounty*, for instance) only the young and the tight were apparently retained, whereas the old and the flabby were systematically sent home. In older films, furthermore, they were not to be overly light—otherwise their state of undress was deemed to be shocking and unacceptable.

Some larger projects (e.g., *Memoirs of a Geisha*) apparently had serious research done about appropriate costumes and props. But most of the time, exoticism is a mere Western fantasy product. Many blockbusters dress younger and more sympathetic strangers in more modern and Westernized clothes, whereas they dress older and more antipathetic strangers in more traditional local dress (also in the Indiana Jones films). The good guys in Western popular culture are often dressed lighter and whiter (hats, costumes, accessories), the bad guys in darker or black ones—for instance, in cowboy movies, but also in more recent space films like the Star Wars series, which, in spite of its creator's claims, does not succeed in transcending its own Manichaeism.

PROPS, SETS, AND DESIGN

In 2006, Russian director Alexandr Proshkin made a new version of Boris Pasternak's *Dr. Zhivago*, previously filmed by David Lean. Proshkin changed the hair color of Lara from blonde to the brunette she had been in the novel (albeit rather reddish), replaced the supposedly characteristic Siberian farmhouse with cupolas as completely unrealistic, and also threw out the balalaika as having no place whatsoever in the story. Within Western popular culture and blockbuster movies, huge civilizations from elsewhere are often condensed into a very limited set of ten or twenty easily recognizable stereotypical objects or images, overly familiar from minority restaurants, bazaars, and markets. Disney movies do this time and again (see the discussions of *Aladdin* and *Mulan* in chapter 2), but others also use this facile approach. The problem is that the representation of other cultures hardly ever goes beyond that and that those cultures (for instance, in Disney's theme parks and others) remain closely identified with those few clichés.

Movies about overseas adventures give ample space to exotic animals and plants, even if they are often made interchangeable worldwide: with Asian tigers and elephants in Africa, lions in the jungle instead of the savannah, and so on (for instance in successive versions of *Tarzan*). Exceptional, exceptionally large, or exceptionally large numbers of strange animals such as bats, reptiles, and insects are routinely employed to underline the eternally creepy nature of foreign countries (for instance in the Indiana Jones movies). Horrible dishes—often completely invented—are served to the same effect (live monkey brains, baby snakes, sheep eyes, crawling insects).

Many films and scenes open with establishing shots that seem to provide a mere geographic location for the action but which often (also through their visual rhetoric) carry additional suggestions. We have already seen that the naturalness but also "virginity" of wide-open spaces is often emphasized, as if they are completely uninhabited, belong to nobody, and are only waiting to be penetrated by Western explorers, pioneers, and settlers (particularly in Westerns and colonial adventure movies).

Ruins or monuments of old civilizations are often used as mere lifeless props or sets most of the time; we do not learn anything worthwhile about those cultures (for instance, in the Lara Croft films). Images of major Western metropolises (for instance, European capitals such as London or Paris) are given an ideological tenor as the mainstays of liberty and progress, just as in world news on television (van Ginneken 1998, pp. 178–79). New York and Los Angeles are presented as by far the most developed cities on Earth, not only of the present but also of the distant future (for instance, in many science fiction movies).

Shohat & Stam have already demonstrated that photography and filmmaking have thrived on bringing closer whatever was distant and exploiting contrasts. When the small screen began to keep people at home, the wide screen raised its bid in adding further production value: with brute rulers and strange crowds in extravagant sets (for instance, in antiquity and Bible movies). Most viewers assumed that these were reconstructions based on substantial research, more or less true to reality—but they were often gratuitous fantasies.

Such movies are also drawn toward the paranormal or metaphysical, furthermore, because of the ample opportunities for special effects. "Miracles" in the Old and New Testaments (such as Moses's parting of the waters of the Red Sea) are always eagerly embraced and further embellished; new findings (that it may just have been a reference to the phenomenon of ebb and flow in a Reed Sea) are of course ignored. The historic past is also made more spectacular than it probably was in many other ways (think of the ultramodern super explosions, rather than the modest thuds of eighteenth-century cannons, in the recent *The Last of the Mohicans*).

SOUND, LANGUAGE, AND SPEECH

Even background sounds may become a cliché. Think of the stereotypical sounds that always accompany jungle images, such as threatening drums, group chanting, and wild cries of the eternal savage native tribe at some close distance. Traditional popular music from elsewhere is often copied or para-phrased, and copyrights are not always respected (think of the example of the global hit "The Lion Sleeps Tonight," originally the African hit "Uyim Mbube," also used in *The Lion King*). The other extreme is that musical themes used to locate a scene elsewhere often bear only a distant relationship to the musical culture there (think of the eternal "pling-plang-plong" scores meant to denote Asia or the "characteristic" sweet string music in South Sea movies, which bears no relationship to traditional Polynesian culture). But Western classical music is often used as nonspecific and quasi-universal (for instance in *Black Hawk Down* and other tragic war scenes).

Strange peoples often remain literally speechless in Hollywood block-busters. They are seldom allowed to speak for themselves in a way that stirs un-derstanding and empathy. Sometimes this of allowed to children or other dependents, but hardly ever of independent adults. If something needs to be explained about the strange culture, this is usually done by a white "mediator" in the scene. In many films, natives can only utter a few unintelligible sounds—like "Ugh!"—or speak just a few broken sentences (think of the older Western cowboy movies).

Often the utterances of "others" in blockbuster movies used to remain un-translated. One has to admit that the introduction of very strange languages may have contradictory effects: It should bring others closer but often further alienates them (think of the discussion in chapter 9 about *The Passion of the Christ*). Even invented languages (such as Klingon in the Star Trek series) of-ten emphasize apparently rude and barbaric sounds. But dubbing in a famil-iar language, voice-overs, or subtitling are all imperfect means to restore linguistic equilibrium. Even if the audience is familiar with another language, nuances are often lost on it—for instance, accents indicating social class or position in the cultural hierarchy, frequently coupled with dominance or in-sistence (not allowing interruption or contradiction, for instance, in the speech of dominant white characters). This is particularly noteworthy when God himself, his prophets, or the saints are speaking in religious movies. Apart from that, there are dialects referring to a particular region or ethnic minor-ity (even in futuristic movies like the Star Wars trilogies). But there is also tone of voice, or pitch, in big adult men or small adult women. The latter are often made to speak with emphatically high or infantile voices (think of East Asian geisha-like characters).

Finally, it is not only important what is present in image and sound but also what is absent—what is "ex-nominated." All kinds of power structures remain in the background and are taken for granted. This often holds for gender roles and class distinctions, ethnicity and nationality—also in colonial and segregationist times (e.g., in the Indiana Jones movies). Young white males in Western audiences are hardly ever made aware that purely because of biological and geographic chance they possess a package of legal and financial privileges that puts them in the top few percent of the world population. This awareness is almost absent.

A WHITE VIEW OF THE WORLD

Hollywood is often called the Dream Factory: Blockbuster successes provide appealing new dreams (and nightmares) to the larger part of the world population every week. Most people, however, are made to share other people's dreams, to look through the eyes of others—not only at themselves, but also at their neighbors—because those movies are primarily made by and for a very small part of the world's population. The top of the social pyramid in a globalized world provides much of the cultural prism through which world history and the present world situation are presented, not because they have more talent to make movies, but because they have better education and more opportunities and means to do just that.

The makers of those blockbusters largely come from the middle class but become multimillionaires, or are determined to become so as soon as possible. Most come from the West Coast and East Coast of the United States, from a handful of cities in the other major Anglophone settler states, or from their former colonial heartland, Great Britain. To a lesser extent they also come from the four larger countries on the European continent, with just a few exceptions. Most are also white. They consider themselves to be broad-minded and open to change, albeit often in a very specific manner. They are full of good intentions but often show little insight in the limitations of their apparently cosmopolitan worldviews, which means that many of the aforementioned clichés and stereotypes remain unchallenged.

The key frame of reference of many Hollywood directors is that of youngsters driving their own stock car at sixteen, hanging out in fast-food restaurants and at the shops in the mall (as in George Lucas's first success, *American Grafitti*). The similar television series *Happy Days* and its many spin-offs had slightly more of a working-class accent, as did the 1970s movie *Saturday Night Fever*. But the 1990s saw the triumph of sitcoms constructed around groups of relatively privileged, white "young urban professionals," with only a few bohemian accents (as in the television series *Seinfeld* and *Friends*). Even female yuppies were represented in a whole new genre of "chick shows" made for prime-time television, from *Ally McBeal* on.

This is because sponsors and advertisers want young consumers with purchasing power in the main roles, and no real social problems in sight. Ethnicity is vaguely present, but mostly as shades of whiteness (Irish and Poles, Italians and Greeks); some colored roles are written in only after several seasons and persistent protests. For the 1999–2000 season, the four major American networks announced twenty-six new drama series, but not a single main writer or main character came from an ethnic minority (even though some were aliens from outer space). Two critics said: "America's storytellers need—and some indeed have—to stop seeing the world as a crowd of 'extras' with turbans, burkas, slanted eyes, or sombreros but no depth or central role."[2]

This media situation is increasingly at odds with everyday social reality, even at home. It is true that for a very long time the United States had a three-quarters majority of European origin. But today it has shrunk to two-thirds, and by the middle of the century it will have become less than half. At this point in time, influential states such as California and Texas already have a majority of minorities, and New York State is close, even if some newspapers tripped up in a headline announcing the emergence of a "nonwhite" majority in California—thus defining Hispanics as "colored." In many European metropolises, the same trend is already visible.

It is true that blacks play a prominent role in present-day American popular culture, but they are still largely limited to well-defined domains, roles, and circumstances (Nederveen Pieterse 1992). One commentator wrote in the *New York Times*: "It's hard to argue that America is becoming more colorblind when one benchmark is still missing: When will Hollywood dare release a major movie in which Denzel Washington and Reese Witherspoon fall passionately in love? For all the gains in race relations, romance on the big screen between a black man and a white woman remains largely a taboo."[3]

That same spring, Ed Leibowitz wrote in the same newspaper about the animated cartoon *Madagascar* and three other big movies Hollywood was releasing about Africa at the time. Two were again about animals and two about "adventures," always with the same standard conventions or clichés about the Dark Continent: "From the Johnny Weissmuller *Tarzan* movies of the 1930s and '40s to *King Solomon's Mines* in 1950 to the recent *Mummy* film starring Brendan Fraser, adventure movies set in Africa have typically featured white heroes besting evil in empty deserts or overgrown jungles."

He continued: "In Sydney Pollack's *Out of Africa* and Michael Radford's *White Mischief,* African locales provided romantic (if threatening) settings for the heated lovemaking of gorgeous white stars." Since then, there have been a few Africa films with other themes. But he added: "Hollywood's reluctance to dramatize Africa in all its complexity is symptomatic of a larger problem." He quoted producer Willam Horberg, who said, "There are very few movies where foreigners are the protagonists and are at the moral center of the film."[4]

Thus, we hardly ever learn to look at the world through the eyes of ethnic or cultural others.

We should be careful to point out that American and European movies are not more ethnocentric than those from other continents, and they are possibly less so. But as we saw in chapter 1, they are commercial products primarily made with a very precise target group in mind, with a preference for young white males with reasonable purchasing power in the most influential cities. In the context of colonial adventure movies these are also called "armchair conquistadores." It is their narcissism that is being stimulated, their ego that is being spared. There are other target groups as well, but in second place: women, the elderly, nonwhites, whoever lives in the faraway countryside and has less money to spend. Although these films are exported and shown worldwide, audiences outside the Western world do not seem to count for very much—although things are slowly beginning to change, as Hollywood is increasingly searching for coproducers in the worthwhile emerging markets of Russia, India, and China.

One might, of course, object that the bad guys in Hollywood movies are not always strangers. They may even be representatives of American corporations or the American government—particularly in liberal or radical films with social criticism. Yet media psychology teaches us that most of us tend to perceive and code them in a different manner—namely, as simply fantasy or caricature, as the exception to the rule, rather than as representative of the "normal" everyday situation. We have many other experiences on which to draw. With bad guys from elsewhere, this pattern is often reversed in our minds—as we have little else to rely on. Yet the emphatic glamour and paranoia in Hollywood films may indeed have paradoxical effects abroad.

Change in all this is slow. In our popular culture, we have all become accustomed to a certain approach to the encounter between more- and less-dominant groups. In it, someone's supposed skin color or ethnicity is still presented as a fundamental aspect of someone's identity—for instance, in the encounter between white and "colored" people in feature films, television series, musicals, and the like. We have even come to expect this approach and derive pleasure from new variations on the same old themes and genres. Apparently, it is not easy to cut loose from this whole heritage: neither for the makers nor for the viewers. It is like a flywheel that only needs little to keep turning and turning and turning.

Glossary

Abolitionist: Literally, in favor of abolition; usually of slavery, during the nineteenth century.

Agitprop: A combination of agitation and propaganda used to stir unrest and change.

AIDA: A persuasion model distinguishing between the successive phases of attention, interest, desire, and action.

Android: From Greek: of humanlike form; a robot in science fiction movies.

Animation: From Latin: endowing with life, breath, or soul; usually the "bringing to life" of sequences of successive drawings, clay figures, or virtual forms in a movie.

Anthropomorphic: Literally, conceived in a human form; used for certain animated object, plant, and animal characters (or aliens) in stories and movies.

Archaic: From Greek: old; the earliest, original, or primitive form of something.

Archetype: From Greek and Latin: an original mold or model; the typical example of something.

Background projection: A technique whereby dangerous scenes or faraway locations are filmed separately, then projected onto the background with the actors in the studio playing the scene in front of it.

Bioessentialism: The idea that the essential characteristics of an individual derive from his or her biology; often applied to race or gender.

Blockbuster: An expression used to denote a very effective and successful cultural product or a best seller, usually a movie.

Box office: Literally, the ticket office at the entry of a theatre; used to describe the direct income generated by a movie at the box office.

Camp: An ambiguous style in which certain clichés are slightly overdone, with an implicit wink to the audience, thus adding new layers of complexity and reflectivity; for example, in gay spoofs of opera divas.

Casting: Literally, giving a particular shape to a substance by pouring it in liquid state into a mold and then letting it harden; in film, finding the right actors for the right roles in a movie, usually with a view to their appearance, image, and previous acting history.

CGI: Abbreviation for computer-generated images.

Chauvinism: Excessive or even blind patriotism, as in political or war movies; derived from Nicholas Chauvin, a legendary French soldier very much devoted to Napoleon.

Chick flicks: Films appealing primarily to girls or young women; "mainstream" films were usually made to be primarily appealing to men.

Clichés: *See* Stereotype.

Composite picture: A photograph or still composed of a number of other pictures, either by combining details or by superposing them, as in portraits of suspected criminals sought by the police.

Computer graphics: *See* CGI.

Demonizing: Ascribing an "evil spirit" or essence to others, usually one's enemies.

Dolchstoss Legende: German: the legend of the "dagger thrust" (into someone's back); the archetypical idea that a lost war could have been won if only the politicians would not have let the military down, dating from after World War I but revived after the Vietnam war; for instance, in the *Rambo* movies.

Dystopia: An imaginary place that is depressing, wretched, and fearful. *See also* Utopia.

Embedded journalists: Journalists integrated into, or traveling with, military units, usually provoking some sort of identification with them and with their fate; an old practice revived during the 2003 invasion of Iraq.

Enemy images: Representations of an adverse party, discrediting it and thus preparing one's own side for conflict; ironically, research has shown that enemy images on both sides often display certain common features.

Epos: A heroic story.

Escapist: Literally, fleeing from; diversion of the mind to a purely imaginative activity or entertainment to dodge unwelcome routines or reality.

Establishing shots: Shots at the beginning of a scene or report that show and set the stage.

Ethnocentrism: Literally, putting one's own group at the center and rating all others in comparison to it (usually in a negative sense).

Eurocentrism: Ethnocentrism concerning the peoples of European or white descent, usually including those of the Americas and elsewhere.

Exhibitionism: Deriving pleasure from one's own indecent exposure. *See also* Voyeurism.

Ex-nomination: Literally, naming something away, or not naming it at all; a way of obscuring unwelcome parts of reality in discourse; for instance, social inequality or power relations.

Expatriate (expat): A person living outside his or her own country; often reserved for upper- and middle-class foreigners, whereas lower-class ones are simply called (im)migrants.

Femme fatale: A (usually attractive) woman, instrumental in bringing destiny to the protagonist.

Founding myth: The myth, or set of myths, on which a collective creed is primarily based; for instance, that of a religion or a nation.

Franchise: The "renting out" of a brand name, a copyrighted character, or film material to others. *See also* Licensed products; Merchandising.

Geisha: A Japanese girl trained in the various traditional arts of entertaining men, including poetry and music, not necessarily or exclusively in sexual ways, but often seen or depicted as such.

Gender: From Latin: sort or type; primarily applied to sexual differences, but with an emphasis on social roles rather than biological distinctions.

Genre: From Latin and French: kind or class: a sort or type of cultural product, such as books or films; genres can be distinguished in many different (often overlapping and contradictory) ways: by technique, subject, emotion, and so on.

Ghostwriter: A professional author, often staying in the shadows, who helps a less experienced person to write his or her own story.

Golem: From Yiddish/Hebrew: something shapeless; a clay or artificial figure in human form, often giant or otherwise fear inspiring.

Hegemonic: From Greek: guide or leader; a preponderant influence or dominant force; for instance, a class, state, or alliance.

Highbrow: Possessing (or pretending to have) strong intellectual interests or even superiority; people favoring arty or cultural films are traditionally deemed highbrow.

High concept: A salient film idea that can easily be explained in a single sentence, still, or trailer.

Icon: A simple and easily recognizable image referring to an object, character, or theme; for example, the profile of Indiana Jones, with his fedora hat and whip.

Ideology: A systematic scheme or coordinated body of ideas or concepts, especially with regard to human life, society, and difference; often implying a worldview.

Intertextual: Literally, between texts; concerning implicit or explicit references to other works.

Libido: From Latin: desire or lust; a hypothetical mental energy deriving from primitive biological urges like sex, in psychoanalytical theory.

Licensed products: Articles produced and distributed with permission of the copyright holder. *See also* Franchise; Merchandising.

Lowbrow: Inferior, without intellectual or cultural interest; a label often used for pulp, soaps, and similarly unpretentious genres.

Macho, Macha: Macho is Spanish for a very masculine and virile man; Macha is a new, feminist variation, indicating a very strong or self-confident girl or woman.

"Making of" documentaries: Documentaries made during and about the production of a major movie, usually to be shown on television as a promotional device.

Manichaeism: An ancient interpretation depicting man and society as the scenes of a struggle between pure good and pure evil; a black-and-white view of conflict.

Manifest destiny: The idea that the "obvious fate" of a nation is to be exceptional and to lead all others.

Merchandising: Developing and selling merchandise deriving from a book or film; for instance, gadgets, toys, games, theme park rides. *See also* Franchise; Licensed products.

Metanarrative: A deeper and more archetypical story hidden beneath the surface of a story.

Metaphor: A figure of speech in which a phrase or word denoting one kind of object or action is used in place of another, to suggest a likeness or analogy; also applied to symbols or images, as in images of a steam engine or a fountain as a metaphor for the sexual act and fulfillment.

Miscegenation: Literally, mixing stock; romance or sex between different races, which was emphatically forbidden in Hollywood movies when segregation was prevalent in the United States.

Mise-en-scène: Preparation of a story for the stage (or the screen), mostly by the director.

Missing in action (MIA): Soldiers who were captured or otherwise disappeared in action; it is unclear whether they are dead or alive, captured or free, a key subject of commando movies such as the Rambo series.

Modernism: A general way of thinking that prevailed in the West from the Enlightenment and Industrial Revolution onward, in which every social phenomenon was easily and neatly categorized as progressive or conservative, left or right, high or low, and so on. *See also* Postmodernism.

Monologue intérieure: French: "interior monologue"; as if someone is talking to him- or herself alone.

Morale: The attitude of an individual or group with relation to the tasks ahead.

Morphology: Relating to form and structure; for instance, the outward appearance of the face or body of an individual or a group.

Multiculturalism: The idea that most major cultures deserve a degree of respect and can live together peacefully; sometimes challenged as overly relativist.

Naturalization: Literally, making something (seem) natural; accomplished in literature and film by the use of certain rhetorical devices. Economic or political inequalities and power relations are often described in natural terms to make them appear self-evident.

Nostalgia: Longing to return to another age or place.

Nouvelle vague: The "new wave" of French filmmaking in the 1960s, which questioned and changed certain traditional cinematic practices.

Occidentalist: A stereotypical view of the West among Easterners. *See also* Orientalist.

Orientalist: A stereotypical view of the Orient and the East (in particular of Arabs and other Muslims) among Westerners.

Orthodox: Adhering to the supposedly original, right, or "true" interpretation of a creed; as in the orthodox church in Christianity or orthodox Marxism or capitalism.

Pan: Short for the panoramic movement of the camera; usually a horizontal scan of a landscape or scene.

Pantheon: Literally, a temple built for all gods, often on a hill; a collection of cultural heroes or a place were they assemble.

Paradigm: Literally, a model or example; an influential grid of interpretation or school of thought within an art form or scientific discipline.

Peplum: Latin: hanging shirt or dress; the genre of antiquity movies, particularly with regard to Greece and Rome.

Permissiveness: A tendency to condone behavior that is frowned upon by others; for instance, sexual permissiveness.

Philology: Literally, the study of language; the study of written source material in order to reach conclusions about its authenticity and veracity; for instance, concerning early versions of Holy Books.

Plagiarism: The copying or stealing of texts, images, or ideas in order to pass them off as one's own.

Pogrom: Russian: devastation; the organized looting and abuse of helpless people by mobs, often tolerated by authorities, especially of minorities such as Jews.

Politically correct (PC): A term originally used to demand more respect for others: nonwhites, nonmales, etc.; today it is mostly employed in a sarcastic sense—that is to say, to denounce supposed exaggerated zeal in combating stereotypes and prejudice.

Polygamous: Having a plurality of wives, husbands, or marriages.

Polysemy: From Latin: multiplicity of meanings; a term indicating that most things do not carry a single meaning but potentially a wide range of them, sometimes even contradictory ones.

Populist: Claiming to represent the rank and file of the ordinary people, often in somewhat simplistic or demagogic ways.

Postmodernism: A philosophy based on an increasing awareness of the multiplicity of possible meanings and values, depending on one's social position, for example, as a woman, gay, or "nonwhite" person.

Prejudice: Literally, preconceived judgment, often on the basis of outward appearances of people (e.g., their gender or race); judging before having had the opportunity to really get to know someone or something.

Prequel: A film made later than the original but telling a story that precedes the original story's time frame.

Production code: A set of guidelines for producers and distributors, stipulating what is and what is not permissible in American movies; the Hollywood Production Code was in force between the 1930s and 1960s before it was replaced by a rating system.

Production value: Those elements in a movie, apart from the story itself, showing the amount of money and energy spent on making it attractive and appealing to a wide audience; for instance, attractive locations, lavish sets, elaborate costumes, famous stars.

Projection: Literally, throwing something forward; in film, images "thrown" onto a screen; in psychoanalysis, ascribing one's own hidden motives to another.

Promiscuity: Indiscriminate mixing with different people; for instance, sexual promiscuity.

Propaganda: Material that promotes a particular worldview.

Proto-: An early, original, or primitive form of; for instance, protofascism or protocommunism.

Pseudonym: Literally, fake name; a name adopted by someone (often an artist) who does not want to use his or her given name.

Quest: An elaborate search, for example, for a material treasure or for spiritual enlightenment; central storylines of a certain type of adventure movies, such as the Indiana Jones and Lara Croft series.

Race: A large group with shared ancestry and common traits that often lived in a similar environment or continent for a considerable amount of time; often arbitrarily linked to skin color.

Racism: The belief that some races are fundamentally better than others.

Rating system: A way of categorizing films, primarily based on their suitability for particular age groups.

Reactionary: Reacting against the current state of affairs, usually by striving to return to an earlier stage of political development (e.g., a feudal state or elitist society).

Red Scare: Widespread fear, after the world wars, that "Red" or socialist revolutions overseas might spread to the United States; partly fanned by parties with an interest in maintaining the status quo.

Regression: A fallback to an earlier stage along the ladder of civilization; for instance, in mental development, when an adult comes to behave in childish ways or a human in animalistic ways.

Revisionism: A concerted attempt to fundamentally change an established view; for instance, concerning the submission of the Native Americans in America or the genocide of the Jews in Europe.

Robinsonades: Stories of inventive survival on an uninhabited island or territory, similar to that of Daniel Defoe's *Robinson Crusoe*.

Saga: A term originally referring to legendary stories from Iceland and Norway about the heroic exploits of the Vikings, usually a mixture of historic facts and fictional embellishments.

Scopophilia: Literally, the lust of looking; for instance, of men looking at (pictures of) women, (semi)nude or otherwise.

Selective articulation: The inevitable selection of elements and emphasis, the organization of coherence and plausibility, in any account, whether supposedly factual or fictional.

Semiology: The study or art of signs and the ways in which meaning is conveyed and organized.

Settler myths: The ensemble of stories and themes concerning the mythical encounter between white settlers and nonwhite natives overseas.

Social Darwinism: The idea (incorrectly ascribed to Darwin) that human progress ultimately stems from the ongoing battle for "the survival of the fittest" among races, nations, classes, and other social groupings.

Stereotype: Literally, something reproduced without variation; an oversimplified, standardized impression of a group of people. *See also* Prejudice.

Subtext: Literally, the hidden text; deeper meaning that lies below the obvious surface meaning of a text.

Synthetic images: A combination of "real" and virtual images.

Tilt: Vertical camera angle, often suggesting a difference in status between the viewer and whoever or whatever is seen.

Unidentified flying object (UFO): Usually implied to be a flying saucer or other spaceship carrying alien visitors, as in Steven Spielberg's *Close Encounters* and *E.T.*

Utopia: An imaginary state or epoch with ideal conditions, as described by the British statesman Thomas More.

Voyeurism: From French: someone looking; deriving pleasure from looking at something, often not meant to be looked at by others, such a nudity or intimate encounters. *See also* Exhibitionism.

White Anglo-Saxon Protestants: Long the dominant group in Great Britain, as well as in the United States and other settler countries.

White man's burden: The idea, expressed by the British author Rudyard Kipling and others, that God or destiny had assigned the white race to colonize and educate the others.

Xenophobia: The fear and rejection of strangers and their habits.

Notes

PREFACE

1. Written in English. A first Dutch translation was published by Boom in Amsterdam in 2006.

CHAPTER 1

1. Conversely, one American dollar corresponded to 0.77 Euros and 0.51 British pounds (February 2007).

2. Dutch quality daily *NRC Handelsblad*, weekly edition, August 5, 2003.

3. Jews were excluded for many centuries from the possession of agricultural land and certain traditional professions in many European countries (for instance, those controlled by guilds), so they tended to turn to modern professions and enterprises instead, also using diaspora networks, as well as to intellectual and cultural skills, which could not be taken away whenever they were forced to flee.

CHAPTER 2

1. Analyzed by me in a previous Dutch book *Comic Strip Heroes on the Couch: The Riddle of the Obsessions of Asterix, Babar, Donald, Superman and Tintin* (van Ginneken 2002).

2. Details in van Ginneken (1998), chap. 1, among others.

3. "Disney lyrics Grate on Arab Americans," *International Herald Tribune*, July 5, 1993, p. 5. The version that was ultimately adopted was slightly different. Also see Bernstein & Studlar 1997, p. 17 n. 20; van Willigen 1995, p. 172; Wasko 2001, p. 140.

4. Recently, they released a brand-new feature-length film, *Leo, King of the Jungle*, directed by Yoshio Takeuchi.

5. See the interview with him about this on the Animated World Network site, www.awn.com/issue1.5/articles/deneroffadd1.5.html.

6. See an item to this effect in the "People" column of the *IHT*, September 9, 2004, and Sharon Lafranière, "Song's Success Finally Returns Home: 'Lion Sleeps Tonight' Income Arrives Many Decades Late," *NYT/IHT*, March 16, 2006.

7. The major Internet sites with critical information are www.powhatan.org and www.lib.berkeley.edu/MRC/Pocahontas.html.

8. For example, Jacquelyn Kilpatrick, "Disney's 'PC' Pocahontas (Race in Contemporary American Cinema)." *Cineaste* 21, no. 4 (Fall 1995).

9. *Encyclopaedia Britannica*, 1973–74 edition, vol 11, pp. 590–91.

10. *Encyclopaedia Britannica*, vol. 11, pp. 590–91.

11. *Encyclopaedia Britannica*, vol. 11, pp. 590–91.

12. See Michael Winerip, "For Some Indians, Thanksgiving without the Pilgrims," *New York Times/IHT*, November 27, 2003.

13. Sheryl Gay Stolberg, "Picture an Artistically Correct US Capitol," *New York Times/IHT*, August 19, 2003.

14. Michael Laris, "China Agrees to Allow Disney Show to Go On," *Washington Post/IHT*, February 9, 1999; "Faith in Disney Magic Helps Lift Hong Kong," *Washington Post/IHT*, December 4–5, 1999.

15. Shen Qipeng, "Chinese Lawmakers Show High Concern over Cultural Security," www.chinaview.cn; quoted in Liu 2004, pp. 6, 11.

CHAPTER 3

1. Claude Aziza, "Hercule contre les tyrans de Babylone: La psychanalyse du pauvre," *Le Monde*, August 7–8, 1994, radio & television supplement, p. 9.

2. In reaction, African American scholars claimed the opposite. See the September 23, 1991, *Newsweek* cover: "Was Cleopatra Black?" A dozen years later, Francesca T. Royster published a fascinating study on the cultural struggle to appropriate an ambiguous symbol: *Becoming Cleopatra: The Shifting Image of an Icon*.

3. Ancient Egypt long ruled Nubia to its south and thus received a significant influx of darker-skinned citizens. Between approximately 750 and 650 BCE the roles were even reversed, with five successive Nubian pharaohs ruling Egypt. But after their overthrow, most of their images were destroyed. See the 2005 Swiss television documentary *On the Traces of the Black Pharaohs* by Stéphane Goël and Sylvie Rossel, broadcast on the Franco-German Arte channel.

4. A multivolume study on this subject written by Martin Bernal (son of a famous historian of science and technology) stirred considerable controversy. It was hailed

as a major breakthrough by some famous scholars of the Orient (Joseph Needham, Edward Said, Perry Anderson) but derided by others as overly "PC."

5. *The Times*, June 23, 2000; quoted in a Netherlands Press Agency (ANP) dispatch, printed the next day as "Piramiden in deeltijd gebouwd" in the daily *NRC Handelsblad*, June 24, 2000.

6. Quoted from his memoirs in the television documentary *The True Curse of the Mummy*, directed by Bryn Higgins for Stone City Productions in 2002 and broadcast in the Avro *Close Up* program on the first channel in the Netherlands.

7. *The Curse of Tutankamon*, directed by Susannah Ward for Take 3/The Travel Channel and Pioneer Productions, broadcast in France on the Fifth Channel (for culture and education).

8. The 2002 German documentary *The Gladiators*, directed by Günther Klein; the 2003 British BBC docu-fiction *Gladiators!* coproduced with France and directed by Tilman Remme; the 2003 German-Austrian television feature *The Honour of the Gladiators*, directed by Jorgo Papavassiliou.

9. See the article by Kevin O'Brien, "German Film Tax Break May Not Make Cut," *IHT*, December 13, 2004.

10. Professor Fik Meijer of Amsterdam University, for one, had a monograph on the death of the Roman emperors followed by further monographs on their horse races and gladiators. The latter (Meijer 2003) estimated that most gladiators, fighting two or three times a year, probably died between the ages of twenty and thirty with some five to thirty-four fights to their names. Emperor Augustus boasted in his testament that no fewer than ten thousand men had fought to the death in the eight gladiatorial contests he had held. Under Claudius, nine thousand prisoners engaged in one mock sea battle alone. (Also see the review of the 2005 English translation by William Grimes in the *NYT/IHT*, December 15, 2005).

11. See the overview on the question in Dienekes Pontikos, "Racial Type of the Ancient Hellenes," http://dienekes.angeltowns.net/articles/hellenes/.

12. Quoted in the "People" column, *IHT*, January 7, 2005, p. 10. One might add that homosexuality is one area where Hollywood insiders and their mass audiences differ markedly. Over the last ten years no fewer than "seventeen actors or actresses have been nominated for Academy Awards for playing gay characters," but only two of the movies nominated for an Oscar "containing substantial homosexuality" made more than $100 million, according to a December 1, 2004 column by Ben Shapiro on the website www.townhall.com.

13. See his article "Into battle with Alexander" in the *Times*, May 8, 2004; also available at www.timesonline.co.uk/article/0,,7434-1101601,00.html.

14. Bob Baker, "The Historical Battle in Making *Alexander*," *New York Times/IHT*, November 18, 2004. Also see Fox 1973, p. 11.

15. The *New York Times* review of the film by Manohla Dargis (in the *IHT*, November 30, 2004) was appropriately called "The Soft-Pedaling of a Monster."

16. Dispatch by Anthony Breznican, AP, November 22, 2004; also see www.mercurynews.com/mld/mercurynews/news/breaking_news/10247251.htm.

17. Dick van den Heuvel, "Oliver Stone strijdbaar over zijn 'Alexander': 'Ze begrijpen me niet,'" *De Telegraaf*, December 23, 2004, p. T21.

18. Dispatch by Anthony Breznican, posted on November 22, 2004 (as in note 16).

CHAPTER 4

1. Interview in the French radio and television weekly *Télérama*, November 9, 2005.

2. One of the most famous American recruitment posters for World War I, which the directors had probably seen as recruits, depicted Germany as a big and dark ferocious gorilla carrying a smaller and white crying woman away—exactly as in *King Kong*—with "Destroy this mad brute" above and "Enlist" under the picture in large letters. See Keen 1991, p. 76, item 1. Nazi propaganda posters later in turn associated black U.S. soldiers with apes and rape.

3. Clive D. L. Wynne (associate professor of psychology at the University of Florida), "Kissing Cousins: King Kong's Origins," *IHT*, December 13, 2005.

4. As late as 1958, a poll found "that 96 percent of whites disapproved of marriages between blacks and whites": Nicholas D. Kristof, "Blacks, Whites and Love in America," *New York Times/IHT*, April 25, 2005. (Also see his article referred to in the first note of chap. 6).

5. Also see the overview documentary *The Blonde and the Beast*, which Kevin Burns and Kim Sheerin made for Prometheus Entertainment in 2004 (together with Animal Planet and Fox), broadcast on Dutch public television in the *Close Up* slot on December 18, 2005.

6. Brent Staples, "Finally Getting to Know the Real Godzilla," *New York Times/IHT*, May 4, 2005.

7. The central television anchorman in the film calls Godzilla's actions "the worst act of destruction since the bombing of the World Trade Center." He means the "minor" bombing of 1993, not the airplane attack of 2001. Some observers noted that the event and the reporting on 9/11 resembled such Hollywood disaster films and may have been co-inspired by it. Others even likened Osama bin Laden to Godzilla.

8. On the unprecedented merchandising effort in France, see for example P. P., "Dinomania: Comment l'invasion a été programmé," *L'Evenement du Jeudi*, August 26–September 1, 1993, pp. 68–69; Henri Béhar & Danièle Heymann, "Les profitosaures: Une monstrueuse série B," *Le Monde*, October 20, 1993, pp. 14–15; and

Philippe Baverel, "Les déçus de la 'dinomania,'" May 3, 1994, econ. suppl., p. II, and many others.

9. In a television overview documentary *The Wild Africa of the Movies*, which Michel Viotte made in 2003 for La Compagnie des Indes, broadcast by Arte in France and Germany and on Dutch public television in the *Close Up* slot.

10. The studio had reportedly bought off his original wife with $10,000, but his widely publicized later romances were no success either, and his five further marriages all ended in divorce. He was briefly hired as a "gambling guest greeter" by Caesar's Palace in Las Vegas, but drank. He ended up on welfare in a hotel room in Acapulco, Mexico, and not one Hollywood superstar came to his low-key burial. Loudspeakers played his yell as his coffin sank into the grave. (According to the documentary *Tarzan, the One and Only*, made by his Romanian "compatriot" Florin Iepan for West End Film & Television, broadcast during a Tarzan night for the Franco-German Arte channel on August 22, 2004, and in Avro's *Close Up* on the first Dutch public channel on September 5, 2004.

11. See, for instance, Roos Kuiper, "Three Hundred People on an Uninhabited Island," *Intermediair* [The Netherlands], October 16, 2003, pp. 36–39.

12. Tom Shales, "The Grand Finale of a Television Obsession," *Washington Post/IHT*, August 25, 2000, p. 22.

13. Quoted by correspondent Koert Lindijer in his article "Overleef Kenia en win 1 miljoen," *NRC Handelsblad*, June 27, 2001, p. 4.

14. *IHT*, January 12, 2000, p. 6.

CHAPTER 5

1. The National Congress of American Indians and other organizations recently filed a detailed and documented lawsuit on behalf of three hundred thousand U.S. Indians, claiming they had been cheated out of the equivalent $137.2 billion (in present-day terms) over the years. See Joel Brinkley, "Indians Hand US a Bill," *New York Times/IHT*, January 8, 2003.

2. The famous Chilean author Isabel Allende (a cousin of the murdered president) published *Zorro: The Novel* in 2005. Even the famous Mexican Zapatista guerrilla leader Commandante Marcos adopted some of his traits.

3. In May 2002 Disney's boss Michael Eisner said he wanted to "capture the post–9/11 surge in patriotism" by investing $107 million in a movie about the Alamo, to be released by Christmas of the following year. The intended blockbuster proved a dud. Sharon Waxman, "For Disney, a Battered Journey to 'The Alamo,'" *NYT/IHT*, March 26, 2004, p. 9.

4. Riva Palacio was named Vicente after his maternal grandfather Guerrero, the first "colored" president of the country.

CHAPTER 6

1. Nicholas Kristof, "Mixing the Races in America," *International Herald Tribune*, December 7–8, 2002.

2. "People" column, *IHT*, March 3, 2005.

3. There is a famous similar incident from the history of the mainstream *National Geographic Magazine*. Photographers reported that the editors once corrected the color of naked overseas breasts from whitish to brownish, in order to make them supposedly "less offending" to its middle-class readers.

4. Alan Riding, "Gauguin's Tahitian Paradise Visits Paris," *NYT/IHT*, October 10, 2003.

5. Olivier Cena "Vahinés et vanités," in the French radio and television weekly *Télérama*, October 1, 2003, and a special issue "hors série." Also see Alan Riding, "Gauguin"s Tahitian Paradise," *New York Times/IHT*, October 10, 2003.

6. Claire Harvey, "Trouble in Paradise: Sex Scandal in Pitcairn," *New York Times/IHT*, October 20, 2004. Also see the shorter AP items during the period before and after that: "7 *Bounty* Descendants to Be Tried in Attacks, September 29, 2004; "6 Men Convicted in Pitcairn Trials, October 26, 2004.

7. Broadcast as *Les filles des mers du Sud* in France (and Germany) on the Arte channel, January 30, 2005, and around that same time as *De betovering van de hoela hoela meisjes* in the Avro *Close Up* program on the Dutch first channel, January 16, 2005.

8. An assumption challenged in great detail by Obeyesekere 1992.

9. He refers to a specific scene in *Bird of Paradise* that seems to derive from the famed "monkey dance" in Bali, a small Hindu island east of Java, the main Muslim island of Indonesia.

10. One of the early successfully exported present-day Chinese movies, *Shanghai Triad* (by the famous couple of director Zhang Yimou and actress Gong Li), also gave the "pleasure girl" such different characteristics.

11. Dutch daily *NRC Handelsblad*, April 7, 2004, p. 4

12. Ivan Wolffers, "Iedereen moet naar het Westen willen: De witte wereld van Miss Saigon," *NRC Handelsblad*, December 27, 1996, cultural supplement, p. 5.

13. "I Love '75," in the series *I Love the '70s*, broadcast in the Netherlands on Net 5, April 18, 2004.

14. There is some confusion over what ultimately happened to the franchise. An Internet search seems to yield at least seven installments of the original French series up to 1993, another seven American ones with the same name from 1994 on, and two individual Italian titles.

CHAPTER 7

1. For example, the French *Télérama*, October 24, 2001, p. 123; and the Dutch *Vpro-gids*, June 1, 2003, p. 33.

2. Also see the revealing television documentary *The White King, Red Rubber and the Black Mountain*, which Peter Bate made for Periscope productions in 2004 and was broadcast on the Franco-German Arte channel on November 2, 2005.

3. A 1966 study by Suleiman Mousa, for instance, said that many of his claims about exploits were demonstrably wrong and that his views on Arabs and their independence at the time were later misrepresented by himself and others. Also see Asher 1998.

4. By Richard Andrews and Georg Graffe (Germany 2001), rebroadcast in prime time on the Franco-German Arte channel, November 29, 2003.

5. Philip Bowring, "Hollywood Can't Get Royal Siam Right," *IHT*, November 24, 1998; Keith B. Richburg, "'Anna' Raises a Royal Furor in Thailand," *Washington Post/ IHT*, January 19, 2000. Also see the *IHT*, of December 9, 1998; August 27, 1999; November 23, 2001.

6. Bowring, "Hollywood Can't Get Royal Siam Right."

7. According to a Quatermain website, the name William Quaterman is mentioned near that of the father-in-law of Samuel Pepys, who reportedly asserted in 1667 that he had discovered those same mines.

8. "Allan Quatermain," Who2, www.who2.com/allanquatermain.html.

9. "Allan Quatermain," The British Empire Library, www.britishempire.co.uk/ library/allanquatermain.htm.

10. They created problems with the "all ages" PG rating, so that Hollywood especially created the "PG-13" rating. Some spooky scenes and the mine car chase were designed to be licensed to theme parks such as Disney.

11. Fundamentalist Jews want to look for them under the Temple Mount, whereas fundamentalist Muslims see this as an attempt to undermine the Al Aqsa mosque on top of it. See the Israeli TV documentary on *The Ark of the Covenant* by Nir Toib, rebroadcast among others by EO on the Dutch first public channel September 23, 2003.

CHAPTER 8

1. More about the ongoing discussion: Hochman (2002). Also see *IHT*, November 13 and 22, 2002.

2. Michiko Kakautani, "Review of Stephen Winder's *The Man Who Saved Britain*," *IHT*, November 28.

3. Stephen Winder, "Her Majesty's Sacred Service," *IHT*, November 22, 2006. Also see *IHT*, November 15 and 28, 2006.

4. In the television documentary *The James Bond Story*, directed by Chris Hunt for Iambic productions in 1999, around the release of *The World Is Not Enough*, and rebroadcast on the Paris Première channel on April 27, 2003, and also in the Avro *Close Up* program on the first Dutch channel.

5. In a one-hour 2002 U.S. portrait documentary, broadcast in Europe a few months after his death on the Franco-German Arte channel, January 25, 2007.

6. Professor Michael Rogin, of the University of California at Berkeley (*IHT*, September 21–22, 1985). More in Rogin 1988.

7. Reuters, July 31, 1985; carried the next day in the *International Herald Tribune* as "In U.S., 'Rambomania' Has Struck a Rich Vein: 'Rambo' Paraphernalia Sell Briskly."

8. Think of the Hungerford massacre in the U.K. and a long list of similar copycat events.

9. In another microphone test during the same period, he joked that he had just outlawed Russia: "The bombing begins in five minutes." (Quoted by Kellner 1995, pp. 70 and 91, n. 17).

10. See the editorial comment "When Photo-ops Go Bad," *IHT*, October 31, 2003.

11. The liaison office was subject to two recent elaborate TV documentaries: the longer and more historical French *Opération Hollywood*, directed by Emilio Pacull for "Les Films d''Ici" in 2004, broadcast during a "theme night" and repeated on the Franco-German Arte channel on October 18, 2006 (and earlier broadcast in the Netherlands on the Avro *Close Up* program on the first public channel, November 10, 2005), and the shorter and more topical *Hollywood and the Pentagon: A Dangerous Liaison*, directed by Marie Pia Mascaro and Jean-Marie Barrère for Capa Films in 2003, made for Canada, Australia, and half a dozen Northern European countries, broadcast in the *Ram* program, by Vpro on the third Dutch public channel, December 28, 2003. The Strub quotes are from both.

12. Paul Farhi discusses five examples in "Network TV Puts US Agents in the Crosshairs," *Washington Post/IHT*, August 10, 2001.

13. In the 2003 TV documentary *All the President's Movies*, by Brett Hudson and Burt Kearns, narrated by Martin Sheen (the president in the successful TV series *The West Wing*), broadcast in the *Het uur van de wolf* timeslot on the third Dutch public channel, May 9, 2005.

14. Elvis Mitchell, "Good at Action Films, Maybe Too Good," *NYT/ IHT*, September 19, 2001; Rick Lyman, "Wanted: Hollywood Villains for a New Climate," *NYT/IHT*, October 9, 2001; James W. Hall, "A New Script for Thriller Writers," *New York*

Times/IHT, November 22, 2001; Sharon Waxman, "Hollywood Puts Out More Flags," *Washington Post/IHT*, February 12, 2002.

15. Sharon Waxman, "Hollywood Exhales as Sales Hit Record Despite Sept. 11," *Washington Post/IHT*, February 12, 2002; also see Paul Hegeman, "Hollywood na 11 September," Dutch *VPRO* TV guide.

16. Jamie Malanowski "A Film of War, Without Any Answers," *NYT/IHT*, December 21, 2001.

17. Malanowski, "A Film of War."

18. Malanowski, "A Film of War."

19. John M. Broder, "Senior Officers in Qatar Watched Private's Rescue by Video," *NYT/IHT*, April 3, 2003, p. 4; Kenneth N. Gilpin, "Private Lynch Returns to Enthusiastic Welcome," *NYT/IHT*, July 23, 2003, p. 5; David Lipsky, "Review of Rick Bragg's *I Am a Soldier: The Jessica Lynch Story*," *NYT/IHT*, December 23, 2003; Jim Rutenberg, "A Multimedia Strategy: CBS Interview Bid Offers So Much More," *NYT/IHT*, June 17, 2003, p. 14. Also see the smaller items on July 10, August 9–10, September 3 and 17, November 7.

20. See the subsequent television special *War Spin*, broadcast on the *Correspondent* program, on BBC2, immediately after the war.

21. Vloet, "Saving Private Lynch," *NRC Handelsblad*, May 17–18, 2003, p. 57.

22. The first interview was almost snatched away from ABC by CBS, which reportedly uses vague promises of extensive multimedia deals to land such scoops.

23. Also see "A Death Embellished," *IHT*, March 29, 2007, p. 6; and "Army Lied, U.S. Athlete's Brother Says," compiled from news reports, in the *IHT*, April 25, 2007.

CHAPTER 9

1. American Philip Dye made a two-part overview television documentary *The Bible according to Hollywood* (1994), broadcast on the Planète channel in France on December 13, 2005.

2. *The Bible Unveiled*, broadcast on the Franco-German Arte channel just before Christmas 2006.

3. Compare the baby incubator hoax preceding the first American invasion of Iraq, for instance, and the long march preceding the founding of Communist China, respectively.

4. Original publication in German in 1914, quoted here from the English translation published by Vintage/Random House/Knopf, New York 1964, pp. 14–5, 11.

5. As the Nazis forced him to leave the European continent and to lead many of his disciples across channel and ocean to the conquest of the Anglo-American world. For a synopsis of his Moses theory, see Freud (1973), pp. 514–35.

6. Rebroadcast in the Netherlands by the Evangelical Broadcaster EO on the first public channel, September 30, 2003, and in France on the Histoire theme channel, April 13, 2004.

7. According to the 1999 edition of the annotated *Groot Nieuws Bijbel*, an official collaborative project of the Dutch (Protestant) Bible Society based in Haarlem, and the Catholic Bible Foundation based in Hertogenbosch, integrating historical research and maps provided by Oxford University Press. See the notes to Exodus 12:37, 12:41, etc.

8. Also see Solomon 2001, p. 242. He also notes on p. 250 that the 1954 movie *The Egyptian* had similarly turned the biblical Joseph into an influence on the pharaoh Akhenaton, the one who first tried to introduce monotheism. (Compare the Freud essay, quoted above, on this same theme).

9. See Sarah Vowell, "The Top Ten Commandments," *IHT*, July 19, 2005.

10. See *Tsippora*, the second book of his trilogy on women in the Bible, by the present-day Jewish writer Marek Halter (Paris: Laffont 2004) and the review in the weekly *Jeune Afrique*, January 25–31, 2004, pp. 82–83.

11. Geraldine Fabrikant, "DreamWorks Dreams Big." *New York Times/IHT*, December 29, 1998.

12. Bernard Weinraub, "Jeffrey Katzenberg Bets All on *Prince of Egypt*" *NYT/IHT*, December 16, 1998.

13. Weinraub, "Jeffrey Katzenberg Bets All on Prince of Egypt."

14. Weinraub, "Jeffrey Katzenberg Bets All on Prince of Egypt."

15. "Prince of Egypt: Three Perspectives." *Tikkun* 14, no. 1 (1999): 8–10.

16. Laura M. Holson, "Pitching a DVD to the Faithful," *New York Times/IHT*, September 1, 2004.

17. See, for instance, Jean-Claude Loiseau et al., dossier "L'Affaire Jésus," in the French weekly *Télérama*, March 24, 2004, pp. 13–24.

18. The supposed "distortion" of the original faith and particularly about Mary Magdalene was also one of the main themes of Dan Brown's mega-bestseller *The Da Vinci Code*, later turned into a blockbuster movie (2006). It was savaged by reviewers but made $750 million anyway. The storyline derived mostly from a much earlier book, *The Holy Blood and the Holy Grail* by Michael Baigent, Richard Leigh, and Henry Lincoln (London: Jonathan Cape/Corgi, 1982/1994). Both wove ancient

stories about the Merovingans, Templars, and so forth together into a superplot spanning millennia, masterminded by a mythical "Priory of Sion"—an obvious and gross invention of French origin.

19. Produced and directed by Roel Oostra for CTC/Cresset Communications, in coproduction with the main German public channels WDR/ARD, the Belgian VRT, the Dutch educational Teleac/NOT, and the Cobo Fund. Among the noteworthy Bible scholars interviewed about these subjects were Elaine Pagels and Gilles Quispel, the aforementioned Keith Hopkins, Timothy Freke, and Peter Gandy (authors of *The Jesus Mysteries* and *Jesus and the Goddess*).

20. Rudi Fuchs (former director of the famous Stedelijk Museum of Amsterdam), "Kroon van Bloed" (Crown of Blood), Dutch quality daily *NRC-Handelsblad,* April, 23, 2004.

21. The documentary *Jesus in the Picture,* produced by Dutch evangelical broadcaster EO, was broadcast on April 1, 2004. It included an interview with Tatum and fragments from many of the films he discussed in his book. Most exposure, however, was given to an "exemplary" 1979 American evangelical dramatic documentary production based on the Gospel of Luke, *Jesus*—once again portrayed with blond hair and blue eyes.

22. The play had long retained its anti-Semitic overtones, and Hitler used its three-hundredth anniversary to reaffirm his anti-Jewish stance (Plate 2004, p. 7).

23. It reportedly received one hundred thousand worried phone calls a few years later, after Christian fundamentalists suggested its logo revealed that it was owned by the devil in person. The classical rumor case was inspired by the supposedly satanic number 666, which people saw in its logo. See van Ginneken (1993).

24. "Using carbon-14 dating tests in 1988, a group of scientists dated the cloth between 1260 and 1390 and ruled that it was probably a medieval forgery": Jason Horowitz, "Computer Creates Face of 'Young Jesus.'" *New York Times/IHT,* December 27, 2004.

25. *In the Footsteps of Jesus,* broadcast as *Sur les traces de Jésus* by France 3 on three successive Sundays around Christmas, December 23, 2001–January 6, 2002. Note that there was later a similar controversy over a historically correct BBC reconstruction of the face of Santa Claus/Saint Nicholas as a Turk with a boxer's nose.

26. According to San Francisco pastor Mark Stanger in the webzine Salon.com, Laurent Rigoulet, "La Dernière Tentation de Mel Gibson," French weekly *Télérama,* February 18, 2003, pp. 28–30.

27. Michael Lerner, "Mel Gibson Revives an Old Message of Hate," *IHT,* April 1, 2004.

28. Details in Ton Crijnen, "JP II maakt omstreden Anna zalig", *Trouw* [The Netherlands], October 2, 2004. According to Amy-Jill Levine, she also "promoted the obscene 'blood libel,' that Jews kill Christian children and use their blood to prepare mazzo, the unleavened bread eaten during Passover" (Plate 2004, p. 140).

29. Radio 620 AM. The transcript is now on many Internet sites: for instance, www.moviecitynews.com/notepad/2004/040303_npd.html.

30. Frank Rich, "Gibson's 'Passion' Publicity Juggernaut", *NYT/ IHT*, September 20–21, 2003; "'Passion' and the U.S. Culture War," *NYT/ IHT*, March 6–7, 2004; "The Campaign against Christmas," *NYT/ IHT*, December 18–19, 2004.

31. Sharon Waxman, "Will 'Passion' Destroy a Career?" *IHT*, February 27; and Rich, "'Passion' and the U.S. Culture War."

32. A. O. Scott, "Another Angle on 'The Passion': Jesus as a Box Office Hero," *IHT*, March 10, 2004.

33. Rich, "The Campaign against Christmas"; see also "The Christmas Miracle," *Newsweek*, December 10, 2004, www.msnbc.msn.com/id/6650997/site/newsweek.

34. Victor Frölke, "Vrolijk Pasen met een hippe kruisigingsspijker," *NRC Handelsblad*, April 3–4, 2004.

35. Diederik van Hoogstraten, "Amerikanen geven schuld vaker aan joden na 'Passion,'" *De Volkskrant*, April 5, 2004, p. 12.

36. David M. Halbfinger, "Mel Gibson Plans TV Mini-Series on Holocaust," *NYT/IHT*, December 6, 2005.

CHAPTER 10

1. A series of TV magazines on television spots, *Culture Pub* on the French commercial channel M6, once also had a complete installment with images of aliens from ads.

2. The documentary *The Dark Side of the Moon* (*Opération Lune*) was made for Point du Jour Productions, shown on the Franco-German Arte channel and in the Netherlands on the third public channel by VPRO (February 12, 2003).

3. In the television documentary *Star Trek Story*, produced and directed by Richard Curson Smith and Russell England, broadcast on a BBC Star Trek night, on August 26, 1996.

4. Quoted in Neal Stephenson, "Now We Take the Jedi Geeks Offline," *IHT*, June 18–19, 2005; A. O. Scott, "*Sith* Is Better Than *Star Wars*," *New York Times/IHT*, May 17, 2005; and Henry Marchand, "The Unfading Dark Side," *Boston Globe/IHT*, May 31, 2005.

5. Also see the 2004 promotional documentary on Star Wars, which Edith Becker

and Kevin Burns directed for Prometheus Entertainment, in cooperation with Fox and Lucasfilms, broadcast on May 16, 2005, as *L'empire des rêves* by the major French commercial channel M6.

6. Tim Weiner, "U.S. Seeks 'God's-Eye View' of Warfare," *NYT/ IHT*, November 15, 2004; editorial "A Science-Fiction Army," *IHT*, April 1, 2005; Tim Weiner, "Air Force Asks Bush to Put Arms in Space," *NYT/ IHT*, May 19, 2005; editorial "Weapons in Space," *NYT/ IHT*, May 25, 2005; Richard Reeves, "Star Wars, All Over Again," *IHT*, May 25, 2005; editorial "Bush's Star Wars Fantasy," *NYT/IHT*, June 25–26, 2005; Robert Park, "The Dark Side of the Moon," *IHT*, September 23, 2005.

CHAPTER 11

1. A. O. Scott, "A Showman's Bloody-Minded Epic," *IHT*, December 6, 2006; Cécile Mury, "Faut que ça saigne," *Télérama*, January 10, 2007; Olivier Kerkdijk, "Matten met de Maya's," *Vpro gids*, early January 2007.

2. Nathan Gardels & Mike Medavoy, *IHT*, June 15, 2006.

3. Nicholas D. Kristof, "Blacks, Whites and Love in America," *NYT/IHT*, April 25, 2005.

4. *IHT*, April 13, 2005.

References

Altman, Rick. (1999). *Film/Genre.* London: British Film Institute.

Andrillon, François, et al. (1991). *Racisme, donker continent: Clichés, stereotypen en fantaziebeelden over zwarten.* Brussels: NCOS.

Arberry, A. J. (1953). Introduction to the translanslation of Scheherazade, *Tales from the Thousand and One Nights.* London: Allen & Unwin.

Asher, Michael. (1998). *Lawrence: The Uncrowned King of Arabia.* London: Viking/Penguin.

Baird, Robert. (1998). "Going Indian: *Dances with Wolves,*" pp.153–69. In Peter C. Rollins & John E. O'Connor (eds.), *Hollywood's Indian: The Portrayal of the Native American in Film.* Lexington: University Press of Kentucky.

Bauval, Robert, & Adrian Gilbert. (1994). *The Orion Mystery.* New York: Crown. In Dutch: *Het Orion mysterie.* Houten: Fibula/Unieboek, 1994.

Bakker, Hans, & Martin Gosman. (1988). *De Oriënt, droom of dreiging: Het Oosten in westers perspectief.* Kampen: Kok Agora.

Bennett, Tony, & Janet Woollacott. (1987). *Bond and Beyond: The Political Career of a Popular Hero.* London: MacMillan.

Berger, Arthur Asa. (1992). *Popular Culture Genres: Theories and Texts.* Newbury Park, CA: Sage.

Bergmans, Noortje. (2002). *Selective Articulation in* The Prince of Egypt. Unpublished paper, Amsterdam University/International School.

Bernal, Martin. (1987, 1991). *Black Athena: The Afroasiatic Roots of Classical Civilization.* 2 vols. London: Free Association.

Bernstein, Matthew, & Gaylin Studlar, eds. (1997). *Visions of the East: Orientalism in Film.* London: Tauris.

Biagi, Shirley, & Marilyn Kern-Foxworth. (1997). *Facing Difference: Race, Gender and Mass Media.* Thousand Oaks, CA: Pine Forge.

Bligh, W. (n.d.). *Selections of His Writings/A Book of the "Bounty."* London: Dent.

Blofeld, John. (1972). *King Maha Mongkut of Siam.* Singapore: Asia Pacific Press; New York; Thai-Am, 1976.

Boersma, Kim. (2000). "Big Brother: Real Life Soap, de voorgeschiedenis van een genre." Master's thesis, Amsterdam University.

Bogle, Donald. (1992). *Toms, Coons, Mulattoes, Mammies and Bucks: An Interpretive History of Blacks in American Films.* Expanded edition. New York: Continuum.

Boorstin, Daniel. (1980). *The Image: A guide to Pseudo-events in America.* New York: Atheneum.

Bourget, Jean-Loup. (1992). *L'histoire au cinema: Le passé retrouvé.* Paris: Gallimard.

Bristowe, W. S. (1976). *Louis and the King of Siam.* London: Chatto & Windus.

Browne, Nick, ed. (1998). *Refiguring American Film Genres: History and Theory.* Berkeley and Los Angeles: University of California Press.

Bryman, Alan. (1995). *Disney and His Worlds.* London: Routledge.

Bulgatz, Joseph. (1992). *Ponzi Schemes, Invaders from Mars & More Extraordinary Delusions and the Madness of Crowds.* New York: Harmony.

Buruma, Ian, & Avishai Margalit. (2004). *Occidentalism: The West in the Eyes of Its Enemies.* New York: Penguin.

Catherine, Lucas. (1993). *Vuile Arabieren: Bedlectuur voor Vlaams Blokkers.* Antwerpen/Baarn: Hadewych.

Chevalier, Jean, & Alain Gheerbrant. (1969). *Dictionnaire des symboles.* Paris: Laffont/Jupiter.

Cittati, Simon. (2003). "Black Hawk Down: From a Defining Battle to a Blockbuster Movie." Unpublished paper, Amsterdam University/International School.

Clarke, James. (2001). *Steven Spielberg.* Harpenden, AL: Pocket Essentials.

Clegg, Jenny. (1994). *Fu Manchu and the "Yellow Peril."* London: Trentham.

Crawley, Tony. (1994). *Dictionary of Film Quotations.* Ware, UK: Wordsworth.

Creeber, Glen, ed. (2001). *The Television Genre Book*. London: British Film Institute.

Curtis, Sandra. (1998). *Zorro Unmasked: The Official History*. New York: Hyperion.

Dalby, Liza Crihfield. (1983). *Geisha*. Berkeley and Los Angeles: University of California Press.

Daniel, Norman. (1963). *Islam and the West: The Making of an Image*. Oxford: One World.

Davies, Jude, & Carol R. Smith. (1997). *Gender, Ethnicity and Sexuality in Contemporary American Film*. Edinburgh: Keele University Press.

De Bougainville, Louis. (1967). *A Voyage around the World*. Amsterdam/New York: Israel/Da Capo.

Defoe, Daniel. (1972). *The Life and Strange Surprizing Adventures of Robinson Crusoe of York, Mariner*. London: Oxford University Press.

DeMause, Lloyd. (1984). *Reagan's America*. New York: Creative Roots.

Dening, Greg. (1992). *Mr. Bligh's Bad Language: Passion, Power and Theatre on the Bounty*. Cambridge, UK: Cambridge University Press.

De Vroet, Elise. (2003). "Black, Brown, Red, White, Yellow . . . or Blue? Transcending Racial Categories in *Little Bill*." Master's thesis, Amsterdam University.

Dichter, Ernst. (1969). *The Strategy of Desire*. London: Boardman.

Dorfman, Ariel, & Armand Mattelart. (1975). *How to Read Donald Duck: Imperialist Ideology in the Disney Comic*. New York: International General.

Downer, Lesley (2003). *Madame Sadayakko: The Geisha Who Bewitched the West*. New York: Gotham.

Dyer, Richard. (1997). *White*. London: Routledge.

Ehrman, Bart D. (2003). *Lost Christianities: The Battles for Scripture and the Faith We Never Knew*. Oxford: Oxford University Press.

Eliot, Mark. (1993). *Walt Disney: Hollywood's Dark Prince*. New York: Carol/Birch Lane.

Elley, Derek. (1984). *The Epic Film: Myth and History*. London: Routledge & Kegan Paul.

Entman, Robert M., & Andrew Rojecki. (2001). *The Black Image in the White Mind: Media and Race in America*. Chicago: University of Chicago Press.

Evans, Martin, & Ken Lunn. (1997). *War and Memory in the Twentieth Century*. Oxford: Berg.

Fausset, David. (1994). *The Strange Surprising Sources of Robinson Crusoe.* Amsterdam and Atlanta: Rodopi.

Finkelstein, Israel, & Neil Asher Silberman. (2002). *The Bible Unearthed: Archeology's New Vision of Israel and the Origin of Its Sacred Texts.* New York: Touchstone.

Fox, Robin Lane. (1973). *Alexander the Great.* London: Penguin.

Frayling, Christopher. (1998). *Spaghetti Westerns: Cowboys and Europeans from Karl May to Sergio Leone.* London: Tauris.

Freeman, Derek. (1983). *Margaret Mead and Samoa: The Making and Unmaking of an Anthropological Myth.* Cambridge, MA: Harvard University Press.

———. (1999). *The Fateful Hoaxing of Margaret Mead: A Historical Analysis of Her Samoan Research.* Boulder, CO: Westview.

Freer, Ian. (2001). *The Complete Spielberg.* London: Virgin.

Freud, Sigmund. (1973). *Standard Edition of the Complete Psychological Works.* New York: International Universities Press.

Gabler, Neil. (1988). *An Empire of Their Own: How the Jews Invented Hollywood.* New York: Anchor/Doubleday.

Goldblatt, Dan, Michael Lerner, & Laura Geller. (1999). "*Prince of Egypt*—Three Perspectives. *Tikkun* 14, no. 1, pp. 8–10.

Golden, Arthur. (1998). *Memoirs of a Geisha.* New York: Vintage.

Goldstein, Norm. (1991). *The History of Television.* New York: Portland/Random House.

Griswold, Alexander Brown. (1961). *King Mongkut of Siam.* Bangkok: Siam Society; New York: Asia Society.

Gross, John, ed. (1983). *Aphorisms.* Oxford: Oxford University Press.

Gustavii, Anna-Lisa. (2004). "Anna and King Mongkut: A Case Study in Ethnocentrism." Master's thesis, Amsterdam University, Department of Communication Studies.

Haggard, H. Rider. (n.d.). *Allan Quatermain.* New York: Lupton.

Halter, Marek. (2004). *Tsippora.* Paris: Laffont.

Hamelink, Cees. (1994). *The Politics of World Communication: A Human Rights Perspective.* London: Sage.

Harrison, Taylor, Sarah Projansky, Kent A. Ono, & Elyce Ray Halford, eds. (1996). *Enterprise Zones: Critical Positions on Star Trek.* Boulder, CO: Westview/Harper Collins.

Hayward, Susan. (2003). *Cinema Studies: The Key Concepts.* 2nd ed. London: Routledge.

Hermes, Joke, & Maarten Reesink. (2003). *Inleiding televisie-studies.* Amsterdam: Boom.

Hes, Jan. (1989). *Utopia in opspraak: Utopisme, chiliasme, science fiction en de film.* Assen and Maastricht: Van Gorcum.

Hinckle, Warren, & William Turner. (1981). *The Fish Is Red: The Story of the Secret War against Castro.* New York: Harper & Row.

Hobsbawm, Eric J. (1959). *Primitive Rebels.* Manchester: University Press.

———. (1969, 2001). *Bandits.* London: Abacus.

Hochschild, Adam. (1998). *King Leopold's Ghost.* London: Macmillan.

Hopkins, Keith. (1999). *A World Full of Gods: Pagans, Jews and Christians in the Roman Empire.* London: Weidenfeld & Nicholson.

Horvilleur, Gilles, dir. (1988). *Dictionnaire des personnages du cinéma.* Paris: Bordas.

Hunter, Allan, ed. (1991). *Film and TV Handbook.* London: Chambers.

Jacquin, Philippe, & Daniel Royot, dir. (1993). *Le mythe de l'Ouest américain et les 'valeurs' de la frontière.* Paris: Ed. Autrement.

James, T. G. H. (2001). *Howard Carter: The Path to Tutankhamun.* London: Tauris Parke.

Jansen van Galen, John, Huib Schreurs, & Erik Smink. (1999). *Gekte: Rages in de Lage Landen.* Utrecht: Bruna.

Jeffords, Susan (1984, Winter). "The New Vietnam Films." *Journal of Popular Film and Television*, pp. 186–94.

Jelot-Blanc, Jean-Jacques. (1993). *Télé feuilletons.* Paris: Ramsay.

Jenkins, Henry. (1992). *Textual Poachers: Television Fans & Participatory Culture.* New York and London: Routledge.

Jessen, Freya J. (2003). "Jessica Lynch: Ordinary Soldier or Legendary War Hero?" Unpublished paper, Amsterdam University/International School.

Kabbani, Rana. (1986). *Europe's Myths of the Orient.* Basingstoke, UK: Macmillan.

Katz, Wendy R. (1987). *Rider Haggard and the Fiction of Empire.* Cambridge, UK: Cambridge University Press.

Keen, Sam. (1991). *Faces of the Enemy: Reflections of the Hostile Imagination.* San Francisco: HarperCollins.

Kek, Corina. (2003). "Suzie Wong: Master Text of Orientalism?" Unpublished paper, Amsterdam University/International School.

Kellner, Douglas. (1995). *Media Culture: Cultural Studies, Identity and Politics between the Modern and the Postmodern*. London: Routledge.

Kempadoo, Shamanee. (2002). "Anna and the King." Unpublished paper, Amsterdam University/International School.

Kilpatrick, Jacquelyn. (1999). *Celluloid Indians: Native Americans and Film*. Lincoln: University of Nebraska Press.

King, Geoff, & Tanya Krzywinska. (2002). *Science Fiction Cinema: From Outer Space to Cyber Space*. London: Wallflower.

Kirchner, Klaus. (1974). *Flugblätter: Psychologische Kriegsführung*. Munich: Hanser.

Kleinen, John (2004, September). "Framing 'the Other': A Critical Review of Vietnam War Movies." *Leidschrift* 19, no. 2, pp. 2–29.

Kochberg, Searle. (2003). "Gladiator." In Jill Nelmes (ed.), *An Introduction to Film Studies*, 3rd ed. London: Routledge.

Kreetz, Tanja. (1998). "On the Star Trek Film *The Undiscovered Country*." Unpublished paper, Amsterdam University/International School.

Kroes, Eva. (2002). "Black Hawk Down." Unpublished Paper, Amsterdam University/International School.

Landon, Margaret. (1944). *Anna and the King of Siam*. In Dutch: *Anna en de koning van Siam*. Amsterdam: Amsterdam boek, 1974.

Lendering, Jona. (2004). *Alexander de Grote: De ondergang van het Perzische rijk*. Amsterdam: Atheneum/Polak & Van Gennep.

Leonowens, Anna. (1873). *The Romance of the Harem*. Boston: Osgood.

Leutrat, Jean-Louis. (1987). *Le western—Archéologie d'un genre*. Lyon: Presse Universitaire de Lyon.

Lewis, Jon E., & Penny Stempel. (1998). *Cult TV/The Comedies: The Ultimate Critical Guide*. London: Pavilion.

Lie, Nadia, & Theo D'Haen, ed. (2002). *Zorro & Co.: Populaire personages en het koloniale verleden*. N.p.: Uitg. Vantilt.

Liu, Yang. (2004). *Eurocentrism in Disney's Movie* Mulan. Unpublished paper, Amsterdam University/International School.

Lowery, Shearon, & Melvin De Fleur. (1983). *Milestones in Mass Communication Research*. New York: Longman.

Maalouf, Amin. (1984). *Les croisades: Vues par les Arabes.* Paris: Lattès.

Maas-Despain, Arwen. (2003). *Indian Stereotypes in Children's Media.* Unpublished paper, Amsterdam University/International School.

Maltby, Richard. (2003). *Hollywood Cinema.* 2nd ed. Oxford: Blackwell.

Mamet, David. (2006). *Bambi vs. Godzilla: On the Nature, Purpose, and Practice of the Movie Business.* New York: Pantheon.

Mattson, Vernon E. (1988, January). "West as Myth." *Journal of the History of the Behavioral Sciences* 24, pp. 9–13.

Mauduy, Jacques, & Gérard Henriet. (1989). *Géographies du western.* Paris: Nathan.

Maxwell, Richard. (1995). *The Oxford History of the American West.* Oxford: Oxford University Press.

Maynard, Richard A. (1974). *Africa on Film: Myth and Reality.* Rochelle Park, NJ: Hayden.

McIntyre, Jaimie. (2003). "Pocahontas: An Entertaining Piece of Faction." Unpublished paper, Amsterdam University/International School.

Meijer, Fik. (2005). *The Gladiators: History's Most Dangerous Sport.* New York: St. Martin's Press. In Dutch: *Gladiatoren: Volksvermaak in het Colosseum.* Amsterdam: Polak & Van Gennep, 2003.

Meijer, Irene C., & Maarten Reesink, eds. (2000). *Reality Soap! Big Brother en de opkomst van het multimedia concept.* Amsterdam: Boom.

Melis, Isabel. (1998). *Colonial Discourse in Tarzan.* Unpublished paper, Amsterdam University/International School.

Miller, Toby, & Robert Stam. (2004). *A Companion to Film Theory.* Oxford: Blackwell.

Moine, Raphaëlle. (2002). *Les genres du cinéma.* Paris: Nathan.

Mok, Ineke, & Marian Van't Hoff. (1992–1993). *En hij noemde hen Indianen: Beelden in geschiedenisboeken en jeugdliteratuur.* Utrecht: Parel, 3 vols.

Mönnich, C. W., et al. (1984). "Utopie en Anti-utopie rond Orwells jaar 1984." *Mededelingen, Van der Leeuw Stichting,* Afl. 60.

Morgan, Susan, ed. (1991). *The Romance of the Harem by Anna Leonowens.* Charlottesville: University Press of Virginia.

Mousa, Suleiman. (1966). *T. E. Lawrence: An Arab View.* London: Oxford University Press.

Neale, Steve, ed. (2002). *Genre and Contemporary Hollywood.* London: British Film Institute.

Nederveen Pieterse, Jan. (1992). *White on Black—Images of Africa and Blacks in Western Popular Culture.* New Haven, CT: Yale University Press.

Negra, Diane. (2001). *Off-White Hollywood: American Culture and Female Stardom.* London: Routledge.

Nelmes, Jill, ed. (2003). *An Introduction to Film Studies.* 3rd ed. London: Routledge.

Nordhoff, Charles, & James Norman Hall. (1932). *Mutiny on the* Bounty. Boston: Little, Brown.

O'Barr, William M. (1994). *Culture and the Ad—Otherness in the World of Advertising.* Boulder, CO: Westview.

Obeyesekere, Gananath (1992). *The Apotheosis of Captain Cook: European Mythmaking in the Pacific.* Princeton, NJ: Princeton University Press.

Odell, Colin, & Michelle Le Blanc. (2000). *Vampire Films.* Harpenden, UK: Pocket Essentials.

Oon, Helen. (2004). *Malaysia.* London: New Holland/Globetrotter.

Oranje, Elske. (2004a). "De Indiaan in *Dances with Wolves.*" Unpublished paper, Amsterdam University/International School.

———. (2004b). "De Griekse mythe in de film *Troy.*" Unpublished internship paper, Amsterdam University/Department of Communication Science.

Osgerby, Bill, & Anna Gough-Yates, eds. (2001). *Action TV: Tough Guys, Smooth Operators and Foxy Chicks.* London: Routledge.

Panati, Charles. (1991). *Fads, Follies and Manias.* New York: Harper Perennial.

Pinel, Vincent. (2000). *Écoles, genres et mouvements au cinéma.* Paris: Larousse-Bordas/HER.

Plate, S. Brent, ed. (2004). *Reviewing* The Passion*: Mel Gibson's Film and Its Critics.* New York: Palgrave/MacMillan.

Porybná, Tereza. (2003). *Robinson Crusoe.* Unpublished paper, Amsterdam University/International School.

Postman, Neil. (1985). *Amusing Ourselves to Death.* New York: Viking/Penguin.

Rank, Otto. (1964). *The Myth of the Birth of the Hero.* New York: Random House/Vintage.

Read, Donald. (1983). *England 1868–1914.* London: Longman.

Redford, Donald B. (1992). *Egypt, Canaan, and Israel in Ancient Times.* Princeton, NJ: Princeton University Press.

Robb, James. (2002). *James Cameron*. Harpenden, UK: Pocket Essentials.

Rogin, Michael. (1988). *Ronald Reagan: The Movie, and Other Episodes in Political Demonology*. Berkeley and Los Angeles: University of California Press.

Rollins, Peter C., & John E. O'Connor. (1998). *Hollywood's Indian: The Portrayal of the Native American in Film*. Lexington: University Press of Kentucky.

Royster, Francesca T. (2003). *Becoming Cleopatra: The Shifting Image of an Icon*. New York: Palgrave/MacMillan.

Russell, Jamie. (2002). *Vietnam War Movies*. Harpenden, UK: Pocket Essentials.

Ryan, Michael, & Douglas Kellner. (1988). *Camera Politica: The Politics and Ideology of Contemporary Hollywood Film*. Bloomington: Indiana University Press.

Said, Edward W. (1978). *Orientalism: Western Conceptions of the Orient*. London: Penguin.

Saunders, John. (2001). *The Western Genre: From Lordsburg to Big Whiskey*. London: Wallflower.

Sayre, Nora. (1982). *Running Time: Films of the Cold War*. New York: Dial Press.

Schickel, Richard. (1986). *The Disney Version*. London: Pavilion.

Schnaars, Steven P. (1989). *Megamistakes: Forecasting and the Myth of Rapid Technological Change*. New York: Free Press.

Schulpen, Sanne. (1998). "The Lion King." Unpublished paper, Amsterdam University/International School.

Schwartz, Nancy Lynn. (1982). *The Hollywood Writers' Wars*. New York: Knopf.

Seesslen, Georg. (1996). *Geschichte und Mythologie des Abenteuerfilms*. Marburg: Schüren.

Searles, Baird. (1990). *Epic! History on the Big Screen*. New York: Harry Abrams.

Sherden, William A. (1998). *The Fortune Sellers: The Big Business of Selling and Buying Predictions*. New York: Wiley.

Shohat, Ella, & Robert Stam. (1994). *Unthinking Eurocentrism: Multiculturalism and the Media*. London: Routledge.

Showalter, Elaine. (1997). *Hystories: Hysterical Epidemics and Modern Culture*. London: Picador.

Simmon, Scott. (2003). *The Invention of the Western Film: A Cultural History of the Genre's First Half-Century*. Cambridge, UK: Cambridge University Press.

Simpson, Paul, ed. (2001). *Cult Movies.* London: Rough Guides/Penguin.

———. (2002a). *Cult TV.* London: Rough Guides/Penguin.

———. (2002b). *James Bond.* London: Rough Guides/Penguin.

Slotkin, Richard (1998). *Gunfighter Nation: The Myth of Frontier in Twentieth-Century America.* Norman: University of Oklahoma Press.

Smith, Jim. (2003). *George Lucas.* London: Virgin.

Smith, Jim, & Stephen Lavington. (2002). *Bond Films.* London: Virgin.

Smith, Julian. (1975). *Looking Away: Hollywood and Vietnam.* New York: Scribner.

Smoodin, Eric, ed. (1994). *Disney Discourse: Producing the Magic Kingdom.* New York: Routledge.

Sobchack, Vivian. (1997). *Screening Space: The American Science Fiction Film.* Rev. ed. New Brunswick, NJ: Rutgers University Press.

Solomon, Jon. (2001). *The Ancient World in the Cinema.* New Haven, CT: Yale University Press.

Stinton, Judith, ed. (1979). *Racism & Sexism in Children's Books.* London: Writers and Readers.

Stringer, Julian. (2003). *Movie Blockbusters.* London: Routledge.

Tanzil, Nila Lestari. (2003). *An Analysis of the Disney Version of Mulan.* Unpublished paper, Amsterdam University/International School.

Tatum, W. Barnes (1997). *Jesus at the Movies: A Guide to the First Hundred Years.* Santa Rosa, CA: Polebridge.

Telotte, J. P. (2001). *Science Fiction Film.* Cambridge, UK: Cambridge University Press.

Troncarelli, Fabio. (2001). *Guillén Lombardo le rebelle: À l'origine de la légende de Zorro.* Paris: Privat.

Valkeman, Vanessa. (2000). "De weerspiegeling van zichzelf in de ander: Verborgen ideologieën in de beeldcultuur over India." Master's thesis, Amsterdam University.

van den Berg, Harry, & Peter Reinsch. (1983). *Racisme in schoolboeken: Het gladde ijs van het westers gelijk.* Amsterdam: Sua.

van der Heide, Mariëtte. (2005). "De speech van Colin Powell onder de loep." Master's thesis, Amsterdam University.

van Ginneken, Jaap. (1986, April 17). "Hoe Amerika het Vietnam-trauma verwerkt." Unpublished lecture, Soeterijn Theatre/Royal Tropical Institute, Amsterdam.

———. (1992). *Crowds, Psychology and Politics.* New York: Cambridge University Press. In Italian: *Folle, psicologia e politica.* Rome: Pieraldo, 1991.

———. (1993). *Rages en Crashes: Over de Onvoorspelbaarheid van de Economie.* Bloemendaal: Aramith.

———. (1998). *Understanding Global News: A Critical Introduction.* London: Sage. In Dutch: *De schepping van de wereld in het nieuws.* 2nd rev. ed. Alphen aan de Rijn: Kluwer, 2002.

———. (2002). *Striphelden op de divan: De ontraadseling van de complexen van Asterix, Babar, Donald, Kuifje en Superman.* Amsterdam: Nieuwezijds.

———. (2003). *Collective Behavior and Public Opinion: Rapid Shifts.* Mahwah, NJ: Erlbaum.

———. (2007). *Mass Movements.* Amsterdam: Spinhuis.

van Hise, James. (1991). *The Unauthorized History of Trek.* New York: Harper Prism.

van Rij, Jan. (2001). *Madame Butterfly: Japonisme, Puccini and the Search for the Real Cho-Cho-San.* Berkeley, CA: Stone Bridge.

van Willigen, Rein. (1995). *Mouse Entertainment: Walt Disney & Company.* Nijmegen: Sun.

Verkaik, Kasper. (2007). "The Media's Lessons from Iraq: Defining Internal and External Constraints." Master's thesis, Amsterdam University.

Viviani, Christian. (1982). *Le western.* Paris: Veyrier.

Walker, Janet, ed. (2001). *Westerns: Films through History.* London: Routledge.

Walsh, Jeffrey, & James Aulich. (1989). *Vietnam Images: War and Representation.* London: Macmillan.

Wasko, Janet. (2001). *Understanding Disney: The Manufacture of Fantasy.* Cambridge, UK: Polity.

Weverbergh, Julien, & Ion Hobana. (1991). *De triomf van de droom.* Antwerpen/Baarn: Hadewijch.

Williams, Linda. (2001). *Playing the Race Card: Melodramas of Black and White, from Uncle Tom to O. J. Simpson.* Princeton, NJ: Princeton University Press.

Wilson, Clint C., Félix Gutiérrez, & Lena M. Chao. (2003). *Racism, Sexism and the Media: The Rise of Class Communication in Multicultural America.* 3rd ed. Thousand Oaks, CA: Sage.

Winder, Stephen. (2006). *The Man Who Saved Britain.* New York: Farrar, Strauss & Giroux.

Winkler, Martin M. (2004). *Gladiator: Film and History*. Oxford: Blackwell.

Wood, Robin. (1986). *Hollywood: From Vietnam to Reagan*. New York: Columbia University Press.

Zheng, Xiaohe. (2002). "The Imagination of Chineseness in Martial Arts Films." Unpublished paper, Amsterdam University/International School.

FURTHER REFERENCE

Dictionnaire des personnages. (1990). Paris: Laffont.

Encyclopédie Alpha du Cinéma. (1976). Lausanne: Grammont.

Film Guide. (2001). 10th ed. London: Virgin.

Halliwell's Who's Who in the Movies. (2003). London: HarperCollins.

Speelfilmgids. (1993). 2nd ed. Haarlem: Luitingh—Sijthoff.

UNESCO Statistical Yearbook. (1992). Paris: UNESCO.

Index

abuse, sexual. *See* Japan; *Pocahontas*; slavery; South Sea paradise

accents, 20, 29, 35, 73, 94, 217, 219, 230

Afghanistan, 132, 142, 167, 175

Africa, North. *See* Arabs

Africa, sub-Saharan, 26–30, 70–74, 81, 108, 124, 132–33, 140, 154, 171, 224–28, 232. *See also* Blacks; *individual countries*

African Americans. *See* Blacks

Aladdin, 23–26, 185–86, 227–28

Alexander, 52, 58–61, 142, 227

Allan Quatermain (character), 67, 128, 132, 141, 144, 148–49, 226, 232

America. *See* United States

American anti-colonialism, 85–86, 89

American Dream, 36, 85, 96

anachronism, 97–98, 229. *See also* perspectivistic slant

Angélique (French movie series), 124–25, 226

Anglo-Saxon (Anglo-American) culture, 5–6, 53, 86, 128, 134, 146, 158, 219, 223

animal characters, 20, 26–30, 64–69, 225, 232

animals and repulsive food, 51, 146, 228–29

animated cartoons, 19–41, 225. *See also individual movies*

Anna and the King, 128, 130, 134–39, 227

anthropomorphism, 235. *See also* animal characters; animated cartoons; robots

antiquity, 43–62. *See also* Bible

anti-Semitism, 7, 8, 188, 195–200, 219, 243nn1–3, 252n5, 253n22. *See also Passion of the Christ, The*

apartheid, 73. *See also* segregation

Apocalypse Now, 67, 97, 142, 160, 165

Apocalypto, 224

Arabs, 4, 23–26, 51, 54, 84, 110, 124–25, 133–34, 145–48, 159, 167, 171, 179–88, 219, 226–27. *See also individual countries*

archaeology. *See* antiquity; Bible; *Indiana Jones; Justine*

art direction, 187
Asia, 108, 159, 211, 227–28, 230. *See also individual countries*
audiences of movies, 3, 9–10. *See also* target groups
Aunt Jemima and Uncle Ben stereotypes, 109, 115
Australia, 75, 81, 188
auteur theory of filmmaking, 8
awards ceremonies, 12

Babylon. *See* Iraq
background projection, 65, 235
Baden-Powell, R. S. Smyth, 63, 133, 142
beauty ideals, 38, 46, 110, 149
"better native than the natives" theme, 227. *See also* Rambo; *Tarzan*; Western movies
bias, 16, 129, 164
Bible, 3, 177–200, 216, 219, 223
Big Brother television format, 74, 79
bin Laden, Osama, 55, 167–68
black and white, 84. *See also* Blacks; Manichaeism; skin color; splitting
Black Hawk Down, x, 151, 167–72, 174, 227, 230
Blacks, 26–30, 54–56, 66, 72–73, 77, 101, 108–10, 159, 171, 184, 199, 204, 211–13, 218–19, 225, 232, 244n3
blockbusters, 231, 235; economy of, 10–11; format of, 11–13
"blond hair/blue eyes" theme, 35, 46, 55, 58, 66, 123, 146, 153, 173, 184, 193, 218–19, 225–26, 228
body-builder heroes, 45, 71. *See also* Schwarzenegger, Arnold; Stallone, Sylvester
box office earnings, 9–11, 235

Brando, Marlon, 112
British Empire, 5, 49, 51, 53, 57, 72, 76, 127–43, 152. *See also* Allan Quatermain; *Anna and the King*; colonial adventure; James Bond; *Lawrence of Arabia*; *Mutiny on the Bounty*; *Pocahontas*
Brooke, James, 132, 142
Brown, Dan, 252n18
Bruckheimer, Jerry, 165–66, 168, 170
Brynner, Yul, 48, 137, 184, 227
Buffalo Bill, 88–89, 95
Burroughs, Edgar Rice, 70
Bush, George H. W., 26, 166–67
Bush, George W., 60–61, 166–67, 172, 220

California, 6–7, 147, 161, 193. *See also* "Southern" movie genre
camera work, 226
camp (style), 51, 126, 144, 157, 159, 211, 236
cannibalism. *See* "human sacrifice" theme
Castaway television format, 74, 79
"castaway" theme, 74–82
casting, 193, 226, 236. *See also* "blond hair/blue eyes" theme
censorship, 66, 68, 80, 117, 170
CGI. *See* computer-generated images
Chaplin, Charlie, 104, 203–4
Chicago World Exhibition/Fair, 86–87, 89
"chick flicks" and "chick shows," 30, 231, 236
"chieftain's daughter" fantasy, 33, 115, 141
children, lost in the wild, 64, 69. *See also* *Jungle Book, The*; *Tarzan*

children's television programming, 11, 92
China, 4, 5, 9, 37–40, 110, 118–19, 130,
    140, 146, 148–49, 158, 161, 216, 225,
    233
Christianity, 33, 44, 57, 76–77, 84,
    135–36, 145, 147, 158, 177–200, 223.
    See also Jesus Christ
civil rights movement (in U.S.), 27, 95,
    211. See also segregation
Clarke, Dorothy (Mrs. Elwin Wilson),
    183, 186
class contrast, 73, 231. See also accents
Cleopatra, 46–47, 53
clichés. See stereotypes
Clinton, Bill, 39
Cody, William Frederick. See Buffalo Bill
Cold War, 152–67, 184, 204
colonial adventure, 127–49, 229–30
colors. See skin color; stereotypes: and
    colors
commando movies, 160–72
computer-generated images (CGI), 39,
    57, 227, 236
concentration, vertical and horizontal
    (of movie-making), 10
condensation in media products, 3–4
Congo, 133, 142
Congo Free State, 133, 142
Conrad, Joseph, 140, 142, 160
controversy, 12, 74, 79
copyright, 6, 22, 29–30, 230
corporate frameworks around studios,
    8–9. See also concentration, vertical
    and horizontal
Costner, Kevin, 93–99
cowboy. See Western movies
cross-cultural appeal, 5. See also special
    effects

cruelty, 33–34, 60, 72, 85, 138, 147, 152,
    160, 164, 173–75, 182, 190, 194, 196,
    198. See also massacre
cultural invasion fears, 39
cultural prism, 15, 231
cultural relativism, 16. See also
    postmodernism
culture, 15. See also cross-cultural
    appeal; intercultural communication;
    individual countries; individual ethnic
    groups; individual language areas;
    individual regions
curse of the pharaoh. See Egypt;
    Mummy, The

Dances with Wolves, 93–99
Da Vinci Code, The (Brown), 252n18
Defense Department, U.S. See Pentagon
Defoe, Daniel, 75–78, 212
DeMille, Cecil B., 46, 93, 179–80,
    183–86, 193
deregulation, 10. See also concentration,
    vertical and horizontal
desexualization. See sex and
    sexualization
design, 226. See also art direction
disguises, 12
Disney, Walt, 8, 20–21, 69, 204
Disneyfication, 205
Disney Studios, 19–42, 69–74, 92, 104,
    166, 185–86, 225, 227–28. See also
    theme parks; individual characters
    and movies
distortion, 16
Dolchstoss Legende (dagger thrust legend,
    Germany), 163, 236
Donald Duck, 24, 37
DreamWorks SKG, 40, 185–88, 198

Dutch traders and settlers, 132. *See also* East India Company; South Africa
Dyer, Richard, 45–46, 109, 225

East India Company, 75, 120
Eastwood, Clint, 89, 92, 161, 165
Eco, Umberto, 156
ego, 127, 233
Egypt, 44, 46–51, 133, 140, 145–48, 178–88, 190
Eisner, Michael, 21, 185
embedded journalists, 172, 236
Emmanuelle (French soft-porn movie series), 125, 226
Emmerich, Roland, 68, 214
emotional experience, 3
enemy images, 36, 83, 151–52, 236
Enlightenment, 23, 114, 129
escapist entertainment, 4, 154, 236
establishing shots, 229, 236
ethnic role actors. *See* Brynner, Yul; Quinn, Anthony; Sharif, Omar
ethnic sidekicks, 77, 79–82, 93
ethnocentrism, 15, 20–22, 100, 130, 179, 219, 223, 233, 236
Eurocentrism, x–xi, 187, 224, 237
European films, 4–5. *See also individual countries*
eviction. *See* ex-nominations
ex-nominations, 27, 237, 230; of people, in sub-Saharan Africa, 27–28
Exodus, 179–88, 227
Expedition Robinson television format, 75, 79
"expendable beauty" theme, 159, 165. *See also Madame Butterfly; Miss Saigon*

expert advice on movie subjects, 3, 25, 36, 223. *See also* antiquity; Bible
exploitation strategies of movies, 8–9. *See also* merchandising; release dates and patterns
"explorer as god" theme, 116. *See also Apocalypse Now; Heart of Darkness* theme; "The Man Who Would Be King"
export of media material, 6. *See also* United States: market size of
extras, 57, 113, 184, 193, 227, 231

fans, 208–10
femme fatale, 58, 237. *See also* gender roles and relations
film libraries, 8, 21
Fleming, Ian. *See* James Bond
foreign participation in U.S. movie industry, 6–7
founding myths, 237. *See also* antiquity; Bible; colonial adventure; *Pocahontas*; Western movies
France, 69, 124–25, 128–29, 132, 135–36, 146–47, 203
franchising. *See* merchandising
free fantasy, 29. *See also* cultural prism; social pyramid
Freemasonry, 103, 143, 149
"free states." *See* Congo; South Africa
Freudian-type arch-conflict, 59
Friday (character). *See* ethnic sidekicks; *Robinson Crusoe*
frontier myth, 86–87, 89, 94, 209

Gauguin, Paul, 36, 114
geishas, 237; American fascination with, 110–11, 118; and *Madame Butterfly*,

120–24; and *Memoirs of a Geisha*, 117–18, 227, 228; and *Mulan*, 38; as myths, 1–2; stories of in theatre and film, 120–24. *See also* Japan

gender roles and relations, 30–32, 35, 37, 46, 155, 159, 209, 211, 217, 224, 226, 230, 237. *See also* romance and eroticism

genres, 13–15, 237

geography and culture, 43–44, 48–49

Germany, 52, 57, 128–29, 134, 145–48, 153, 158, 163–64, 217

ghost writers, 70, 174, 208, 237

Gibson, Hutton, 197–98

Gibson, Mel, 112, 188, 194–200, 224

Gladiator, 52

Godzilla, 68

gold, looking for, 36, 50, 72, 85, 100, 133, 141, 149, 158

good guy, bad guy. *See* Manichaeism; splitting

grandiosity, 57–58. *See also* founding myths

Great Britain, 127–49, 231. *See also* British Empire

Greece, 54–57, 140, 189–90, 194, 209, 216

Greene, Graham, 141, 153, 159

Greystoke: The Legend of Tarzan, 73. *See also* Tarzan

"Gunga Din" (Kipling), 143, 145. *See also* Indiana Jones

Haggard, H. Rider, 70, 132, 140–42

Hamelink, Cees, x, xii

Hawaii, 113, 116–17

Heart of Darkness theme, 65, 67, 97, 133, 142, 156. *See also Apocalypse Now*

Hebrews. *See* Jews

"high concept" idea, 11, 237

Hiroshima, 67

Hispanic. *See* Latino

historical revisionism: concerning Jewish Holocaust, 197–98; concerning Native Americans, 93–99

Hollywood: crises in, 7; movies of, 7–10. *See also* blockbusters

Hollywood Production Code, 66, 117, 192

homosexuality, 56, 91, 107, 245n12

"hula girl" theme, 111, 115–17

"human sacrifice" theme, 20–21, 33, 65–66, 72, 75, 126, 138, 148, 224

Hussein, Saddam, 24, 167, 172, 174. *See also* Iraq

icons, 47, 84, 116, 144, 191, 208, 237

IHT (*International Herald Tribune*), xi

India, 4, 5, 23, 25, 132, 140, 145–48, 155, 216, 224, 233

Indiana Jones, 8, 51, 67, 93, 105, 128, 139, 141, 143–49, 226, 228–29, 231

Indians. *See* Native Americans

individuality, 226–27. *See also* uniformity of exotic faces and bodies

input, into movies, 17. *See also* cultural prism; social pyramid

intercultural communication, 16

International Herald Tribune. See IHT

Internet distribution, 11, 13

intertextuality, 15, 144, 238

Into the West (television series), 2

Invasion from Mars, The, 213–14

Iran (Persia), 23–24, 43–44, 54–55, 59–61, 124, 181, 190

Iraq, 24, 44, 48, 59, 61, 167, 172–75, 181–82, 221
Islam, 44, 49, 60–61, 84, 147, 167, 170, 180, 182, 185, 190. *See also individual countries*
Israel. *See* Exodus; Jews; Palestine; Passion story
Italy, 45–46, 51–54, 104, 140, 179, 188–200, 216, 218

Jackson, Peter, 64, 67
Jamaica, 155, 157, 219
James Bond, 144, 151, 153–59
Japan, 37–38, 110–11, 117–24, 128, 136, 158, 164, 216, 227, 230
Jesus Christ, 97, 164, 177–78, 188–200, 227
Jews, 7, 8, 140, 147, 177–200, 243nn1–3. *See also* anti-Semitism
Judaism. *See* Jews
Jungle Book, The, 20, 64, 69, 74, 142
jungle man movies, 69–74
Jurassic Park, 67
Justine (American soft-porn movie series), 126, 148

Katzenberg, Jeffrey, 21, 27, 40, 180, 185–86, 198
Kennedy, John F., 159, 206, 209
Kenya, 27, 29, 81, 170
Khomeini, Ayatollah, 24, 167. *See also* Iran
killings, eluded, 29
Kimba the Lion, 28
King and I, The, 130, 137. *See also Anna and the King*
King Kong, 65–67, 224, 227
King Solomon's Mines. See Allan Quatermain

Kipling, Rudyard, 20, 70, 132, 140, 142
Kubrick, Stanley, 161, 207

landscapes, 26, 85, 91, 129, 193, 225–26, 229
language: areas and markets and, 5–6, 128, 224; strangeness of, 194, 213, 224, 230; translation or subrepresentation in, 94, 97, 188–89, 194, 230. *See also* accents; Anglo-Saxon culture
Lara Croft, 51, 149, 229
Latino, 4, 146, 148, 159, 227, 232
Lawrence of Arabia, 95, 128, 134, 146, 185
Lean, David, 228. *See also Lawrence of Arabia*
Leopold II, King of Belgium. *See* Congo
libido, surplus of (ascribed to non-white people), 46, 65–66, 82, 228. *See also* Cleopatra; romance and eroticism
licensing. *See* merchandising
light and dark appearance and dress, 28, 46, 84, 111–12, 194, 219–20, 228. *See also* skin color
lighting conventions, 225
Lion King, The, 26–30, 74, 185, 230
"The Lion Sleeps Tonight" (song), 29–30, 230
living room environment, of television viewing, 3, 30. *See also* television vs. theatrical film
lore masters, 15. *See also* social pyramid
Lucas, George, 8, 139, 143–45, 147, 210, 215–21, 231
Lynch, Jessica, 172–75

Madame Butterfly (opera), 118–24. *See also* Japan

"making of" documentaries, 11, 29, 32, 238

Manichaeism, 4, 84, 95, 97, 182, 220, 228, 238

manifest destiny, 85, 238. *See also* United States; Western movies

"The Man Who Would Be King," 132, 142–43

MASH (movie and TV series), 160, 163

massacre, 34, 60, 85, 88, 96–98, 113, 194

McDonald's tie-ins, 38–39, 68, 199

Mead, Margaret. *See* Samoa

Memoirs of a Geisha, 117, 120, 227–28

merchandising, 11, 20, 30–31, 68–69, 74, 99, 105, 163, 186, 199, 208, 216–17, 238

Mesopotamia. *See* Iraq

metropolises, 202, 225, 229

Mexico, 93, 224. *See also* "Southern" movie genre; Zorro

"MIA/POW" theme, 162–63, 168, 238

Middle East. *See* Arabs

miniature models, 65

miscegenation, 35, 66, 73, 78, 98, 110, 211, 238

Miss Saigon (musical), 119, 123–24

modernism, 16. *See also* Enlightenment; postmodernism

Monroe doctrine. *See* United States: expansion of

monster movies, 64–69

montage, 125

moon landing, 206–7

Moses, 179–88, 209, 218, 227

"movie brat" directors, 7, 192, 216

movie data websites, xi

movie theater seating, 3, 30. *See also* emotional experience; television vs. theatrical film

Mulan, 37–40, 185, 227–28

multiculturalism, 16, 60, 208, 211, 239

Mummy, The, 47, 49–51, 232

music. *See* stereotypical sounds and music

Muslims. *See* Islam

Mutiny on the Bounty, 111–15, 228

Nagasaki harbor. *See* Hiroshima; Japan; *Madame Butterfly*

narcissistic confirmation, 41, 233. *See also* ego

Native Americans ("Indians"), 2, 20–21, 127, 146, 164, 225, 247n1. *See also* "Southern" movie genre; Western movies

naturalization, 16, 20, 49, 128, 225, 239

Nazis, 29, 36, 65, 145, 147–48, 163, 206, 252n5

NCDO. *See* Netherlands National Commission on Sustainable Development

Nederveen Pieterse, Jan, xi, 109

Netherlands. *See* Dutch traders and settlers

Netherlands National Commission on Sustainable Development (NCDO), xii

news about other cultures, 16, 223

"New Spain." *See* Mexico; "Southern" movie genre

"new world" theme: as applied to the Americas, 86, 96; as applied to the rest of the world, 25. *See also* Iraq; Native Americans; Pax Americana; *Pocahontas*

9/11. *See* World Trade Center attack

Nixon, Richard, 159, 161, 167, 207

"noble savage" concept, 114, 138, 141, 213

noses, 20, 25, 227
nouvelle vague (France), 203, 239
nuclear bombs, 67–68, 123, 217. *See also*
    Hiroshima; Nagasaki harbor
nudity, 34, 66–67, 71–73, 108, 124, 127,
    227. *See also* South Sea paradise

Occidentalism, 15–16, 239
oppositions in movie scripts, 65–66, 100
Orientalism, 15, 125, 129, 136, 148, 184,
    216, 239. *See also Aladdin; Anna and
    the King;* Islam; *Madame Butterfly;
    Miss Saigon; Mulan; individual
    countries; individual regions*
others and otherness, 107–8, 212–13,
    225, 230–31, 234

Pacific, 225. *See also* Japan; *King Kong;*
    South Sea paradise
Palestine, 15, 44, 53, 140, 181
Passion of the Christ, The, 177–78, 188,
    196, 230
Passion story, 147, 188–200, 227
Pax Americana, 26, 54
PC. *See* political correctness
Pearl Harbor, 151, 166
Pearl Harbor naval base, 116, 166–67.
    See also Hawaii
Pentagon, 160–61, 163–67, 172, 175,
    250n11
peplum genre, 45, 239. *See also* antiquity
Persia. *See* Iran
perspectivistic slant, 55
Peter Pan, 20–21
physique, 108, 113. *See also* casting;
    uniformity of exotic faces and bodies
Pitcairn (island), 113–15
plagiarism. *See* copyright

Pocahontas, 32–36, 99
political correctness (PC), 16, 32, 80,
    134, 149, 155, 209, 225, 240
Polynesia, 110–17, 230
polysemic details, 17
popular novels and pulp fiction, 70, 87,
    104, 124, 132, 140, 147, 157
postmodernism, 16, 144, 157, 225, 240
presidents' favorite movies, 167–68
pressure groups, 27, 178–79, 185, 192,
    223
Prince of Egypt, The, 40, 48, 177–78, 180,
    185–88
producer role, 5
promiscuity. *See* Polynesia
promotion, 11. *See also* publicity, free
propaganda, 68, 163, 165, 214. *See also*
    British Empire; Pentagon
props. *See* stereotypical props,
    characters, and situations
prostitution, 116–24
psychological projection, 128, 221
publicity, free, 10, 12. *See also* awards
    ceremonies; controversy; star system
Puccini, Giacomo (composer). *See
    Madame Butterfly*

Quinn, Anthony, 93, 134, 227

Rambo (character), 93, 151, 161–66,
    168, 170, 172, 228
Reagan, Ronald, 161, 163, 165–66, 198,
    204, 220
reality TV, 74, 79, 81
Red Scare. *See* Cold War
release dates and patterns, 9–11, 52
religion, 177–200, 219, 230. *See also*
    Christianity; Islam; Jews

remote control. *See* living room
    environment, of television viewing
research for movies, 3, 22, 228–29
"revenge" theme, 168. *See also* Rambo
reversal, 85, 163, 168
"Robinsonades" theme, 77, 241
Robinson Crusoe (Defoe), 75–78, 212
robots, 203, 212, 220, 225
Rocky, 162
Roddenberry, Gene, 208, 212
romance and eroticism, 107–26, 129
Rome. *See* Italy
Russia, 128, 132, 153, 158, 217, 233. *See*
    also Soviet Union

"safari park" stereotype (of Africa), 26–27,
    72–74. *See also* animal characters
Said, Edward, 15. *See also* Orientalism
Samoa, 113, 116
Schwarzenegger, Arnold, 161, 168, 203
science fiction (SF), 201–21, 225
scouting, 144–45. *See also* Baden-Powell,
    R. S. Smyth
segregation, 66, 110, 211, 223, 230. *See*
    also apartheid; civil rights movement;
    miscegenation
selection, 178, 241
"selective articulation," 16, 127, 223
sequels, 12, 51, 67, 71
sets, 229. *See also* landscapes;
    stereotypical props, characters, and
    situations
settlers, 78, 85, 188, 229, 231; lore of, 33,
    140, 241
settler states, 5, 128. *See also* Australia;
    colonial adventure; South Africa;
    "Southern" movie genre; Western
    movies

sex and sexualization, 35, 38, 56, 66–67,
    71, 82, 184, 228. *See also* romance
    and eroticism
SF. *See* science fiction
Sharif, Omar, 134, 227
Shohat, Ella, xi, 36, 94, 110, 143, 148,
    229
"Singapore girl" image, 110. *See also*
    gender roles and relations; Japan
Sitting Bull (Sioux chief), 88, 95
skin color, 20, 28, 46, 48, 55, 72, 83, 108,
    112–13, 125, 131, 142, 184, 193–94,
    224–25, 227, 231–33
slavery, 49, 77, 109, 118, 125, 133, 136,
    138, 181, 212, 218–19, 224, 225
social Darwinism, 70, 241
socialization, 19, 28, 35, 83–84, 108
social pyramid, 15, 231
Somalia, 151, 168–72
sound. *See* stereotypical sounds and
    music
South Africa, 27, 29–30, 132–33, 140–41,
    144
"Southern" movie genre (Mexico),
    99–105
South Sea paradise, 80, 111–17, 230
Soviet Union, 158, 161–62, 167, 169,
    206, 212–13, 220
space adventure, 201–21
special effects, 13, 51, 64, 182, 184, 217,
    229
speech, 230. *See also* accents; language
Spielberg, Steven, 1, 40, 52, 185; as
    director, 1, 8, 68, 139, 143–44,
    147–48, 205, 210, 213–14; as
    producer, 2, 99, 101
splitting (in good and bad, us and
    them), 4, 36, 83, 96–97, 129, 148,

166–67, 178, 182, 186, 201, 215, 218, 220, 224. *See also* Manichaeism
spy movies, 152–59
Stallone, Sylvester, 161–66, 174
Stam, Robert, xi, 36, 94, 143, 148, 229
Stanley, H. M., 72, 132–33, 141
Stargate, 149
star system, 12, 53, 56
Star Trek (movies and television series), 93, 208–13, 225, 230
Star Wars, 8, 93, 144, 215–21, 225, 228, 230
stereotypes, 20, 124, 144, 159, 219, 231, 241; and colors, 225–26. *See also* light and dark appearance and dress; skin color
stereotypical props, characters, and situations, 20–22, 25, 38, 94, 100, 105, 228
stereotypical sounds and music, 38, 72–73, 105, 117, 170–71, 227–30
Stone, Oliver, 52, 56–61, 159, 161
struggle between races, 71
studios, 8, 13
superheroes, 12, 54, 155
survival games, 64
Survivor television reality show, 80
"swords and sandals" genre, 45
synthetic images, 67, 225, 242

Tahiti, 111–15
target groups (prime), 4, 10, 14, 31, 74, 152, 210, 231–32
Tarzan, 40, 64, 69–74, 164, 225, 228, 232, 247n10
television vs. theatrical film, 3, 7, 45, 92, 156, 208, 229
temple (Jerusalem), 180, 189, 195

temples (East Asian), 130, 146, 229
Temptation Island television format, 81–82
Ten Commandments, The, 48, 177–79, 185, 227
"tent poles" (relative hits), 9
terrorism, 154, 158. *See also* World Trade Center attack
Thailand, 125, 130, 134–39, 227
Thanksgiving, 34
theme parks (Disney), 3, 20–21, 37, 39–41, 68–69, 79, 89, 105, 184
Tintin (Belgian comic strip hero), 144
Top Gun, 165–66
top two hundred best-selling movies, ix, xi, 9
torture. *See* cruelty
tourist industry, 27, 112, 116–17
treasure, 24, 40, 64, 78, 85, 129, 142, 146. *See also* gold, looking for
trek, 91, 94, 181
tribes, primitive, 63, 66–67, 72, 129, 227, 229
Troy, 52, 58, 227
truth claims, 32, 59, 100, 128, 130–31, 134–39. *See also* Bible
Turkey, 23, 124, 134, 145–48, 189. *See also* Greece
Turner, Frederick Jackson, 86

UFO, 204, 242
uniformity of exotic faces and bodies, 39, 53, 137, 227
United States, 128, 136, 188, 197, 202, 212, 221, 230; expansion of, 86, 94, 102–4, 142; market size of, 5, 128. *See also* Native Americans; Pentagon; "Southern" movie genre;

South Sea paradise; war; Western movies
University of Amsterdam, x, xii
us and them. *See* splitting

Vietnam, 92, 95, 111, 125, 160–67, 170, 212. *See also Miss Saigon*

War of the Worlds, The, 213–14
war movies, 160–72, 230
WASP (White Anglo-Saxon Protestant), 100, 242
Wayne, John, 89, 160–61
weapons of mass destruction (WMD), 24, 145, 164, 172, 205

Wells, H. G., 202, 213
Western civilization, 43
Western movies, 2, 83–99, 144, 209, 226, 229
White Anglo-Saxon Protestant (WASP), 100, 242
"white man's burden," 78, 142, 242
wilderness adventure, 63–82
WMD. *See* weapons of mass destruction
World of Suzie Wong, The, 110, 118
World Trade Center attack, 167–68

Zaïre. *See* Congo
Zorro (character), 99–105, 144

About the Author

Jaap van Ginneken is an independent author and lecturer based in France, who has published seventeen books in thirty-two editions and five languages. A psychologist by training, he long taught at the Section for Entertainment Studies within the Department of Communication Science at the University of Amsterdam in the Netherlands as associate professor, covering two specialties: collective behavior and intercultural communication.

His belated doctoral dissertation *Crowds, Psychology and Politics* (1992) was received "with distinction" to rave reviews at the time; he recently published a sequel, *Mass Movements* (2007). His *Collective Behavior and Public Opinion* (2003) had earlier tried to give the field a new impetus and was hailed for its innovative approach to rapid shifts, drawing on chaos and complexity theory.

Having traveled widely in his younger years, on the other hand, he is also fascinated by the (mis)representation of other cultures. His book *Understanding Global News: A Critical Introduction* (1998) took a close look at the various sources of unintentional bias in international reporting. A smaller Dutch book looked at comic strips, and this current book does the same for feature films.

Meanwhile, the author has done a lot of media work himself over the years, in a wide variety of roles: from newspaper columnist to broadcasting consultant, including occasional advice for television soaps, sitcoms, and feature films.